REGNUM STUDIES IN



# Celebrating Life in Community

## Reflections in Social Ethics and the Church, Essays in Honour of Murray W. Dempster

## Series Preface

Regnum Studies in Mission are born from the lived experience of Christians and Christian communities in mission, especially but not solely in the fast growing churches among the poor of the world. These churches have more to tell than stories of growth. They are making significant impacts on their cultures in the cause of Christ. They are producing 'cultural products' which express the reality of Christian faith, hope and love in their societies.

Regnum Studies in Mission are the fruit often of rigorous research to the highest international standards and always of authentic Christian engagement in the transformation of people and societies. And these are for the world. The formation of Christian theology, missiology and practice in the twenty-first century will depend to a great extent on the active participation of growing churches contributing biblical and culturally appropriate expressions of Christian practice to inform World Christianity.

REGNUM STUDIES IN MISSION

# Celebrating Life in Community

## Reflections in Social Ethics and the Church, Essays in Honour of Murray W. Dempster

Edited by

**Kenneth J. Archer and Zachary Michael Tackett**

First published 2023 by Regnum Books International

Regnum is an imprint of the Oxford Centre for Mission Studies
St. Philip and St. James Church
Woodstock Road
Oxford, OX2 6HR, UK
www.regnumbooks.net



**British Library Cataloguing in Publication Data**
A catalogue record for this book is available from the British Library

ISBN: 979-8-8898-3315-4
eBook ISBN: 979-8-8898-3316-1

Typeset by Words by Design



Distributed by Fortress Press in the US, Canada, India, and Brazil

# Contents


REFLECTIONS ON MURRAY W. DEMPSTER

Foreword: From President to President: An Appreciation
*Kent Ingle* vii

Introduction and Acknowledgements
*Zachary Michael Tackett and Kenneth J. Archer* ix

Reflections on a Forever Friend
*Douglas P. Petersen and Byron D. Klaus* xiii

SCRIPTURAL AND THEOLOGICAL CONCEPTS

1. The Old Testament as a Source for Ethics for the Pentecostal Community
*Jacqueline Grey* 1

2. Justice and Righteousness, Israel's Kingship Ideology, and the Spirit of God
*Wonsuk Ma* 13

3. 'I Stand at the Door and Knock': Eucharist, Homelessness, and the Paradox of Hospitality
*Chris E.W. Green* 27

4. The Synaptic Mind of James Forbes: A Delta of Theology
*Nimi Wariboko* 35

5. On the Way Toward Pneumatological Ecclesiology
*Peter Kuzmic* 53

6. Jesus, Pentecostalism, and the Encounter with (Religious) Others: Pentecostal Christology and (the Wider) Ecumenism in North America
*Amos Yong* 59

PEACEMAKING AND THE CHRISTIAN WITNESS

7. Does Jesus Sometimes Want Christians to Kill Their Enemies?
*Ronald J. Sider* 75

8. The Christian Moral Witness of Dietrich Bonhoeffer
*David P. Gushee* 87

9. Desire Redirected: Hermeneutical Shifts Regarding War and Peacemaking
*Kenneth J. Archer* 99

10. Toward Individual Conscience: The Assemblies of God and World War II
*Zachary Michael Tackett* 117

11. A Pentecostal/Charismatic Response to the 'Red Scare' as Portrayed in *The Voice of Healing*
*Lisa Millen* 135

CHURCH AND COMMUNITY


12. Why Should Pentecostals Engage in Social Ethics? Ecumenical Considerations
*Jean-Daniel Plüss* 147

13. Manifest Lament: Pentecostals, Lukan Hospitality, and Indigenous Decolonisation
*Martin W. Mittelstadt* 159

14. The Value of the Human Soul: Radicalising Adolf von Harnack's Social Gospel
*Frank D. Macchia* 173

15. CARE (Christian Action Research and Education) as a Model for Social Action
*William K. Kay* 191

16. Saints vs Heroes: The Triumph of Spectacle in American Culture and Film
*Robby Waddell* 205

Abridged Curriculum Vitae of Murray W. Dempster 219

Contributors 221

Index 225

# Foreword

## From President to President: An Appreciation

Kent Ingle, President, Southeastern University

Congratulations Dr Murray Dempster on this publication celebrating your academic and ministry achievements! In your decades of service, you have greatly impacted the lives of thousands of leaders, faculty members, coworkers, and students. Through pursuing a life of academic excellence, you have contributed greatly to the advancement of Christian theological studies.

They say there are one or two people in your life you simply cannot tell your story without mentioning. For me, Dr Murray Dempster is one of those people. Dr Dempster's great character and teaching of theology have been incredibly influential to me over the course of my life.

When I was working in Springfield, Missouri, as a broadcaster I was offered a job to work in Los Angeles, California. I transferred my undergraduate work to Vanguard University in Costa Mesa, California. It was during one of my first courses at Vanguard, Introduction to Theology and Ethics, that I first met Dr. Dempster. Then, ten years later, when I returned to Vanguard to start my graduate work in theological studies, Dr. Dempster had become the provost of the university. He would later go on to serve as president, and then chancellor.

In the classroom, Dr Dempster taught me what it means to assess one's personal theological and moral identity, and the distinctive theological characteristics of the Word of God. His teachings guided me in understanding the great theologians such as Karl Barth, Dietrich Bonhoeffer, and Paul Tillich while incorporating his jovial and unpredictable sense of humour. He taught me how to embrace humanity with a true Christian ethic.

Throughout my years as a student under his guidance, Dr Dempster's leadership, teachings, and passion for God greatly shaped my own life and leadership. Years later, when I became a professor myself, I took to heart all that Dr Dempster had taught me; I wanted to model his way of teaching and inspiring students in my own classroom.

With all the places my vocational track would take me, I never could have imagined that I would end up at Southeastern University (SEU) in 2010 to become the new president. When I arrived, I soon learned that Dr Dempster was a part of the faculty. I knew it was a God-ordained encounter. In many ways, his example, as a leader and professor at Vanguard, helped mould and shape me even before arriving at SEU. In his leadership, Dr Dempster displayed the great characteristics it takes to uphold responsibility. And, in his own personal walk, he had always been instrumental in creating a solid awareness of the things that mattered in life.

On the eve of my inauguration as the president of SEU, Dr Dempster gifted me with the book *Legitimacy in the Academic Presidency*[1] from his personal library. He gave me this book because it had made a tremendous difference in his life. He had tucked a congratulatory note inside the book along with something I didn't expect. It was a copy of a paper I had completed for his class during my undergraduate studies. Dr Dempster explained that he knew I was destined for a position of significant leadership based on my ability to grasp complex ideas at an early age. He knew even then that if I could decipher what I needed to for that particular assignment, I was uniquely gifted to handle significant tasks and responsibilities.

Dr Dempster kept my paper all those years because it inspired him. He explained that he used my paper as an example for other students until he left the classroom for university leadership. This gesture was a moment of affirmation for me and what God had planned for my life. As I stepped into a new role as president, it was extremely encouraging to have the moral support of an influential professor and leader like Dr Dempster. I was able to lean into his wisdom and insight as I navigated the challenges of leading a university.

Throughout the most critical points of transition in my career – from broadcasting, ministry, teaching, and then in my role as president – Dr Dempster has always been there to support me. I was blessed to be able to continue to be mentored by him while he was a faculty member at SEU. For someone who served as the president of Vanguard University, his leadership insights and guidance were invaluable to me.

Up until his retirement in 2020, Dr Dempster continued to invest in my life and the SEU community. He was an integral part of our university, teaching and designing courses in the undergraduate and graduate programmes. His research has made great contributions to Pentecostalism and the interaction of Christianity and social ethics. He was also highly instrumental in the development of the Global Pentecostal Center at SEU. Dr Dempster encouraged, challenged, supported, and led students into academic rigor, while spurring students into a deep personal relationship with Christ.

Dr Dempster's life, teachings and leadership have been pivotal in my personal and professional life. And, I know Dr Dempster has made a significant impact on the lives of many on our campus, as well as at the other university campuses and churches where he served.

---

[1] Rita Bornstein, *Legitimacy in the Academic Presidency: From Entrance to Exit* (Westport, Connecticut: American Council of Education, Praeger Series on Higher Education, 2003).

# Introduction and Acknowledgements

## Zachary Michael Tackett and Kenneth J. Archer

We, Ken Archer and Zach Tackett, are pleased to be able to honour Murray W. Dempster, an outstanding scholar, academician, and friend, with this *festschrift*. We are also gratified with the array of scholars who have contributed to this volume as a statement of tribute. The contributors are from the variety of Murray's interests in the academy and the church.

Contributors include longtime friends with whom he cut his scholastic teeth as a student, pastor, and young professor, Doug Petersen, Byron Klaus, Peter Kuzmic, and Frank Macchia. Having reached well beyond his denomination, Murray is honoured by representatives of this community of ethicists through the writings of Ron Sider and David Gushee. Scholars who represent his global values include William Kay, Jacqueline Grey, Martin Mittelstadt, Jean-Daniel Plüss, and Nimi Wariboko. Murray contributed to the academy as a dean, a provost, and a university president. Thus, we are hearing the voice of representatives of these communities, Wonsuk Ma and Amos Yong. Finally, there are those who came to know Murray when he rightfully had become recognised as the leading social ethicist in American Pentecostal studies, Chris Green, Lisa Millen, Robby Waddell, and the editors, Ken Archer and Zach Tackett.

Thank you very much Kent Ingle, President of Southeastern University, Lakeland, Florida, for providing a foreword and tribute to Murray's work. Murray came out of retirement to conclude his academic journey at Southeastern as Distinguished Professor of Social Ethics. Kent had been a student of Murray's at Southern California College (Vanguard University). Southeastern is also where Ken and Zach serve as professors in the School of Divinity, where we came to know Murray closely.

The essays presented in this volume reflect the diversity of interests presented in Murray's writings. In that Murray is a Pentecostal, many of the essays intersect with Pentecostal themes. Yet that is not the case in all the essays. Most notably, Ron Sider and David Gushee reflect the respect Murray receives from the larger academic community in social ethics.

Two very important essays unveil the project. First, Kent Ingle in the Foreword speaks to Murray Dempster, president to president, university administrator to university administrator, amplifying the value Murray has given to the academic community. The second is provided by two of Murray's lifelong friends and academic colleagues, Doug Petersen and Byron Klaus. Together the three edited two books, including what is perhaps Murray's, and their, most-known contribution, *Called and Empowered: Global Mission in Pentecostal Perspective*. In a personal manner that only Doug and Byron can do, they tell their story. Recognising that unique relationship, the Society for Pentecostal Studies in 2016 presented the three together with SPS's Lifetime Achievement Award.

The first section of essays addresses biblical and theological themes. While Murray was diverse in his thought, his Christian faith pushed him to insist that social ethics are to be grounded through Christian expression. Jacqueline Grey and Wonsuk Ma address the foundation of Christian social ethics within Scripture, particularly focusing upon the Old Testament. Thereafter, four essays contextualise issues through theological encounter. Chris Green, Nimi Wariboko, Peter Kuzmic, and Amos Yong engage theological and ethics issues via Christology, pneumatology, ecclesiology, and ecumenism.

The second collection of essays addresses peacemaking. This is a significant topic within Murray's writings. He is a pacifist who sees pacifism as active, as a prophetic action that calls for and empowers peacemaking. Two of the essays address the moral witness of peacemaking, those of Sider and Gushee. The next two essays engage shifts within American Pentecostalism, from a community that prioritised pacifism to a community that now prioritises the conscience of the individual. The articles by Archer and Tackett work together. They also reflect differences in approaches, with Archer advocating active pacifism in a manner similar to that of Dempster, and Tackett advocating what Glenn Stasson has identified as Just Peacemaking,[1] a concept that encourages pacifist and just war advocates to work together in arresting violence and pursuing peacemaking. The final essay in this collection, by Lisa Millen, addresses a particular dynamic within the twentieth century, that of the Cold War.

The third collection addresses ecclesiology and the specific dynamics of the church and community. Jean-Daniel Plüss, in a call to ecumenism and social action, asks the question of Pentecostals, "Why should Pentecostals engage social ethics?" Thereafter, four essays engage specific dynamics related to community. Marty Mittelstadt, as a fellow Canadian with Murray, addresses the problematic relationship of the church, particularly the Pentecostal community, to Indigenous communities in Canada. Frank Macchia considers the work of church historian Adolf von Harnack, focusing on how his theory of history contributes to social engagement. William Kay looks at a particular model of social action that developed in a community in England. Finally, Robby Waddell brings to us the ubiquitous movie screen, asking us to consider the distinction between how culture creates heroes and how the church recognises her saints.

At the end of each essay is a series of questions that have been written by the editors. The discussion questions are designed to elicit thought from the reader. Also, the questions are provided so that when the text is used in a classroom setting, a discussion prompt is provided.

Each of the writers in this volume were invited to comment on their relationship with Murray. Some began with a short recognition. Others wove an appreciation into their essays.

---

[1] Glenn H. Stassen, *Just Peacemaking: Transforming Initiatives for Justice and Peace* (Louisville: Westminster/John Knox Press, 1992); Stassen (ed.), *Just Peacemaking: The New Paradigm for the Ethics of Peace and War* (Cleveland, Ohio: The Pilgrim Press, 2008).

## Editors' Reflection: Ken Archer

Murray Dempster is one of the few very first academically trained Pentecostal social ethicists. Dr Dempster did not hide his Pentecostalism, but instead has allowed his Pentecostal tradition and experience to shape his ethical perspectives in the most creative and positive ways. The Day of Pentecost is woven into the very fabric of his writings, sometimes overtly, many times inconspicuously, yet always present in significant ways. The Holy Spirit and the outpouring of the Spirit upon all flesh have shaped his theological social ethics. My theological perspectives have been enriched through Murray's writings, and my life has been significantly enriched through our friendship, especially during our time together at Southeastern University.

I want to say a very special thank you to Zach Tackett. We have been working on this project for some time – planning the volume, inviting contributors, and sharing the editing of the drafts. However, Zach took on the responsibility for being on point with most of the follow up communication through emails, locating a publisher, and organising the final essays thematically, and then formatting the entire compilation. He wrote most of the abstracts and put together the final questions for discussion that appear at the end of each chapter. Our desire was to make this a volume that would be used as a reader for undergrad and grad courses in theological ethics. He has worked tirelessly towards that end. He has been the one who has brought this collaborative project to its final destination: thank you Zach!

## Editors' Reflection: Zach Tackett

The quality and passion of Dempster's scholarship attracted me when I was first introduced to his writings. I had been introduced to his scholarship from his editorship of *Pneuma: The Journal of the Society for Pentecostal Studies* and through his co-editing *Agora*, an academic but popular journal that gained traction in new areas of academic and ecclesial Pentecostalism. I was fascinated by his passioned, quality scholarship in engaging Pentecostalism and ethics.

The first time that I met Murray Dempster, I was in my PhD studies. I was presenting a paper at a meeting of the Society for Pentecostal Studies on the influence of Fundamentalism upon early- and mid-twentieth-century Pentecostalism, the first paper that I had presented at an academic forum. I expected persons to show up to hear the other presenters in the session in which I was presenting; I did not expect anyone to come to hear my presentation. To my amazement, Murray Dempster and a couple of other well-known scholars were front and centre. To this day I wonder how I made it through that session as the powerhouses of Pentecostal scholarship sat in front of me. Dr Dempster's words of encouragement at the conclusion of the presentation spoke to me then as they continue to speak to me today.

Toward the end of his career, Murray was encouraged by the dean at the time, Robert Houlihan, to come out of retirement to teach in the College of Ministry and Theology at Southeastern University. I am so very pleased that he did, for although I knew him prior to his coming to Southeastern, it has been as a colleague of Murray that I have been privileged to engage the fullness of his personhood. Dr Dempster become a friend, as he is to many. We have even had season tickets together at the college football games. “Murray, wasn’t that an incredible catch?! Go Fire!”

Finally, thank you to my colleague, Ken Archer. He floated the idea of a *festschrift* well before we decided to take on the project. He is the one who encouraged many, if not most, of the scholars to contribute. He is the driving force that enabled this plane to get off the ground. Thank you, Ken.

# Reflections on a Forever Friend

Douglas P. Petersen and Byron D. Klaus

This chapter will explore Murray's roots of faith in Canada and foundations for scholarship at the Northwest Bible College in Edmonton, Alberta, and the University of Southern California. We will talk about how our friendships developed and were deepened by our collaborative work. We would want to paint an authentic picture of our friend, Murray W. Dempster, as a Pentecostal scholar worth admiring and emulating: a Pentecostal scholar who epitomised the description of Pentecostal scholarship by Russ Spittler (our colleague at Southern California College, now Vanguard University) as *the right to enquire and the might to believe*.

The world of the academy yields relationships fostered by interactions with the works of a scholar. We sometimes presume to know a person through the evaluation of their writings. We have had the privilege to know Murray not just as a colleague and scholarly collaborator, but most importantly as a close friend. Surely we can call each other *forever friends*.

Our friendships developed through a somewhat circuitous pathway that began in the prairie provinces of Canada for Murray and Doug and the midwestern USA for Byron. Eventually our paths intersected in Southern California and more specifically at Southern California College. Murray was clearly the most brilliant of the "three amigos," but our lives and ministries were slowly woven together in our first co-edited book entitled *Called and Empowered: Global Mission in Pentecostal Perspective*[1] published in 1991.

The work on that first volume moved each of us into a deep commitment to friendship and the belief that sharp minds and passionate hearts belonged together. We were all weary of scholars discovering this burgeoning Pentecostal movement, applying their pet paradigms onto Pentecostals to define us and offering their explanations for our global expansion. We just wanted to speak for ourselves and name our world as insiders. We were not ashamed of our humble roots. We could embrace our Pentecostal "distinctives" that some would scoff at, but we knew we had been shaped at Pentecostal altars and were happy to tell the world who we were. We weren't willing to allow the scholarly efforts that dominated to define Pentecostals without our voices speaking clearly about issues critical to all who called themselves Christians. We knew who we were, and we wanted to show the academic world that these "new kids on the block" could speak on issues critical to interrelationships within the Christian family and manage the encounters with those who were not Christian. To that end, Murray clearly was the person whose sheer intellectual prowess gave a framework to our scholarly endeavours.

---

[1] Murray W. Dempster, Byron D. Klaus, and Douglas Petersen, ed. *Called and Empowered: Global Mission in Pentecostal Perspective* (Peabody, MA: Hendrickson, 1991).

Our second volume of work together was entitled *The Globalization of Pentecostalism: A Religion Made to Travel* (1999).[2] While *Called and Empowered* had represented Pentecostal scholars speaking for themselves about who Pentecostals were, this volume represented an interaction with Christianity that was becoming increasingly global and Pentecostal. The metrics of David Barrett, in his annual report on Global Christianity published in the *International Bulletin of Missionary Research* (*IBMR*), was chronicling the global growth of Pentecostalism. Harvey Cox had published *Fire from Heaven*[3] in 1995 and posited that twenty-first-century Christianity would bear the distinctive flavour of Pentecostal spirituality. It was from Cox that we "borrowed" the descriptive phrase "a religion made to travel."

This volume was intentionally framed around an international consultation that took place in San José, Costa Rica, in the summer of 1996. Murray was now serving as the provost at Southern California College, and the three of us had all been working throughout the last decade of the twentieth century to establish the College's Study Center at CINCEL (Centro de Investigaciones y Estudios Lingüísticos). The consultation that yielded the volume was a triangulation of financial support from SCC and President Wayne Kraiss and resources from a great friend of the College as well as a result of Doug's leadership of Latin America ChildCare[4] (now ChildHope). That supporter was Margaret Smith, whose gracious and vital support allowed this significant array of international scholars to be together in Costa Rica. As with our first volume, Murray's brainpower shaped the framework of the *Globalization* volume. Doug and I would have ideas that we thought were outstanding. Murray would simply reframe those "outstanding ideas" into something so much better and we would mutter to ourselves, "you are right, that's what we meant to say!" This volume was recognised by the *International Bulletin of Missionary Research* in its annual listing of significant books published on mission in 1999.

## The Rest of the Story

### *Byron's Recollections*

I came from getting my seminary degree to Southern California College in 1975 to serve on the student life team. I observed the highly charismatic Murray Dempster. He was the brilliant philosophy professor who was finishing his doctoral work at the University of Southern California. He was the cool professor whom students wanted to emulate. We knew each other only by name during this short period of time. Within a year we had both returned to local church

[2] Murray W. Dempster, Byron D. Klaus, and Douglas Petersen (eds), *The Globalization of Pentecostalism: A Religion Made to Travel* (Oxford, UK: Regnum, 1999).

[3] Harvey Cox, *Fire from Heaven: The Rise of Pentecostal Spirituality and the Reshaping of Religion in the Twenty-First Century* (Reading, MA: Addison-Wesley, 1995).

[4] ChildHope (formerly Latin America ChildCare) is a ministry of compassion providing food, medical care, a quality education and the good news of the gospel to 100,000 impoverished children in 300 schools throughout Latin America.

ministry. Murray became pastor of a church in nearby Fullerton, and I joined the staff of a church in the Los Angeles area. I remember Murray coming to preach at our church one weekend after he had been with our young adult group for a retreat. He preached a sermon on Job and his "friends." I was mesmeried by the narrative that Murray could weave from that ancient book. I was in awe of brilliance and (for lack of a better descriptor) old time Pentecostal fire that combined in one person. The sharp mind and passionate heart that I saw in Murray was of the calibre of the icon of Pentecostal scholar/preacher, Gordon Fee.

Several years later our paths again crossed as we both returned to Southern California College. We became colleagues and friends and here we are over four decades later looking back at the treasure this friendship has been. Murray's conceptual prowess was always something that I admired but knew I could never match. His theological positions, at times, would leave me wondering, who is this guy anyway? But his brilliance was not connected to haughtiness, snarkiness, or contempt for alternative opinion that can so easily be the DNA of topflight scholars. Murray could tear apart my opinions on critical subjects, leave my ideas in shambles, and yet never stop smiling. That smile was not pride at demolishing a colleague's position; it was the genuine expression of the centre of his being that valued enduring friendship over brainpower. We hold some very polar opposite opinions about a variety of issues, but because we grew up praying at the same kinds of simple Pentecostal altars, we knew whose power we had to rely on every day. No matter what professional prowess we might have attained, we still believed that "it is not by power nor by might, but by my Spirit saith the Lord!"

If you were to ask me what is the single most significant influence Murray's scholarly work had on my life, I would respond that it is rooted in a paper he presented at the 1983 meeting of the Society for Pentecostal Studies held in Cleveland, Tennessee. This paper was based on his study of the philosopher Ludwig Wittgenstein. Murray adapted that work to his personal Pentecostal perspective in a paper entitled "Soundings in the Moral Significant of Glossolalia."[5] He stated in this paper that glossolalia allows a person to bring previously unimagined possibilities out of already existing perceptions of reality. He argued that the Spirit-empowered community had an inherent hunger not only for God, but to act under the compulsion of the Spirit to make Him known. This paper has led me from a posture of defending Pentecostal "distinctives" to a posture of affirming the empowered life in the Spirit that is the guarantee of Pentecost. I look to this early work of Murray's scholarship as the root of the deep commitment to my Pentecost heritage and confidence in a ministry trajectory that has allowed me to serve in the broadest and most diverse expressions of Christian community.

---

[5] Murray W. Dempster, "Soundings in the Moral Significance of Glossolalia" (presentation, Society for Pentecostal Studies, Cleveland, TN, 3–5 November 1983).

### *Doug's Recollections*

Murray Dempster was born and raised in Saskatchewan, Canada. His family was Pentecostal. After watching his parents go through a difficult divorce, he left the church and spent his teen years in a rock 'n roll band named the "Black Cats," playing rhythm guitar. After graduating from high school, he was offered a scholarship from the University of Alberta to study pharmacology. Murray's mother prayed for her son every day, and before Murray left for university, his mother made one request. A young evangelist holding a week of special meetings at the church – would Murray attend just one service? Out of love for his mother, Murray agreed. That first night Murray responded to the altar call and surrendered his life to Christ. The next night, he was baptised in the Holy Spirit; Murray never missed another service. By the time the special meetings ended, Murray felt called into the ministry. In the fall of 1960, within weeks of his encounter with the Lord, Murray entered Northwest Bible College in Edmonton, Alberta.

That's when I met Murray Dempster for the first time. The Bible School, housed in the basement of Central Pentecostal Tabernacle, sent out students on the weekends to minister in the churches, large and small, throughout the province. Students would stay the Saturday night with a family from the local church and one weekend Murray stayed at our house.

You would have to know Murray for this to make any sense. He was eighteen; I was twelve. He was 6′2″; I wasn't 5′2″. Murray treated me like we were "hanging out" together. By the time the weekend was over, I believed Murray was my friend.

It was a Sunday, three years later before I saw Murray again. After graduating from Bible School, Rev. R.W. Taitinger invited Murray to be his associate pastor at Central Tabernacle.[6] Mark Buntain, a missionary to Kolkata, India, had returned to his home turf to speak at the Tabernacle. Mark's father, D.N. Buntain, had pastored the church from 1945 to 1955 and founded the Bible School in 1946. Everyone in our little Pentecostal world knew about Mark Buntain. Like so many others throughout the province, my parents made the long drive from our town to the city to hear the stories of this famous missionary. When I walked into the foyer of the church that evening, I spotted Murray. I was too shy to approach him. But as soon as he saw me, his face lit up into a big smile, and he said, "Doug Petersen, how great to see you!" Murray Dempster knew my name! After chatting for a few minutes, Murray said, "Let me introduce you to my fiancé, Coralie Erickson. She's up in the balcony." Coralie, I was soon to discover, was a stunning blonde, and easily the prettiest girl in the church.[7] From that moment, I wanted to be just like Murray.

In the spring of 1969, I graduated from Northwest Bible School. That summer I was invited to be one of the speakers for a youth camp in Hungry Horse,

---

[6] R.W. Taitinger pastored Central Pentecostal Tabernacle from 1955 until he was elected general superintendent of the Pentecostal Assemblies of Canada in 1971.

[7] Coralie's parents named her after Coralee Haist, a Pentecostal Assemblies of Canada (PAOC) pioneer missionary to China whose career spanned fifty years. However, Coralie'sfather misspelled her name on the birth certificate!

Montana. To my delight, and not a little intimidated, I discovered Murray was the other speaker. Four years earlier, Murray and Coralee had moved from Edmonton to Southern California to be an associate pastor at First Assembly of God in Long Beach. Down the freeway from Long Beach, Southern California had just become the first school in the Assemblies of God to be granted regional accreditation. Even though our little Canadian Bible School wasn't accredited, Murray had the reputation as the best student the Bible School ever produced. By the summer of 1969, Murray had enrolled as a student at Southern California College, graduated with a BA from SCC, and earned an MA in Social Ethics from the University of Southern California. I wanted to follow in Murray's footsteps. During our week together at Hungry Horse, we really did become friends. We started to envision the possibility of someday working together.

Early one Monday morning, a year or so later, the phone rang. It was Murray and he was excited with his news. "Doug, you're going to get a call in a few minutes from the pastor of First Assembly in Santa Ana. He needs a youth pastor. I recommended you. It's a great opportunity." Then Murray cautioned me, "Don't tell the pastor I called." Within a few weeks, visa in hand, my wife, Myrna, and I arrived in Southern California.

Life didn't turn out quite like we planned. I did follow Murray to Southern California College. But shortly after graduation, my wife and I were off to Central America – our home for the next twenty-five years. However, our missionary life just provided Murray and me (and soon Byron) with more opportunities.

We were living in San José, Costa Rica, when the three of us (Murray, Byron, and myself) dreamed up what became the volume, *Called and Empowered*. We divvied up our writing assignments. I was a novice scholar with a recently completed MA under my belt and I was a bit over my head. I struggled with my assignments. On our next trip back to Southern California, I gave Murray and Byron a copy of my drafts. A few days later, Murray returned the draft complete with a raft of edits and arrows pointing everywhere. Always the diplomat, Murray was quick to tell me the writing was just wonderful! It was easy to identify with the student who, after reviewing Murray's comments on his essay, remarked, "I never felt so good about getting a C!"

Despite the geographical distance between us, I saw quite a lot of Murray during our Central American years. Every year we taught courses together at Vanguard University or at the Costa Rica Study Center.[8] Murray was a favourite speaker for missionary retreats. Murray is a superb preacher and the missionaries loved him. On a personal note, when our daughter, Christie, was getting ready to graduate from her secular High School in San José, she convinced the school administrators to invite Murray Dempster as the commencement speaker. The leadership was worried that they might get a sermon. Not to worry … Murray

---

[8] I published a journal article based on a course I often taught with Murray. There was so much of "Murray" in the article that at the last minute I decided to submit it under both of our names. I sent Murray a note: "Just to let you know you just published an article with me!" See Douglas P. Petersen with Murray W. Dempster, "Redemption and Transformation: A Theology of New Life in Christ," *Asian Journal of Pentecostal Studies* 16:1 (2013), 17–29.

was brilliant! Even some of the recently graduated Ivy-League teachers, doing a two-year overseas stint to burnish their CVs, were impressed. Murray's commencement address was a subject of school conversation for days!

For almost four decades, Murray, Byron, and myself worked on one project after another. My role was to think up stuff, Byron made things happen, and Murray made sure we had something to say. In 2015, the Society of Pentecostal Studies awarded the three of us with a Lifetime Achievement Award. It was fitting that we could celebrate this honour together!

When Murray retired after forty years at Vanguard University and moved to Florida (soon to be named Distinguished Professor of Social Ethics at Southeastern University), my wife Myrna said to me, "Do you know what I miss most about Murray? I miss his joy!"

Since I was a twelve-year-old kid, Murray was present through my adolescence and at every stage of my career. How could I ever repay him? I couldn't. I didn't have anything to give that Murray needed. But what I could do was take the generosity, perseverance, patience, and kindness that Murray extended to me and pay them forward to others the Lord places in my life.

## Some Final Thoughts from Doug and Byron

There is a poignant statement in John 15:15 where Jesus calls those closest to him "friends." The following verse adds the statement "you did not choose me, but I chose you." While the context of this text certainly describes the rich uniqueness of relationships between our Lord and his followers, we have experienced a small glimpse into the dynamic of this text in our human relationships with Murray. He has called both of us friend and we did nothing that could impress or convince him to give us that moniker. He simply chose to be our friend because that's who Murray is. He was always the smartest guy in the room and could have used that gift to propel himself into the stratosphere of academia and its rarefied air of eliteness. But he chose us as friends simply because he could, and it gave him great joy to do so. Whenever *los tres amigos* are together (which now is all too infrequent), we never fail to remind each other that we are forever friends: and Doug and Byron are the fortunate ones!

## Bibliography

Cox, Harvey. *Fire from Heaven: The Rise of Pentecostal Spirituality and the Reshaping of Religion in the Twenty-first Century*. Reading, MA: Addison-Wesley, 1995.

Dempster, Murray W. "Soundings in the Moral Significance of Glossolalia." Paper presented at the Society for Pentecostal Studies, Cleveland, TN, 3–5 November 1983.

Dempster, Murray W., Byron D. Klaus, and Douglas Petersen, Eds. *Called and Empowered: Global Mission in Pentecostal Perspective*. Peabody, Massachusetts: Hendrickson, 1991.

Dempster, Murray W., Byron D. Klaus, and Douglas Petersen, Eds. *The Globalization of Pentecostalism: A Religion Made to Travel*. Oxford, UK: Regnum, 1999.

Petersen, Douglas P. with Murray W. Dempster. "Redemption and Transformation: A Theology of New Life in Christ.". *Asian Journal of Pentecostal Studies* 16:1 (2013), 17–29.

# Chapter 1

# The Old Testament as a Source for Ethics for the Pentecostal Community

Jacqueline Grey

## Abstract

The chapter addresses the use of Old Testament texts in ethical decision-making for the Pentecostal community. First, it provides an overview of the work of Pentecostal scholar, Murry Dempster, before discussing the challenges of using texts from the Old Testament as a source of ethics. The Old Testament reveals that at the heart of God's character and actions is liberation, salvation, healing, and freedom – particularly for the poor, marginalised and powerless. The covenant community is expected to live *imitatio Dei* as revealed by the narrative of God's character and actions. Secondly, this chapter suggests that texts from the Old Testament must be considered dialogically – reading them both in their own *context* and reading them *intertextually* – as part of the story of Scripture. The meta-narrative of Scripture provides the pattern by which Pentecostals seek to live and reorient their lives towards as they join the story as ongoing participants in this drama of Scripture. For Dempster, a landmark event in this story is the Pentecost Feast. Spirit baptism can be understood as including an empowerment to apply the covenant values to new situations and contexts. In this way, the Spirit empowers the contemporary Pentecostal community through Spirit baptism to live in ethical consistency and loyalty with the story of Scripture. The Old Testament then, and indeed all of Scripture, provides the foundation for ethical living and moral decision-making – not by cut-and-pasting the past expressions of moral behaviour and thinking onto the present, but by an empowering of the Spirit to live consistently and creatively imitating God's actions and character as revealed in the biblical narrative.

## Introduction

Murray Dempster was initially known to me through his writings and editorial work, particularly the *Pneuma* journal. As I am based in Australia, opportunities to personally meet scholars based out of North America, such as Murray, were limited. It was then through my involvement as part of the executive of the Society for Pentecostal Studies I had the great pleasure of becoming acquainted with Murray in person. The occasion was the presentation of the SPS Lifetime Achievement Award (jointly awarded to Murray, Doug Petersen and Byron Klaus) at the Annual Meeting of 2016. Through both the preceding correspondence and meeting, I came to appreciate the gracious manner and care for others that Murray exhibited in all his interactions. It is no surprise then to reflect that Murray's academic contribution has, among his diverse interests, reflected this same concern for ethical integrity and care for others. With this in mind, I will turn to an exploration of Old Testament sources of ethics from a Pentecostal perspective.

Pentecostals are people of the Book. It is on the rock-bed of Scripture that they orient their lives, activities, and theological reflection. Therefore, the need for a scriptural foundation for ethical decision-making is of the utmost importance. Yet, what do we do with the Old Testament? With its superseded laws, outdated cultural restrictions, and nationalistic outlook it may seem to be irrelevant to the community today. However, we recognise its value, at least in theory, as part of God's revelation. This chapter explores the use of the Old Testament as a source for ethics. Of course, it is impossible to study the value of the Old Testament for developing a Pentecostal social ethic without bumping into the work of Murray Dempster. So, first, this chapter will provide an overview of some of the key ideas promoted by Dempster in his exploration of a social ethic from the Old Testament. For Dempster, the covenant community is expected to live *imitatio Dei* as revealed by the narrative of God's character and actions. This leads secondly to consider how ethical texts from the Old Testament should be handled. That is, how do we interpret ethical texts of the Old Testament from our post-Pentecost location? I would like to suggest that texts from the Old Testament must be considered dialogically – reading them both in their own *context* and reading them *intertextually* – as part of the story of Scripture. The meta-narrative of Scripture, thirdly, provides the pattern for the Pentecostal community to integrate their lives. A key event in this narrative is what Dempster identifies as the "Pentecost Feast," where the Spirit is given for the empowerment of the covenant community. According to Dempster, the "confession of being Spirit baptized should lead to a passionate concern about justice, enhancing public morality and changing the plight of the underprivileged and marginalized."[1] Spirit baptism, it is argued, includes a creative empowerment to live in ethical consistency and loyalty with the story of Scripture. The Old Testament then, and indeed all of Scripture, provides the foundation for ethical living and moral decision-making – not by cut-and-pasting the past expressions of ethical decisions onto the present, but by an empowering of the Spirit to live consistently and creatively imitating God's actions and character as revealed in the biblical narrative.

## Dempster's Contribution to the Study of Biblical Ethics

Dempster has been one of the few voices within the community of Pentecostal scholars to articulate the significance of the Old Testament corpus for a biblical ethic. Dempster's direct contribution to social ethics is recognised by his work

[1] Murray W. Dempster, "The Structure of a Christian Ethic Informed by Pentecostal Experience: Soundings in the Moral Significance of Glossolalia," in Wonsuk Ma and Robert P. Menzies (eds), *The Spirit and Spirituality: Essays in Honor of Russell P. Spittler* (London and New York: T&T Clark, 2004), 108.

in developing a biblical mandate for social justice from a Pentecostal perspective.[2] While this theme is evident in much of his writing,[3] it was specifically in his 1987 *Pneuma* article that Dempster identified the need for a social ethic for the Pentecostal community, and that the role of Scripture was central to underpin this construction. To do this, Dempster began with the Old Testament (OT). He wrote "it is the Old Testament that presents social justice as the will of God for society and mandates the people of God to pursue it."[4] Dempster identified five ethical principles from the OT moral tradition to encourage a concern for social justice among the Pentecostal community. The five principles (the theocentric foundation of the OT; its concept of the Imago Dei; its portrayal of the covenant people; its prophetic tradition of social criticism, and its Jubilee teachings)[5] were then integrated into a reading of Luke-Acts. According to Dempster, God's character, laws, and will stood at the centre of Jewish life in the Old Testament. As God was considered morally good, the role of the community was to imitate God. The self-disclosure of God recorded in Scripture, particularly through the mighty, kind (*hesed*), and liberating acts of God, provided the basis for understanding the moral character of God whom they were to reflect. This theological foundation became the platform for social reform from which the prophets of the Old Testament could petition.[6]

At the heart of this ethical structure was a theocentric approach to ethics (based on theological definism) and its application to moral decision-making for the contemporary Pentecostal community. Dempster described this approach as a like a "silver thread" that runs throughout the biblical canon. Each text that reveals God's character and actions prescribes the standard to which the people of God should aspire in their own character and actions.[7] Therefore, the moral life of the community should be grounded in the *imitatio Dei*.[8] Yet, while Dempster emphasised this theocentric approach, he also complemented it with an anthropological perspective. He suggested that since all people are created in the image of God they should be treated with dignity and fairness. Dempster wrote, "the Old Testament teaches that persons are entitled to just treatment on the basis that they are persons created in the divine image, nothing more or

---

[2] Murray W. Dempster, "Pentecostal Social Concern and the Biblical Mandate of Social Justice," *Pneuma* 9:2 (Fall 1987), 129–53.

[3] This includes, but is not limited to, the following articles and chapters: "Eschatology, Spirit Baptism, and Inclusiveness: An Exploration into the Hallmarks of a Pentecostal Social Ethic," in Peter F. Althouse and Robert C. Waddell (eds), *Fresh Perspectives on Pentecostal Eschatologies* (Eugene, OR: Pickwick, 2010), 155–88; "Christian Social Concern in Pentecostal Perspective: Reformulating Pentecostal Eschatology," *Journal of Pentecostal Theology* 2 (April 1993), 53–66; "Evangelism, Social Concern, and the Kingdom of God" in Murray W. Dempster, Byron D. Klaus and Douglas Petersen (eds), *Called and Empowered: Global Mission in Pentecostal Perspective* (Peabody, MA: Hendrickson, 1991), 22–43; "The Structure of a Christian Ethic," 108–40.

[4] Dempster, "Pentecostal Social Concern," 129.

[5] Dempster, "Pentecostal Social Concern," 129.

[6] Dempster, "Pentecostal Social Concern," 130–31.

[7] Dempster, "The Structure of a Christian Ethic," 114.

[8] Further discussion by Dempster on the concept of the *imitatio Dei* can be found in "The Structure of a Christian Ethic," 114–15.

nothing less."[9] This must include those on the margins of society such as the alien, the poor, and oppressed.

Dempster also connected the mighty and liberating acts of God with the social concern reflected in the covenant obligations of the Old Testament people of God. As God had rescued the Israelites from slavery at the Exodus, so they were to mirror kindness to those in need of liberation, whether their situation be of metaphorical economic, social, or ethnic slavery.[10] For the liberated covenant community, the law provided tangible ways to live in right relationship with God and each other. The law promoted social justice in the everyday life of the faithful community, particularly through its measures to provide justice for and protect those on the margins.[11] Dempster considered the implications of these covenant principles of the Old Testament for the Pentecostal community to be enormous. He concluded,

> Thus, the church is empowered by the Spirit to provide a visible demonstration of what all of life should look like in the new covenant established in Jesus Christ which "fulfils" the Old Covenant. Accordingly, social justice should be proclaimed as God's will for the global community, and most significantly, it should be modelled within the pentecostal community as a social witness to the power of the Gospel.[12]

The social action of the church provides a "signpost" that this is, indeed, the covenant community in bringing healing and restoration to our alienated world.[13]

This concern for the right behaviour of the covenant community identified by Dempster in the law and self-revelation of God is also reflected in the prophets of the Old Testament. The prophets, as Fee and Stuart emphasise, are covenant enforcers.[14] That is, the prophets contextualise for each new generation the covenant requirements of the people of God. The prophets regularly remonstrated against the people for their unjust and unethical behaviour. For Dempster, this was particularly evident in the message of the eighth-century prophets. He wrote of Amos that "he explicitly identified justice as a fundamental moral quality of God's character."[15] Amos's message was one of indictment against the rich, ruling elite for their inhumane exploitation of the poor and vulnerable. The significance of the prophetic message of justice for the Pentecostal community was not lost on Dempster. He wrote, "the prophetic tradition stands as authoritative testimony that the social concern of God's people requires a prophetic cutting edge in its engagement with society."[16] In this way, Dempster prioritised the Old Testament in providing a foundational social ethic to challenge the Pentecostal community towards being an agent of social change.

---

[9] Dempster, "Pentecostal Social Concern," 132.
[10] Dempster, "Pentecostal Social Concern," 137.
[11] Dempster, "Pentecostal Social Concern," 135.
[12] Dempster, "Pentecostal Social Concern," 137.
[13] Dempster, "Pentecostal Social Concern," 137.
[14] Gordon D. Fee and Douglas Stuart, *How to Read the Bible For all its Worth*, 3rd ed. (Grand Rapids, MI: Zondervan, 2003), 184.
[15] Dempster, "Pentecostal Social Concern," 138.
[16] Dempster, "Pentecostal Social Concern," 142.

## Sources of Ethics within the Old Testament

What is (hopefully) clear in this summary of some of Dempster's contributions to biblical ethics is his reliance on the law and prophets of the Old Testament. This raises not only issues in using particular texts from the Old Testament as sources of ethics, but also issues raised by using the Old Testament in general as a source of ethics for the New Testament church. Jacqueline Lapsley identifies two primary approaches to biblical ethics of the Old Testament; that is, descriptive and constructive. Descriptive approaches focus on the ethics of ancient Israel; the ethics "behind" the world of the text. This approach is exemplified by scholars such as John Barton, who focus on the values and content of the Old Testament texts within their own history and development.[17] In comparison, according to Lapsley, constructive approaches explore how the Old Testament has informed and can inform understandings of key topics (such as creation, humanity, etc.) that guide or impact the moral and ethical norms of contemporary societies.[18] This second approach focuses on the application of Old Testament texts for today. For the Pentecostal community with both a high view of Scripture and a tendency towards pragmatism, this is of most interest. Pentecostals value Scripture and seek to follow the patterns of behaviour they see modelled in the text. As Wolfgang Vondey writes, "Pentecostals relate their experience to scripture, to stories and events in the Bible, because they interpret and authenticate their present experiences as participating in the biblical events thrust anew into the present."[19] Yet this sometimes works backwards for Pentecostals in the task of reading Scripture. Attempting to be true to Scripture, readers sometimes "cut-and-paste" texts from the Old Testament onto their daily life without recognition of the historical and cultural differences in the text. This propensity to interpret the Bible both literally and acontextually can too easily lead to misappropriation of the text.[20] Such acontextual readings divorce the text from its historical and cultural anchor.

Instead, the approach to reading Scripture for the Pentecostal community should be to understand each text in its own context and to apply the text in the direction to which Scripture points.[21] This is not an attempt to retrieve the original intention of the author, but to acknowledge and honour the actions and voice of God engaging the covenant community in the past. If the Pentecostal community believes and seeks the voice of God for today, then they must acknowledge and value the voice of God in the past and seek to understand that message as it was received by the historic community. To read the text in context

[17] See as an example, John Barton, *Ethics in Ancient Israel* (Oxford: Oxford University Press, 2014).

[18] Jacqueline E. Lapsley, "Ethics: Hebrew Bible/Old Testament," *Encyclopedia of the Bible and its Reception,* Vol. 8 (Berlin: de Gruyter, 2014), 98.

[19] Wolfgang Vondey, *Pentecostal Theology: Living the Full Gospel* (London: Bloomsbury/T&T Clark, 2017), 16.

[20] Jacqueline Grey, *Three's A Crowd: Pentecostalism, Hermeneutics, and the Old Testament* (Eugene, OR: Pickwick, 2011), 120–21.

[21] See Richard D. Israel, et al., "Pentecostals and Hermeneutics: Texts, Rituals and Community," *Pneuma* 15:2 (1993), 143. It is noted that Dempster was editor of *Pneuma*, in which this article appeared.

is to acknowledge God speaking to the covenant community in a different historic and cultural point in time. This also emphasises the diversity of God's revelation to the previous covenantal communities of the Old Testament, and the need to consider the diversity of texts which can be sources of ethics for the present. In this sense, the sources of ethics from the Old Testament must be considered dialogically – both reading them in their own *context* and reading them *intertextually* – as part of the integration process for the contemporary Pentecostal community. As Kenneth Archer recognises, there is a "necessary distance between the reader and the text by emphasizing the important contributions of both the text and reader in the making of meaning. This space between the reader and text creates a real conversation."[22]

As the process of reading Scripture in context has been detailed by numerous scholars,[23] it will not be attempted in this chapter other than to offer a brief comment concerning some of the challenges in reading Old Testament texts as a source of ethics for the Pentecostal community. This is particularly troubling when there appear to be "double standards" in the ethical expectations of the covenant community. That is, when God instructs or condones behaviour that is ethically dubious, especially when read as part of the meta-narrative of Scripture.[24] Other challenges occur when the cultural expectations of the Old Testament are misapplied to the contemporary context by Pentecostal readers. This tendency towards literalistic readings (as noted above) can result in a confusion of culture as though the Bible has direct universal application and has somehow escaped the vicissitudes of history.[25] Instead readers must recognise that, while the text makes a claim about the world, it is a claim that is made within a historical and cultural context. This leads then to the second aspect of the above statement that the sources of ethics from the Old Testament must be considered dialogically – read both *contextually* and *intertextually* – as part of the integration process for the contemporary Pentecostal community. While intertextuality can be understood in a variety of ways (including exploring the resonances between two independent texts), the focus here will be on the interconnection of the Old Testament text as part of the story of Scripture.

## The Old Testament as a Source for Ethical Decision-Making

A narrative approach to the reading of the whole of Scripture has much appeal to the Pentecostal community. Archer highlights the Pentecostal understanding

[22] Kenneth J Archer, *The Gospel Revisited: Towards a Pentecostal Theology of Worship and Witness* (Eugene OR: Pickwick, 2011), 123.

[23] For a Pentecostal perspective on this process, see Craig Keener, *Spirit Hermeneutics: Reading Scripture in Light of Pentecost* (Grand Rapids, MI: Eerdmans, 2016).

[24] For reflections on this theme from a Pentecostal perspective, see Andrew Davies, *Double Standards in Isaiah: Re-evaluating Divine Justice and Prophetic Ethics* (Leiden: Brill, 2000), and Andrew Davies, "Reading in the Spirit: Some Brief Observations on Pentecostal Interpretation and the Ethical Difficulties of the Old Testament," *Journal of Beliefs and Values* 30:3 (2009), 303–11.

[25] Kenneth J. Archer, "Early Pentecostal Biblical Interpretation," *Journal of Pentecostal Theology* 9:1 (2001), 36.

of Scripture "as a grand meta-narrative with the Gospels and Acts as the heart of the Christian story."[26] This narrative provides the pattern for which Pentecostals seek to live as they join the story – integrating and reorienting their lives as ongoing participants in the drama of Scripture. The Pentecostal community understand themselves as a continuation of the biblical narrative. This idea of the Scripture as a story is not simply because much of the Bible is in narrative form. The idea of the Bible presenting a kind of meta-narrative comes internally from within Scripture itself. There are various points within the Bible that provide summaries of the story thus far.[27] Yet, as Richard Bauckham has identified, while there are numerous texts in the Old Testament that provide summaries of part of the overarching history of Israel and some comparable summaries in the New Testament, it is only in Acts 13:17-41 that the narratives of the Old and New Testament are unified in a singular story.[28] As Acts identifies, the Bible as story is driven by the idea that Scripture as a whole is a witness to God's saving activity in human history. Bauckham continues, "Throughout the New Testament, of course, the story of Jesus is treated as the continuation of the story of Israel and as initiating the fulfilment of the prophetic promises to Israel."[29] The story of Scripture tells a somewhat unified and cohesive narrative of God's purpose for the world.[30] Importantly for ethical reflection, Bauckham also notes that the story of Scripture demonstrates God's continual and active care of the powerless and marginal.[31]

Yet one of the challenges with this meta-narrative approach is that some of the most significant texts from the Old Testament for ethical thinking and moral reasoning do not fit easily into a narrative framework.[32] The ethics of the wisdom writings of the Old Testament closely align to virtue ethics.[33] They emphasise the moral formation of the person and purity of character, rather than just purity of sacrifices as stressed in the law and prophets.[34] Instead, the focus in some of the wisdom writings is on a kind praxis: good thinking influences, or results in,

---

[26] Archer, *The Gospel Revisited*, 120.

[27] Bauckham identifies various partial summaries of the story of Israel, including Deuteronomy 6:20-24 (exodus to occupation of the land); Deuteronomy 26:5-9 (settlement in Egypt to occupation of the land); Joshua 24:2-13 (Abraham to occupation of the land); Nehemiah 9:6-37 (creation + Abraham to return from exile); Psalm 78 (exodus to David); Psalm 105 (Abraham to occupation of the land); Psalm 106 and 1 Chronicles 16:8-16 (exodus to exile); Psalm 135:8-12 (exodus to occupation of the land); Psalm 136 (creation + exodus to occupation of the land); Acts 7:2-50 (Abraham to Solomon). See Richard Bauckham, *The Bible in the Contemporary World* (Grand Rapids, MI: Eerdmans, 2015), 4–5.

[28] Bauckham, *The Bible in the Contemporary World*, 5.

[29] Bauckham, *The Bible in the Contemporary World*, 4.

[30] Bauckham, *The Bible in the Contemporary World*, 1.

[31] Bauckham, *The Bible in the Contemporary World*, 15.

[32] Of course, non-narrative material can be grafted onto the story via its canonical connections (such as connecting the wisdom literature to characters (such as Solomon) or to the relevant general historical period of pre-exilic or exilic material). But it is still somewhat an artificial connection.

[33] Barton, *Ethics in Ancient Israel*, 60.

[34] Barton, *Ethics in Ancient Israel*, 162–63.

good practice. For Pentecostals, this potentially has much resonance with the process of sanctification by which the Spirit transforms the heart (and character) of the believer to produce godly fruit (Gal. 5:22-23). Yet these ethical texts, such as the wisdom writings, are often missed in narrative approaches to Scripture because the texts are not "events" orientated towards the story of Scripture. Yet despite such limitations, the meta-narrative approach has much to offer the Pentecostal community as a framework for incorporating the Old Testament into their ethical thinking.

The understanding of Scripture as presenting a meta-narrative is well established in broader biblical scholarship. Among others,[35] N.T. Wright offers a compelling framework for the bible as an unfinished drama. Wright uses the analogy of a Shakespearean play of which the fifth (and final) act was missing. What if the actors immersed themselves in the first four acts and then were told to improvise the final act based on their knowledge of the story thus far but which brought the story to a proper conclusion (also provided from the consistency of the first four acts)? This would require the actors to continue the story "with both *innovation* and *consistency*." Wright outlines the five acts as being: "(1) Creation; (2) Fall; (3) Israel; (4) Jesus. The New Testament would then form the first scene in the fifth act, giving hints as well (Rom 8; 1 Cor 15; parts of the Apocalypse) of how the play is supposed to end."[36] One of the issues of this model, that Wright himself highlights, is what to do with the Old Testament when it appears to have been made somewhat obsolete by the New Testament. The sacrificial system was a grace in its time, but it is no longer to be directly applied by New Testament believers. Other aspects of the law of the Old Testament, such as the food or purity laws, have no functional role in the church, despite their usefulness as pointing to the character of God (such as holiness) for *imitatio Dei*. But perhaps this is the very point of their usefulness. As Dempster has emphasised, the concept of *imitatio Dei* that is very present in the Old Testament cannot just be discarded but continues in the "story" of Scripture through Jesus to the early church. He writes, "This ethical axiom of the *imitatio Dei*, which is embedded in the theological indicative/moral imperative structure of Old Testament ethical thinking, rests at the heart of Jesus' ethics."[37]

While Wright's framework is helpful, it is not the only option to consider. Dempster outlines four epochs in the story of Scripture: The Exodus; the rise of

---

[35] Other key scholars that utilise a meta-narrative approach to Scripture include, C.G. Bartholomew and M.W. Goheen, *The Drama of Scripture: Finding Our Place in the Biblical Story* (Grand Rapids, MI: Baker Academic, 2014); Bauckham, *The Bible in the Contemporary World*; Alister E. McGrath, *Narrative Apologetics: Sharing the Relevance, Joy, and Wonder of the Christian Faith* (Grand Rapids, MI: Baker Books, 2019).

[36] N.T. Wright, "How Can the Bible be Authoritative?" Accessed 27 January 2020, http://ntwrightpage.com/2016/07/12/how-can-the-bible-be-authoritative/, originally published in *Vox Evangelica* 21 (1991), 7–32.

[37] Murray W. Dempster, "Eschatology, Spirit Baptism, and Inclusiveness: An Exploration into the Hallmarks of a Pentecostal Social Ethic," in Peter Althouse and Robby Waddell (eds), *Perspectives in Pentecostal Eschatologies: World Without End* (Eugene, OR: Pickwick, 2010), 168.

the prophetic movements; the advent of Jesus Christ, and the Pentecost Feast. For Dempster, these landmark "events" are anchored in God's own character, which is demonstrated in acts of salvation and creative power.[38] It is clear in this narrative outline that the Old Testament does have an important role in the testimony of Scripture. The Old Testament provides important landmark events[39] that set the story of salvation on its trajectory. This includes the Exodus as a landmark event of liberation in which God acts on behalf of his covenant community to defeat oppressive powers. The prophets enforced the covenant requirements of justice and loyalty to Yahweh alone. Jesus continued the work of the prophets in proclaiming the kingdom of God: Jesus our saviour, sanctifier, Spirit baptiser and coming king – which leads to the Pentecost Feast. Dempster writes, "At the Pentecost festival, the same Holy Spirit who had earlier anointed and empowered Jesus of Nazareth was outpoured to call out and empower the disciples to form the church in order to perpetuate Jesus' mission, ministry and message."[40] The contemporary church now continues the story of the early church. The eschaton to which the story moves is both realised now and in the future. In the meantime, the Pentecostal community must be shaped by the story in which they find their place and meaning. To be shaped by the narrative is to act, in the words of Wright, with both *innovation* and *consistency*. In the words of Dempster, it is to live *imitatio Dei* as revealed by the story of God's character and actions. And as Dempster has argued, at the heart of God's character and actions are liberation, salvation, healing, and freedom – particularly for the poor, marginalised, and powerless. Yet what might be a distinctly Pentecostal contribution to interpreting the Old Testament as a source of ethical data?

## Conclusion: Pentecostal Perspectives

As noted above, Dempster has argued that a Pentecostal ethic should be characterised as theocentric.[41] This is modelled within the Old Testament narrative whereby the covenant community mirror the character and actions of God (*imitatio Dei*). Of course, the narrative of the Old Testament culminates in the person of Jesus Christ, as described in the New Testament. The Spirit of Jesus is then poured out on the covenant community in Acts, described by Dempster as including a "divine-human glossolalic encounter." He identifies an important outcome of this encounter as a "creative power." For Dempster, this idea of power is "the ability to translate purpose into action" – a kind of empowering to live out the purposes of God. This includes "the capacity to bring out new and previously unimagined possibilities out of existing realities."[42] According to Dempster, glossolalia functions as a symbol and model for the need to transform rational thinking into imaginative thinking, albeit including reflection on

---

[38] Dempster, "The Structure of a Christian Ethic," 121.

[39] This phrase is adopted from Bauckham, *The Bible in the Contemporary World*, 7.

[40] Dempster, "Eschatology, Spirit Baptism, and Inclusiveness," 162.

[41] Dempster, "The Structure of a Christian Ethic," 119.

[42] Dempster, "The Structure of a Christian Ethic," 117–18.

theological foundations.[43] In addition, it is also helpful to reflect upon glossolalia as an embodied phenomenon; it is outworked in active speech within a particular context.[44] So also moral decision-making must be outworked in concrete action within the Pentecostal community.

Yet while Dempster closely focuses his discussion on the linguistic act of glossolalic utterance,[45] I would like to suggest that his ideas can be broadened to the more general concept of Spirit baptism. That is, Spirit empowerment can stimulate new directions for considering the use of the Old Testament (and indeed the whole of Scripture) as an ethical resource. The God who is experienced as a "creative power" at Pentecost is the same God who has acted in redemptive and creative ways throughout the history.[46] This same God continues to empower the contemporary Pentecostal community through Spirit baptism to live in ethical consistency and loyalty with that history as revealed in Scripture. However, as this ethical consistency is not prescribed, it requires the creative empowerment of the Spirit to "bring out new and previously unimagined possibilities." Unlike in the second epoch of "the rise of the prophetic movements" identified by Dempster in the story of Scripture, it is not just a few selected individuals that are now imbued with this creative power, but now the whole covenant community. Therefore, for the Pentecostal community the Old Testament can provide a foundation for ethical living and moral decision-making – not by cut-and-pasting the past expressions of ethical decisions onto the present, but by an empowering of the Spirit to live consistently and creatively, imitating God's actions and character as revealed in the story of Scripture in new and concrete contexts.

## Discussion Questions

1. As identified by Grey, how might we in two or three sentences summarise Dempster's theocentric approach to ethics that leads to moral decisions?
2. How does a meta-narrative approach to hermeneutics, particularly within the OT, enhance the development of ethics? What are the limitations and how does narrative address those limitations?
3. Summarise the concept of *imitatio Dei* as developed within a meta-narrative approach to hermeneutics.

---

[43] Dempster, "The Structure of a Christian Ethic," 126–27.

[44] For further reflection on embodiment and tongues, see Michael Wilkinson and Peter Althouse, *Catch the Fire: Soaking Prayer and Charismatic Renewal* (DeKalb, IL: Northern Illinois University Press, 2014).

[45] Dempster is specific in his emphasis on glossolalia as the key to the creative empowerment rather than just Spirit baptism in general because glossolalia has the potential to critique those forms of constructed knowledge of God through human reasoning and language that can become a substitution, and perhaps even idol, for a relational knowing of God. See "The Structure of a Christian Ethic," 120.

[46] Dempster, "The Structure of a Christian Ethic," 124.

## Bibliography

Archer, Kenneth J. "Early Pentecostal Biblical Interpretation." *Journal of Pentecostal Theology* 9:1 (2001), 32–70.

Archer, Kenneth J. *The Gospel Revisited: Towards a Pentecostal Theology of Worship and Witness*. Eugene OR: Pickwick, 2011.

Bartholomew, C.G. and M.W. Goheen. *The Drama of Scripture: Finding Our Place in the Biblical Story*. Grand Rapids, MI: Baker Academic, 2014.

Barton, John. *Ethics in Ancient Israel*. Oxford, UK: Oxford University Press, 2014.

Bauckham, Richard. *The Bible in the Contemporary World*. Grand Rapids, MI: Eerdmans, 2015.

Davies, Andrew. *Double Standards in Isaiah: Re-evaluating Divine Justice and Prophetic Ethics*. Leiden: Brill, 2000.

Davies, Andrew. "Reading in the Spirit: Some Brief Observations on Pentecostal Interpretation and the Ethical Difficulties of the Old Testament." *Journal of Beliefs and Values* 30: 3 (2009), 303–11.

Dempster, Murray W. "Pentecostal Social Concern and the Biblical Mandate of Social Justice." *Pneuma* 9:2 (Fall 1987), 129–53.

Dempster, Murray W. "Evangelism, Social Concern, and the Kingdom of God." In *Called and Empowered: Global Mission in Pentecostal Perspective*. Eds Murray W. Dempster, Byron D. Klaus and Douglas Petersen. Peabody, MA: Hendrickson, 1991, 22–43.

Dempster, Murray W. "Christian Social Concern in Pentecostal Perspective: Reformulating Pentecostal Eschatology." *Journal of Pentecostal Theology* 1:2 (April 1993), 53–66.

Dempster, Murray W. "The Structure of a Christian Ethic Informed by Pentecostal Experience: Soundings in the Moral Significance of Glossolalia." In *The Spirit and Spirituality: Essays in Honor of Russell P. Spittler*. Eds. Wonsuk Ma and Robert P. Menzies. London and New York: T&T Clark, 2004, 108–40.

Dempster, Murray W. "Eschatology, Spirit Baptism, and Inclusiveness: An Exploration into the Hallmarks of a Pentecostal Social Ethic." In *Perspectives in Pentecostal Eschatologies: World Without End*, edited by Peter F. Althouse and Robert C. Waddell, 155–188. Eugene, OR: Pickwick, 2010.

Fee, Gordon D. and Douglas Stuart. *How to Read the Bible For All Its Worth*. 3rd ed. Grand Rapids, MI: Zondervan, 2003.

Grey, Jacqueline. *Three's A Crowd: Pentecostalism, Hermeneutics, and the Old Testament*. Eugene, OR: Pickwick, 2011.

Israel, Richard D. et al. "Pentecostals and Hermeneutics: Texts, Rituals and Community." *Pneuma* 15:2 (1993) 137–61.

Keener, Craig. *Spirit Hermeneutics: Reading Scripture in Light of Pentecost*. Grand Rapids, MI: Eerdmans, 2016.

Lapsley, Jacqueline E. "Ethics: Hebrew Bible/Old Testament." *Encyclopedia of the Bible and its Reception*. Vol. 8. Berlin: de Gruyter, 2014, 98.

McGrath, Alister E. *Narrative Apologetics: Sharing the Relevance, Joy, and Wonder of the Christian Faith*. Grand Rapids, MI: Baker Books, 2019.

Vondey, Wolfgang. *Pentecostal Theology: Living the Full Gospel*. London: Bloomsbury/T&T Clark, 2017.

Wilkinson, Michael and Peter Althouse. *Catch the Fire: Soaking Prayer and Charismatic Renewal*. DeKalb, IL: Northern Illinois University Press, 2014.

Wright, N.T. "How Can the Bible be Authoritative?" Accessed 27 January 2020. http://ntwrightpage.com/2016/07/12/how-can-the-bible-be-authoritative/. Originally published in *Vox Evangelica* 21 (1991) 7–32.

# Chapter 2

# Justice and Righteousness, Israel's Kingship Ideology, and the Spirit of God

Wonsuk Ma

**Abstract**

In Israel's history, kingship takes centre stage in the shaping of its society and theology. This study explores the nature and development of Israelite kingship and its ideology to set the context. The main discussion focuses on the maintenance and execution of justice and righteousness as a primary royal duty, and the role of the presence of God's Spirit upon selected leaders/kings as a critical part of kingship ideology. This study is intended to serve as a useful biblical foundation for engagements with social issues seeking justice and righteousness as an important theme for Pentecostal mission.

## Reflection on Murray Dempster

Pentecostal mission has evolved into a significant player in witnessing the gospel for slightly more than a century of its existence. Caring for the needy, or diakonic mission, has a strong presence in the Pentecostal mission scene, although its articulation came only recently. Advocating and working toward justice as an area of Pentecostal mission engagement are slowly emerging.[1] However, a plea to push the boundaries of Pentecostal mission to justice issues was passionately raised in the 1990s. At the centre of this prophetic voice was and has been Murray Dempster.[2]

To honour his scholarship and activism in campaigning for Pentecostals to take justice as an important mission agenda, this study investigates "justice and righteousness" in relation to Israel's kingship ideology and the Spirit's empowering role upon selected leaders. Kingship is singled out for its paramount role in the welfare and fate of the nation. This study aims to provide a useful

---

[1] For a discussion, see Julie C. Ma and Wonsuk Ma, *Mission in the Spirit: Towards a Pentecostal/Charismatic Missiology* (Oxford: Regnum Books, 2010), 7–14 (under the heading, "Three Ripples of Pentecostal Mission"). For an expanded discussion, Wonsuk Ma and Julie C. Ma, "Missiology: Evangelization, Holistic Ministry, and Social Justice," in Wolfgang Vondey (ed.), *Routledge Handbook of Pentecostal Theology* (London: Routledge, 2020), 279–89.

[2] Murray W. Dempster, Byron D. Klaus, and Douglas. Petersen (eds), *Called & Empowered: Global Mission in Pentecostal Perspective* (Peabody, MA: Hendrickson, 1991).

biblical and theological layer to the argument that justice is a crucial element in fulfilling God's mission today.

## Views of Kingship in Israel

The Old Testament appears to maintain an inconsistent attitude towards Israel's kingship. These contradictory views may reflect a specific social time and circumstance from which positive and negative views were held toward kingship.

First, there is a clearly negative sentiment about kingship. The narrative of 1 Samuel 8 describes the elders' request for a king as a rejection of Samuel's leadership and ultimately, God's kingship over Israel (8:7). This rebellious attitude, according to God, had been deeply rooted in the beginning of Israel's history: "As they have done from the day I brought them up out of Egypt until this day, forsaking me and serving other gods, so they are doing to you" (8:8, NIV). Up to this historical point, God had provided a unique type of leadership which combines several key roles, while positioned between God and his people. For example, Moses combines the priestly, prophetic, and political/military leadership roles. Because of this complex leadership which includes religious and political leadership, Moses and subsequent leaders such as Joshua, the judges, and now Samuel, are placed as a regent of God: ruling God's people under God's authority and legitimation.

This unique leadership system comes with weakness from the point of view of the people: the uncertainty of the succession process. The successions between Moses and Joshua and one between Eli and Samuel had no time gap. However, reading the book of Judges gives the reader a chaotic impression when people are without a judge for an extended period. This period without a leader is part of God's deliberate action to judge the nation's (or tribe's) infidelity to God. For instance, after the death of Joshua and his elders, a new generation arose "who knew neither the Lord nor what he had done for Israel … and who did evil in the sight of the Lord and served the Baals" (Judg. 2:10-11).

This underlying systematic uniqueness of succession in their leadership greatly influences their social structure. Because God is the ultimate king and the leader is his regent or visible representative among the people, it is God's prerogative as to who and when the next leader will be appointed. The succession, therefore, is unpredictable, adding uncertainty and instability to society. An uncertain environment for succession is the perfect environment where a "charismatic" leader could emerge. Even if the next leader has been chosen, there still is a process for the community to recognise and accept the new leader. This authentication process is found in several individuals in the Old Testament. For example, God had called Gideon as a judge, but his own clan and tribe were reluctant to acknowledge his legitimacy. Indeed, Gideon himself found it a difficulty that he was now chosen by God (Judg. 6:11-24). It took a national crisis in which his divine appointment was ratified through the coming of the Spirit (6:34), successful mobilisation of an inter-tribal army (6:34-39), and decisive victory over the enemy (Judg. 7). Equally limited is the nature of leadership and the power of the leader. It is God's will, not the best judgement of the leader, to discern and execute. It might have been easier to determine God's will if the leader combined both priestly and political roles as in Eli and Samuel.

In order to ensure the unique design of Israelite kingship, the prophets and priests functioned as a counterbalance when the monarchy was established. Before a military campaign, the priest was to give the king a divine sanction by offering a sacrifice before the war. Saul first failed in this test (1 Sam. 13:8-13). But it is the prophets who could interfere with the king's policy and action. They interfered with the king's spiritual life, criticised his ill intention, and condemned any violation against God's expectation. They did not wait for the king's invitation; they just appeared at their will. Prophet Nathan's rebuke over King David's action to violate Bathsheba, then murder her husband Uriah, and then take Bathsheba as his own wife in order to cover up his sinful acts (2 Sam. 11:1) represents an ideal role of the prophet (2 Sam. 12:7-12).[3] All the kings, both of Judah and Israel, were evaluated by the standards set by the prophetic tradition, and for this reason, the books of Samuel and Kings are part of the Former Prophets. They are judged by how faithful they were in keeping God's laws and ordinances rather than how ably they protected national interests. For example, Asa's positive "grade sheet" lists all the pious acts rejecting idol worship and restoring temple worship:

> (Asa) expelled the male shrine prostitutes from the land and got rid of all the idols his ancestors had made ... Although he did not remove the high places, Asa's heart was fully committed to the Lord all his life (1 Kgs. 15:12, 14).

In terms of Israelites viewing kingship in a positive light, the book of Judges and Israel's expectation of the continuing role of the king in the restored age are two helpful sources. The book of Judges, especially in its latter chapters, frequently attributes the chaotic, anarchic, and lawless state of the nation to the absence of the king. The typical expression is, "In those days Israel had no king; everyone did as they saw fit" (Judg. 17:6). Chapter 18 records an act of deception and violence by the Danites in their search for a settlement, and the whole story is prefaced by the familiar expression, "In those days Israel had no king" (18:1). Again, the following chapter reports appalling violence against the concubine of a Levite and a war against the Benjamites. This chapter also begins with the statement, "In those days Israel had no king" (19:1). The book ends with the same but expanded statement, "In those days Israel had no king; everyone did as they saw fit" (21:25).

Although one may be quick in concluding that the experiment with the judges is a failure, it is important to point out that all the four occurrences of the statement appear after Samson, the last recorded judge, died (16:31). The writer of the book, therefore, may attribute the lawless incidents to the absence of a leader. If so, why is the word "king" used to refer to the leader? Would the writer or the final redactor of the book see the lack of a national leader (versus the tribal

---

[3] Concerning David's abuse of Kingly authority see Jacqueline N. Grey, "A Prophetic Call to Repentance: David, Bathsheba, and the Royal Abuse of Power," in Cheryl Bridges Johns and Lisa P. Stephenson (eds), *Grieving, Brooding, and Transformation: The Spirit, The Bible, and Gender* (Leiden and Boston: Brill, 2021), 36–52.

nature of each judge's leadership) as the primary cause of the politically fragmented and morally degenerated state of the nation? The overall sense of the book of Judges is an affirmation of strong political leadership. This sentiment that is carefully placed in the latter part of the book and connected with the failed leadership of Eli (1 Sam. 2:12–4:21) may build a case for the people's request for a king.

On the other hand, some of Israel's expectations of the restored age includes the presence and role of a king or kingly figure. In an unspecified historical context which points to a crisis, the prophet Isaiah announced the appearing of the future king whose rule would fulfil all the spiritual, ethical, and political expectations:

> For to us a child is born,
> to us a son is given,
> and the government will be on his shoulders.
> And he will be called
> Wonderful Counselor, Mighty God,
> Everlasting Father, Prince of Peace.
> Of the greatness of his government and peace
> there will be no end.
> He will reign on David's throne
> and over his kingdom,
> establishing and upholding it
> with justice and righteousness
> from that time on and forever.
> The zeal of the Lord Almighty
> will accomplish this (Isa. 9:6-7).

It is observed that Old Testament eschatology has two contrasting views of the future: one is the continuation of the present order and the other is radical discontinuation. Naturally, the expectation of the future king is part of the former eschatological trend. Since most features of the ideal future king or leadership figure are the subject of the discussion on kingship ideology, it suffices to point out these issues.

## Sources of Israelite Kingship Ideology

As already observed, Israelite kingship ideology was developed through the contribution of various experiences. The first was the pre-monarchical vision of national leadership. Moses was the archetype, embodying the religious and political leadership roles in one person. His leadership legacy is found in his intimate relationship with God. He is the only one who saw God's glory and yet survived. This unusual relationship is attested in various incidents. Only Moses went up to Mountain Horeb to be in God's presence for forty days and forty nights (Exod. 34:28). God descended on the Tent of Meeting, and only Moses could enter the tent (Exod. 33:9). God's glory remained on the face of Moses, which the people could not withstand (Exod. 33:11). This ideal model of theocratic regency continues in Joshua, several judges, and Samuel. Israelite monarchy, therefore, has a different nature of kingship from the surrounding systems.

The second source of Israelite kingship ideology is the general expectation of kingship in the ancient Near East. Most kings traced their origin in divinity as observed in mythologies such as the Sumerian King List and Gilgamesh Epic. The preamble of the Code of Hammurabi (c. 1800 BCE) is perhaps the best example illustrating the nature of ancient kingship:

> … Anum and Enlil named me to promote the welfare of the people; me, Hammurabi, the devout, god-fearing prince, to cause justice to prevail in the land, to destroy the wicked and the evil, that the strong might not oppress the weak, to rise like the sun over the black-headed (people), to light up the land. Hammurabi, the shepherd, called by Enlil, am I; the one who makes affluence and plenty abound; who provides in abundance all sorts of things for Nippur-Duranki; the devout patron of Ekur; the efficient king, who restored Eridu to its place; … the one who strides through the four quarters of the world; who makes the name of Babylon great.[4]

The divine appointment or origin of Babylonian kingship is reiterated by invoking various deities but comes short of claiming one deity as the king of the nation. The Egyptian traditions go one step further by understanding each Pharaoh as the incarnate of the principal deity. It is the expectation or duties of the king that was prevalent throughout the ancient world. Ancient expectations of the king included a ruler to be powerful in securing the land, expanding the national borders, and subjugating neighbouring territories. He was also to be a "shepherd" providing benevolent care to his people, bringing prosperity to the nation, and maintaining law and order. Finally, he was to ensure the weak members of the nation were protected by destroying "the wicked and the evil," and preventing the powerful from oppressing the weak.

The third source of the ideology is the failure of fulfilling kingship roles. Although the beginning of Israelite monarchy encountered hindrances, David's ascendancy to kingship had abundant divine sanction. The most obvious is God's covenant offered to his household through the prophet Nathan: "Your house and your kingdom will endure forever before me; your throne will be established forever" (2 Sam. 7:16). However, as observed above, Israelite kingship generally failed to meet God's expectation. Judah, the southern kingdom, occasionally had kings who received affirming evaluations, but almost all the northern kings failed. The failure of the kings led to widespread abuses by the powerful of society. The judicial system became corrupt, the rights and welfare of the weak were not protected, and the moral standards of the nation collapsed. As the prophetic tradition pointed out, the destruction of a city was the reflection of the king's infidelity to God, the true king (Jer. 18:11). Ironically, such failure often took place amid political stability and economic prosperity. Religious leaders, who were called to counterbalance political power, were equally corrupt, often endorsing the evil of the leaders. That is why the eighth-century prophets, both from the south and the north, were extremely critical of political and religious leaders. The destruction of the nations and the exile of the people were the ultimate consequences due to the failed kingships and nations.

---

[4] James B. Pritchard (ed.), *Ancient Near Eastern Texts: Relating to the Old Testament*, 3rd ed. with suppl. (Princeton, NJ: Princeton University Press, 1969), 164.

## Kingship and the Spirit of God

The presence of God's Spirit upon selected leaders of Israel is a long-held tradition. The book of Judges and 1 Samuel are particularly rich in historical records of the Spirit upon leaders. The nature of the Spirit found among the leaders is often referred to as "charismatic" because of their unusual abilities and exploits. In the context of Israelite leadership, the "charismatic" process begins with the election of the leader. Due to its unique nature of leadership/kingship, as discussed above, it is God's prerogative who the next leader was and when and how he would raise him up.

In this "unstable" succession system, the Spirit of God plays a key role in verifying God's election of the leader. In this authenticating process, the coming of the Spirit is visibly demonstrated through "prophesying" as a common sign. For example, when the Spirit came upon the seventy elders, they "prophesied" (Num. 11:25). Since they were expected to function not as prophets but as administrators, the temporary prophetic experience was to serve as a proof of God's approval of Moses' selection of the seventy. Similarly, after Samuel anointed Saul in a private setting, the Spirit of God came upon him as he met the company of the prophets and prophesied (1 Sam. 10:7, 10, 11). In both cases, the verb for "prophesy" is in the hithpael form, which is believed to denote a certain behaviour which was readily understood as a sign of the Spirit's presence.[5] Again, he was not to be part of the company of the prophets, as the riddle suggests, "Is Saul also among the prophets?" (10:11). As in the seventy elders, the passage does not refer to any oracular activity. There is no doubt that this sign served first Saul himself and Samuel secondarily.[6] Ancient kingship in the ancient Near East shared a common feature of its divine origin, as seen above. Different from Egyptian or Mesopotamian traditions, Israelite kingship nonetheless claims a special divine sanction. The psalmist calls the king "God's anointed" (Ps. 2:2) who became his God's "son," and he is the king's "father" (2:7). This special and intimate relationship is illustrated by the placement of his vital quality or faculty on the human agent. This pattern of "election" is seen in the creation of humans in God's image (Gen. 1:26) and the breathing of his breath into the man's nostril (Gen. 2:7). This is exactly what the coming of the Spirit achieved in selected leaders of Israel: authenticating God's election and his special relationship with the leader.

The second function we observe in the presence of the Spirit is the equipping of leaders for specific tasks. In many cases, the leader rose to respond to a unique national crisis. Saul experienced for the second time the coming of the Spirit. This incident was clearly placed in the context of a military threat from the Ammonites: to "gouge out the right eye" of everyone in Jabesh Gilead, thus to "bring disgrace on all Israel" (1 Sam. 11:2). Upon hearing the loud weeping of the people, "the Spirit of God came powerfully upon him [Saul], and he burned with anger" (11:6). His call for war among Israelite tribes was met with a

---

[5] Robert R. Wilson, *Prophecy and Society in Ancient Israel* (Philadelphia: Fortress, 1980).

[6] Robert R. Wilson, "Prophecy and Ecstasy: A Reexamination," *Journal of Biblical Literature* 98 (1979), 321–37.

successful organisation of a large inter-tribal army as the "the terror of the Lord fell on the people, and they came out together as one" (11:7). The sweeping victory is attributed to the divine empowerment of the leader. The Spirit equipped him to exercise an unusual ability in organising the army and leading the campaign. There is no indication that the Spirit's presence or empowerment continued beyond this campaign. However, the enabling of the Spirit also had an authenticating role. His appointment as the king was unanimously accepted by the people (11:12-14). Although the empowering gift of the Spirit does not guarantee successful leadership,[7] it is this function which is directly linked to the king's obligation to administer justice and righteousness among the people. The "sign" role in the Spirit upon leaders would signify that their mandate towards the people came from God.

## Justice and Righteousness in Kingship Ideology

There are two areas in the king's duty: his relationship with God and one with the people. This relationship aspect is often referred to as "righteousness" or "doing right." Historical narratives link these two as an integral whole: if the king is faithful in his worship to God, he will also be faithful in governing the nation.

### *Isaiah 11:1-5*

This passage, often dated in the eighth century BCE, is one of the most important passages in the study of Israelite kingship ideology:

> A shoot will come up from the stump of Jesse;
> from his roots, a Branch will bear fruit.
> The Spirit of the Lord will rest on him –
> the Spirit of wisdom and of understanding,
> the Spirit of counsel and of might,
> the Spirit of the knowledge and fear of the Lord –
> and he will delight in the fear of the Lord.
> He will not judge by what he sees with his eyes,
> or decide by what he hears with his ears;
> but with righteousness, he will judge the needy,
> with justice, he will give decisions for the poor of the earth.
> He will strike the earth with the rod of his mouth;
> with the breath of his lips he will slay the wicked.
> Righteousness will be his belt
> and faithfulness the sash around his waist.

The exact setting of this passage has been debated, but one convincing contention is the priestly prayer of blessing at the coronation of a prince, next in line for the throne, or a new ruler.[8] The prayer stipulates the two dimensions of a king's obligation as discussed above: to God, the real king of Israel (or Judah

---

[7] See Wonsuk Ma, "Tragedy of Spirit-Empowered Heroes: A Close Look at Samson and Saul," *Spiritus: ORU Journal of Theology* 2:1 & 2 (2017), 23–38.

[8] Hans Wildberger, *Isaiah 1–12* (trans. Thomas H. Trapp; Minneapolis: Fortress, 1991), 63.

in this case) and to the people whom God entrusted to his rule. The idea of his upward relationship has two elements: the Spirit of God bestowed on him and the fear of the Lord as his response to God. The Spirit equips him with valuable qualities: wisdom, understanding, counsel, might, knowledge, and the fear of the Lord (11:2). The action also points to the equipping role of the Spirit: "judging with righteousness" and "deciding with justice" while "striking the earth" and "slaying the wicked" (11:4). His rule is summed to be "righteous" and "faithful," presumably in his relationship with the people and with God (11:5).

"Justice" and "righteousness" appear together more than thirty-two times either as a pair of words or in parallel lines in the Old Testament. Several of them specifically refer these traits to the king. 1 Kings 10:9 (also 2 Chr. 9:8) colours Israelite kingship as God's delight and an expression of his love for Israel, and the king is to "maintain justice and righteousness." Isaiah 9:7 also stipulates the task of the king as "establishing and upholding [the kingdom] with justice and righteousness."

Although these virtues are almost always used as one larger whole, each also distinguishes itself from the other. "Righteousness" (*ṣedeq*) in the Old Testament is a relational concept: "doing right" in the context of relationships. One's relationship embraces both God and fellow citizens. Therefore, "faithfulness" is an essential virtue in maintaining righteousness: faithful to God and the people. As God has demonstrated his faithfulness to his people through the covenantal relationship, the people are expected to reciprocate to God through their faithfulness. "Justice" (*mišpat*), on the other hand, is often linked to the judicial system of Israel, as in Isaiah 28:6, "a spirit of justice to him who sits in judgment." The same word is also translated as "judgment."[9] To properly "judge," wisdom for discernment is an essential virtue. The passage brilliantly highlights this discerning ability as the empowering gift of the Spirit for the king who acts as the final arbiter (cf. Solomon, 1 Kgs. 3:16-28). Wildberger sees justice as referring to the extrinsic activities while righteousness deals with intrinsic relationships.[10]

If upholding justice and righteousness was the priority of the kingly task, decisive dealing with the enemies of justice and righteousness in the community was an essential part of the kingly obligation. The "might" (v. 2) refers not to the military or political might but to the authority and power to administer justice and righteousness. This power is particularly exercised to "strike the earth" and "slay the wicked" (v. 4). For this reason, several scholars notice that the ideal king is less royal than historical kings.[11] This interpretation is well supported by how he is to wield his power to judge the evildoers: "with the rod of his mouth" and "the breath of his lips."

---

[9] See below on Isaiah 42.

[10] Wildberger, *Isaiah 1–12*, 64.

[11] E.g. Patricia K. Tull, *Isaiah 1–39* (Macon, GA: Smyth & Helwys, 2010), 228, "[the six virtues] are more at home in wisdom literature."

### Justice and Righteousness, and the Powerless

If we deconstruct and reconstruct the parallel lines of vv. 3b and 4a, we may read:

> He will judge the needy not by what he sees with his eyes but with righteousness,
> or decide for the poor of the earth not by what he hears with his ears but with justice.

Justice and righteousness specifically refer to the protection of the weak members of the community. The wholeness of Israelite society is, often, measured by the extent the weak are properly cared for. Throughout the Old Testament, the weak include orphans (or fatherless), widows, and foreigners. They were easy prey for exploitation in Israel (Ps. 94:6, also Mic., passage above). Thus, Israelite laws prohibit taking advantage of their powerlessness (e.g. Exod. 22:22; Deut. 24:17; 27:19; Zech. 7:10). Indeed, God becomes their protector: "A father to the fatherless, a defender of widows, is God in his holy dwelling" (Ps. 68:5); "Leave your fatherless children; I will keep them alive. Your widows too can depend on me" (Jer. 49:11). Therefore, the whole community and leaders were urged to uphold the rights and welfare of the orphans, widows, and foreigners who had little or no legal right in society: "Learn to do right [or "righteousness"]; seek justice. Defend the oppressed. Take up the cause of the fatherless; plead the case of the widow" (Isa. 1:17; cf. Jer. 22:3).[12]

However, the administration of justice and maintaining righteousness are not merely royal tasks. They are the key virtues and qualities flowing from a special relationship with God through his Spirit upon the ruler. Therefore, he is to be also just and righteous in relationship with God and the people. For this reason, a prayer is offered for the king: "Endow the king with your justice, O God, the royal son with your righteousness. May he judge your people in righteousness, your afflicted ones with justice" (Ps. 72:1-2). The king's failure, on the other hand, brings a moral failure to the nation (e.g. Mic. 3:1-3).

When the king moves astray from his duty of righteousness and justice, it is the prophet who confronts the ruler by reminding him of God's demand. The prophet Nathan's confrontation of David over his adultery and murder showcases this prophetic role. Therefore, when the prophet fails, it spells a fatal disaster to the nation: "[The prophets] lead the people astray, they proclaim 'peace' if they have something to eat, but prepare to wage war against anyone who refuses to feed them" (Mic. 3:5).

However, there was the lone voice of a true prophet who publicly declared his allegiance to God: "But as for me, I am filled with power, with the Spirit of the LORD, and with justice and might, to declare to Jacob his transgression, to Israel his sin" (3:8). Here, as with the king, the prophet full of God's Spirit and justice and might now courageously pointed out sins and transgressions of the powerful leaders, including fellow prophets. He announced God's judgement for the total collapse of spiritual, moral, and social order by singling out the failure of the leaders:

---

[12] For the "powerless" and "powerful," see James Limburg, *The Prophets and the Powerless* (Atlanta: John Knox, 1977), 25–53.

> Hear this, you leaders of Jacob, you rulers of Israel, who despise justice and distort all that is right; who build Zion with bloodshed, and Jerusalem with wickedness. Her leaders judge for a bribe, her priests teach for a price, and her prophets tell fortunes for money. Yet they look for the Lord's support and say, "Is not the Lord among us? No disaster will come upon us." Therefore because of you, Zion will be plowed like a field, Jerusalem will become a heap of rubble, the temple hill a mound overgrown with thickets (3:9-12).

### *Isaiah 42:1-4*

We have already noted the critical role that the Spirit plays in the life of the king and his administration of justice and righteousness. By looking at selected pre-exilic prophetic oracles, one can suspect that Israel's kingship ideology took justice and righteousness as key virtues, values, and tasks of the king largely due to the failure of the kings, both in Israel and Judah. Then how did the people envision the coming king who would fulfil kingship ideology? As alluded to above, Israel's eschatology was not uniform: one tradition expected the continuation of the present order, including kingship, whereas another anticipated the direct rule of God without human intermediaries. This discussion takes a look at the former tradition. Perhaps the most known passage would be Isaiah 42:1-4:

> Here is my servant, whom I uphold, my chosen one in whom I delight; I will put my Spirit on him, and he will bring justice to the nations. He will not shout or cry out, or raise his voice in the streets. A bruised reed he will not break, and a smoldering wick he will not snuff out. In faithfulness, he will bring forth justice; he will not falter or be discouraged till he establishes justice on earth. In his teaching, the islands will put their hope.

In this so-called "First Servant Song," God introduces his servant to the unknown audience. About his servant, he uses a catalogue of affirmations indicating his approval: "my servant," "uphold," "my chosen," and "delight." This overwhelming approval is followed by God's bestowal of his Spirit and his mission: bringing justice to the nations. "Justice" appears three times in the passage, making it the main emphasis. The nature of "justice" is not immediately clear. For example, John Watts translates the word as "verdict" or "judgment" to the nations in the literary context of the trials between God and the idols (40:1-5, 9-10).[13] Similarly, Goldingay interprets it as "Yahweh's just purpose in the world" as the servant "conveys and implements Yahweh's decision."[14] Oswalt further argues that the servant's mission to establish justice is ultimately to bring God's salvation to the nations by establishing the "life-giving order" restoring the creation … in accordance with the design of its Lord."[15] If nations and the coastland are receiving the servant's ministry of justice and God's teaching (or *torah*), then, as Goldingay contends, Isaiah 2:2-4 may provide the vision of the

---

[13] John D.W. Watts, *Isaiah 34–66, Word Biblical Commentary* (Waco, TX: Word Books, 1987), 113, 119.

[14] John Goldingay, *Isaiah* (Peabody, MA: Hendrickson, 2001), 240.

[15] John N. Oswalt, *The Book of Isaiah Chapters 40–66* (Grand Rapids, MI: Eerdmans, 1998), 110.

nations coming to Zion to worship Yahweh and receive his instruction (*torah*).[16] And this mission is accomplished by the presence of God's Spirit upon the servant.

Particularly significant is the manner in which the servant would fulfil his mission. In contrast to the traditional "charismatic" features of the Spirit upon the recipients, the servant will exhibit the Spirit's empowerment by persevering pursuit for the task. Devoid of the old connection between military or physical prowess and the Spirit, he will endure hardship and approach the weak with tenderness (vv. 2-3). This internalised "empowerment" of the Spirit would demonstrate God's solution to the world that awaits God's justice. Although Oswalt may read this passage with other Servant Songs, the meekness of the Spirit's presence is well expressed: "God's answer to the oppressors of the world is not more oppression nor is his answer to arrogance more arrogance; rather in quietness, humility, and simplicity, he will take all the evil into himself and return only grace. That is power."[17]

## Recapping: The Spirit and Life

This brief essay has observed the uniqueness of Israelite kingship in its development and ideology. Although it shared the "sacral" nature of the institution, Israel's claim was distinct from its neighbouring traditions. As seen in passages, justice and righteousness are God-given qualities, principles, attitudes, and goals of the king's dealing with the people. These qualities flow from the king's intimate relationship with God and are best tested in the care or lack thereof for the needy and weak as it pertains to the Israelite laws. The Israelite king is the regent of Yahweh, the God of Israel. The king's priority of justice and righteousness, therefore, reflects God's priority for his people.

Following the ancient tradition, the endowment of God's Spirit upon the ruler, therefore, had both authenticating and empowering functions. The presence of God's Spirit established the source of the ruler's legitimacy and authority while reminding him of his accountability to God. However, there is a significant shift in the understanding of the "charismatic" nature of rulership. Isaiah 11 undermines any military or political aspect of the king's rule through the Spirit's empowerment. Isaiah 42 takes it further to remove any external demonstration of superhuman ability. At the same time, the servant's single focus for the fulfilment of the "mission" is attributed to the presence of the Spirit.

There are two more important observations to be made in both passages. The first one looks at the passages that link the Spirit upon the ideal ruler/leader to the fullness of life. From the literary composition in Isaiah 11, the full restoration of harmony and peace of creation is the extension of the Spirit-empowered leader's just rule (11:6-9). The scene of the returned "paradise" reaches back to the perfect original intent of God's creation ("good" and "very good" in Gen. 1). There is no hint of violence, and this world of shalom is finally realised through the just rule of the king, who has been in turn endowed with the Spirit of the true

---

[16] Goldingay, *Isaiah*, 240.

[17] Oswalt, *The Book of Isaiah*, 111.

king, God. In the case of Isaiah 42, the emphasis is a bit different, but the focus on "life" is still evident. Immediately following the passage, v. 5 picks up the prevailing creation motif introduced in ch. 40. "The Creator of the heavens, who stretches them out, who spreads out the earth with all that springs from it, who gives breath to its people, and life to those who walk on it." Although in the earlier passages the creation motif plays a prominent role in setting the God of Israel far above the idols (e.g. 40:17-20) his supreme wisdom and power are now directed to his people and their mission to the nations: "I will keep you and will make you to be a covenant for the people and a light for the Gentiles, to open eyes that are blind, to free captives from prison and to release from the dungeon those who sit in darkness" (vv. 6b-7). Although the immediate impression is more of a micro-vision of the restoration of life, Israel (and the servant) serves as "the covenant for the people and a light for the Gentiles [or nations]." If the paradise scene in ch. 11 is the outcome of the restoration plan, ch. 42 depicts the process of the same plan. Similar work is repeated in ch. 61. In the vision of the restoration of the world through the Spirit-empowered ruler/servant, the "charismatic" power and the restoration of life merge.[18] After all, it is the same Spirit of God creating and renewing his creation (Gen. 1:2 and e.g. Ezek. 47).

The second important point looks at the community identity of the servant in Isaiah 42, important as in other passages, in what is called Second Isaiah (e.g. 41:8; 44:1; 45:4; 49:3). The beginning part of the chapter leans more towards an individual identity, and so do other "servant" passages (e.g. Isa. 53:1-10). Isaiah 42:5, by the literary transition, links justice to life while expanding the servant from the individual to the corporate identity. However, this does not resolve the mystery surrounding the identity of the servant. It is possible that the identity of the servant was left ambiguous, or the double-identity was intentional. After all, the king represented the people of God as much as he ruled with God's entrusted authority. In the same way, the servant could represent the people of God. And this mixed identity is further developed in the New Testament. The Gospel writers identify Jesus as the Servant by quoting Isaiah 43 at his baptism (Matt. 3:16-17; Mark 1:10-11; Luke 3:21b-22). The descending of the Spirit is crucial as he was soon to be tested by the leading of the Holy Spirit (Matt. 4:1; Mark 1:12). Yes, through the empowering work of the Spirit, he performed miracles and wonders (Acts 10:38), and more importantly, he bore the cross through the empowering presence of the Spirit (Heb. 9:14). Through his righteous "rule," he restored right relationships, ushered in God's kingdom, and inaugurated the new era (Luke 4:19:18-19; also Isa. 61:1-3). Equally important is the establishment of the church as his people and body in the world through the life-giving and empowering work of the Holy Spirit (Acts 2). Both Jesus and his church share the same mandate of proclaiming God's salvation and the empowerment of the Holy Spirit. It is no wonder that the first sermon by Peter on the Day of Pentecost was from the Joel passage. As the selected leaders received the Spirit, the whole people of God anticipated the pouring out of the Spirit in the last days (Joel 2:28-29). Although "social justice and righteousness" is a crucial dimension of

[18] Wonsuk Ma, "Isaiah," in Trevor J. Burke and Keith Warrington (eds), *A Biblical Theology of the Holy Spirit* (London: SPCK, 2014), 34–45.

mission in the Spirit, it is part of the larger work of restoring God's creation through the Spirit: righting the broken relationship and justifying the undeserved. That's the call which the Spirit-empowered people of God have received to take to the ends of the earth!

## Discussion Questions

1. What is meant by the prophets and priests functioning as a counterbalance to the monarchy of Israel?
2. In what ways did the Spirit of God authenticate leaders?
3. In what ways do justice and righteousness provide protection to the weak members of the community?
4. How might the present community of the people of God participate in the restoration of God's creation through the Spirit?

## Bibliography

Dempster, Murray W., Byron D. Klaus, and Douglas Petersen, Eds. *Called & Empowered: Global Mission in Pentecostal Perspective*. Peabody, MA: Hendrickson, 1991.

Goldingay, John. *Isaiah*. Peabody, MA: Hendrickson, 2001.

Grey, Jacqueline N. "A Prophetic Call to Repentance: David, Bathsheba, and the Royal Abuse of Power." In *Grieving, Brooding, and Transformation: The Spirit, The Bible, and Gender*. Eds. Cheryl Bridges Johns and Lisa P. Stephenson. Leiden and Boston: Brill, 2021, 36–52.

Limburg, James. *The Prophets and the Powerless*. Atlanta: John Knox, 1977.

Ma, Julie C. and Wonsuk Ma. "Three Ripples of Pentecostal Mission." In *Mission in the Spirit: Towards a Pentecostal/Charismatic Missiology*. Oxford: Regnum Books, 2010, 7–14.

Ma, Wonsuk. "Isaiah." In *A Biblical Theology of the Holy Spirit*. Eds Trevor J. Burke and Keith Warrington. London: SPCK, 2014, 34–45.

Ma, Wonsuk. "Tragedy of Spirit-Empowered Heroes: A Close Look at Samson and Saul." *Spiritus: ORU Journal of Theology* 2:1 & 2 (2017), 23–38.

Ma, Wonsuk and Julie C. Ma. "Missiology: Evangelization, Holistic Ministry, and Social Justice." In *Routledge Handbook of Pentecostal Theology*. Ed. Wolfgang Vondey. London: Routledge, 2020, 279–89.

Oswalt, John N. *The Book of Isaiah Chapters 40–66*. Grand Rapids, MI: Eerdmans, 1998.

Pritchard, James B., Ed. *Ancient Near Eastern Texts: Relating to the Old Testament*. 3rd ed. Princeton, NJ: Princeton University Press, 1969.

Tull, Patricia K. *Isaiah 1–39*. Macon, GA: Smyth & Helwys, 2010.

Watts, John D.W. *Isaiah 34–66, Word Biblical Commentary*. Waco, TX: Word Books, 1987.

Wildberger, Hans. *Isaiah 1–12*. Trans. Thomas H. Trapp. Minneapolis: Fortress, 1991.

Wilson, Robert R. "Prophecy and Ecstasy: A Reexamination." *Journal of Biblical Literature* 98 (1979), 321–37.

Wilson, Robert R. *Prophecy and Society in Ancient Israel*. Philadelphia: Fortress, 1980.

# Chapter 3

# "I Stand at the Door and Knock": Eucharist, Homelessness, and the Paradox of Hospitality

Chris E.W. Green

Those who become Jesus' understudies will abide with the unclean.

Theodore Jennings

The Christian vision of the restoration of all things in Christ is kindled at the altar.

Donald MacKinnon


## Abstract

This essay explores what it means to invite the outsider into the community while also holding faithfully to the way of wholeness and holiness. The essay considers the paradox of exclusion and embrace. The focus of this exploration is set in the homelessness of God. Via the incarnation, Jesus is the foreigner who offers hospitality.


## Introduction

Four or five years ago, I heard a seminary student share his testimony in a chapel service, and I remember his story every time I'm forced to think about hospitality. He told us about the year he had spent as a Christian student in a Muslim school in Cairo. They had accepted him graciously, he said, assuring and reassuring him that he belonged, respecting his faith, welcoming his questions, patiently responding to his concerns. When the time came for graduation, he and the head of school exchanged gifts. As soon as he graduated, however, he began to pray for God to force the school's closure. The room broke into applause when he said it had been in fact been shut down only a short time after his departure.

This story forces difficult questions, does it not? It seems wrong for him to have responded to their hospitality as he said he did. Jesus commanded us to bless those who curse us, and whatever else he meant, he surely did not intend for us to curse those who have blessed us. But it may be that I misheard the student's story. English was not his first language, and he was describing a life I do not know at all. Even if I heard him rightly, even if he meant exactly what I took him to mean, you could argue that he was not wrong to do what he did or to feel what he felt about it. The apostle Paul tells the Galatians to count as "accursed" anyone who "proclaims to you a gospel contrary to what you received" (Gal. 1:9) and warns the Romans against presuming on God's graces:

"Note then the kindness and the severity of God" (Rom. 11:22). He admonishes the Corinthians against mingling with the unfaithful:

> Do not be mismatched with unbelievers. For what partnership is there between righteousness and lawlessness? Or what fellowship is there between light and darkness? What agreement does Christ have with Beliar? Or what does a believer share with an unbeliever? What agreement has the temple of God with idols? For we are the temple of the living God … (2 Cor. 7:14-16).

Similarly, the apostle John directs those in his community not to "receive into the house or welcome anyone who comes to you and does not bring this teaching [that Jesus Christ has come in the flesh]," arguing that to do so is "to participate in the evil deeds of such a person" (2 John 1:10-11). So – what, then? Is holiness the limit of hospitality? In the Scriptures, "God's challenge to invite the alien and outsider is accompanied by the equally challenging command to remain distant from the transgression and wickedness of the world."[1] The question, then, is how these commands are to be reconciled. Can they be lived at once, as one? If so, how? By whom? To what end?

## Exclusion as Embrace

Contemporary "Western" societies have been labelled, not entirely misleadingly, pluralist, postcolonial, post-Christian.[2] Unsurprisingly, under the cross-pressures of these times, within the struggle to learn how to live well with one another, hospitality has emerged as a prevailing theme for philosophers and theologians. Richard Kearney, for example, has argued that Scripture is "made up of struggles between two different ways of responding to the alien."[3] And it has taken this shape, he believes, because the Abrahamic traditions – Jewish, Christian, and Islamic – are themselves defined by that struggle, determined at every point by the defining difference between conflict and openness, exclusion and embrace.

> Three of the earliest books of the Bible are about hosting strangers – Job, Ruth and the Song of Songs. Job challenges Yahweh before finally accepting his strange ways. Ruth is a Moabite alien welcomed by Boas into his home, thereby initiating a long line of hybrid descendants including David and Jesus. And the Song of Songs may be cited as paradigmatic of the coming together of Israel and its Egyptian rival – King Solomon hosts the foreign "Shulammite" woman, defying tradition to embrace this "black and beautiful" stranger as his bride.[4]

Kearney concludes – rightly, I think – that the Abrahamic traditions offer a wisdom worth heeding. It is right and good to take the side of the stranger and to offer welcome to outsiders. For some in those traditions, if not all, "hosting your

---

[1] Wolfgang Vondey, *People of Bread: Rediscovering Ecclesiology* (Mahwah, NJ: Paulist, 2008), 103.

[2] See Matthew Kaemingk, *Christian Hospitality and Muslim Immigration in an Age of Fear* (Grand Rapids, MI: Eerdmans, 2018).

[3] Richard Kearney, "Guest or Enemy? Welcoming the Stranger," *ABC Religion and Ethics* (21 June 2012), http://www.abc.net.au/religion/articles/2012/06/21/3529859.htm. (accessed 13 January 2023).

[4] Kearney, "Guest or Enemy?" n.p.

Other is more divine than protecting your own," because "the divine, as exile, is in each human other who faces us, defenseless and vulnerable." Heirs of Abraham's faith should know that the face of a stranger reflects the face of God in ways a familiar face cannot.[5]

But even if Kearney is right, as I think he is, more, much more, needs to be said. For Christians, at least, hospitality must be understood paradoxically, because Jesus, the divine and human one, is "the only definition of love."[6] In him, two glories, the glory of the Creator and the glory of the created, cohere and cooperate fully and fulfillingly, without anything like competition or discord. For just that reason, however, his life is also a sign of contradiction, a life lived in conflict with the powers that "make things happen" in the world. Jesus loves us, unconditionally. But his unconditional love conditions us absolutely. So, the promise of the gospel, which assures us that all things shall be conformed to his likeness, is in a very real sense also a threat – not to us exactly, but to so much of what we regard as good and necessary.

We see these paradoxes at play in the story of Zacchaeus (Luke 19:1-10). Thinking he has sought out Jesus, Zacchaeus finds, to his delight, that he is the one who has been pursued. Caught off guard, he finds he cannot help but offer Jesus the same welcome Jesus has offered him. And in that reciprocation, he is freed to be true to himself by doing right by his neighbours. His exchange with Jesus leaves no doubt: precisely because "he too is a son of Abraham," the only way he can return home is by offering to others the same welcome his fathers offered to and received from God. Jesus, in a single act, both vindicates Zacchaeus and convicts him, offering him a reassurance that pressures him toward healing and integration. So, in the end, Zacchaeus learns what we all must learn: salvation comes as kindness and severity, a making and an unmaking, life and death. Or to say the same thing another way, grace not only gives what it demands but also makes the last demand on us in that giving, freeing us not from responsibility but into it. The Zacchaeus story suggests that Christ's hospitality is at home even in this homelessness, that the invitation into the Father's house begins with a visitation from the wandering Son.[7] God, Luke means to teach us, is a guest who gives his hosts their hospitality, a host who became a guest so we might become his hosts and co-hosts.

## The Homelessness of God

If Jesus' story tells us anything, it is that God is hospitable. Indeed, all of God's works – creation and providence, redemption and consummation – are acts of hospitality. And not only his works: God is hospitable in and for himself. Immanently, then, God is lover, beloved, and love itself, and so also host, guest, and hospitality. In their missions, however, Jesus and the Spirit are met at nearly

---

[5] Kearney, "Guest or Enemy?" n.p.

[6] Dietrich Bonhoeffer, *Ethics* (New York: Simon & Schuster, 1995), 53–54.

[7] Bryne Lewis, "Not At-Home: Rethinking Hospitality and Homelessness," *The Other Journal* (7 January 2012), https://theotherjournal.com/2012/01/07/not-at-home-rethinking-hospitality-and-homelessness-3/.

every turn with inhospitality. Mary welcomed them, of course. As did others, including Simeon, John the Baptist, Mary and Martha and Lazarus. But they are the exceptions. At almost every moment of time, God comes to his own and his own receive him not.

We know, of course, how Jesus' story ends. But, as Mark's Gospel tells us, long before anyone in Jerusalem has heard of him, Jesus is met in the synagogue in Nazareth with furious resistance. These people – his neighbours, his kinfolk – have known him his entire life. They're so familiar with him and his family, in fact, that they're sure they know all they need to know about him, sure he has no right to speak and act in such ways. Their question is tellingly smug: "Where did this man get all this?" Here is how Mark tells the story:

> Jesus came to his hometown, and his disciples followed him. On the sabbath he began to teach in the synagogue, and many who heard him were astounded. They said, "Where did this man get all this? What is this wisdom that has been given to him? What deeds of power are being done by his hands! Is not this the carpenter, the son of Mary and brother of James and Joses and Judas and Simon, and are not his sisters here with us?" And they took offense at him. Then Jesus said to them, "Prophets are not without honor, except in their hometown, and among their own kin, and in their own house." And he could do no deed of power there, except that he laid his hands on a few sick people and cured them. And he was amazed at their unbelief.[8]

If Jesus met with inhospitality then, "in the days of his flesh," he meets with it now even more. Siobhán Garrigan suggests that this is the truth in the old Irish tradition of leaving a candle in the window on Christmas Eve: Jesus roams the earth, a stranger looking for shelter, for rest, and he needs a "signal of welcome" before he can approach.[9] More provocatively, it might be said that he is the legendary Jew cursed to wandering.[10] The same can be said of the Spirit, the dove that returns again and again to the Ark, restlessly, the fire that is all too easily quenched.

No doubt, the sufferings of Christ and the Spirit expose the cold hostility of our world, laying bare our wearied lack of concern for the needs of others, as well as the cruelties of power systems we've made (and been made – or unmade – by). But Christ and the Spirit are at ease with their homelessness, and the hospitality they offer is essentially paradoxical. In Christ, God has become a guest of the human so we might become hosts of the divine. Or to the say the same thing another way, we are a home for God just as we open our lives for others.

---

[8] Mark 6,1-3.

[9] Trinity College Dublin, "Professor Siobhán Garrigan Calls for a New Understanding of 'Home' in Inaugural Lecture," *News and Events* (Dublin: Trinity College, 3 November 2014), https://www.tcd.ie/news_events/articles/professor-siobhan-garrigan-calls-for-a-new-understanding-of-home-in-inaugural-lecture/ (accessed 13 January 2023).

[10] In the legend, of course, the man is doomed to wander because he taunted Jesus on his way to the cross. But if Jesus is who Christians confess him to be, then he not only does not curse those who curse him, he *blesses* them – and not merely in word: in deed.

### The Presence of God and the Presence of My Enemies

In Luke's Gospel, the Zacchaeus story is the seventh story of meals Jesus shared with strangers and friends.[11] The first is the story of a meal shared with Levi (Luke 5.27-32):

> After this he went out and saw a tax collector named Levi, sitting at the tax booth; and he said to him, "Follow me." And he got up, left everything, and followed him. Then Levi gave a great banquet for him in his house; and there was a large crowd of tax collectors and others sitting at the table with them. The Pharisees and their scribes were complaining to his disciples, saying, "Why do you eat and drink with tax collectors and sinners?" Jesus answered, "Those who are well have no need of a physician, but those who are sick; I have come to call not the righteous but sinners to repentance."

In this story, Jesus extends an invitation to Levi, an invitation that moves the tax collector to throw a big party, and to invite all the wrong people to the celebration, a move that some scribes and Pharisees cannot help but find bothersome. Jesus seems to answer their complaints, explaining he has come to call sinners to repentance. But as they must have immediately realised, he meant for them to change, not the tax collectors. He addresses them as the sinners, the diseased. And although they hold Jesus in high regard, they cannot, as a group, make themselves make that change. Because they are enthralled to the powers that make the world go around, they feel their lives depend on the difference established between "sinners" and "the righteous." So, when Jesus calls that difference into question, he unsettles them – like a mother bird stirring her chicks out of the nest.

Luke's table theology is deeply Psalmic, calling up the promise/threat of Psalm 23, in particular: God prepares his feast for us always and only in the presence of our enemies (Ps. 23.5). Why? So that we might serve them as he has served us. We are invited to the Lord's Table not as guests but as co-hosts, his fellow slaves, bent to the same tasks. This is the secret Christ shares with the Twelve at his last meal with them before his death (Luke 22:24-27):

> A dispute also arose among them as to which one of them was to be regarded as the greatest. But he said to them, "The kings of the Gentiles lord it over them; and those in authority over them are called benefactors. But not so with you; rather the greatest among you must become like the youngest, and the leader like one who serves. For who is greater, the one who is at the table or the one who serves? Is it not the one at the table? But I am among you as one who serves."

As Theodore Jennings argues, religious and political "systems of division and domination ensure their rule through the threat of the body, the threat, above all, of torture, humiliation, and death."[12] In his torturous passion, dying among thieves as another godforsaken one, Jesus not only denounces these systems as

---

[11] See Luke 5:27-32; 7:36-50; 9:10-17; 10:38-42; 11:37-52; 14:1-24; 19:1-10. After these meals, Jesus shares the Last Supper with the Twelve (22:14-38), breaks bread with two disciples at Emmaus (24:28-32), and eats in the presence of the disciples (24:36-43).

[12] Theodore W. Jennings, Jr. *Transforming Atonement: A Political Theology of the Cross* (Minneapolis: Fortress, 2009), 118.

wicked, but also "breaks the back of pollution taboos," revealing that holiness is not achieved or safeguarded or defended but only always shared. Love for Jesus "keeps the Christian community riveted upon the bodies of those who suffer," not only because "every broken and suffering body is a recognizable mirror of the body of the Crucified" but also because every broken and suffering body is recognised as itself in the mirror of Jesus' crucifixion. Thus, as Jennings says, "those who become Jesus' understudies will abide with the unclean."[13]

## Conclusion

"Behold I stand at the door and knock" (Rev. 3:20). On their own, these words read as a sign that the Laodiceans, like Dostoevsky's inquisitor, have excluded Jesus, leaving him out of their "ministries." But in the flow of the text, they take on another significance. In the message to the angel of the church of Philadelphia, Christ offered his assurance: "Look, I have set before you an open door" (Rev. 3:8). And immediately following the message to the angel of the church of Laodicea, the Revelator looks and sees a door standing open (Rev. 4:1). Welcomed in, he finds himself before the throne of God, in the presence of the Almighty. And eventually, exactly as promised, he is invited to eat: "So I took the little scroll from the hand of the angel and ate it; it was sweet as honey in my mouth, but when I had eaten it, my stomach was made bitter" (Rev. 10:10). He becomes what he eats, taken up by the Spirit and transfigured into a witness of Jesus – his robes washed in the Lamb's blood.

This passage draws together so many threads, reminding us of the mystery at the heart of our calling: we must do for Jesus what he alone can do for us. To talk about drinking the cup he himself did not want to drink and eating the "visible word" offered to us, a word that is bitter and sweet (but not bittersweet!), is to acknowledge that the life we are called to live is a life that not only ends in death, as all lives do, but is lived at every moment as a "living sacrifice" offered continually for the good of our neighbours. And we can do this because Jesus has done it for us. As the divine-human one, he bodied forth in his life and his death the fullness of God's kindness and God's severity – the kindness that leads to repentance, the severity against all that is false in us, all that is foul. Precisely in that way he reveals that holiness is hospitality and that love for God and love for neighbour are necessarily identical.[14]

This, in the end, is why the student's story I shared at the beginning is so troubling for me. It presupposes a basic competition between love for God and love for neighbour, a finally irreconcilable conflict between the holiness God desires for us and the hospitality our neighbour needs from us. Such thinking is as mistaken as it is common. As Rahner explains,

> When we look at the average Christin life, it would seem that the notion prevailing in the normal Christian's moral consciousness is that we have "loved our neighbor" when we have done nothing evil to him or her, and have met the objective claims

---

[13] Jennings, *Transforming Atonement*, 119.

[14] I try to make this argument at length in *Sanctifying Interpretation: Vocation, Holiness, Scripture* (2nd ed., Cleveland, TN: CPT Press, 2020).

> he or she may justly have against us. The truth, however, is that what we are commanded to by the "commandment" to love our neighbor, in its oneness with the commandment to love God, is the demolition of our selfishness – the overthrow of the notion that love of neighbor is basically really only the rational settlement of mutual claims, that it demands only giving and taking to the mutual satisfaction of all parties. In reality, Christian love of neighbor attains its true essence only where no more accounts are kept – where a readiness prevails to love without requital – where, in the love of neighbor as well, the folly of the cross is accepted and welcomed.[15]

We need to take these words, this wisdom, to the hilt. What might change, Rahner asks, if we "spontaneously and unquestionably heard 'Save your soul' as 'Save your neighbor'?" The answer, obviously, is everything.

## Discussion Questions

1. Green begins and concludes with a student's story. What does Green mean, in light of this story, by the limits of hospitality and its relationship to holiness?
2. Green offers the story of Zacchaeus as one of exclusion and embrace. What are other stories from Jesus and what are biblical stories beyond the gospel narratives that might provide a paradoxical example of exclusion and embrace?
3. How might the story of Jesus himself reflect a paradoxical example of exclusion and embrace?
4. How can we resolve the assumed irreconcilable conflict between the holiness desires of God for us and the need to be hospitable?

## Bibliography

Bonhoeffer, Dietrich. *Ethics*. New York: Simon & Schuster, 1995.

Green, Chris E.W. *Sanctifying Interpretation: Vocation, Holiness, Scripture*. 2nd ed. Cleveland, TN: CPT Press, 2020.

Jennings, Theodore W. Jr. *Transforming Atonement: A Political Theology of the Cross*. Minneapolis, MI: Fortress, 2009.

Kaemingk, Matthew. *Christian Hospitality and Muslim Immigration in an Age of Fear*. Grand Rapids, MI: Eerdmans Publishing, 2018.

Kearney, Richard. "Guest or Enemy? Welcoming the Stranger." *ABC Religion and Ethics*. 21 June 2012. http://www.abc.net.au/religion/articles/2012/06/21/3529859.htm (accessed 13 January 2023).

Lewis, Bryne. "Not At-Home: Rethinking Hospitality and Homelessness." *The Other Journal*. 7 January 2012. https://theotherjournal.com/2012/01/07/not-at-home-rethinking-hospitality-and-homelessness-3/.

---

[15] Karl Rahner, *The Love of Jesus and the Love of Neighbor* (New York: Crossroad, 1983), 83–84.

Rahner, Karl. *The Love of Jesus and the Love of Neighbor*. New York: Crossroad, 1983.

Trinity College Dublin. "Professor Siobhán Garrigan Calls for a New Understanding of 'Home' in Inaugural Lecture." *News and Events*. 3 November 2014. https://www.tcd.ie/news_events/articles/professor-siobhan-garrigan-calls-for-a-new-understanding-of-home-in-inaugural-lecture/ (accessed 13 January 2023).

Vondey, Wolfgang. *People of Bread: Rediscovering Ecclesiology*. Mahwah, NJ: Paulist, 2008.

# Chapter 4

# The Synaptic Mind of James Forbes: A Delta of Theology

Nimi Wariboko

**Abstract**

This essay uses the scholarship and practices of James Forbes to develop a theology of social engagement that is Pentecostal in orientation and driven by praxis. The notion of a river's delta, where life is developed in a convergence of lands and waters which lead into an ocean, provides a metaphor for this praxis. Forbes self-identifies as a Progressive Pentecostal whose theology has been influenced by Tillich's focus in which the Spirit provides an impetus for social transformation. Such a focus provides a corrective to Pentecostals' emphasis upon the work of the Spirit within the individual but commonly does not have an emphasis upon social engagement.

## Introduction

The architectonics of James Forbes's theological thought is deltaic. Its formation is akin to the fan-like assemblage of landform and tributaries of a delta. Its signature orientation is that of change, making a difference in America's social existence, as the mathematical sign of Δ (delta) that denotes change or difference. In finance, delta measures the risk of an option: the change in price of an option as the underlying asset changes. In over fifty years of scholarship and active ministry, Forbes has kept his eyes and trained America's ears on the risk that confronts the option of the poor for flourishing life as the underlying culture or ethos of the nation changed. Deltas like those of the Mississippi, Nile, or Niger are formed when rivers carrying sediments run into slower moving bodies of water, forcing them to proliferate, fan out in rhizomes of earth and water. Forbes's ministry is a river of ideas springing from the Spirit (pneumatology), spiritedly transporting ancient and contemporary sedimented theological wisdoms into the body politic of America that is slow at social transformation. Consequently, his thought and ministry are forced to take multiple byways and pathways to his envisioned America's destiny of egalitarian democracy unburdened by racism, poverty, patriarchy, homophobia, eco-injustice, and militarism. These byways and pathways converge into dynamic hybrid formations such as the secular-spiritual, Pentecostal-mainline Christianity, pulpit-preaching social activism, black-liberation poverty elimination, prayer-protest, and pastor-scholar. Finally, my resort to the metaphor of delta to characterise Forbes's scholarship and ministry helps us to steal a look at the *intellectual synapses* that encode the channels of his complex mind – how he thinks, imagines, feels, and sets forth his provocative ideas. My goal here is to elucidate the philosophy and methodology of his works, to chart the paths and connections, warp and woof, gaps and tensions of his mesh of theological creativity. This is an effervescent creativity that is simultaneously *in*, *toward*, *about*, and *for* God and not God, and its deltaic, relational movement is marked by the principle: *to serve God is to serve people.*[1]

The foregoing may have rightly described the architectural structure of Forbes's theological thought but not its dynamic foundation, not the grinding of the tectonic plates underneath the huge edifice. The dynamo is the Pauline-messianic outlook or deep structure that forms the point of departure, the originating site of Forbes's theology. In the next section of this chapter, I will carefully work out this connection between Paul and Forbes.

## From Jesus to Paul via Luke: The Messianic Intensity of Forbes

While going over the essays, books, and sermons of James Forbes, one quickly gets the impression that the programmatic disposition of his scholarship and ministry is drawn from Jesus' inaugural manifesto as stated in Luke 4:18: "The Spirit of the Lord is upon me, because he has anointed me to preach the good news to the poor." Forbes calls himself Tillichian Pentecostal or "Progressive Pentecostal" because he wants to relate the work of the Spirit to the prophetic ministry of social transformation, dismissing the notion that it is incongruous to connect the ontological power of the Holy Spirit to black liberation or social activism with zeal. The mainline churches, the non-Pentecostal churches, he believes have often ignored the power of the Holy Spirit in the personal life of Christians. The Pentecostal churches, on the other hand, lack a deep commitment to transformative social action.[2] The Spirit anoints, he argues, so that preachers, and all Christians for that matter, can bring the good news of liberation to the poor and to captives. In one of his early essays, "The Ministry of Hope from a Double Minority," published in 1973, he states at length the nature of his ministry and I beg your indulgence to quote from it at length here.

> How could *Holy Ghost* preachers have missed this connection? Jesus was in the power of the Spirit, but there was no escaping the realities of "… this world, with devils filled who threaten to undo us." He was led by the Spirit into the wilderness to get a sharpened focus of the forces with which he would be engaged in deadly conflict. What he saw in the wilderness made it clear that people needed something other than getting their stomachs filled or their souls saved. He saw everything from individual need to corporate structures of evil. His ministry would have to operate on more than one level.
>
> On the other hand, the liberation preachers do not seem to put sufficient emphasis upon the *Holy Spirit* as power in the believers by which they may participate in

[1] Stanislas Breton, *The Word and the Cross* (trans. Jacquelyn Porter; New York: Fordham University Press, 2002), 101. I have borrowed phrases and ideas from a very different context to convey my thoughts here.

[2] James A. Forbes, *The Holy Spirit and Preaching* (Nashville: Abingdon Press, 1989), 15.

> God's work of liberation. The great text of liberation in Luke 4:18 must be read in the context of Jesus "being full of the Holy Spirit," returning into Galilee "in the power of the Spirit" and standing up and saying: "The Spirit of the Lord is upon me…" How can apostles of liberation miss this connection? It is naïve to challenge the church to be about the work of liberation and not to remind her that she cannot expect to be victorious in her own strength alone. It is only in the power of the Holy Spirit that we can expect to confront the forces of bondage with the full authority of God. For the Spirit is about the work of liberation.
>
> I believe, therefore, that I have been given a ministry of hope – with implications for spiritual renewal and social reform. I am a black Pentecostal preacher who believes that the Holy Spirit empowers us to witness better for Jesus Christ, and also equips us to engage in warfare against the forces and structures of oppression. I am committed to black liberation (not excluding other kinds of liberation) through the power of the Holy Spirit.[3]

I have given you the manifesto of Forbes's ministry, which derives from Jesus' Luke 4 inaugural proclamation. We are now ready to connect his orientation to the fundamental sensibility of Saint Paul, which is, somewhat, a radical reduction of Jesus' understanding of the Word, the law and prophet. "No dual commandment, but rather *one* commandment. I regard this as an absolutely revolutionary act," writes the Jewish philosopher Jacob Taubes.[4] Paul, claiming to stand in the messianic time inaugurated by Jesus, reinterprets Jesus' understanding of the law and political ethics of believers in ways that appear to circumscribe it (Rom. 13:8-14). We see that Forbes, claiming to stand in Jesus' ministerial manifesto, is also doing the same thing from a different angle. Jesus has argued that the whole Bible is summed up in a dual commandment. In response to a question from the lawyer about which commandment in the law is the greatest, Jesus answered, "'You shall love the Lord your God with all your heart, and with all your soul, and with all your mind.' This is the greatest and first commandment. And a second is like it: 'You shall love your neighbor as yourself.' On these two commandments hang all the law and the prophets" (Matt. 22:35-40). But Paul in summing up the law omitted the command to love God: "Owe no one anything, except to love one another; for the one who loves another has fulfilled the law. The commandments, You shall not commit adultery; You shall not murder; You shall not steal; You shall not covet; and any other commandment, are summed up in this word, Love your neighbour as yourself. Love does no wrong to a neighbor; therefore, love is the fulfilling of the law" (Rom. 13:8-10).

Paul sublates the command to love God into the love of the neighbour without even the force of divine mandate as in Leviticus 19:18: "You shall not take vengeance or bear a grudge against any of your people, but you shall love your neighbor as yourself: I am the Lord." As L.L. Wellborn, New Testament historian, puts it: "Without the divine mandate, it is scarcely possible to imagine

---

[3] James A. Forbes, "A Ministry of Hope from a Double Minority," supplement, *Theological Education*, 9:4 (1973) 307–8; italics added. Note his use of Holy Ghost and Holy Spirit.

[4] Jacob Taubes, *The Political Theology of Paul* (trans. Dana Hollander; Stanford: Stanford University Press, 2004), 53.

that one could undertake something as unreasonable and difficult as loving neighbor as oneself."[5] Paul's call to mutual love, not even backed by the force of a divine mandate as in Leviticus, is very radical. The neighbour in Paul's injunction – unlike that of Leviticus 19:17-18 is not a brother, sister, or kinsperson – but the *other* by reason of class, race, ethnicity, gender, and so on.

> The obligation of mutual love not only traverses these distinctions, but embraces "the other," as the embodiment of difference. Paul's choice of the word "other," rather than "neighbor" or "brother," was no doubt intended to short-circuit the widespread assumption in Greco-Roman society that true love depended upon sameness, affinity, and familiarity, and that the true friend was a "mirror of the self." The sweeping nature of Paul's formulation suggests that Paul had in mind not just particular cases, but the ethic of the community: a community that practices love of "the other" can never be a totality – that is, a group closed upon itself. A people that practices love of "the other" is perpetually incomplete.[6]

Why would a Christian undertake a task as difficult as loving "the other" or the neighbour without a divine mandate? Even with a divine mandate, it is a very difficult task as indeed Sigmund Freud informs us in his commentary on Leviticus 19:18. He evaluates the injunction to love the neighbour at different degrees of propinquity to the recipients of our love. He starts from the case of a neighbour who is not a perfect stranger.

> We will adopt a naïve attitude towards it, as if we were meeting it for the first time. Thereupon we find ourselves unable to suppress a feeling of astonishment, as at something unnatural. Why should we do this? What good is it to us? Above all, how can we do such a thing? How could it possibly be done? My love seems to me a valuable thing that I have no right to throw away without reflection. It imposes obligations on me which I must be prepared to make sacrifices to fulfill. If I love someone, he must be worthy of it in some way or other … He will be worthy of it if he is so like me in important respects that I can love myself in him; worthy of it if he is so much more perfect than I that I can love my ideal of myself in him.[7]

Freud goes on to examine the injunction in the light of loving a stranger:

> But if he is a stranger to me and cannot attract me by any value he has in himself or any significance he may have already acquired in my emotional life, it will be hard for me to love him. I shall be doing wrong if I do, for my love is valued as a privilege by all those belonging to me; it is an injustice to them if I put a stranger on a level with them. But if I am to love him (with that kind of universal love) simply because he, too, is a denizen of the earth, like an insect or an earthworm or a grass-snake, then I fear that but a small modicum of love will fall to his lot and it would be impossible for me to give him as much as by all law of reason I am entitled to retain for myself. What is the point of an injunction promulgated with such solemnity, if reason does not recommend it to us? (58–59).

Freud then reasons that the stranger actually deserves his hostility:

---

[5] L.L. Wellborn, *Paul's Summons to Messianic Life: Political Theology and the Coming Awakening* (New York: Columbia University Press, 2015), 3.
[6] Wellborn, *Paul's Summons*, 58.
[7] Sigmund Freud, *Civilization and its Discontents* (trans. Joan Riviere; New York: Doubleday Anchor Books, 1951), 57–58.

> To be honest, I must confess he has more claim to my hostility, even to my hatred. He does not seem to have the least trace of love for me, does not show me the slightest consideration. If it will do him any good, he has no hesitation in injuring me, never even asking himself whether the amount of advantage he gains by it bears any proportion to the amount of wrong done to me. What is more, he does not even need to get an advantage from it; if he can merely get a little pleasure out of it, he thinks nothing of jeering at me, insulting me, slandering me, showing his power over me; and the more secure he feels himself, or the more helpless I am, with so much more certainty can I expect his behavior from him towards me … If the high-sounding commandment had run, "Love thy neighbor as they neighbor loves thee," I should not take objection to it (59).

Freud brings his objection to Leviticus 19:18 to a crescendo when he writes:

> The bit of truth behind all this – one so eagerly denied – is that men are not gentle, friendly creatures wishing for love, who simply defend themselves if they are attacked, but that a powerful measure of desire for aggression has to be reckoned as part of their instinctual endowment. The result is that their neighbor is to them not only a possible helper or sexual object, but also a temptation to them to gratify their aggressiveness on him, to exploit his capacity for work without recompense, to use him sexually without his consent, to seize his possessions, to humiliate him, to cause him pain, to torture him and to kill him. *Homo homini lupus*; who has the courage to dispute it in the face of all evidence in his own life and in history?[8]

Where did Paul get the courage to dispute such a story of humankind? How did Paul embrace or assume away the strangeness of the neighbour who in Freud's term cannot be loved? What new communal consciousness did Paul think himself capable of awakening in Christians that could work the magic? How do we seek to clarify "Paul's eschatological faith [that] enables his confidence in a community capable of obligating itself to mutual love"?[9] More importantly, why did Paul lift the burden of loving God from the new messianic community, from the new people of God?

Before we answer these provocative questions let us examine how Forbes handles the primordial core of the dual commandment in the church today. Does Forbes believe that he has been called by God to summon Americans to an awakening? Whatever may be the answer, he has got himself a version of the reduction of the dual commandment, the refocusing on love of the other. Does he provide a rationale for his version of the reduction? The reader may even now have a question for me. Why not address the scintillating questions about Paul's theology before whetting our appetite with those of Forbes's theology? My rationale for first addressing the questions relating to Forbes's reduction of the dual commandment rather than addressing those relating to Paul is that Paul's reasoning provides the key to deciphering what we think is going on in Forbes's mind. Once we have laid out Forbes's style of dealing with the dual commandment, we will go to Paul to get the key – and the oceanic depths in which Forbes's style originates will be unlocked. Without first knowing the lay of the land of Forbes's reduction of the dual commandment, the force of the similarity in the deep structure meanings between Paul's thinking and that of

---

[8] Freud, *Civilization and its Discontents*, 60–61.

[9] Wellborn, *Paul's Summons*, 10.

Forbes might not adequately open our eyes to the trenchant beauty of Forbes's theological scholarship.

In his sermon "Whatever Happened to the Golden Rule?" preached at the Riverside Church in New York City on 10 April 1989, he lays out his vision of the Christian political ethics, which like Paul's Romans 13:8-10 put its weight on one part of the dual commandment. Commenting on Jesus' discussion of the so-called Golden Rule in Matthew 7:7-12, Forbes zeroed in on a phrase and posited that the whole of Christian social ethics is encapsulated within it. "In everything do to others as you would have them do to you; for this is the law and the prophet" (7:12). He calls upon his listeners to pay close attention to this verse in this way:

> Now, two observations. Did you notice at the end of the Golden Rule – "in everything do to others as you would have them do to you" – that was not the end of the sentence? That there was a semicolon? And, following the semicolon, these words: "for this is the law and the prophets"? This suggests that the Golden Rule is not just some voluntary principle or reciprocity; it is at the heart of the gospel. The core of Christian conduct is found right in these words: "Do unto others as you would have them do unto you." I think it is such a strong admonition that persons who call themselves Christians who do not at least attempt to live by the Golden Rule might, on one day of harsh judgment, be required to turn in their membership card.[10]

I hope just as Forbes wanted the Riverside Church congregation to observe, that you too have noticed his emphasis on caring for others as the *sine qua non* of Christianity, of Christian ethics. He goes further to state that the Golden Rule must be properly situated in Jesus' earlier proclamation in the chapter: "Ask and it shall be given; seek and you shall find; knock and the door shall be opened unto you" (Matthew 7:7). This staggering claim, according to Forbes, is about the kingdom of God, which he translates as the *commonwealth of love*, love of the other. It is important to quote at length Forbes's interpretation of the kingdom of God, Jesus' claim, and the work of the church as it goes to undergird our point that, like Paul, Forbes has radically reduced the dual commandment to the love of the other. There is no explicit mention of loving God with all our heart, soul, and strength; the focus is squarely on the people, God's children. For Forbes this singular focus on love of the neighbour presupposes a community of believers in Jesus who are committed to the ideals of the faith, have experienced the love of God themselves, and actively recognise the suffering of Jesus for all of God's children.

> Jesus is talking about a new community, a new arrangement that will obtain when God's reign has become the order of the day. In that time, people who have needs because of the equality of life in the beloved community would ask and it would be given; they would seek and find; they would knock and doors would be opened unto them. It is Jesus' projection of what it will look like when the church configures its life or when society configures its life, according to the dream in the mind of the Creator … When God's reign and the principles of justice and mercy and equality have become the Magna Carta of the people of faith, when you could

[10] James A. Forbes, "What Happened to the Golden Rule?" in G. Lee Ramsey (ed.), *Care-Full: From Sermon to Caring Community* (St. Louis: Chalice Press, 2000), 149.

ask and it would be given. It is within this kind of projection of a caring community that Jesus then says, "Do unto others as you would have them do unto you."[11]

Now we can turn to Paul and seek the reason for the radical reduction of the dual commandment. Following Wellborn, I argue that Paul lifted the burden of the love of God because he believed he was in the messianic time. For those who have experienced the calling of the Messiah to a new community, those who now recognise that while they were still sinners God commended his love toward them and the Messiah died for them, the weak, the ungodly, and enemies (Rom. 5:5-11), there are no longer two imperatives, but one – to love the one for whom Christ died. This is at once a recognition and affirmation of the kenotic movement of the divine love which not only led to the sacrificial death of God, but has also "sublated the first commandment."[12] Wellborn brings his reflection on Paul's radical reduction of the dual commandment to a close by drawing an inference: "One who has awakened to the messianic nature of his or her own existence is empowered to do the most difficult thing – the thing that Freud, as Paul's spiritual heir, rightly judged to be unreasonable and impossible in human terms: to love the neighbor."[13]

We all can now interpret Forbes's radical reduction of the dual commandment. It is based on the Pauline sensibility that those who are called into messianic community have only one imperative: to love the other as themselves. As per his reasoning, Christians' commitment to their membership, the messianic calling, their gratefulness to God's offering of Jesus to the world and Christ's suffering for them, and their awareness of their embodiment of God's tender care for all humanity compel in them the love of the neighbour. This is all about grace as can be easily understood from Romans 5. In Forbes's reckoning, the grace of God that was shed abroad on all God's children calls them to the love of the other. According to theologian G. Lee Ramsey, Forbes's prioritisation of grace allows Forbes to "develop the Golden Rule as an indicative within the Christian community, not simply an imperative. Christians live by the Golden Rule because, as members of the 'realm of God's tender, loving care,' we are set free from inordinate preoccupation with our own security and well-being. By grace, we are free to live according to the values indicated by the Golden Rule."[14] In this new community where the Golden Rule is an indicative, the love of God by its members is presupposed. The love of neighbour (the other) is implied in the love of God – as its presupposition. The love of God (as in both God's love for people and people's love for God) is the constituting power of the community. The first part of the dual commandment is the *constituting love* of the second part, the *constituted love*. The first is the violence of passion, so to speak, that posits the law of neighbourly love.

This awakening to the messianic foundation of Christian social ethic for both Paul and Forbes does not have the individual as the solitary subject, but the community; individuals within a community. In the portion of the sermon we

---

[11] Forbes, "What Happened to the Golden Rule?" 150.

[12] Wellborn, *Paul's Summons*, 2.

[13] Wellborn, *Paul's Summons*, 60.

[14] Ramsey, *Care-Full*, 156.

quoted above, Forbes was talking about a *new community*. Paul in Romans 13:8 has a *collective subject* in mind, an "awakened communal consciousness" as both the verb and the pronouns are in plural form in the original Greek.[15] Now a question quickly arises: how does Forbes understand this collective subject, the collective subjectivity that has grasped the full import of God's tender, loving care?

## "Love of the Other" as Cultural and Cosmological Authentications of Theology

Forbes's theology of God's tender, loving care unfolds as a creative interplay between *bios*, which is the physical life of the other, and *mythos*, which not only enables us to tell the story of the being-in-the-world of the community, but also to transcend and revise the order of *bios*. Following Frantz Fanon and Jamaican literary critic Sylvia Wynter, I will investigate Forbes's theological anthropology as already indicated as an intersection of *bios* (ontogenesis and phylogenesis) and *mythoi* (sociogenesis), biology and culture. We are hybridly human. As Wynter puts it: "So here you have the idea that with being human *everything* is *praxis*. For we are not purely biological beings!"[16] In this light, our being-in-the-world or theological anthropology is best interrogated and comprehended at the registers of the genetic and the symbolic (discourse, language, culture) for maximum insights. In the United States, and for that matter other places where black persons or minorities are severely oppressed, the scientific codes of phylogenetic and ontogenetic theories fall far short in enabling us to understand their being-in-the-world, their collective subjectivity. As Fanon puts it: "The alienation of the black man is not an individual question. Alongside phylogeny and ontogeny, there is also sociogeny … Society, unlike biochemical processes, does not escape human influence. Man is what brings society into being."[17] The lived experience of blacks in the United States is that sociogeny (*mythoi*) is daily converted into ontogeny in the untiring mechanism of racialisation. This constitutes a monumental political violence which, in the words of Alexander Weheliye, "simultaneously serves to create not-quite humans in specific acts of violence and supplies the symbolic source material for racialization."[18]

Recognising the power of the "racializing assemblages" working to enact, recalibrate, reinvent, and re-impose negative stereotypes on blacks, Forbes names racism as *demonic* and identifies racialisation as not only degrading the humanity of blacks, but also defining, degrading, and distorting the Christianity

---

[15] Wellborn, *Paul's Summons*, 61.

[16] Sylvia Wynter and Katherine McKittrick, "Unparalleled Catastrophe for our Species? Or, to Give Humanness a Different Future: Conversations," in Katherine McKittrick (ed.), *Sylvia Wynter: On Being Human as Praxis* (Durham, NC: Duke University Press, 2015), 33–34.

[17] Frantz Fanon, *Black Skin, White Masks* (trans. Richard Philcox; New York: Grove Press, 2008), xv, quoted in Alexander G. Weheliye, *Habeas Viscus: Racializing Assemblages, Biopolitics, and Black Feminist Theories of the Human* (Durham, NC: Duke University Press, 2014), 26.

[18] Weheliye, *Habeas Viscus*, 28.

of white Americans. How can this demon be exorcised in America? He counselled that,

> The heart of the matter in exorcising racism is whether people in power will be accountable to the God who made them or whether they will continue to play God by daring to attach to racial difference distinctions which the Creator never intended.
>
> When people of this nation learn that racism is a form of demonic possession, they may cry out to God for deliverance. And if we ask with repentant heart: "What must we do to be saved?" we may be told *rethink*, *redefine*, *restructure* and *redistribute*, until nothing in this nation makes it appear that being white makes one a favorite child of God.[19]

An integral part of his fifty-plus years of pulpit ministry, academic career, and social activism is to give language, hope, and courage to blacks, minorities, homosexuals, the marginalised, and the oppressed to construct new *mythoi* for themselves, to craft stories of their unshakable Christian identity of being fully selected and accepted by God that will liberate their sense of worth. In all these, Forbes considers serving God as concretely caring and serving all of God's children.

All theology is anthropology, so says Ludwig Feuerbach. This is so true to the thought of Forbes, but not exactly as Feuerbach would want us to believe. In a very important sense, Forbes's theology is a study and reflection of being black (oppressed) and Christian in the United States. This takes the form of weaving the warp-threads of black collective experience on the woof of theology. Second, his scholarship is an anthropological (as in the social sciences discipline) inquiry into the "tribe" of African Americans and progressive black Pentecostals, and their specific engagement with reality traversed by divine energy. Owing to these fundaments of his scholarship, Christian theology, that is, Western-Christianity-dominated Christian theology, in his hands goes through a process of what anthropologists call *cultural* and *cosmological authentications*, forging a process that makes it "authentic" (new and improved) African American Pentecostal theology.

Nigerian cultural theorist Tonye Erekosima and American anthropologist Joanne Eicher define the process through which a culture imports foreign (meaning from outside or from an earlier generation) artefacts, transforms them through adaptation and reinterpretation, and integrates them into the harmony of its worldview as *cultural authentication*.[20] For the Kalabari society (Niger Delta, Nigeria) that provoked this theorisation by Erekosima and Eicher, it is a way of adapting foreign elements by modifying, enriching, and bringing them into the

---

19 James A. Forbes, "Racism as Demon Possession," *Christian Century* 95 (18 January 1978), 48.

20 Tonye V. Erekosima, "The Tartans of Buguma Women: Cultural Authentication" (paper presented at the African Studies Association Annual Meeting, Los Angeles, CA, October 1979); Tonye V. Erekosima and Joanne B. Eicher, "Kalabari Cut-Thread Cloth: An Example of Cultural Authentication," *African Arts* 14:2 (February 1981), 48–51, 87; Tonye V. Erekosima and Joanne B. Eicher, "Why Do They Call it Kalabari? Cultural Authentication and the Demarcation of Ethnic Identity," in J.B. Eicher (ed.), *Dress and Ethnicity* (Washington, DC: Berg Publishers, 1995), 139–64.

core of their culture through a process of selection whereby only those foreign artefacts which promote human flourishing and stability or harmony with their worldview are assimilated. On the other hand, *cosmological authentication*, according to American anthropologist Annette Weiner, designates the process of "how material resources and social practices link individuals and groups with an authority that transcends present social and political action. Because this authority is lodged in past actions or representations and in sacred or religious domains, to those who draw on it[,] it is a powerful legitimizing force."[21]

We will examine the process of authentication in Forbes's theology and ministry from two different facets. What gives his Progressive Pentecostalism, or lately his Progressive Protestantism, its "aura" are the connections to his interpretation of Jesus' manifesto (Luke 4:18) as focused on freedom and inclusiveness. He believes that what he has been doing for over half a century is ingesting and reinterpreting current events and relationships to make them fit within the harmony of the gospel as he understands it. He also feels that his ministry is authenticated through the authority of his ancestors. Connections to the legitimising force of his late father and eponymous ancestor authenticate his version of liberal Christianity. This is how he tells his story:

> My father [a Pentecostal preacher] preached about the powerful symbols in biblical stories that could open our understanding and transform our lives. His was also a liberal spirit, focusing more on grace than judgment. His sermons were characterized by inclusiveness. Just as there was room at our family table for neighbors and strangers, he preached that God's table had room for all sorts and conditions of people.[22]

He also tells the story of another ancestor who had the dogged determination and fervent courage to preach the gospel to the captives and the poor. This is the paternal ancestor from whom the family got its name.

> My ancestor C.C. Forbes … I did not know about him until recently. He was down at a slave plantation on Route 58 between Snow Hill and Stantonsburg [North Carolina]. I'm going to eat from the table [communion] because it's [courage] in my blood. C.C. Forbes was a preacher to slaves. He preached to the slaves down in the brush harbor. When the boss came down, the slave master shot him in the leg and said, "You can't preach here anymore." The slave master said to him, "Don't you come down here no more. I shot you in the leg as a warning that if you preach anymore, I'm going to kill you." C.C. Forbes stood up on that shot leg and said, "Well, you just as well go 'head and shoot me now because I'll be back. I'm going to preach here until I die. Go ahead and kill me anyhow!" That's what he said. And the slave master was so dumbfounded by this courage that he said, "All right, go ahead. Y'all can have this little plot of land."
>
> If you go down Route 58 between Snow Hill and Stantonsburg, you'll see a church called Courage Baptist Church.[23]

---

[21] Annette B. Weiner, *Inalienable Possessions: The Paradox of Keeping-While-Giving* (Berkeley: University of California Press, 1992), 4; see also 42.
[22] James A. Forbes, *Whose Gospel? A Concise Guide to Progressive Protestantism* (New York: New Press, 2010), 7.
[23] James A. Forbes, "The Call for Courage," *African American Pulpit* (Fall 2004), 54.

Let me now turn to the second facet of authentication used by Forbes in his theology and ministry. The second facet is about how he culturally and cosmologically authenticates his *mythoi*. We earlier stated that an integral part of his theology, pulpit ministry, and social activism is to enable the oppressed to construct new *mythoi* for themselves. This process is about how he evaluates the *mythoi* he constructs or helps others to craft or the *mythoi* that are pressed into service by churches and communities: Are they "authentic," acceptable, or absorbable into the fabric of his Progressive Protestantism? As we are by now familiar with how his thought fans into deltaic structure, the authentication of *mythoi* branches into two socio-theological streams: cultural authentication and cosmological authentication.

In what I am calling the process of cultural authentication of theology, Forbes sieves every story, sermon, explanation, or variety of gospel through the meshes of black liberation and grace. The word, the *logos* of anyone – or even from the Bible – must be authenticated by the richness of black religious and social experience. He rejects the American *mythoi* that blacks are inferior and not-quite human. In his own sermonic language, he names the two predominant *mythoi* on race as two contrasting "gospels": "gospel of racial exceptionalism" and "gospel of human race equality of being."[24] The former he would characterise as inauthentic insofar as it is not just and righteous for Christians who want others to do unto them as they want to do to others, and as it does not follow the Spirit in a community-building mission.[25] In this regard, if the social positions of the church on issues are not shot through with grace, they are also unacceptable, not authentic to the core message of the gospel. "God has a *special caring* for those who have been despised and rejected and abused and oppressed … Everybody in the realm of God's love and tender care is already somebody. You don't have to make a case for being there. By God's grace you are already in. You don't have to go around testing folks all the time, judging other folks; you're in!"[26]

Grace, in Forbes's theology and ministry, not only gestures to the mercy and compassionate caring that the prophetic church and awakened America need to inhabit, but also, and more importantly, to the irruptive force of natality and social transformation operative in the encounter with the Holy Spirit. Grace signals an appearance of something new into creation, human life, human condition – it breaks into the order of things. It allows freedom to appear, to flourish as such. It is a movement toward openness to futural possibilities, dislocating human lives and situations toward their future forms, nudging them toward full actualisation of their potentials. In its dislocating movement, it has a *novum* character signalling it as a response to the current order of things whose potentialities exceed the current structuring of individual and social existence. Grace expresses as well as transcends the hidden potentials of a situation, existence, or life.

All this nicely brings us to the second branch of his authentication process of *mythoi*: cosmological authentication. As Weiner taught us, this form of

---

[24] Forbes, *Whose Gospel?* 79.
[25] Forbes, *Whose Gospel?* 93, 75, 92.
[26] Forbes, "What Happened to the Golden Rule?" 151.

authentication is about how social practices, material resources, or ideas acquire authority by being linked to the sacred domain. Forbes carefully locates his Progressive Protestantism, his emphasis on love of the neighbour, his practical orientation to the Golden Rule within an encounter with the Holy Spirit. He attributes the fundamental disposition of his ministry and theology to the converging of two streams of Christian teaching. The personal model of salvation that is at the heart of his Pentecostal formation and tradition collide with the social gospel agenda of the Holy Spirit of mainline Christianity, and the resulting *novum* is Progressive Pentecostalism. He interprets, locates, and brands Progressive Pentecostalism as both a divine call for and as the hermeneutics of "spiritual renewal" of America. This Spirit-infused-and-traversed self-interpretation of life, scholarship, and ministry – an *inalienable possession*, so to speak – lifts his social and political actions, his reciprocal exchanges of ideas and energies with the world, into the realm of cosmological authenticity.

Given the dynamism of the deltaic networking of his ideas, we should expect that cosmological authentication anchored on the Holy Spirit would have its own downward streams. And it does. When Forbes talks about the Spirit he has two distinct but related notions in mind. In his Pentecostal formation that has not completely dissipated in him he has an ontological, personal view of the Holy Spirit. The Spirit is a being, a person that one encounters. A Christian can actually encounter and hear from the Spirit that anoints him and anoints Jesus to preach as laid bare in Luke 4:18. The Spirit of God can be personally encountered, be spoken to, and he/she is able to speak back. His call narrative bespeaks of this fact.[27] He also mentions with evident delight – doing so in a manner reminiscent of Pentecostal "testimony time" during worship – how God miraculously restored full hearing to a partially deaf man when he preached at a Pentecostal conference in Jerusalem in 1974.[28]

The second stream is more in line with the notion of spirit as the collective energy for social transformation. It is the mutual energies that citizens co-generate and give to themselves in focused interaction and intersubjectivity – and what we claim to receive from what each one of us considers as his or her own ultimate concern. Here the notion of spirit is not ontological or perfection in be-ing, but he deploys it for the sake of highlighting specific observations, contemplations, and questions that can fleetingly point us to something of broader significance. In this way it is for understanding the multi-directional openness of the social life of Americans without presuming a constrictive universalising framework. Eventually these two streams (notions) of the Spirit coalesce into one big sea as they pour into the ocean of healing, the healing of nations. At the end of his hugely successful eighteen-year ministry at Riverside Church, Forbes brings together his Pentecostal spirituality's emphasis on bodily healing and mainline churches' accent on social justice to ultimately define his

[27] Forbes, *Whose Gospel?* 5, 9–10; James A. Forbes, "Prophesy to My People," in James Echols (ed.), *I Have a Dream: Martin Luther King Jr and the Future of Multicultural America* (Minneapolis: Fortress, 2004), 83–95.

[28] Forbes, *Holy Spirit and Preaching*, 97–98.

calling as healing, broadly defined. In a book published in 2010 at age seventy-five he says,

> Progressive spirituality understands that the spirit that works in the hearts and minds of people is the same Spirit that widens the circle of inclusion in the human community and the whole of creation. The Spirit that heals our bodies also brings wholeness to the body politic. As a person of color, I have spent much time working toward racial equality. But the Spirit that liberates me does not get stuck on my issues alone … Because my healing ministry was focused on promoting racial reconciliation and justice, it would be unconscionable for me to ignore other forms of injustice based on prejudice and exclusionary laws or social practice.[29]

Though Forbes developed a brilliant constructive theology for his pulpit ministry and social activism, there is an obvious gap, a missed opportunity to develop a well-rounded theology for practice and vision for which he pressed Luke 4:18 into service. Forbes is rigorous in his thoughtful combination (intuition) of spiritual power and social justice, divine agency and human agency, divine empowerment and human cooperation, but his scholarship cries for a theology of *concursus*. How do divine and human actions interact to produce results, to enact social transformation in the world? The grounding of his theological edifice on the love of neighbour needs a well-thought-out theology of *concursus* to further undergird the connection between Luke 4:18 and Roman 13:8/Matthew 7:12. The works of theologians like Joshua D. Reichard would be helpful to Forbes and anyone contemplating this important connection. Reichard, after identifying three types of *concursus* in the extant theological literature, formulates a new category that synthesizes all three and rebases them on the notion of spiritual empowerment to service (through the working of the Holy Spirit – Spirit baptism – and human cooperation).[30] "Thus, a Pentecostal *concursus* is best described as primarily concurrence with the power of the Spirit through human agency."[31] The theology of *concursus* is a creative impulse that Forbes missed in the actualisation of his thought. He missed this key dimension of his own discovery, that which would have been a major contribution not only to Pentecostal theology, but also to liberal theology.

## Concluding Remarks

This has been a study of the rhizomatic methodology undergirding the theology and ministry of James A. Forbes, Senior Minister Emeritus of Riverside Church, New York, preacher extraordinaire, and a Pauline-Niebuhrian apostle of social justice as love writ large who is enlarging the tracks of spiritual renewal laid down by Martin Luther King for America. In this essay, I have carefully mapped the movements of his theological thoughts as they have unfolded over the years in encounters with multiple social issues and have also worked to identify the agonistic tensions that arose in them as he grappled with enfolding different

[29] Forbes, *Whose Gospel?* 15.
[30] Joshua D. Reichard, "Toward a Pentecostal Theology of *Concursus*," *Journal of Pentecostal Theology* 23:1 (2013), 95–114.
[31] Reichard, "Toward a Pentecostal Theology," 113.

Christian disciplinary formations and doctrinal perspectives into a singular way of being and doing. The following chart, a diagrammatic précis of the arguments of this essay, is my attempt to capture the firing of the synapses of his mind and how they concretely manifest as a visible network of ideas, interests, and real-life experiences. Together, the chart and essay provide us with theoretical and methodological approaches for interpreting, analysing, locating, and assessing Forbes's scholarship.

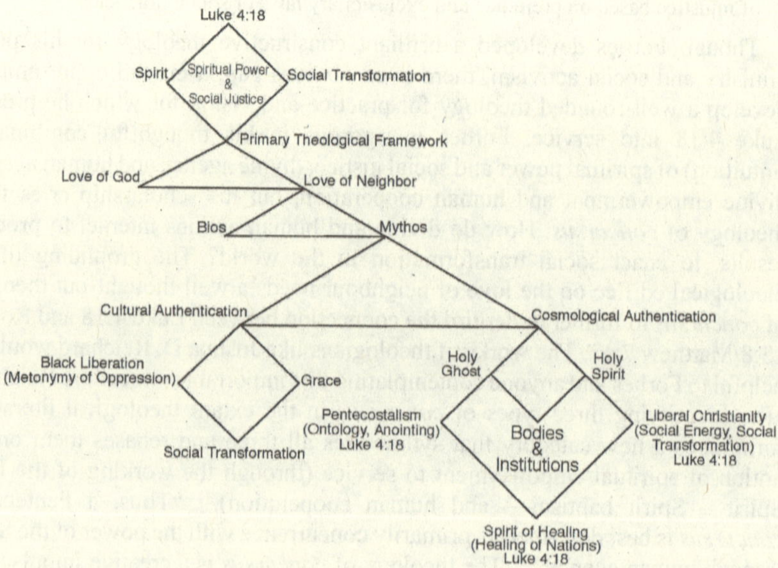


*The Deltaic Synapses of James Forbes's Progressive Protestantism*

At the beginning of this essay, I gave four reasons why I named Forbes's methodology as a delta. Now that we have deeply explored his thoughts and mapped his theoretical and methodological approaches to theology and pastoral ministry, we are able to name the fifth and final reason. The network of his ideas has a *fractal* pattern – more precisely, *Pentecostally fractal*. I support this assertion with two descriptive explanations.

First, in the above diagram, we can see (a) the self-similarity of shapes, (b) scale invariance (every level in the relevant path of the flow of ideas bifurcates and all branches are equally penetrated by the common "spirit" or sense and sensibility of Luke 4:18), and (c) a determined effort by him to keep the part of *the-Spirit-of the-Lord-is-upon-me* (the anointing) and the part of *proclaim-good-news-to-the-poor* (social transformation) in proportion as knowledge and interests flow through or incarnate in the network. As a river branches into multiple distributary channels that flow into the sea, the delta it forms may have the shape of a fractal. Indeed, I venture to say that the deltaic network of Forbes's ideas as I have presented them in this essay is in the shape of a fractal; that is, the repeating patterns of channels and synapses as ideas and interests move from the top of Luke 4:18 to the bottom of Luke 4:18.

Second, the Pentecostal component about all this (i.e. his network of ideas being *pentecostally fractal*) is that – arguably – its implicit generative-replicative dynamism apropos to the repetitive viviparous, self-similar divisions and rhizomatic iterations of Pentecostal movements neither becomes completely chaotic nor reaches pure order. Pentecostalism is never one river flowing majestically into the sea or ocean. It is rather a river ("the flow of anointing") that fans out as it travels, branching into thousands of channels as it pours into the oceanic depths of God's reign on earth. The global flow of Pentecostalism is deltaic in structure; indeed, it is a *delta* of Christianity.

From the above chart and discourse, we surmise that Forbes is a *theologinaut* (*theologia* + *naut*, *nautos*, navigation) for his ability to invent pathways among extant theologies and social issues and navigate them to his desired destiny.[32] He has carved out fragments from Scripture, cultural issues, and social philosophies to create a form of theology that suits his needs, social location, and time – and to prophetically speak to his country, the United States. He carved his own pathways depending on his roots, his starting cultural identity, and worldview. But these roots were not static and reified; instead they were, and still are, very adaptive, dynamic, searching for other roots to establish connections and to be transformed. Forbes has roots that work as routes. Forbes is a *radicant*, to use the neologism of French philosopher Nicolas Bourriaud for today's "postproduction" artists. He writes that a *radicant*

> is a term designating an organism that grows its roots and adds new ones as it advances. To be radicant means setting one's roots in motion, staging them in heterogeneous contexts and formats, denying them the power to completely define one's identity, translating ideas, transcoding images, transplanting behaviors, exchanging rather than imposing.[33]

I have described this *radicant-esque* formation of ideas and interests as deltaic in structure, named it as a force for change (δ), and identified it as a motion toward spiritual rebirth. The energy of the motion is supplied by the creative effervescence surrounding the principle: *to serve God is to serve people*, which supplies the enduring linkages between Forbes's conceptualisation of ecclesiology, affirmation of theological orthodoxy, and unflinching commitment to social transformation.[34]

Finally, let me state that Forbes's theology, always inescapably concrete, always irreducibly an ethic, is life in practice, thought as a disciplined way of being, practising at "love thy neighbour as yourself." Theology therefore is a construction of life, a thought process that engages the whole of a person's

---

[32] This name is inspired by Nicolas Bourriaud, who calls today's artists *semionauts* for their ability to invent pathways among signs. See his *The Radicant* (trans. James Gussen and Lili Porten; New York: Lukas and Sternberg, 2009), 39, 53, 102. See also Bourriaud, *Postproduction Culture as Screenplay: How Art Reprograms the World* (trans. Jeanine Herman; New York: Lukas and Sternberg, 2002).

[33] Bourraiud, *Radicant*, 22; see also his *Postproduction Culture*, 51–53.

[34] Akintunde E. Akinade, "No Time for Foolishness: On the Prophetic and Progressive Projects of James A. Forbes Jr," *Crosscurrents* 66:1 (March 2016): 108–22.

existence in his or her conscious movement toward reunion and reconciliation with the whole of creation, and hence theology is a model of life or life is a model of theology seen as a subjective openness to love. For him, the authenticated roots and routes of theology as a way or form of life will eventually transport us to love, which is the being (life) of God.

## Discussion Questions

1. How does Wariboko describe Jesus' inaugural manifesto (Luke 4:18) as providing the guideposts for developing a Tillichian Pentecostal or Progressive Pentecostal approach to the prophetic ministry and social transformation?
2. How does Forbes distinguish his Pentecostal approach to social engagement distinct from the social engagement commitments of liberal theology?
3. Identify a particular area of social engagement in a particular location that interests you. How might we use Forbes's theology as a guide for developing praxis (theology and practice) within that setting?

## Bibliography

Akinade, Akintunde E. "No Time for Foolishness: On the Prophetic and Progressive Projects of James A. Forbes Jr." *Crosscurrents* 66:1 (March 2016), 108–22.

Bourriaud, Nicolas. *Postproduction Culture as Screenplay: How Art Reprograms the World*. Trans. Jeanine Herman. New York: Lukas and Sternberg, 2002.

Bourriaud, Nicolas. *The Radicant*. Trans. James Gussen and Lili Porten. New York: Lukas and Sternberg, 2009.

Breton, Stanislas. *The Word and the Cross*. Trans. Jacquelyn Porter. New York: Fordham University Press, 2002.

Erekosima, Tonye V. "The Tartans of Buguma Women: Cultural Authentication." Paper presented at the African Studies Association Annual Meeting, Los Angeles, CA, October 1979.

Erekosima, Tonye V. and Joanne B. Eicher. "Kalabari Cut-Thread Cloth: An Example of Cultural Authentication." *African Arts* 14:2 (February 1981): 48–51, 87.

Erekosima, Tonye V. and Joanne B. Eicher. "Why Do They Call it Kalabari? Cultural Authentication and the Demarcation of Ethnic Identity." In *Dress and Ethnicity*. Ed. J.B. Eicher. Washington, DC: Berg Publishers, 1995, 139–64.

Fanon, Frantz. *Black Skin, White Masks*. Trans. Richard Philcox. New York: Grove Press, 2008.

Forbes, James A. "A Ministry of Hope from a Double Minority." Supplement, *Theological Education* 9:4 (1973), 305–16.

Forbes, James A. "Racism as Demon Possession." *Christian Century* 95 (18 January 1978): 48.

Forbes, James A. *The Holy Spirit and Preaching*. Nashville: Abingdon Press, 1989.

Forbes, James A. "The Call for Courage." *African American Pulpit* (Fall 2004), 52–54.

Forbes, James A. "What Happened to the Golden Rule?" In *Care-Full: From Sermon to Caring Community*, by G. Lee Ramsey, 148–59. St. Louis: Chalice Press, 2000.

Forbes, James A. "Prophesy to My People." In *I Have a Dream: Martin Luther King Jr and the Future of Multicultural America*. Ed. James Echols. Minneapolis: Fortress, 2004, 83–95.

Forbes, James A. *Whose Gospel? A Concise Guide to Progressive Protestantism*. New York: New Press, 2010.

Freud, Sigmund. *Civilization and its Discontents*. Trans. Joan Riviere. New York: Doubleday Anchor Books, 1951.

Ramsey, G. Lee. *Care-Full: From Sermon to Caring Community*. St. Louis: Chalice Press, 2000.

Reichard, Joshua D. "Toward a Pentecostal Theology of *Concursus*." *Journal of Pentecostal Theology* 23:1 (2013), 95–114.

Taubes, Jacob. *The Political Theology of Paul*. Trans. Dana Hollander. Stanford: Stanford University Press, 2004.

Weheliye, Alexander G. *Habeas Viscus: Racializing Assemblages, Biopolitics, and Black Feminist Theories of the Human*. Durham, NC: Duke University Press, 2014.

Weiner, Annette B. *Inalienable Possessions: The Paradox of Keeping-While-Giving*. Berkeley: University of California Press, 1992.

Wellborn, L.L. *Paul's Summons to Messianic Life: Political Theology and the Coming Awakening*. New York: Columbia University Press, 2015.

Wynter, Sylvia and Katherine McKittrick. "Unparalleled Catastrophe for Our Species? Or, to Give Humanness a Different Future: Conversations." In *Sylvia Wynter: On Being Human as Praxis*. Ed. Katherine McKittrick. Durham, NC: Duke University Press, 2015, 9–89.

# Chapter 5

# On the Way Toward Pneumatological Ecclesiology

Peter Kuzmic

**Abstract**

A holistic pneumatology that engages Christology provides a foundation for an ecclesiology that engages Word and Spirit, democratising and empowering the clergy and people of the church. Such a view of the church challenges the limitations of institutionalization and self-serving organisational structures. The positive recent expressions of Pentecostal-Charismatic revival-renewal has led to an increasing recognition that the doctrine of the church must also be founded on pneumatology. A pneumatological ecclesiology also engages the apostolic witness of the early church, in which the Holy Spirit was the life of the church. This essay calls the church to evaluate and incorporate a pneumatological ecclesiology that has the potential of moving beyond the limitations of institutionalisation and engages the fullness of clergy and people through the work of the Spirit into the mission of Christ.

## Introduction

In theological thinking of the past, Christology has usually been considered the basis for ecclesiology. The connection of the two was often seen in ontological terms, which has not infrequently led to a very static view of the church. Such a view was further fostered by the institutionalisation of the church, whose primary concerns were its own doctrine, order of worship, and self-serving organisational structures. The powerlessness and sterility of such churches became evident as soon as and whenever they lost the support of worldly powers and had to stand on their own. Dissatisfaction with such negative developments, along with the more positive recent expressions of Pentecostal-Charismatic revival-renewal, led to an increasing recognition that the doctrine of the church must also be founded on pneumatology.

## The Spirit Addresses Institutionalisation

The pneumatological aspect of the church brings into focus the dynamics and power of the kingdom of God, especially when the Spirit's role in energising the believing community for its mission in the world is acknowledged. It is now increasingly and rightly recognised that in the church, the charismatic must have priority over the purely institutional. Fossilised institutionalism, lifeless sacramentalism, and narrow-minded legalism can all be signs of the absence of the Spirit of Christ. Such churches are without power and joy. "For the kingdom of God is not a matter of eating and drinking, but of righteousness, peace and joy in the Holy Spirit" (Rom. 14:17 NIV).

When the Spirit of God is given freedom to move, the church also moves away from the unbiblical dichotomy between clergy and laity and a process of "democratisation" takes place, leading to the discovery of the gifts of the Spirit by the members of the congregation and to the ministry of the whole body of Christ. For the churches that give no freedom to the Spirit of God to work, the following description of Richard Lovelace in the *Dynamics of Spiritual Life* often applies, "The spiritual gifts of the laity have atrophied, while the responsibilities of ministers and administrators have hypertrophied."[1]

Such congregations are impoverished with respect to two of the basic components of a biblical church – the priesthood of all believers and the true sense of Christian fellowship and its biblical dynamics of unity and diversity. Both their mission and their nature are incapacitated. Their assembling turns out to be the private show of the pastor or his/her private audience. Often the result is that instead of mutual care for the well-being of each and all, growing into a fellowship of the Spirit, the pastor and members have, as W.A. Visser 't Hooft stated, "degenerated until they consist of unrelated individuals who attend Church services for private reasons."[2] The Christian church which takes the kingship of Christ seriously will be a church continually filled, renewed and controlled by the Holy Spirit. Otherwise, it will easily become (and this may be a temptation for liberal ecumenism) "the prey of secular social forces ... influenced by the inexorable laws of sociology rather than by the creative force of the Holy Spirit."[3]

Lesslie Newbigin argued in 1953 in the context of ecumenical (pre-Orthodox) discussion about the nature of the church for a three-cornered understanding of the church which, in addition to emphasis on right teaching, namely apostolic witness (Protestantism) and true order, i.e. continuation of the apostolate (Catholicism), must also include the Pentecostal emphasis on the role of the life-giving Spirit of God. He illustrates his criticism of the distortion and deficiency of the first two views by contrasting scriptural and church-traditional criteria and practice.

> The apostle asked the converts of Apollos one question: "Did you receive the Holy Spirit when ye believed?" and got a plain answer. His modern successors are more inclined to ask either, "Did you believe exactly what we teach?" or "Were the hands that were laid on you our hands?" and, if the answer is satisfactory, to assure the converts that they have received the Holy Spirit even if they don't know it. There is a world of difference between the two attitudes.[4]

---

[1] Richard Lovelace and Timothy Keller, *Dynamics of Spiritual Life: An Evangelical Theology of Renewal* (Downers Grove, IL: IVP Academic, 2020), 172.
[2] Willem Adolph Visser 't Hooft, *The Kingship of Christ: An Interpretation of Recent European Theology* (New York: Harper, 1948), 76.
[3] Hooft, *Kingship of Christ*, 76.
[4] Lesslie Newbigin, *Household of God: Lectures on the Nature of the Church* (Eugene, OR: Wipf and Stock Publishers, 2008), 104.

## Beyond a Bourgeois Church

The beginning of the Pentecostal movement in the West along with its rapid spread and phenomenal growth in the countries of the Third World witnesses unmistakably to the fact that the Holy Spirit is not synonymous with the bourgeois spirit for which much of the Christian establishment seemed to have mistaken him in their monopolising approach to the kingdom of God. "The Spirit (like wind) moves (blows) wherever he (it) pleases" (John 3:8). The underdogs of any society, the poor and the oppressed, the working class and the despised and uneducated peasantry are nowadays recipients of the saving grace of Christ and participants in the powerful manifestations of the Holy Spirit's workings. This truly is the sign of the kingdom, for our Lord himself was anointed by the Spirit "to preach good news to the poor … sent to proclaim freedom for the prisoners and recovery of sight to the blind, to release the oppressed …" (Luke 4:18).

If our mission is to be modelled after the mission of Jesus, as we evangelicals and Pentecostals have rightly emphasised (especially since Lausanne), then we must be consistent and face up to the challenge of the supernatural aspects of Jesus' and the apostles' ministry and the legitimate role of "signs and wonders" in the mission of the church. Spiritualising such passages as the above inaugural statement of Jesus so as to suggest, for example, that Jesus "was talking about healing blinded hearts in captivity to sin …" does no justice to the plain meaning of the text. Even a greater violation of Scripture takes place when this and other Spirit-power texts – due to a secularised worldview and with the help of the "horizontalized hermeneutics" of the interpreter – have the meaning of their text reduced to an (ideologically inspired) socio-political import, contrary to the intent of the author and of the general biblical context. With the collapse of communism some of the socio-politically based liberal theologians and activists have been forced to not only undergo an ideological *metanoia* but also to undertake a radical change in their hermeneutical grid.

The ecumenically orientated Western protestants should, however, in their legitimate concern for relevance beware of the subtle modern temptation of simply replacing the "socio-political" with an "ecological" reductionism in their use of scriptures. Countless numbers of examples could be cited of hermeneutical abuses and unbelievable exegetical misconstructions, all obvious twisting of the scriptural text, in order to avoid the clear challenge of the full-fledged biblical pneumatology and to justify the powerlessness of much of the contemporary Christian church. The sad fact is that even many evangelicals, who swear their allegiance to an authoritative and inerrant Bible, often were (and are) guilty of the most gross abuse of Scripture in this respect. It is not hard to provide evidence to illustrate how Christians of various persuasions are guilty of hermeneutical inconsistencies and sheer lack of obedience to the full counsel of God.

## Word and Spirit

We Pentecostals and Charismatics are to beware of all sensationalism, superficial charismatic triumphalism, and selfish searching for miracles. We are to be critical whenever and wherever miracles are sought after without the obedient acknowledgement of the lordship of Christ and his sovereignty. We are also to distrust those who speak more about the gifts than the Giver. At the same time, however, we must face the totality of the biblical teaching on the mission of the church, including the role of the supernatural in the spreading of the gospel (especially in frontier and pioneering situations), and acknowledge the importance of the full range of the gifts of the Spirit for the proper understanding and healthy "functioning" of the church.

Conservative Christians must realise that "preaching the word" alone is not enough. Evangelical churches may be known for excellent biblical preaching and yet at the same time they may be impotent in evangelism. My experience in the Pentecostal movement, where preaching has regrettably often been poor in both content and form, has nonetheless convinced me that the presence of the Spirit is (as Wolfhart Pannenberg would say) "much more suggestive and inspiring than dozens of sermons delivered by inhibited preachers."[5]

Donald Gee, one of the better-known Pentecostal pioneers and Bible teachers, known for his balance and ability to express it, aphoristically pointed the way:

> The Word alone will make you dry up,
> The Spirit alone will make you blow up.
> The Word and the Spirit together will make you grow up.

"Without the *pneuma* there is no soma" is a poignant way of summarizing Pauline pneumatological ecclesiology. Let us, however, humbly recognise that the Holy Spirit is not our possession and can neither be controlled nor confined by the church. He is never called "the Spirit of the church" and no church body (no Orthodox who has a strong and highly developed Trinitarian-based pneumatology and not even any Pentecostal or Charismatic!) has any right to boast that they "have the Spirit." The Spirit of God is nobody's property! Let us instead altogether ecumenically confess that the whole church repeatedly needs a new infusion of the Holy Spirit in order to be renewed in its nature and empowered for the biblically promised end-time harvest both locally and globally. Let us humbly recognise that the church of Jesus Christ is dependent on the Holy Spirit for its very life and that he is the chief and powerful executor of Christian mission. In that confession and recognition, we will discover the ecclesiastical dimension of the kingdom of God which will qualify us to redemptively minister to the world and contribute to the Spirit-yearned renewal of the whole creation (Rom. 8:19-22).

## Toward a Pneumatological Ecclesiology

For the continuous and credible Christian search for a vital and coherent theology it is imperative that we take theologically and seriously the full discovery of a holistic biblical pneumatology. The late Canon David Watson, a prominent Anglican pastor and evangelist, speaks to the church with prophetically relevant admonition which neither ecumenicals nor evangelicals dare to ignore.

---

[5] Wolfhart Pannenberg, *Theology and the Kingdom of God* (ed. Richard John Neuhaus, Louisville, KY: Westminster/John Knox Press, 1969), 90.

> There is no guaranteed bestowal of the Spirit at baptism, confirmation or ordination. The Spirit will not be tied to the church, nor to any ecclesiastical office within the church. The church which tries to tie the Holy Spirit to its institutionalized forms, to its traditional patterns, or to its doctrinal statements, will quickly find itself moribund and powerless. True spiritual life and freedom will come only insofar as the church submits to the Spirit, listens to the Spirit and obeys the Spirit. At every stage we must learn to hear what the Spirit is saying to the churches, even if that word is sometimes a word of rebuke, or a warning of judgment. God gives the Spirit to those who obey him.[6]

In the apostolic church, the Holy Spirit was the very life of the church, not replacing but rather centralising and always exalting Christ, which is the Spirit's primary mission. Christ rules when the Spirit moves, for the coming of the dynamics of the kingdom in the convicting, transforming, and enabling power of the Holy Spirit is the beginning of the end of everything that opposes the rule of God.

## Discussion Questions

1. What distinguishes Kuzmic's Christological ecclesiology and pneumatological ecclesiology?
2. What identifiers does he give for a bourgeois in contrast to a democratised church?
3. What are the implications of a democratised church for the life and mission of the church?
4. Kuzmic speaks primarily to evangelicals and Pentecostals, thus focusing on the dynamics of those communities. If this essay were to be primarily addressed to what Kuzmic identifies as ecumenists, what elements of his essay might he emphasise?

## Bibliography

Hooft, Willem Adolph Visser 't. *The Kingship of Christ: An Interpretation of Recent European Theology*. New York: Harper, 1948.

Lovelace, Richard and Timothy Keller. *Dynamics of Spiritual Life: An Evangelical Theology of Renewal*. Downers Grove, IL: IVP Academic, 2020.

Newbigin, Lesslie. *Household of God: Lectures on the Nature of the Church*. Eugene, OR: Wipf and Stock Publishers, 2008.

Pannenberg, Wolfhart. *Theology and the Kingdom of God*. Ed. Richard John Neuhaus. Louisville, KY: Westminster/John Knox Press, 1969.

Watson, David. *I Believe in the Church*. Grand Rapids, MI: Eerdmans Publishing, 1979.

[6] David Watson, *I Believe in the Church* (Grand Rapids, MI: Eerdmans, 1979), 48.

# Chapter 6

# Jesus, Pentecostalism, and the Encounter with (Religious) Others: Pentecostal Christology and (the Wider) Ecumenism in North America

Amos Yong

**Abstract**

Historical Pentecostal theologies of religious others are addressed herein. The concomitant Christological commitments and their role in Pentecostal views regarding intra-Christian ecumenism and the wider ecumenism of the interreligious encounter are emphasised. The essay contends that Pentecostal theological thinking in Christology, ecumenism, and a theology of interreligious relations is best illuminated via the other two domains, providing implications for contemporary Pentecostal belief and practice.

## Introduction

This chapter seeks to trace Pentecostal theologies of (religious) others historically through three periods: early classical Pentecostalism, the Charismatic renewal, and the contemporary emergence of academic Pentecostal theology in the twenty-first century, especially in North America.[1] I have elsewhere already charted this periodisation;[2] what is new here is an explication of the concomitant Christological commitments and their role in Pentecostal views regarding intra-Christian ecumenism and the wider ecumenism of the interreligious encounter.[3] We will identify changing Pentecostal theological

---

[1] I am delighted to be able to honour Murray Dempster with this essay that attempts to contribute to a vision of social cohesiveness that he long sought to articulate and to do so via suggestions regarding how people from divergent faith and religious traditions can live together while also sharing out of their deepest convictions. This piece also gives me the opportunity to revisit some of my earlier work on theology of religions and theology of interfaith encounter after spending almost a decade in various other spheres and arenas, in order to confirm both what remains pertinent from the previous efforts even as some indication is given about how I might articulate things a bit differently in the present time (with the footnotes providing many of these dual cues).

[2] Initially in the published version of my doctoral dissertation, *Discerning the Spirit(s): A Pentecostal-Charismatic Contribution to Christian Theology of Religions* (Journal of Pentecostal Theology Supplement Series, 20: Sheffield, UK: Sheffield Academic Press, 2000), ch. 6.

[3] Peter Phan (ed.), *Christianity and the Wider Ecumenism* (New York: Paragon House, 1998).

instincts in light of their Christological convictions and sensibilities as these have been shaped by developments within and external to the movement and unfolded in their relationships with other Christians and with those of other faiths during the last century. In effect, we will be attempting to map three concurrent historical trajectories of Pentecostal theological reflection: a set of Christological beliefs that have continuously evolved; a Pentecostal ecumenism in its various guises; and an expanding Pentecostal set of intuitions and practices vis-à-vis interreligious interactions. I will argue that Pentecostal theological thinking in each of these arenas – Christology, ecumenism (or views regarding other churches or denominations), and theology of interreligious relations (theology of religions) – is illuminated when refracted through the other two domains, with normative implications for contemporary Pentecostal belief and practice. The concluding section will briefly overview this interwoven threefold cord of Pentecostal Christologies, ecumenical theologies, and theologies of pluralism and interfaith encounter, and anticipate future developments.

## Early Pentecostal Exclusivism

Early modern Pentecostals were thoroughly Christocentric, resolutely anti-ecumenical in one sense (although also paradoxically deeply ecumenical in another sense), and staunchly exclusivist with regard to the religions. Each of these threads is interconnected. We shall unfold them in turn.

In a very real sense, Pentecostal spirituality and piety have revolved perennially around Jesus. Pentecostals have been from the beginning in love with Jesus, the person of whom they believed "in him dwelleth all the fulness of the Godhead bodily" (Col. 2:9).[4] Note that this focus on Jesus is not exclusive of Christ, although most Pentecostals would not understand the difference between the Jesus of history and the Christ of faith opened up by historical-critical scholars in the nineteenth century. Instead, the Christ is not a title but rather simply the "last name" of the Jesus whom they loved.

Pentecostals inherited this Jesus-centred piety from their Holiness forebears. A.B. Simpson (1843–1919), the founder of the Christian and Missionary Alliance movement (in 1887), published his *The Four-Fold Gospel* originally in 1890, and in it proclaimed Jesus as saviour, sanctifier (resulting, in holiness parlance, in separation from sin and dedication to God), healer (against all forms of medical, metaphysical, magnetic, and spiritualist healing), and coming Lord. The early Pentecostals who had been shaped by the holiness movement often just added the baptism in the Holy Spirit as a third work of grace (following after justification or salvation and sanctification), resulting in various renditions of

---

[4] Unless otherwise noted, all biblical quotations will be from the King James Version, since this is the one that most North American Pentecostals have relied on until fairly recently.

what has come to be known as the five-fold gospel.[5] What is important to note, however, is the centrality of Jesus to Pentecostal spirituality.

This is not to say that Pentecostals did not have differing Christological beliefs amidst their Jesus-centricity. Oneness Pentecostals, for example, emphasised that Jesus was not merely one of three persons in the Godhead but *the* personal name of God as revealed in the Scripture,[6] as opposed to the majority Trinitarian counterparts who adhered to the classic Nicene formulation. But both Oneness and Trinitarian Pentecostals were committed to the deity of Jesus; more importantly, Jesus was their saviour, sanctifier, baptiser in the Holy Spirit, healer, and soon-coming king. In short, Jesus was the centre of their doctrinal beliefs, and the heart of their religious devotion.

Simultaneously, most early modern Pentecostals believed that the Jesus who baptised his people with the Holy Spirit was absent from many if not most churches that claimed his name. Like many of their Holiness predecessors in the nineteenth and early twentieth centuries,[7] Pentecostals who were seeking for more of Jesus and of his Spirit left their existing churches and formed new congregations, fellowships, and movements which they believed would be purveyors of a more dynamic and vital form of Christian faith. They recalled that St Paul had urged the Corinthians, "come out from among them, and be ye separate, saith the Lord" (2 Cor. 6:17a), and believed this divinely sanctioned injunction applied to anyone who found him or herself enmeshed among institutions discerned as "[h]aving a form of godliness, but denying the power thereof" (2 Tim. 3:5). Thus were Pentecostals new embodiments and expressions of the long tradition of separatism and come-outism characterising Anglo-American Christianity and religion.[8] They also were looking for a restoration of apostolic Christianity, replete with the signs and wonders that Jesus promised would be performed in his name and by the power of his Spirit. In short, they wielded what has been called a primitivist hermeneutic,[9] one that led them to read the Scriptures, in particular the apostolic narratives, as a template for how to live faithfully in the modern world.

But Pentecostal come-outism and separatism only tell part of the story. The other part of the story highlights a unique form of what might be called a

[5] Amos Yong, *In the Days of Caesar: Pentecostalism and Political Theology – The Cadbury Lectures 2009* (Sacra Doctrina: Christian Theology for a Postmodern Age, Grand Rapids, MI: Eerdmans, 2010), see ch. 3.1.3.

[6] See David A. Reed, *"In Jesus' Name": The History and Beliefs of Oneness Pentecostals* (Journal of Pentecostal Theology Supplement Series, 31: Blandford Forum, UK: Deo Publishing, 2007).

[7] See Steven L. Ware, *Restorationism in the Holiness Movement in the Late Nineteenth and Early Twentieth Centuries* (Studies in American Religion, 80: Lewiston, NY: Edwin Mellen Press, 2004).

[8] See Meic Pearse, *The Great Restoration: The Religious Radicals of the 16th and 17th Centuries* (Carlisle, UK: Paternoster, 1998); Thomas S. Kidd, *The Great Awakening: The Roots of Evangelical Christianity in Colonial America* (New Haven: Yale University Press, 2007), ch. 12.

[9] Grant Wacker, "Playing for Keeps: The Primitivist Impulse in Early Pentecostalism," in Richard T. Hughes (ed.), *The American Quest for the Primitive Church* (Urbana, IL: University of Illinois Press, 1988), 196–219.

Pentecostal ecumenism, which Pentecostals explicitly repudiated in those terms, but manifested in their ecclesial practices.[10] What Pentecostals had rejected in the early days of their movement and continued to denounce through at least this first period under review were the incipient but formal efforts among the established Protestant churches to overcome denominational divisions through discussions about doctrinal differences, reconfigurations of ecclesial practices, and the arrangements regarding the merging of traditions. For them, the solution to the divisiveness of denominational Christianity during the first half of the twentieth century lay not in "man-made" attempts to bridge the chasms but in the prayer of Jesus and the answer related to the work of the Holy Spirit. So Jesus' prayer for unity in John 17 was predicated upon the arrival of the promised Paraclete earlier during the Supper, and it was this outpouring of the Spirit which birthed the united people of God. Thus Pentecostals believed, for example, that fresh outpourings of the Spirit in their times were the prerequisite for new forms of Christian unity. Those who attended the Azusa Street revival, for example, were convinced that the true unity of the Church was to be found in the experience of the baptism of the Holy Spirit into divine love, one that overcame divisions based on ethnicity and race, on class and social status, and on denominational or church backgrounds.[11] Many others felt that the new Pentecostal revivals were occasions for celebrating the return of apostolic Christianity that would get behind, or move beyond, the existing institutional and denominational structures of "dead and life-less" Christianity. For them, Jesus as the baptiser of the Spirit would reinvigorate the united church, one "not of the letter, but of the spirit: for the letter killeth, but the spirit giveth life" (2 Cor. 3:6).

The same outpouring of the Spirit, however, was the occasion not only for the renewal of the one true, holy, and united church, but also for the animation and empowerment of the Great Commission of the church so that the "gospel of the kingdom shall be preached in all the world for a witness unto all nations; and then shall the end come" (Matt. 24:14). For the early Pentecostals, the most important reason for Jesus' gift of the Spirit was so that his followers would be enabled to bear testimony to the gospel: "But ye shall receive power, after that the Holy Ghost is come upon you: and ye shall be witnesses unto me both in Jerusalem, and in all Judaea, and in Samaria, and unto the uttermost part of the earth" (Acts 1:8). The gifts of tongues, for example, were even thought by some to provide the means for missionaries to share the good news in the languages of

---

[10] Veli-Matti Kärkkäinen, "'Anonymous Ecumenists'? Pentecostals and the Struggle for Christian Identity," *Journal of Ecumenical Studies* 37:1 (2000), 13–28; Wolfgang Vondey, "Pentecostalism and Ecumenism," in Cecil M. Robeck, Jr and Amos Yong (eds), *The Cambridge Companion to Pentecostalism* (Cambridge: Cambridge University Press, 2014), 273–93; and Amos Yong, "Pentecostalism and Ecumenism: Past, Present, and Future," in Corneliu Constantineanu and Christopher James Scobie (eds), *Pentecostals in the 21st Century: Identity, Beliefs, and Praxis* (Eugene, Ore.: Cascade Books, 2018), 202–36.

[11] Dale T. Irvin, "'Drawing All Together in One Bond of Love': The Ecumenical Vision of William J. Seymour and the Azusa Street Revival," *Journal of Pentecostal Theology* 3:6 (1995), 25–53; see also Yong, *Spirit of Love: A Trinitarian Theology of Grace* (Waco, TX: Baylor University Press, 2012), ch. 4.

"natives" since the time was too short to spend having to learn foreign languages.[12] Many were soon disabused of this notion, but they nevertheless remained fervently committed to their missionary and evangelistic vocations.[13]

As catalysts for the twentieth-century dynamic of the Protestant missionary movement, Pentecostals approached those in other religions as being trapped in darkness and awaiting the light of the Spirit of Christ. In doing so, they were one with much of the conservative Protestant missionary thinking of the first part of the twentieth century with regard to other religions.[14] As the apostles had testified, "Neither is there salvation in any other [name than Jesus]: for there is none other name under heaven given among men, whereby we must be saved" (Acts 4:12). If the light of Christ was to be scarcely found even among those who claimed to know him (Matt. 7:22-23), then it was surely unknown among the unevangelised. Thus it fell upon those who were empowered by the Spirit of Jesus to go to those at ends of the earth: "To open their eyes, and to turn them from darkness to light, and from the power of Satan unto God, that they may receive forgiveness of sins, and inheritance among them which are sanctified by faith that is in [Jesus]" (Acts 26:18). This image of the world residing in darkness awaiting the light of the gospel remains a powerful one in much of the popular Pentecostal consciousness.[15]

In short, during this first period of Pentecostal history, roughly the first half of the twentieth century, it may be said that Pentecostals inhabited a Jesus-centred piety and a Christ-centred theology. This Christocentricity amounted simultaneously and paradoxically to an ecumenical exclusiveness on the one hand (vis-à-vis the efforts to seek Christian unity among the formally organised denominations) but an ecumenical sensitivity on the other hand (vis-à-vis those who were open to being defined according to their experience of having been baptised in or filled with the Spirit of Jesus and his love). By extension, however, it was the ecumenical exclusiveness that characterised Pentecostal views regarding those in other faiths; such were "pagan" or "heathen," lost without the light of Christ and the power of the Holy Spirit.

---

[12] See James R. Goff, *Fields White unto Harvest: Charles F. Parham and the Missionary Origins of Pentecostalism* (Fayetteville, AR: University of Arkansas Press, 1988), esp. chs 4–5.

[13] Allan Anderson, *Spreading Fires: The Missionary Nature of Early Pentecostalism* (London: SCM Press, 2007); Gary B. McGee, *Miracles, Mission, and American Pentecostalism* (Maryknoll: Orbis Books, 2010).

[14] J.E. Godbey and Allen Howard Godbey, *Light in Darkness: or, Missions and Missionary Heroes – An Illustrated History of the Missionary Work Now Carried on By All Protestant Denominations in Heathen Lands* (Boston, Eastern, 1888); cf. Thomas Pakenham, *The Scramble for Africa: White Man's Conquest of the Dark Continent from 1876 to 1912* (New York: Avon, 1992).

[15] See Clifton Clarke, "Rulers of Darkness: Towards a Pentecostal Missiology of Poverty and Underdevelopment in Africa" (paper presented at the annual meeting for the Society for Pentecostal Studies, Eugene, Oregon, 26–28 March 2009); cf. Amos Yong, "'The Light Shines in the Darkness': Johannine Dualism and the Challenge of Christian Theology of Religions Today," *Journal of Religion* 89:1 (2009), 31–56.

## Charismatic Renewal and an Emerging Inclusivism

We now turn to the next phase of our inquiry, one focused generally on the period of the Charismatic renewal that overtook the mainline Protestant denominations and the Roman Catholic Church. During this time, basically the last half of the twentieth century – the dates are not important, although the *terminus a quo* would be the late 1950s or early 1960s – we find that Pentecostals were challenged on many theological fronts. Chiefly, their soteriology and ecclesiology were interrogated in and through the process of encountering Spirit-filled believers who remained in their established churches and denominations. Additionally, their understandings of Christ were re-envisioned by those who held to other views of Jesus. Finally, and not surprisingly, Pentecostal views regarding other religions would also be probed and expanded in the process.

The Charismatic renewal jolted the Pentecostal world because they presumed that only by coming from out of the institutionalised denominations could the life of the Spirit be experienced. But the renewal showed that the winds of the Spirit were now blowing also within these same churches and traditions. Whereas many Pentecostals had been brought up to say, "I grew up in the ____ [fill in with Presbyterian, Lutheran, Catholic, etc.] church, but I got saved and came to know Jesus personally when I attended a ____ [fill in with your typical Pentecostal] church," now people were not only finding Jesus in these denominations and traditions but their spirituality and piety were also being nurtured in these contexts. In other words, no longer could Christianity be separated between "dead denominations" and "Spirit-filled churches." Hence the soteriological and ecclesiological lines were being re-drawn.

The Charismatic renewal in the Roman Catholic Church was and probably remains the most challenging for Pentecostals. Having allied themselves with fundamentalists and conservative evangelicals in the early twentieth century, most Pentecostals did not question the classic anti-Catholic stereotypes going all the way back to Luther and the Protestant Reformation. For them, then, the Catholic Church was the "whore of Babylon," the Pope was the Antichrist, and Catholic spirituality involved nothing less than ritualistic prayers to the saints rather than to the triune God. Hence the fact of the Charismatic renewal across the Catholic world, starting in North America in 1967 but quickly spreading to Latin America and then from there around the world,[16] came indeed, to use a Pentecostal formulation applied to their own origins, "suddenly, from heaven!"[17]

In particular, Catholic Christologies – both their formal theological views sanctioned by their councils and practices prevalent among the piety of the masses – posed both ecumenical and interreligious questions. With regard to popular Catholic spirituality, for instance, Jesus is not merely the Son of God but also the Son of Mary; this itself is not disconcerting for most Pentecostals until

---

[16] Susan A. Maurer, *The Spirit of Enthusiasm: A History of Catholic Charismatic Renewal, 1967–2000* (Lanham, MD: University Press of America, 2010); Edward L. Cleary, *The Rise of Charismatic Catholicism in Latin America* (Gainesville, FL: University Press of Florida, 2011).

[17] Carl Brumback, *Suddenly ... From Heaven: A History of the Assemblies of God* (Springfield, MO: Gospel Publishing House, 1961).

the declaration of the Council of Chalcedon is factored in, i.e. that Mary is also thereby understood as *Theotokos*, or literally "the mother of God." Mary thus plays a much more substantial role in Catholic (and ecumenical) belief and practices, which has taken seriously what the third evangelist recorded Mary to have prayed in the Magnificat, that "from henceforth all generations shall call me blessed" (Luke 1:48b). Mary thus stands much closer to Jesus for Catholic theology and spirituality than most Pentecostals are comfortable admitting.[18]

Further, for the Catholic theological tradition, as with most mainline Protestant views, Jesus is also recognised as the incarnate Logos, the "true Light, which lighteth every man that cometh into the world" (John 1:9). Hence as far back as the church fathers, Jesus as the Logos has been thought to be cosmically available to humankind, through the "seeds of the Logos," as Justin the Martyr had put it.[19] Not surprisingly, then, the Second Vatican Council that met on the eve of the Charismatic renewal in the Catholic Church – some observers say that the Council made possible, if not initiated, the renewal[20] – made pronouncements about the religions that signalled a shift from the exclusivist position of earlier times toward a more open and inclusive stance.[21] This is not to say that Catholics adopted a lower Christology; rather, many Catholic theologians, in light of the conciliar declarations, distinguished between the saving work of God secured in the life, death, and resurrection of Christ, and the accessibility of that salvation even to people in other religions. If in the exclusivist viewpoint salvation was tied in with hearing about, believing in, and confessing Christ (Rom. 10:13-17), a more inclusivist perspective held that the benefits of Christ's saving work were available by the Holy Spirit perhaps even to those who had never heard the gospel but had been judged by God to have responded appropriately to whatever light they might have had (Rom. 2:5-16).

A number of evangelical theologians who had been touched by the Charismatic renewal also gravitated to this more inclusive Christology and theology of religions. Clark Pinnock, a Baptist who was initially exposed to the renewal in the 1960s and then later participated in the Toronto Blessing revival in the early 1990s, was among the most renowned of these. In two separate books,[22] he argued the twin theses regarding the universal scope of the saving

---

[18] Pentecostal theologians have begun to explore the promise of Mary for Pentecostal spirituality, e.g. Sally Jo Shelton, "Jesus' Mother 'Treasured All These Words … in Her Heart' (Luke 2:19): On Using a Spirit Hermeneutic to Reflect Together About Mary," *Spiritus* 2:2 (2017): 57-75.

[19] See Jacques Dupuis, *Toward a Christian Theology of Religious Pluralism* (Maryknoll: Orbis Books, 1997), ch. 2; cf. John Gravey, *Seeds of the Word: Orthodox Thinking on Other Religions* (Yonkers, NY: St. Vladimir's Seminary Press, 2005), 83–86.

[20] See, for example, Joseph Bagiackas, *The Future Glory: The Charismatic Renewal and the Implementation of Vatican II* (South Bend, IN: Charismatic Renewal Services, 1983).

[21] René Laurentin and Josef Neuner, *The Declaration on the Relation of the Church to Non-Christian Religions* (Glen Rock, NJ: Paulist Press, 1966).

[22] See Clark H. Pinnock, *A Wideness in God's Mercy: The Finality of Jesus Christ in the World of Religions* (Grand Rapids, MI: Zondervan, 1992); Pinnock, *Flame of Love: A Theology of the Holy Spirit* (Downers Grove: InterVarsity Press, 1996).

work of Christ and the universal activity of the Spirit of Christ which together opened up to a more inclusivist theology of religions. Pinnock did not go as far as some Roman Catholic theologians did in affirming the religions as ways of salvation themselves, but he did urge that the universality of Christ's work and the Spirit's activity meant there was no a priori reason why at least some people of non-Christian faith might encounter the saving work of God in and through their religions.[23]

For Pentecostals, then, the ecumenical question was burst wide open with the Charismatic renewal. If, for the first few generations of Pentecostals, a form of Pentecostal triumphalism had nurtured the view that true or authentic Christianity was to be found only in Pentecostal Christianity and not in degenerate and lifeless institutions and denominations, then the Charismatic renewal movement now appeared to suggest otherwise. Those who were considered second-class Christians at best and as non-Christian at worst were now undeniably not only followers of Christ but also fellow brothers and sisters who were filled with the Spirit. The longstanding Pentecostal defence of their distinctive doctrine – that glossolalia, the speaking in tongues that were unlearned, was the evidence of the infilling or baptism of the Spirit – now cut in another direction: if those in other denominations and even those in the Catholic Church were now speaking in tongues, that was irrevocable "proof" that they also were filled with the Spirit of Jesus. In that case, these formerly considered "outsiders" to the faith were now insiders, and perhaps had been so all along. This was especially the case for those (the majority of Pentecostals) who held that the experience of Spirit baptism was subsequent to that of Christian initiation in Christ since, in this scheme of things, it was conceivable that these members of other denominations and churches were believers in Jesus long before they received the empowering gift of the Holy Spirit.

But if the ecumenical question was opened up, then so was the interreligious one. If the salvific status of even Roman Catholics had to be reconsidered, did that not also have implications for understanding members of other faiths? The issue here is similar to the one that persisted for Jews in relationship to Samaritans in the first century.[24] Jews thought that Samaritans were outside the pale of the covenant; they fit, for all practical purposes, those who were of "another faith." Similarly, then, for Pentecostals surprised by the Charismatic renewal, these of "no faith" now turned out to have faith. And if faith in Christ existed for those who were previously thought not to have any, what did that mean for people in other religions? Might it also be possible that people of other faiths have, at least implicitly, faith in Christ, especially through the universally present and active work of the Spirit? Certainly this is not to say that all aspects of all religions are salvific; it is to at least consider the possibility afresh that God might have mysterious and unfathomable means of saving even the

---

[23] See Amos Yong, "Whither Theological Inclusivism? The Development and Critique of an Evangelical Theology of Religions," *The Evangelical Quarterly* 71:4 (1999), 327–48.

[24] See Amos Yong, *The Spirit Poured Out on All Flesh: Pentecostalism and the Possibility of Global Theology* (Grand Rapids, MI: Baker Academic, 2005), 241–44.

unevangelised, through the cosmic Christ and his Spirit who had been poured out "upon all flesh" (Acts 2:17).[25]

## Contemporary Pentecostal Theology in a Pluralistic World

So far, I have suggested that at least some Pentecostals have shifted from a more exclusivist Christology, ecumenical theology, and theology of religions characteristic of the first few generations toward a more inclusive view in the last few decades. In this section, I want to probe more recent Pentecostal scholarly reflections that have been intentional about acknowledging and engaging with the pluralism that characterises the world in the twenty-first century. We will observe openness toward Spirit-Christological formulations as well as more pneumatologically configured theologies of ecumenism and of world religions.

It is undeniable that the world has always been pluralistic, but our knowledge of such pluralism has increased exponentially in the last generation. The forces of globalisation and the practical omnipresence of our telecommunication technologies mean that many of us now live with first-hand awareness of what is happening around the world. Pentecostalism as a global presence has also burst into the limelight.[26] There have been a gradual if not less perceptible pentecostalisation and charismatisation of the world Christian movement, especially in the Global South.[27]

But if our awareness of the expansion of Pentecostal and Charismatic forms of Christianity is escalating, so is our consciousness of the vast diversity within this global renewal movement. There are so many types of Pentecostal and Charismatic movements, many of which do not even go by these names, which leave researchers bewildered. These various movements are characterised by doctrinal differences, ritual variety, and cultural pluralism. There are independent churches and movements, non-denominational and post-denominational forms and expressions, and non-traditional church and parachurch organisations, networks, and dynamics.[28] Many of these would not recognise others in this broad domain as being Pentecostal or Charismatic, or even Christian. If the "old days" were characterised by doctrinal disputes

---

[25] Which is where my own journey led: Yong, *Beyond the Impasse: Toward a Pneumatological Theology of Religions* (Grand Rapids, MI: Baker Academic, 2003; repr. Eugene: Wipf & Stock, 2014).

[26] Philip Jenkins, *The Next Christendom: The Coming of Global Christianity* (2nd ed., Oxford: Oxford University Press, 2011).

[27] Cephas N. Omenyo, *Pentecost Outside Pentecostalism: A Study of the Development of Charismatic Renewal in the Mainline Churches in Ghana* (Zoetermeer, NL: Boekencentrum, 2002).

[28] See Harvey G. Cox, *Fire from Heaven: The Rise of Pentecostal Spirituality and the Reshaping of Religion in the 21st Century* (Reading, MA: Addison-Wesley, 1995); Walter H. Hollenweger, *Pentecostalism: Origins and Developments Worldwide* (Peabody, MA: Hendrickson, 1997); Allan Anderson, *An Introduction to Pentecostalism: Global Charismatic Christianity* (Cambridge: Cambridge University Press, 2004).

between Oneness and Trinitarians, or between come-outers/separationists and those in the mainline, then today's clashes are additionally complicated by those between the "orthodox" and the "syncretists," between conservatives and liberals, and between biblicists and progressivists, among other factions.

Amid this cacophony of voices we cannot hope to delineate the various Christological views and ideas across the spectrum of the global renewal movement. What we can note are some dominant trends, particularly as these impact theologies of ecumenism and interreligious encounter. To be sure, the classical Christological exclusivism persists, especially among Pentecostals who are closely allied with conservative evangelical positions. For these, Jesus remains the unique saviour in a religiously plural world, even as there are also some here who still retain an anti-Catholic or anti-mainline Protestant stance, specifically with regard to how they see the implications of their Christological confessions for other, especially moral, issues.

Some Pentecostals, however, have also taken a turn toward Spirit-Christology.[29] There are at least three advantages of a Spirit-Christology for Pentecostals. First, it highlights the close connections between Christ and the Spirit that are deeply rooted in Pentecostal experience and spirituality. Second, a Spirit-Christological formulation is more organically derivative from the Lukan corpus that underlies the Pentecostal primitivist hermeneutic; both the Gospel of Luke and the book of Acts talk about Jesus as one anointed by the Spirit to do the works of God. Third, a Spirit-Christological approach is more consistent with the narrative base not only of the synoptic witness but also of the rest of the Bible, and this is important especially for Pentecostal and Charismatic renewalists across the Global South that are shaped by oral-cultural sensibilities and worldviews. In these arenas, the Logos-Christological paradigm is too deeply influenced by Western philosophical modes of thinking to be helpful in many cases. This is not to say that Spirit-Christologies need to deny Christ as the Logos or Word of God; it is to say both that Spirit- and Logos-approaches are complementary and that the latter is more comprehensible in terms of the former for much of the global renewal movement.

From an ecumenical and interreligious perspective, however, there are additional reasons for such a pneumatological turn in addition to the Christological benefits. Ecumenically, a pneumatological approach highlights the centrality of the Day of Pentecost narrative for Pentecostal theological reflection.[30] At a broader level, this invites rethinking the broad scope of Pentecostal theology that resists focusing apologetically only on the details of its distinctive doctrine of Spirit baptism. More concretely related to the task at hand, revisiting the Day of Pentecost narrative has implications for reconsidering a

---

[29] See, for example, Jenkins, *A Spirit Christology* (New York: Peter Lang, 2018), and Sammy Alfaro, *Divino Compañero: Toward a Hispanic Pentecostal Christology* (Eugene, OR: Pickwick, 2010).

[30] E.g. Amos Yong and Timothy T.N. Lim, "Acts 2 and Interreligious Engagement: Pentecostal and Evangelical Reflections," in Or N. Rose, Homayra Ziad, and Soren M. Hessler (eds), *Words to Live By: Sacred Resources for Interreligious Engagement* (Maryknoll: Orbis Books, 2018), 41–52.

distinctively Pentecostal and intercultural theology of ecumenism.[31] None of this denies the centrality of Christ or the Jesus-centred piety of Pentecostal spirituality. What it does is recognise this Christocentricity as an open set, one that invites the many Pentecostal voices and the many other ecumenical perspectives around a common table in order that the Spirit might empower a fresh and new witness to the risen Christ.[32] And this is also not to say that all voices are equal; there may well be certain "confessions" that are ultimately deemed to be inadmissible. But discerning what these are will involve a careful process of listening and understanding first, before speaking. Pentecostals have often been more eager to do the latter, usually motivated by the belief that it is their calling and vocation to speak as the Spirit has empowered and enabled. But in this new climate, with many different voices speaking simultaneously already, perhaps there are now occasions when it is just as important to hear one another's testimonies afresh, in order that the important task of discerning the Spirit can take place.

Interreligiously, a pneumatological approach flows right out of the developments that we charted as developing during the latter half of the twentieth century alongside and through the Charismatic renewal.[33] Again, the issue is not that the Spirit saves those in other religions apart from Christ; the Jesus-centred piety of Pentecostals will not usually allow for that. A pneumatological approach to the religions, however, invites us to emphasise not necessarily the historic Jesus but the eschatological Messiah, the one who not only has come but is also yet to come. And this emphasis on the coming Christ has both epistemological and soteriological consequences. With regard to the former, it means that there is perhaps much yet to be revealed about the Christ, although none of that will contradict what humanity now knows: "For now we see through a glass, darkly; but then face to face: now I know in part; but then shall I know even as also I am known" (1 Cor. 13:12). With regard to the latter, the salvific work of Christ and the Spirit will continue to surprise us, just as it did at Azusa Street and through the Charismatic renewal movement, since we cannot predict the comings and

---

[31] See, for example, Samuel Solivan, *The Spirit, Pathos, and Liberation: Toward an Hispanic Pentecostal Theology* (Journal of Pentecostal Theology Supplement Series, 14: Sheffield: Sheffield Academic Press, 1998), 112–18; Frank D. Macchia, "The Tongues of Pentecost: A Pentecostal Perspective on the Promise and Challenge of Pentecostal/Roman Catholic Dialogue," *Journal of Ecumenical Studies* 35:1 (1998), 1–18.

[32] See my essay, "Christological Constants in Shifting Contexts: Jesus Christ, Prophetic Dialogue, and the *Missio Spiritus* in a Pluralistic World," in Stephen B. Bevans and Cathy Ross (eds), *Mission on the Road to Emmaus: Constants, Contexts, and Prophetic Dialogue* (London: SCM Press, and Maryknoll: Orbis Books, 2015), 19–33.

[33] One of the leading Pentecostal theologians who has emerged to reflect and write on these matters is Tony Richie, *Speaking by the Spirit: A Pentecostal Model for Interreligious Dialogue* (Lexington, KY: Emeth Press, 2011) and *Toward a Pentecostal Theology of Religions: Encountering Cornelius Today* (Cleveland, TN: CPT Press, 2013).

goings of the Spirit (John 3:8): so "when he shall appear, we shall be like him; for we shall see him as he is" (1 John 3:2).[34]

From a pneumatological perspective, then, the ecumenical and interreligious questions beg not primarily for doctrinal resolution but for a more variegated theology of mission and evangelism.[35] The lordship of Christ is not in question for Pentecostals, but the Day of Pentecost narrative which records the surprised response of the crowd – that "we do hear them speak in our tongues the wonderful works of God" (Acts 2:11) – suggests that God may still be in the business of speaking through voices that had not been thought of as belonging to God. The Azusa Street revival, the Charismatic renewal movement, the contemporary explosion of the global renewal movement – each of these is vastly different from one another, and has been and is constituted internally by very different voices. Yet if God could work redemptively amidst the cacophony of Pentecost, why is such still not possible through the buzz and boom of our present ecumenical and religiously plural world? More precisely, maybe the many tongues of Pentecost are suggestive of many different forms of witness and evangelism today, ones that include social activism and even interreligious dialogue and hospitality.[36]

## Conclusion

What we have attempted to do in the preceding is to correlate Pentecostal theological developments along three avenues – the Christological, the ecumenical, and the interreligious – as these have unfolded basically across three periods of twentieth-century Pentecostalism. It has been suggested that the Christocentric piety of the first period functioned ecumenically in both exclusivist and inclusivist ways (exclusivist with regard to Pentecostal separatism and come-outism but inclusivist with regard to the spiritual ecumenism that bound Pentecostals together across denominational and ecclesial lines), but worked itself out with regard to other religions according to the reigning exclusivist paradigm characteristic of other fundamentalist and evangelical churches. Then, without abandoning the original Christocentrism, Pentecostals were challenged by the Charismatic renewal movement to understand the uniqueness and supremacy of Christ in more inclusivist ways, especially with regard to other Christian denominations, churches, and traditions, but also as they pertained to the possibility of God being present and active

---

[34] The goal is a more robust Trinitarian theology regarding other faiths, as I attempt to sketch also in my "Toward a Trinitarian Theology of Religions: A Pentecostal-Evangelical and Missiological Elaboration," *International Bulletin of Mission Research* 40:4 (2016), 294–306.

[35] See my "Apostolic Evangelism in the Postcolony: Opportunities and Challenges," *Mission Studies* 34:2 (2017), 147–67.

[36] Amos Yong, *Hospitality and the Other: Pentecost, Christian Practices, and the Neighbor* (Maryknoll: Orbis Books, 2008); also more recently, "Hospitality and Religious Others: An Orthopathic Perspective," in John W. Morehead and Brandon C. Benziger (eds), *A Charitable Orthopathy: Christian Perspectives on Emotions in Multifaith Engagement* (Eugene, OR: Pickwick, 2020), 183–95.

among people in other faiths in mysterious ways, but especially through the Holy Spirit. Finally, in our contemporary pluralistic world, Pentecostals have retained their Jesus-centred spirituality, but now the anti-institutionalism that characterised the first period and that opened up to the interdenominational ecumenism of the second stage has come to what some might consider full flowering, particularly insofar as both Christ and the Spirit are understood to transcend any formalised or institutionalised ecclesial structures. In the present time, then, the Christ who through the Spirit burst forth from out of the strictures of Christendom in the first period and who exploded through the denominational and ecumenical frameworks of the second phase has manifested himself anew: still as the king of kings and lord of lords but now who also works imperceptibly through the Spirit across human organisations, cultures, and even religions. This is not only the cosmic Christ but also the Spirit-anointed Christ who continually pours out his Spirit so that the world may come to experience the loving embrace of the Father.

If the preceding account is anywhere close to the truth, then it is difficult to imagine next steps in the development of Pentecostal Christology, just as it would have been impossible during the first decades of the early modern Pentecostal movement (1900s–1910s) to have anticipated the ecumenical form and interreligious nature of the history of Pentecostalism as it actually unfolded in the rest of the last century. It is not difficult to affirm that Christ will remain central to Pentecostal spirituality and theological reflection. But how to understand Jesus as the one anointed by the Spirit to save the world will remain an open question in part because of the ever-changing nature of the church catholic and the ever-shifting forms of the world's religious traditions. What the lordship of Christ will look like in an increasingly post-Christian and pluralistic world may take on new forms from generation to generation. But for Pentecostals who take seriously the dynamic and unpredictable nature of life in the Spirit, perhaps none of this would be of too much concern.

## Discussion Questions

1. Yong notes that early Pentecostals tended to leave their historic churches and communities to embrace Pentecostalism in new church settings, practising ecclesial exclusivism. At the same time Yong identified these Pentecostals, while repudiating ecumenism, as engaging a type of ecumenism. In light of Pentecostal "come-outism," how was ecumenism understood and practised within early Pentecostalism?
2. Describe the ecumenical shift within mid-century Pentecostalism. What are some specific ways that the Charismatic Movement contributed to a refreshing of Pentecostal ecumenism, at least among some Pentecostals?
3. How might Yong describe a Spirit-Christology? How is such a Spirit-Christology influenced by eschatology?
4. How does a Spirit-Christology approach to eschatology be valuable to engaging religions within a post-Christian and pluralistic world?

## Bibliography

Alfaro, Sammy. *Divino Compañero: Toward a Hispanic Pentecostal Christology*. Eugene, OR: Pickwick, 2010.

Anderson, Allan. *An Introduction to Pentecostalism: Global Charismatic Christianity*. Cambridge: Cambridge University Press, 2004.

Anderson, Allan. *Spreading Fires: The Missionary Nature of Early Pentecostalism*. London: SCM Press, 2007.

Bagiackas, Joseph. *The Future Glory: The Charismatic Renewal and the Implementation of Vatican II*. South Bend, IN: Charismatic Renewal Services, 1983.

Brumback, Carl. *Suddenly ... From Heaven: A History of the Assemblies of God*. Springfield, MO: Gospel Publishing House, 1961.

Clarke, Clifton. "Rulers of Darkness: Towards a Pentecostal Missiology of Poverty and Underdevelopment in Africa." Paper presented at the Annual Meeting for the Society for Pentecostal Studies, Eugene, Oregon, March 26–28, 2009.

Cleary, Edward L. *The Rise of Charismatic Catholicism in Latin America*. Gainesville, FL: University Press of Florida, 2011.

Cox, Harvey G. *Fire from Heaven: The Rise of Pentecostal Spirituality and the Reshaping of Religion in the 21st Century*. Reading, MA: Addison-Wesley, 1995.

Dupuis, Jacques. *Toward a Christian Theology of Religious Pluralism*. Maryknoll: Orbis Books, 1997.

Godbey, J.E. and Allen Howard Godbey. *Light in Darkness: or, Missions and Missionary Heroes – An Illustrated History of the Missionary Work Now Carried on By All Protestant Denominations in Heathen Lands*. Boston: Eastern, 1888.

Goff, James R. *Fields White Unto Harvest: Charles F. Parham and the Missionary Origins of Pentecostalism*. Fayetteville, AR: University of Arkansas Press, 1988.

Gravey, John. *Seeds of the Word: Orthodox Thinking on Other Religions*. Yonkers, NY: St. Vladimir's Seminary Press, 2005.

Hollenweger, Walter H. *Pentecostalism: Origins and Developments Worldwide*. Peabody, MA: Hendrickson, 1997.

Irvin, Dale T. "'Drawing All Together in One Bond of Love': The Ecumenical Vision of William J. Seymour and the Azusa Street Revival," *Journal of Pentecostal Theology* 3:6 (1995), 25–53

Jenkins, Philip. *The Next Christendom: The Coming of Global Christianity*. 2nd ed. Oxford: Oxford University Press, 2011.

Jenkins, Philip. *A Spirit Christology*. New York: Peter Lang, 2018.

Kärkkäinen, Veli-Matti. "'Anonymous Ecumenists'? Pentecostals and the Struggle for Christian Identity." *Journal of Ecumenical Studies* 37:1 (2000), 13–28.

Kidd, Thomas S. *The Great Awakening: The Roots of Evangelical Christianity in Colonial America*. New Haven: Yale University Press, 2007.

Laurentin, René and Josef Neuner. *The Declaration on the Relation of the Church to Non-Christian Religions*. Glen Rock, NJ: Paulist Press, 1966.

Macchia, Frank D. "The Tongues of Pentecost: A Pentecostal Perspective on the Promise and Challenge of Pentecostal/Roman Catholic Dialogue," *Journal of Ecumenical Studies* 35:1 (1998), 1–18.

Maurer, Susan A. *The Spirit of Enthusiasm: A History of Catholic Charismatic Renewal, 1967–2000*. Lanham, MD: University Press of America, 2010.

McGee, Gary B. *Miracles, Mission, and American Pentecostalism*. Maryknoll: Orbis Books, 2010.

Omenyo, Cephas N. *Pentecost Outside Pentecostalism: A Study of the Development of Charismatic Renewal in the Mainline Churches in Ghana*. Zoetermeer, NL: Boekencentrum, 2002.

Pakenham, Thomas. *The Scramble for Africa: White Man's Conquest of the Dark Continent from 1876 to 1912*. New York: Avon, 1992.

Pearse, Meic. *The Great Restoration: The Religious Radicals of the 16th and 17th Centuries*. Carlisle, UK: Paternoster, 1998.

Phan, Peter, Ed. *Christianity and the Wider Ecumenism*. New York: Paragon House, 1998.

Pinnock, Clark H. *A Wideness in God's Mercy: The Finality of Jesus Christ in the World of Religions*. Grand Rapids, MI: Zondervan, 1992.

Pinnock, Clark H. *Flame of Love: A Theology of the Holy Spirit*. Downers Grove: InterVarsity Press, 1996.

Reed, David A. *"In Jesus' Name": The History and Beliefs of Oneness Pentecostals*. Journal of Pentecostal Theology Supplement Series 31. Blandford Forum, UK: Deo Publishing, 2007.

Richie, Tony. *Speaking by the Spirit: A Pentecostal Model for Interreligious Dialogue*. Lexington, KY: Emeth Press, 2011.

Richie, Tony. *Toward a Pentecostal Theology of Religions: Encountering Cornelius Today*. Cleveland, TN: CPT Press, 2013.

Shelton, Sally Jo. "Jesus' Mother 'Treasured All These Words ... in Her Heart' (Luke 2:19): On Using a Spirit Hermeneutic to Reflect Together about Mary." *Spiritus: ORU Journal of Theology* 2:2 (2017): 57-75.

Solivan, Samuel. *The Spirit, Pathos, and Liberation: Toward an Hispanic Pentecostal Theology*. Journal of Pentecostal Theology Supplement Series 14. Sheffield: Sheffield Academic Press, 1998.

Vondey, Wolfgang. "Pentecostalism and Ecumenism." In *The Cambridge Companion to Pentecostalism*. Eds Cecil M. Robeck, Jr. and Amos Yong. Cambridge: Cambridge University Press, 2014, 273–93.

Wacker, Grant. "Playing for Keeps: The Primitivist Impulse in Early Pentecostalism." In *The American Quest for the Primitive Church*. Ed. Richard T. Hughes, 196–219. Urbana, IL: University of Illinois Press, 1988.

Ware, Steven L. *Restorationism in the Holiness Movement in the Late Nineteenth and Early Twentieth Centuries*. Studies in American Religion 80. Lewiston, NY: Edwin Mellen Press, 2004.

Yong, Amos. "Whither Theological Inclusivism? The Development and Critique of an Evangelical Theology of Religions." *The Evangelical Quarterly* 71:4 (1999), 327–48.

Yong, Amos. *Discerning the Spirit(s): A Pentecostal-Charismatic Contribution to Christian Theology of Religions*. Journal of Pentecostal Theology Supplement Series 20. Sheffield, UK: Sheffield Academic Press, 2000.
Yong, Amos. *The Spirit Poured Out on All Flesh: Pentecostalism and the Possibility of Global Theology*. Grand Rapids, MI: Baker Academic, 2005.
Yong, Amos. *Hospitality and the Other: Pentecost, Christian Practices, and the Neighbor*. Maryknoll: Orbis Books, 2008.
Yong, Amos. "'The Light Shines in the Darkness': Johannine Dualism and the Challenge of Christian Theology of Religions Today." *Journal of Religion* 89:1 (2009), 31–56.
Yong, Amos. *In the Days of Caesar: Pentecostalism and Political Theology – The Cadbury Lectures 2009*. Grand Rapids, MI: Eerdmans, 2010.
Yong, Amos. *Spirit of Love: A Trinitarian Theology of Grace*. Waco, TX: Baylor University Press, 2012.
Yong, Amos. *Beyond the Impasse: Toward a Pneumatological Theology of Religions*. Eugene: Wipf & Stock, 2014 [2003].
Yong, Amos. "Christological Constants in Shifting Contexts: Jesus Christ, Prophetic Dialogue, and the *Missio Spiritus* in a Pluralistic World." In *Mission on the Road to Emmaus: Constants, Contexts, and Prophetic Dialogue*. Eds Stephen B. Bevans and Cathy Ross. London: SCM Press, and Maryknoll: Orbis Books, 2015, 19–33.
Yong, Amos. "Toward a Trinitarian Theology of Religions: A Pentecostal-Evangelical and Missiological Elaboration." *International Bulletin of Mission Research* 40:4 (2016), 294–306.
Yong, Amos. "Apostolic Evangelism in the Postcolony: Opportunities and Challenges." *Mission Studies* 34:2 (2017), 147–67.
Yong, Amos. "Pentecostalism and Ecumenism: Past, Present, and Future." In *Pentecostals in the 21st Century: Identity, Beliefs, and Praxis*. Eds Corneliu Constantineanu and Christopher James Scobie. Eugene, OR: Cascade Books, 2018, 202–36.
Yong, Amos. "Hospitality and Religious Others: An Orthopathic Perspective." In *A Charitable Orthopathy: Christian Perspectives on Emotions in Multifaith Engagement*. Eds John W. Morehead and Brandon C. Benziger. Eugene, OR: Pickwick, 2020, 183–95.
Yong, Amos and Timothy T.N. Lim. "Acts 2 and Interreligious Engagement: Pentecostal and Evangelical Reflections." In *Words to Live By: Sacred Resources for Interreligious Engagement*. Eds Or N. Rose, Homayra Ziad, and Soren M. Hessler.Maryknoll: Orbis Books, 2018,41–52.

# Chapter 7

# Does Jesus Sometimes Want Christians to Kill Their Enemies?[1]

Ronald J. Sider

**Abstract**

This essay considers the question of how Jesus and subsequently the church have responded to social institutions regarding the killing of others, focusing upon war, but also addressing abortion and capital punishment. Historical and biblical considerations are given. Jesus' admonition to love one's enemy (Matt. 5:43-44) provides the foundation for the essay. Six statements that contribute to the debate are considered, including murder and adultery, an eye for an eye, and turn the other cheek. Sider concludes by addressing approaches that the church has used to soften the implications of Jesus' ethic of loving one's enemy.

## The Question

Both in my head and in my heart, I understand the just war tradition. Vicious bullies and ruthless dictators – Hitler, Stalin, ISIS – swagger through history. They wreck terrible havoc on hundreds of millions of innocent people. Thoughtful Christians conclude that the only realistic way to stop them and their vile destruction is to kill them. In the face of such massive evil, pacifism seems naïve, simplistic, irresponsible. That has been the official stance of most Christians for at least 1,500 years.

So why revisit this question?

First, as my comprehensive sourcebook *The Early Church on Killing* shows, every time Christian writers up until the time of Constantine discussed killing, they said that all killing of human beings is wrong – whether in abortion, capital punishment, or war. Surely Christians today should ponder why for three centuries all Christian writers who discuss the topic thought Jesus meant to tell his disciples not to kill.

Second, history demonstrates that the typical argument against this view (namely that there are only two options: to kill or do nothing) is simply historically false. My book, *Nonviolent Action: What Christian Ethics Demands but Most Christians Have Never Really Tried*, demonstrates that in every historical situation there's a third option: nonviolent action. And the history of

---

[1] This piece is adapted from my book, *If Jesus Is Lord: Loving Our Enemies in An Age of Violence* (Baker Academic, 2019), and used with permission.

Mahatma Gandhi, Dr Martin Luther King. Jr and many others prove that nonviolent action is often successful.

Third, there have been a striking number of prominent theologically conservative Christians who have been pacifists – including Charles Spurgeon and Dwight Moody. The Assemblies of God was officially pacifist until 1967.

Finally, and most important, all Christians want to be faithful to Jesus. All historically orthodox Christians believe that Jesus is true God and true man, and that Jesus came both to die for our sins and also to show us how he wants his disciples to live now. And Jesus clearly called his disciples to love their enemies.

To understand Jesus' statement in Matthew 5:43- 44, we must understand three things: Jewish messianic expectations in Jesus' time; the messianic violence in Jesus' time; and Jesus' gospel.

In Jesus' day, most Jews eagerly expected a military messiah to drive out the oppressive Roman imperialists with a great military victory. Josephus, the Jewish historian of the 200 years around the time of Jesus, reports repeated violent Jewish rebellions (often with messianic overtones) against Rome. These violent Jewish revolutionaries called on Jews to kill their Roman oppressors. And the Romans regularly squelched them, crucifying thousands.

Jesus did claim to be the long-expected messiah, but he radically reinterpreted the role of the Messiah. Jesus said his dawning messianic kingdom meant both that he would die for our sins and also that his disciples should live what he taught.

The "Sermon on the Mount" in Matthew 5–7 is the largest block of Jesus' teaching in the four gospels. So, we must start there to answer the question: what does Jesus' teaching tell us about whether Jesus wanted his disciples ever to kill?

Near the beginning of chapter 5, Jesus insisted that "until heaven and earth disappear, not the smallest letter … will by any means disappear from the Law until everything is accomplished [or "fulfilled"]" (Matt. 5:17-18). And Jesus condemned setting aside even "the least of these commandments" (v. 19).

It is not surprising that two quite different interpretations of how Jesus "fulfilled" the Old Testament have emerged. One group argues that Jesus did not set aside any Old Testament law or teaching; he merely corrected misunderstandings of the Old Testament held by some of his contemporaries. The other group insists that Jesus fulfilled some parts of the Old Testament precisely by setting aside some of its provisions and calling his disciples to a different, higher norm.

It is quite clear that Jesus claimed the authority to challenge widely understood demands of the law. And the early Christians clearly taught that central demands of the Old Testament law were no longer binding: circumcision, food laws, sacrifices in the temple for forgiveness of sins, the Sabbath. Paul taught that, although the law was a divinely given custodian applicable until the coming of Christ, now "we are no longer under the supervision of the law" (Gal. 3:25). If Matthew 5:17-20 means that the rules of the Old Testament law must be followed the way they were before Jesus came, Matthew would seem to contradict the whole tenor of the New Testament.

The Old Testament included clear food laws which declared certain foods (meat from pigs, camels, rabbits, etc. etc.) unclean (Lev. 11:1-47; Deut. 14:3-

19). But Mark explicitly tells us that Jesus set these food laws aside: "Jesus declared all foods clean" (Mark 7:18-19). The story of Peter's vision in Acts 10:9-16 and the teaching of Paul underline the way the early church abandoned the explicit food laws of the Old Testament.

Jesus' conflict with the Pharisees over the Sabbath is stunning. One of the Ten Commandments (Exod. 20:8) demanded Sabbath observance. Strict observance of the Sabbath was one of the most important parts of Jewish life in Jesus' day. The Gospels report sharp conflicts with the Pharisees because they believed Jesus' and his disciples' actions broke the Sabbath laws (Mark 2:23–3:6; Luke 13:10-17; John 5:16-18). But Jesus dared to claim authority over the Sabbath: "The Sabbath was made for people, not people for the Sabbath. So the Son of Man is Lord even of the Sabbath" (Mark 2:27-28; TNIV). Claiming lordship over a teaching of one of the Ten Commandments certainly suggests that Jesus' "fulfillment" of the Old Testament may involve major modification of its teaching.

Jesus is not denying that the Law and the Prophets are God's word. But he is saying that now what they foretold has actually arrived.

Clearly, contemporary Christian scholars offer two rather different frameworks for approaching the important block of Jesus' teaching in Matthew 5:21-48. In the first, Jesus corrects contemporary misunderstandings of the law but does not set aside any of its ethical demands. In the second, Jesus sometimes fulfils the law by correcting or even declaring some of its demands no longer normative. Careful exegesis of each of the texts will help us decide which framework fits better with the data.

## Six "Antitheses"

*Murder and Adultery*. The first two sets of sayings on murder (5:21-26) and adultery (5:27-30) clearly show Jesus strengthening but certainly not setting aside the Old Testament commands. Not only should Jesus' followers not murder, they should not be angry with a sister or brother but rather seek reconciliation. Not only should they not commit adultery, but they should also avoid dwelling on lustful thoughts.

*Divorce*. The next segment on divorce, however, appears somewhat different. In 5:31, Jesus quotes Deuteronomy 24:1 where the Mosaic law forbids a husband who has divorced a wife (who then marries another man) from taking her back later. The Deuteronomic text does not command divorce, but it clearly allows it. Later, in Matthew 19:3ff, the Pharisees ask Jesus why "did Moses command that a man give his wife a certificate of divorce" (v. 7). Jesus replies that Moses permitted divorce "because your hearts were hard," but that was never God's will. And Jesus insists that his disciples follow the Creator's original intention, rejecting divorce "except for sexual immorality" (v. 9). This teaching of Jesus does not set aside an explicit Old Testament command. But it does set aside what the Mosaic law allowed.

*Oaths*. In Matthew 5:33-37, Jesus condemns all use of oaths: "Again you have heard that it was said to the people long ago, 'Do not break your oath' … But I tell you, do not swear at all … All you need to say is simply 'Yes' or 'No'; anything beyond this comes from the evil one."

The Old Testament explicitly *commands* taking oaths (Num. 5:19-22; Deut. 6:13; Exod. 22:10-11). Jesus seems to explicitly forbid what the Old Testament commanded.

It is interesting that, for the first few centuries, the early church, especially in the East, took Jesus' prohibition of oaths literally. That is clear from the statements of many prominent Christian writers including Justin Martyr, Irenaeus, Tertullian, Origen and others. But after Constantine, this tradition disappeared.

*Eye for an Eye*. Matthew 5:38-42 is a very important text for our question: "You have heard that it was said, 'Eye for eye, and tooth for tooth.' But I tell you, do not resist an evil person. If anyone slaps you on the right check, turn to them the other cheek also. And if anyone wants to sue you and take your shirt, hand over your coat as well. If anyone forces you to go one mile, go with them two miles. Give to the one who asks you, and do not turn away from the one who wants to borrow from you."

An "eye for an eye" had been a central principle of Near Eastern law since the famous Code of Hammurabi (eighteenth century B.C.). And it was certainly the centre of criminal justice for Jewish law in the Old Testament. Exodus 21:23 is clear: "If there is serious injury, you are to take life for life, eye for eye, tooth for tooth …" Leviticus states the same standard: "Anyone who injures a neighbor is to be injured in the same manner: fracture for fracture, eye for eye, tooth for tooth" (24:19-20). Deuteronomy 19 prescribes how to punish someone who gives false testimony in court. If the court discerns that a witness has lied, then "do to the false witness as that witness intended to do to the other party … Show no pity: life for life, eye for eye, tooth for tooth, hand for hand, foot for foot" (19–21).

Jesus' response to this fundamental Old Testament principle is pointed: "But I tell you, do not resist an evil person" (5:39). In a moment, we must examine carefully what the key verb translated in the NIV as "do not resist" actually means. But to try to argue as some do that here Jesus is not setting aside an Old Testament teaching seems to ignore the clear meaning of the text. John Piper is explicit: "Jesus' command not to resist evil (Matt. 5:39-42) demands the opposite of the Old Testament legal principle … they exclude each other; they are contradictory."[2]

Central to an understanding of this passage is the proper translation of the key verb *antistēnai*. The NIV translates it "do not resist" and a number of people (e.g. Paul Ramsey and Reinhold Niebuhr) have concluded that Jesus advocates pure passivity, total nonresistance, in the face of evil.

But if Jesus in Matthew 5:39 is advocating pure passivity in the face of evil, then Jesus again and again contradicted his own teaching. Jesus unleashed a blistering attack on the Pharisees denouncing them as blind guides, fools, hypocrites, and snakes (Matt. 23:13-33). He urged his followers to confront

---

[2] John Piper, *"Love Your Enemies": Jesus' Love Command in The Synoptic Gospels and The Early Christian Paraenesis* (Cambridge: Cambridge University Press, 1979), 89.

members of the church who sin (Matt. 18:15-17). His cleansing of the temple, when he overturned the tables of moneychangers and drove out the animals, was anything but passive.

A careful study of the verb used in this text shows clearly that Jesus is not recommending passivity. *Anthistēmi* is a variant of the word *antistēnai* (used in v. 39) and this word appears in the Greek Old Testament primarily as a military term. In forty-four of seventy-one uses in the Greek Old Testament, the word refers to armed resistance in military encounters (e.g. Lev. 26:37; Deut. 7:24; 25:18; Josh. 7:13; 23:9; Judg. 2:14). Josephus, the first-century Jewish historian, uses the word fifteen of seventeen times to refer to violent struggle. The Greek lexicon by Liddell and Scott defines the word to mean "set against especially in battle." Ephesians 6:13 uses the word *antistēnai* to refer to the spiritual battle against Satan when Christians are armed with the full armour of God. *antistēnai* means to resist *violently*.[3] N.T. Wright summarises the meaning of the word this way: "The word 'resist' is *antistēnai*, almost a technical term for revolutionary resistance of a specifically military variety. Taken in this sense, the command draws out the implication of a good deal of the sermon so far. The way forward for Israel is not the way of violent resistance ... but the different, oblique way of creative non-violent resistance ... Jesus' people were not to become part of the resistance movement."[4]

After prohibiting a violent response to evil, the text describes a proper response in four concrete situations. In each case, the commanded response is neither violent nor passive. Jesus calls his disciples not to turn aside passively or hit back, but rather to confront the evil nonviolently.

Walter Wink has proposed an interpretation of vv. 39b–41 which, if correct, greatly strengthens the claim that, in these statements, Jesus is proposing a vigorously activist (although certainly nonviolent) response to evil and injustice.[5] Some scholars agree with Wink. Others do not. But his argument merits careful evaluation.

*Turn the Other Cheek.* The text says: "If anyone slaps you on the right cheek, turn to them the other cheek also" (v. 39b). There is widespread acceptance by commentators that someone could strike a person on the right cheek only with the back of the hand and that such an action would be the kind of insult that a superior would deliver to an inferior. We know from documents of the time that a backhanded blow to the right cheek was a huge insult. Ancient documents also show that the fine for striking an equal with the (insulting) back of the hand was double that for a blow by one's fist. But no penalty followed for striking slaves that way. A backhanded slap was for inferiors like slaves and wives.

If that is the proper context for understanding the saying, then Jesus' advice to turn the other (left) cheek conveys a surprising suggestion. Normally, an inferior would simply accept the insult (or on occasion fight back). But by

---

[3] See the detailed citations in Ronald J. Sider, *If Jesus Is Lord; Loving Our Enemies in an Age of Violence* (Grand Rapids, MI: Baker Academic, 2019), 35, nn. 32–34.

[4] N.T. Wright, *Jesus and The Victory of God* (Minneapolis: Fortress, 1996), 291

[5] Walter Wink, *Engaging the Powers* (Minneapolis: Fortress, 1992), 175–84; Walter Wink, *The Powers That Be* (New York: Doubleday, 1998), 98–111.

turning the left cheek to the person insulting one, one almost forces the attacker to use his fist if he wants to strike again. (It is much harder to hit the left cheek with a backslap than with a fist.) The effect is that the inferior person astonishes his superior by a dramatic act that asserts his dignity, not by striking back but by forcing his attacker either to stop or use his fist and thus treat him as an equal. Thus, Jesus is urging a nonviolent but nonetheless activist response to evil.

*Sued for One's Shirt*. "If anyone wants to sue you and take your shirt [inner garment], hand over your coat [outer garment] as well" (v. 40). The setting refers to a typical first-century context where debt was widespread among the poor.

In Jesus' example, the person taken to court for an unpaid debt is obviously very poor because he owns nothing of worth to repay the debt except his clothes. As an impoverished person, he has no hope of winning against the richer person. So he loses his inner garment as payment on his debt.

But why would Jesus tell this kind of poor person, who has just lost his inner garment, to also give the person he owes money his outer garment as well? Since many poor people had only one outer garment, that would mean stripping naked in court. And nakedness was a terrible disgrace in Palestinian Jewish society.

The disgrace for nakedness, however, fell not only on the naked person but also on those viewing the naked person. By stripping naked, the debtor exposes the cruelty not only of the creditor but the oppressive system he represents. The system in which rich people abused poor debtors is publicly disclosed. Rather than recommending a passive response to injustice, Jesus urges a dramatic nonviolent protest.

*The Second Mile*. "If anyone forces you to go one mile, go with them two miles" (5:41). The context for this saying is clearly Roman imperialism. The word translated "mile" is a Roman word, not a Jewish word. And the word translated "forces you" is the technical term (*angareia*) very widely known in Roman law to refer to the legal right of Roman soldiers to compel subject people to carry their packs for one mile. There is a large literature that demonstrates both that Roman soldiers often abused this right and also that colonised people hated this burdensome obligation.

Earlier, we saw how angry, violent rebellion against Roman rule and its collaborators kept erupting among the Jews in the century around the time of Jesus. These violent revolutionaries certainly urged fellow Jews to refuse to carry the baggage of oppressive Roman soldiers. What Jesus recommends is the exact opposite of what the violent Jewish revolutionaries promoted. The words used and the context demonstrate that Jesus is clearly rejecting a widespread, popular attitude toward the oppressive Roman imperialists.

But is he recommending passivity? Is he urging fellow Jews to affirm Roman oppression? The soldier knows the colonised person has a legal obligation to carry his pack one mile. But he also knows the law forbids the Roman soldier forcing the person to carry it more than one mile. And he knows his commander may punish him severely for breaking this law. So when they reach the end of the first mile, the soldier asks for his pack back. But the colonised person walks on, intending to carry the pack another mile. Now the soldier is in trouble. He may be disciplined by his superior. So, he begs to be given back his pack. With this action, the oppressed Jew seizes the initiative and asserts his dignity – all in a nonviolent way fully compatible with loving the oppressor without endorsing the oppression.

## "Love Your Enemies"

> "You have heard that it was said, "Love your neighbor and hate your enemy." But I tell you, love your enemies and pray for those who persecute you, that you may be children of your Father in heaven (Matt. 5:43-45).

There is no dispute about the source of the traditional summons to "love your neighbor" which Jesus mentions in v. 43a. It is a verbatim quote from the Greek translation of Leviticus 19:18. The neighbour that one was obligated to love was normally understood to be a fellow Israelite. A different attitude toward Gentiles was expected.

But who are the enemies Jesus summons his disciples to love? It is interesting that in v. 43 ("love your neighbor and hate your enemy") the words for neighbour and enemy are singular. But v. 44 uses the plural: "Love your enemies." Every class of enemy seems to be included.

Some have argued that the word for enemies (*echthroi*) used by Jesus refers not to foreign or military enemies, but to personal enemies because of local squabbles in small Palestinian villages. Therefore, this summons to love one's enemies has nothing to do with the question of whether Jesus opposes killing violent enemies.

Duke Divinity School New Testament scholar, Richard Hays, however, argues convincingly that this argument is wrong. There is nothing in Matthew's text that suggests the kind of precise social situation in small villages that some imagine. Furthermore, the lexicographical evidence does not support this view. "The term *echthroi* is generic. It is often used in biblical Greek of national or military enemies."[6] For example, in Deuteronomy 20:1 (Septuagint), the text says: "When you go to war against your enemies [*echthroi*] and see horses and chariots and an army greater than yours, do not be afraid of them." (It is also interesting that this verse follows immediately after Deuteronomy 19:21 which commands an eye for an eye – the principle which Jesus specifically rejects.) The fact that, in the immediately preceding section, Jesus had urged his followers to carry the packs of Roman soldiers not just the legally mandated one mile but a second mile demonstrates that Jesus is thinking about the situation that the violent Jewish revolutionaries hated. If in v. 41, Jesus is talking about how to respond to Roman imperialists, it is very likely that his command to love enemies included the people the revolutionaries sought to kill.

It is hard to exaggerate either the originality or the importance of Jesus' direct command to love our enemies. It contradicts the practice of every society known to historians. No precise parallel to Jesus' words has been found. New Testament scholars point out that the saying appears both in the earliest sayings tradition of Jesus' words (scholars call it Q) and then Luke (6:27, 35) as well as Matthew.

---

[6] Richard B. Hays, *The Moral Vision of The New Testament* (New York: HarperOne, 1996), 328.

Also striking is the fact that Matthew 5:38-48 is probably the most frequently cited biblical text when one collects all the statements about killing from the early Christian writers before the time of Constantine. Ten different writers in at least twenty-eight different places cite or refer to this passage and note that Christians love their enemies and turn the other cheek. In nine instances, they link this passage from Jesus with a statement that Christians are peaceable, ignorant of war, or opposed to attacking others. Sometimes they explicitly link Jesus' saying to a rejection of killing and war.[7] In every single instance where pre-Constantinian Christian writers mention the topic of killing, they say that Christians do not do that, whether in abortion, capital punishment, or war. And Jesus' statement about loving enemies is one of the reasons cited.

### Side-Stepping Jesus' Teaching

It is not surprising that Christians over the centuries have developed numerous ways to weaken or set aside Jesus' call to love our enemies. His teaching directly contradicts our natural instincts. It challenges the practice of all civilisations. We must examine the most common arguments for setting aside this radical teaching.

*Jesus Came to Die*. Many Christians think that the only important reason Jesus came was to die as the substitute for our sins. The Gospel is limited to the good news that we are forgiven through the cross and can go to heaven when we die. Jesus' ethical teaching is at best relatively unimportant and perhaps irrelevant.

The problem with this understanding is that it simply ignores Jesus' full teaching about his gospel. Jesus' gospel was the good news that the long-expected messianic kingdom was now breaking into history. Certainly, one fundamental part of that good news is that God forgives sinners and that Jesus' death on the cross accomplished our reconciliation with God. But equally central to Jesus' understanding of the gospel is the fact that the new messianic time of peace and justice has already begun, and Jesus' disciples are now summoned to live according to Jesus' teaching.

*An Interim Ethic*. Since Albert Schweitzer at the beginning of the twentieth century, many scholars have thought that Jesus expected an almost immediate end to our space-time world. Since the world was about to end, Jesus could proclaim a radical ethic for this brief interim – an ethic which would be totally unrealistic if the world were to continue.

The problem with this argument, as N.T. Wright clearly demonstrates, is that there is virtually no evidence that any Jew in Jesus' day thought that the arrival of the messianic kingdom meant the end of our space-time world.[8] The apocalyptic language used to describe the arrival of the messianic kingdom was figurative language to underline the sweeping societal change that the Messiah would bring. Since Jesus was not thinking of a very near end to our space-time

---

[7] Ronald J. Sider, *The Early Church on Killing: A Comprehensive Sourcebook on War, Abortion and Capital Punishment* (Grand Rapids: Baker Academic, 2012), 163–95, especially 190–95.

[8] Wright, *Jesus and the Victory of God*, 40, 81, 95–96; N.T. Wright, *The New Testament and The People of God* (Minneapolis: Fortress, 1992), 333–34.

world, the idea of his teaching an interim ethic for the short time before the world ended makes no historical sense. It is a fiction of modern scholarship.

*Jesus' Radical Ethics Calls Us to Repentance, Not Discipleship*. Believing that Jesus' radical ethics are impossible to live, some Christians (Martin Luther among others) argue that their purpose is to reveal our sinful failure and thus drive us to confess our sins and seek forgiveness rather than reveal how Jesus wants his disciples to live.

Jesus' high demands rightly lead us to repentance. But there is not a hint in Jesus that that is all he intends. In fact, repeatedly it is clear that Jesus summons his disciples to obey all that he commands.

*Private vs Public Roles*. Various versions of this argument are probably the most common way that Christians have argued that Jesus' command to love enemies does not mean that Christians should never kill others. (As soldiers or public officials carrying out a judicial decision on capital punishment, Christians rightly kill.) Jesus' teaching about how to respond to a slap of the hand or a demand for one's clothing shows that he is talking about how to respond to personal injury, not about public life.

Careful consideration of this widely used argument is essential. I believe this argument: 1) ignores the historical context of Jesus' teaching; 2) contradicts what seems to be the most obvious meaning of the text; 3) relies on pragmatism to set Jesus aside; 4) historically, has sometimes led to very bad consequences; 5) finally, ignores the first three centuries of Christian teaching about killing.

First, in his historical context, Jesus claimed to be the Messiah of the entire Jewish people. He intended his teaching to show Israel how it should live. Jews of all kinds – common people and religious leaders, ordinary folk and members of the Sanhedrin – heard his teaching. And it is clear that Jesus disagreed with the devout, violent Jewish revolutionaries of his time who, according to Josephus, urged the Jews to rebel against the Roman imperialists and their Jewish collaborators. Rejecting the widespread expectation of a military Messiah, Jesus clearly chose to be a peaceful Messiah who called his followers to love even their enemies – and those enemies, as the saying about carrying Roman soldiers' packs a second mile demonstrates, included even the hated Romans.

Jesus advocated love, even for political enemies, as his response to several centuries of violent Jewish response to foreign oppressors. And there is certainly no hint that Jesus' reason for objecting to the violence of the revolutionaries was that they were unauthorised individuals whose violent sword would have been legitimate if the religio-political leaders of the Sanhedrin had just given the order. Rather, his point was that the revolutionaries' whole approach to enemies was wrong. They offered one messianic strategy. Jesus offered another. But both appealed to the entire Jewish nation to follow their vision and teaching.

Revolutionary violence, Jesus realised, would lead to national destruction as it did in the Jewish revolt (66–70AD) just a few decades later. Jesus' messianic vision offered an entirely different approach. He called the Jewish people to embrace his vision of a peaceful messianic kingdom where people loved their enemies rather than killing them. That kingdom, he said, was now breaking into history and he invited the entire Jewish people to embrace it. Understood in its historical setting, Jesus' call to love enemies clearly cannot be limited to the personal sphere of private life.

Second, the personal–public distinction seems to contradict the most natural, literal meaning of the text. There is no hint in the text of such a distinction. It is true that one or two of Jesus' concrete examples refer to personal life. That is true of the slap on the cheek. To some extent, that is also the case with the statement about how the debtor should respond. But in that case, the setting is a court scene of public law. The call to carry the Roman soldier's pack a second mile clearly speaks of the public political setting where Roman imperialists had the legal right to make oppressive demands. And Jesus' call to reject the principle of an "eye for an eye" refers to the foundational principle of all Near Eastern jurisprudence – i.e. the very centre of public life, not some personal private sphere. The members of the Sanhedrin and other officials surely heard Jesus' teaching. The most natural conclusion is that Jesus intended his words to be normative not just in private but also in public life.

Third, an essential ethical pragmatism often underlies the argument that Jesus could not have meant that his followers should never use lethal violence. In a sinful world which often tramples on nonviolent persons, it is argued by people like Reinhold Niebuhr, violence is necessary to defend oneself and others. Jesus' love ethic, Niebuhr said, is an "impossible ideal" that simply will not work in the real world. This factual claim may or may not be accurate. But what is surely most important for Christians, however, is the essential pragmatism of the argument. The *pragmatic* question of whether Jesus' ethic works in the short run – that is, whether it enables us and others to avoid suffering – dares not be decisive in our analysis of what Jesus actually means. If one confesses, as the church has for two millennia, that Jesus is truly God incarnate, then one simply dares not tell Jesus that his teaching is impractical in the real world and therefore may, even should, be set aside.

Fourth, the consequences of this dualistic distinction between private and public have often been disastrous. German Christians under Hitler, for example, justified their participation in terrible evil on the pretext that it was not right for them to challenge official orders.

Finally, the writings of Christians in the first three centuries clearly do not support the personal–public distinction. In every instance where they discuss killing, they say that Christians do not and should not kill. That holds in both the private realm of abortion and infanticide and also the public realm of capital punishment and war. Writing in the first decade of the fourth century, the Christian orator Lactantius insists: "When God forbids us to kill … He warns us against the commission of those things which are esteemed lawful among people. Thus it will be neither lawful for a just man [a Christian] to engage in military service … nor to accuse anyone of a capital charge, because it makes no difference whether you put a person to death by word or rather by sword, since it is the act of putting to death itself which is prohibited."[9] Repeatedly, they reject the view that Christians may kill in the public role of soldier or executioner.

---

[9] Lactantius, *Divine Institutes*, 6.20; Sider, *Early Church on Killing*, 110.

The most natural interpretation of the Sermon on the Mount certainly seems to confirm that Christians in the first three centuries were right in thinking that Jesus intended to teach his followers never to kill.

The evidence of the New Testament is quite clear. Jesus called his followers to love their enemies, not kill them. One can conclude, with people like Reinhold Niebuhr, that, while that is what Jesus taught, it does not work in the real world. From that perspective, we should not follow what Jesus taught. But that option is simply not available to anyone with an orthodox Christology. If Jesus is true God as well as true man, then it is profoundly heretical to say that Jesus' followers should reject one of his central teachings. Evangelicals and other historically orthodox Christians simply dare not do that.

If Jesus is God incarnate; if Jesus was truly the expected Messiah; if Jesus taught his followers to love, not kill, their enemies; if Jesus' messianic kingdom has begun in his life, death, and resurrection; if the church in the power of the Holy Spirit is called to live now the lifestyle of the already dawning kingdom modelled by Jesus; and if the crucified and risen Jesus is now Lord of all earthly kingdoms: then Christians today must refuse to kill their enemies. Miroslav Volf is right: "If one decides to put on soldier's gear instead of carrying one's cross, one should not seek legitimation in the religion that worships the crucified Messiah."[10]

## Discussion Questions

1. Why does Jesus' call to love one's enemy create a difficult saying for the practices of the church?
2. What is the purpose of the antitheses in Sider's development of his argument for pacifism? How do the arguments that emerged out of the antitheses contribute to Sider's argument?
3. What moderating, side-stepping issues have you seen as most common within the church or society?
4. If you could ask Dr Sider one question regarding his perspective on pacifism, what would be that question? How do you think that he would answer that question?

## Bibliography

Hays, Richard B. *The Moral Vision of the New Testament*. New York: HarperOne, 1996.

Piper, John. *"Love Your Enemies": Jesus' Love Command in the Synoptic Gospels and the Early Christian Paraenesis*. Cambridge: Cambridge University Press, 1979.

Sider, Ronald J. *The Early Church on Killing: A Comprehensive Sourcebook on War, Abortion and Capital Punishment*. GrandRapids, MI: Baker Academic, 2012.

[10]Miroslav Volf, *Exclusion and Embrace* (Nashville: Abington, 1996), 306.

Sider, Ronald J. *If Jesus is Lord: Loving Our Enemies in an Age of Violence*. Grand Rapids, MI: Baker Academic, 2019.
Volf, Miroslav. *Exclusion and Embrace*. Nashville: Abington, 1996.
Wink, Walter. *Engaging the Powers*. Minneapolis: Fortress, 1992.
Wink, Walter. *The Powers That Be*. New York: Doubleday, 1998.
Wright, N.T. *TheNew Testament and the People of God*. Minneapolis: Fortress, 1992.
Wright, N.T. *Jesus and the Victory of God*. Minneapolis: Fortress, 1996.

# Chapter 8

# The Christian Moral Witness of Dietrich Bonhoeffer

David P. Gushee


## Abstract

This essay engages Dietrich Bonhoeffer as an exemplar for developing a moral witness, a prophetic voice to society. Bonhoeffer's home in early- to mid-twentieth-century Germany, where antisemitism pervaded much of the church and the larger culture, sets the scene for developing an exemplar for a present culture that often appreciates a Christian moral witness when such a witness calls for the valuing of minority communities. Significant to the essay are seven inflection points that are significant to the moral journey of Bonhoeffer; points that contributed to shifts in Bonhoeffer's thinking and practices regarding a Christian moral witness. Significantly, most of those points relate directly or indirectly to developments within a German society that was embracing the National Socialism of Adolf Hitler. The essay concludes by pointing to the richness of Bonhoeffer's intellectual tradition, his vibrant and disciplined personal faith, and his commitment to take actions that reflected those dynamics in public life, even when such a moral witness would cost him his life.


## Introduction

Murray Dempster is a significant moral leader in the Pentecostal community, and it is an honour to be asked to participate in this *festschrift* in his honour. I have decided to focus my contribution on the Christian moral witness of Dietrich Bonhoeffer.

I will be drawing partly on materials in my 2017 book, *Moral Leadership for a Divided Age*, written with Colin Holtz.[1] That book marked an effort to respond to the moral, political, and social chaos, injustice, and division of our time (*that* time, so long ago, it now seems) by undertaking a serious historical study of some of history's greatest moral leaders.

As I write, the entire world is facing the threat of COVID-19. Once again, morally serious leadership, or its lack, is determining the very fate of nations, communities, and individuals.

I believe that in this frightening and apocalyptic time, rehearing the story of German theologian and resister Dietrich Bonhoeffer will offer hope. Humanity has faced apocalyptic circumstances before, and we have endured them, though all too often with great loss of life. Perhaps considering Bonhoeffer's story in

---

[1] David P. Gushee and Colin Holtz, *Moral Leadership for a Divided Age: Fourteen People Who Dared to Change Our World* (Grand Rapids, MI: Brazos Press, 2018).

this new context will encourage courageous Christian moral witness on the part of those who enter his journey once again.

As I narrate Bonhoeffer's pilgrimage, I will name seven "inflection points" that proved pivotal in shaping the journey that he took with his life.

## Germany (1871–1932)

Dietrich Bonhoeffer was born into a Germany that was both old and young. Germany was old in its culture but new as a nation, emerging only in 1871 out of independent states and cities. Germany was eager to join the imperial and colonialist game which its near neighbours had long been playing.

In religious and intellectual life, however, Germany was already a leader. Protestantism was born there, of course, with Martin Luther. By the 1800s German philosophers, theologians, and religious studies professors dominated their fields.

The Reformation and the religious warfare that followed left the German peoples predominantly Lutheran, with a substantial Catholic population concentrated heavily in Bavaria. The tiny Jewish minority loomed larger in the deeply antisemitic religious and cultural imagination of Germany than was merited – with disastrous consequences. Martin Luther's bitter antisemitism late in his life contributed greatly to this problem.[2] But antisemitism certainly was not unique to the German or Protestant people. It was an ancient Christian legacy.[3]

Germany entered World War I confident both of success and God's blessing. So, of course, did most of the other European Christian nations. But the war took a turn that no one anticipated: trench warfare, horrific casualties, bloody stalemate lasting four long years.

It is hard enough for people to come to terms with mass wartime death when their side wins. But defeat brings incomparably greater difficulty. Germany lost, bringing not just grief but a sense of incomprehension and humiliation. Not unlike what happened in the white South after the Civil War, for Germany World War I became a "lost cause" that needed not just explanation but reversal, even revenge. Germany was unhinged by frustrated and enraged grief. Meanwhile, Germany's authoritarian, semi-monarchical political system, led by the Kaiser, collapsed.

After the war, the regime of the Kaiser was replaced by a fragile parliamentary democracy. This was young Germany's first experiment in democracy. While it had the support of millions of Germans, conservatives yearned nostalgically for *l'ancien regime*, while on the other side of the spectrum the Left actively sought a Communist revolution as had just occurred in Russia. Democracy is hard enough to sustain when it has universal popular legitimacy and longstanding cultural norms. But the so-called Weimar Republic faced existential threats from

---

[2] Martin Luther, "On the Jews and Their Lies, 1543," *Luther's Works, Volume 47* (Philadelphia: Fortress, 1971), 121–306.

[3] See Rosemary Radford Reuther, *Faith and Fratricide* (Boston: Seabury Press, 1974).

its birth. The fact that in the eyes of many it was associated with hostile foreign powers that had defeated, disarmed, and subjugated Germany did not help.

Periodic waves of economic crisis throughout the 1920s and early 1930s weakened the fragile Republic. Desperate people tend to move toward the political edges. Conservative, militarist, authoritarian, deeply antisemitic nationalists promised a return to national glory and a crushing of Germany's purported internal and external enemies, while the Communists promised their classless utopia. The frustrated lower working (and unemployed) classes were the primary objects of political seduction efforts. Some went left; in the end, more went right – right into the arms of Nazism.

The National Socialist German Workers' Party was born in 1919. In its earliest form it combined nationalist appeals with a socialist focus on improved conditions for working-class Germans. Its nationalist/militarist wing won out under the leadership of the Austrian corporal and Iron Cross winner Adolf Hitler.

The Nazis attempted a coup in 1923. It failed, landing Hitler in jail. His sympathetic jailers gave him the resources he needed in jail to write *Mein Kampf* (*My Struggle*).[4] This turgid, massive, awful book contained plenty of clues as to the frightening character of the man gunning for power in Germany. But the clues were not heeded, or perhaps the desperation overrode all other considerations. Hitler received just over one third of the votes in the last free elections in Germany and was named chancellor (essentially, prime minister) of a coalition government that took office on 30 January 1933.

Within six months, Hitler had strangled the Weimar Republic and instituted what quickly became a totalitarian and murderous dictatorship. Hitler's evil regime forced its citizens to choose between cooperation and resistance. Dietrich Bonhoeffer became famous for his resolute, uncompromising resistance.

## Young Dietrich (1906–1932)

Dietrich Bonhoeffer was born well, in every sense. Entering the world on 4 February 1906, Dietrich enjoyed a happy childhood in one of Germany's leading families. His father was one of the nation's top psychiatrists, and his mother came from an aristocratic German lineage. Any serious biography of Bonhoeffer offers a staggering list of elite characters who crossed his path.[5] In the Bonhoeffer family, it was never a matter of whether one would be a successful professional, but in which particular field one would be so. Later, Bonhoeffer's family, class, and connections offered him extraordinary manoeuvring room and even protected him during most of his resistance to the Nazi state.

*First inflection point*: The interaction of a sturdy, well-placed, upper-crust German family with the social crisis that began with World War I, the rise of a militant Left and Right, and finally a triumphant Nazism, proved pivotal. The

---

[4] Adolf Hitler, *Mein Kampf* (trans. Ralph Manheim; Boston: Houghton Mifflin, 1943).

[5] In my view, the single best biography of Bonhoeffer is Ferdinand Schlingensiepen, *Dietrich Bonhoeffer 1906–1945: Martyr, Thinker, Man of Resistance* (London: T&T Clark, 2010).

social capital provided by such a family to brilliant young Dietrich should be noted. He learned to see the world in a way that ultimately proved impenetrable to any political extremism, including Nazi paganism, racism, and militarism. A broader look shows that the family as a whole, and not just Dietrich as an individual, proved similarly clear and impregnable in its values. Families matter.

In 1918, with the Great War nearing its close, its awful cost came home to the Bonhoeffer family. Dietrich's oldest brother, Walter, was killed only two weeks after leaving for battle. The Bonhoeffer family joined the thousands upon thousands of others also faced with staggering grief.

Dietrich was twelve. By all accounts a quite sensitive child, the loss of Walter affected him deeply. Any student of Bonhoeffer's writing can see the continuing echoes of this pivotal childhood event.

By all accounts a personal religion was not meaningfully present to sustain young Dietrich. His family was Lutheran but not devout or churchgoing. His mother's father and grandfather had been prominent Christian leaders, but a scientific and professional spirit, rather than a religious one, tended to dominate the family.

Thus it came as a shock to the family when Bonhoeffer decided two years later to become a theologian. The family was not particularly enthused. Bonhoeffer later indicated in correspondence that he chose to become a theologian before he became a serious follower of Jesus. Theology was a career path, like any other – especially in a culture in which theology was a career embedded in state university structures. For young Dietrich, it was certainly a way to differentiate himself from the rest of the family.

As a student, Bonhoeffer was a prodigy. He started his theological studies at Tübingen before finishing at the University of Berlin. He studied under legendary church historian Adolf von Harnack, Luther scholar Karl Holl, and theologian Reinhold Seeberg. Like every serious theology student in this period, Bonhoeffer also engaged with the work of Karl Barth, the giant of twentieth-century neo-orthodox Protestant theology who later also resisted the Nazi state and was forced out of his German post. The two became friends and supporters of each other, though Bonhoeffer was a generation younger.

Bonhoeffer completed two book-length doctoral dissertations by the age of twenty-four. The first was a theology of the church.[6] The second was a highly philosophical work on the nature of revelation.[7] Neither is widely read today, but together they qualified him to become a university professor before his twenty-fifth birthday. (My twenty-five-year-old students usually collapse in self-doubt when I tell them this.)

Unlike many of Germany's religion students and professors, Bonhoeffer undertook a parallel educational path toward becoming a pastor. At twenty-two he served as an assistant pastor at a small German church in Barcelona, Spain. He proved to be very effective with children and youth as well as in the pulpit.

---

[6] Dietrich Bonhoeffer, *Sanctorum Communion: A Theological Study of the Sociology of the Church* (Dietrich Bonhoeffer Works, Volume 1: Minneapolis: Fortress, 2009).

[7] Dietrich Bonhoeffer, *Act and Being* (Dietrich Bonhoeffer Works, Volume 2: Minneapolis: Fortress, 1996).

At this point in his journey, a school year spent in New York affected Bonhoeffer deeply. In September 1930, he began what amounted to a post-doctorate at Union Theological Seminary in New York (my own alma mater). He was not much impressed either by Union or the white liberal Protestant churches of New York. He was more deeply affected by several key friends. Two of them were Jean Lasserre, a Frenchman who was a dedicated Christian pacifist with a moral vision rooted in the Sermon on the Mount, and Albert Franklin Fisher, a black Alabamian who introduced Bonhoeffer to Abyssinian Baptist Church and, more broadly, to Harlem and black culture.

Abyssinian was and is one of the leading black Baptist churches in New York. Bonhoeffer opened himself radically to the spirit and vision of Abyssinian and more generally to African American religion and culture. He immersed himself deeply in black literature and music and by all accounts felt deeply the racism that so affected the daily lives of African Americans.

*Second inflection point*: In his book *Bonhoeffer's Black Jesus*, Reggie Williams convincingly argues that Bonhoeffer's fundamental understanding of Jesus changed in Harlem.[8] He came to envision Jesus as the suffering and liberating black Jesus of Abyssinian rather than the lordly white Jesus of high European Christianity. This also appears to be how he really met Jesus. Something about Abyssinian, where he worshipped and even led Bible study, brought him closer to God. He later claimed that before then he had rarely prayed and was mainly an ambitious and self-interested theologue. But after New York, he was a changed man. It is very interesting to wonder who Bonhoeffer would have been without Fisher, Harlem, and Abyssinian. But one must also ask: who was he *already*, to choose to invest so deeply there? Not every European (or American) white student who comes to Union goes north to Harlem for faith and community.

When Bonhoeffer returned home to Germany in 1931, personal faith in Jesus and a commitment to serious personal discipleship focused on simple obedience to the Sermon on the Mount had become central. Dietrich Bonhoeffer was a compelling thinker in 1930, but he came back to Germany from New York in 1931 a serious Christian. He would bring both into his pastoral and academic work from that point forward.

## Bonhoeffer and Hitler Arrive at the Same Time (1931–1938)

Dietrich Bonhoeffer returned to a Germany moving closer to its greatest mistake – handing power to Adolf Hitler. While Hitler was rising, Bonhoeffer was beginning his career in Berlin. He lectured at the University of Berlin, served as a chaplain at a technical college, and taught confirmation classes in a poor section of town. He had a front-row seat as Left and Right fought (quite literally) for the support of struggling working people.

[8] Reggie L. Williams, *Bonhoeffer's Black Jesus: Harlem Renaissance Theology and an Ethic of Resistance* (Waco, TX: Baylor University Press, 2014).

When Hitler was named chancellor, like many others Bonhoeffer and his family were incredulous. Their wonder turned to horror as Hitler gobbled up power, opened concentration camps, and passed laws attacking Jews.

Hitler had dangerous goals both domestically and in foreign policy. At home, he wanted to crush dissent – even its possibility – by synchronising every institution in German society with Nazi ideology. He succeeded in relation to business, education, the arts, and many other areas, but church structures were harder to synchronise. From a Christian perspective, they should have been not just harder but impossible to synchronise. Christians follow Christ, not politicians. Right?

Bonhoeffer was a rising star in the official German Evangelical Church, a youthful scholar and pastor with stature beyond his years. He responded immediately to Hitler's rise by demanding that his Church retain its independence; that is, its fidelity to Christ. Some of his fellow pastors and church leaders agreed completely. Some agreed up to a point, though mainly focusing on the Church's institutional autonomy rather than the broader resistance that Bonhoeffer favoured. Some, shockingly, went all in for Nazism and acted as if it were completely synchronous with Christianity already – including in its militarism, violence, antisemitism, and totalitarianism.

In 1933, at the age of twenty-seven, Bonhoeffer wrote an essay titled "The Church and the Jewish Question," attempting to think through the antisemitism issue theologically.[9] There is much in this essay not to like, including evidence of traditional Christian theological anti-Judaism and a hesitance to bless direct political action on the part of the church. But the most important thing about the essay is that already in 1933 Bonhoeffer was suggesting that the church must not allow the state to impose its discriminatory antisemitism onto itself, and that state antisemitic measures must evoke the church's aid to the victims, and *in extremis* possibly even direct resistance. In this he went much farther than almost any of his peers, or elders, in the German Evangelical Church.

Even though he was so young, Bonhoeffer quickly became one of the leaders of what became known as the *Kirchenkampf* (Church Struggle), the internal fight within the German Evangelical Church over how to respond to Nazi blandishments and seductions. In September 1933, along with the much older war hero/pastor Martin Niemöller and others, Bonhoeffer helped organise the Pastors' Emergency League. This group opposed Nazi meddling in church affairs, particularly the "Aryan Clause," an infamous Nazi law that defined who was Jewish and then banned them from civil service roles. That had already been implemented in other sectors – the Pastors' League sought to prevent it from being forced on the church, as a matter of principle. The main impact would have been in forcing the church to dismiss any pastors of "Jewish" blood.

On this matter as on others, Bonhoeffer was uncompromising and, in his context, utterly radical. Bonhoeffer refused any compromise with the Nazi regime, defended the church's absolute authority to direct its own affairs, and

---

[9] Dietrich Bonhoeffer, "The Church and the Jewish Question," in Geffrey B. Kelly and F. Burton Nelson (eds), *A Testament to Freedom: The Essential Writings of Dietrich Bonhoeffer* (New York: HarperCollins, 1990), 137–40.

resisted the growing Hitler cult and violations of human rights. Even as Hitler's popularity soared and others bent with the wind, Bonhoeffer did not.

*Third inflection point*. It is not all that surprising that during this crucial period Bonhoeffer proved impervious to Nazified Christianity, which was grotesque and utterly foreign to his family's values. It also does not surprise that with his theological sophistication he would join people like Karl Barth in resisting theological or institutional Nazi encroachment on the church. But why did he see the need to resist on the Jewish front, far more than others did? Was it that his beloved twin sister Sabine had married a Jewish man in 1924? Or was it a deeper family sensitivity to antisemitism? We know that his aged grandmother quite visibly violated the 1 April 1933 boycott and terrorisation of Jewish stores. Again, family matters. Bonhoeffer knew who he was and to whom he belonged.

## First Escape and Return to Resistance (Fall 1933-Spring 1939)

In October of 1933, Bonhoeffer left Germany to pastor two German churches in London. It seems mainly to have been an attempt to escape the controversy, though Bonhoeffer's motives were unclear even to himself. His letters reveal a highly stressed young man wondering why he saw things so differently from supposedly wiser and more experienced leaders. Bonhoeffer's pastoral experiences in London were not especially notable, but he did use his time there to develop valuable friendships – including with the Anglican bishop George Bell, who proved to be a valuable ally and friend for years to come.

Back home, by summer 1934 Hitler had tightened his grip, ended any semblance of democracy, ordered the murders of his internal party rivals, and merged the office of chancellor and president to become absolute dictator. The Nazification of Germany and the German Evangelical Church deepened. In May 1934, the resistant part of the German Evangelical Church, now called the Confessing Church, adopted the Barmen Declaration, a historic document that offered theological resistance to the Nazification of the church.[10] Bonhoeffer appreciated this important text but was unhappy that it did not address the Nazi government's cruel measures against German Jews. In the Dahlem Synod of October 1934, the Confessing Church would make official its break with the majority Reich Church. There was now a complete schism in the German Evangelical Church, and Bonhoeffer resolutely served the "Barmen–Dahlem" side for the rest of his life.

In England, Bonhoeffer deepened his reflections concerning how to protect the Confessing Church's moral and theological integrity in the Nazi state. Indeed, he saw the need to prepare hardy ministers ready to die for their faithful confession of Jesus Christ. He knew that this level of resistance would require deeper spiritual roots and a very different kind of theological education. Distressed and looking for resources, he began studying Gandhi, and he even wrote a letter to the Mahatma asking for a chance to visit him and study his community of nonviolent civil disobedience.

---

[10] Schlingensiepen, *Dietrich Bonhoeffer*, Appendix 1.

But there was no time. In 1935 the Confessing Church opened several small new seminaries to train their ministers. Bonhoeffer returned to Germany to direct this new initiative. Surprising his fellow Protestants, in the seminary Bonhoeffer established at Finkenwalde he experimented with creating an atmosphere that followed the rhythms of Catholic and Anglican monasteries. The deep rhythms of prayer, silence, worship, work, and study in a residential community were intended to create a different kind of minister. Bonhoeffer's lovely depiction of this community is found in his famous and accessible little book, *Life Together*.[11]

Bonhoeffer taught at Finkenwalde between 1935 and 1937. Besides running the seminary, he also offered the principal lectures. His lectures on discipleship as taught in the Gospels and Epistles left a profound impression on students. In 1937, his last permitted publication in Germany was the compilation of these lectures under the title *Nachfolge* – commonly known outside Germany as *Cost of Discipleship*, and now simply *Discipleship*.[12]

Reading *Discipleship* today one is struck by the absolute and uncompromising vision of the work. At one level it is a diagnostic work – Bonhoeffer is trying to figure out how a historically Christian country like Germany could fall for Nazism. He attributes much of the fault to "cheap grace," in which Christian identity and a sense of God's forgiveness came cheap, without any corresponding seriousness about the effort to follow the teachings of Jesus. If there had been a serious understanding that Christianity means following the actual teachings of Jesus and the rest of Scripture, the German Evangelical Church – and German Christians as a whole – might have been able to see the godlessness of Nazism and its utter incompatibility with the way of Jesus. But instead, they surrendered to Hitler. Now Bonhoeffer was trying to train a remnant ready to die as martyrs to preserve at least a small community bearing faithful Christian witness.

*Fourth inflection point*: *Discipleship* and *Life Together* reveal Bonhoeffer responding to Nazism theologically, biblically, ecclesiologically, and spiritually. He sees that the susceptibility of Germany and even its church leaders to the grotesqueries and injustices of Nazism reveals a deep vulnerability, a corruptibility, that should not exist in a healthy Christian individual, church, or society. One might say that Nazism was a virus, and the antibodies were missing in Germany's Christian people. Both at the seminary and through the two books from this period, Bonhoeffer was trying to deepen his people's resistance to this diseased ideology.

As Nazi dictatorship deepened, Bonhoeffer's *downward mobility career arc* intensified. In 1936 the government revoked his authorisation to teach at the University of Berlin. In 1937 the Gestapo closed all Confessing Church seminaries. Bonhoeffer was eventually banned from addressing any public gathering or publishing any further books. In April 1938, every pastor in

[11] Dietrich Bonhoeffer, *Life Together* (Dietrich Bonhoeffer Works, Volume 5: Minneapolis: Fortress, 1996).

[12] Dietrich Bonhoeffer, *Discipleship* (Dietrich Bonhoeffer Works, Volume 4: Minneapolis: Fortress, 2003).

Germany was ordered to take an oath of allegiance to Hitler as a birthday present for the Führer. Of course, Bonhoeffer refused. November 1938 brought *Kristallnacht* ("the Night of Broken Glass"), a horrific state pogrom in which mobs destroyed Jewish homes and synagogues. Even the Confessing Church was largely silent. As Nazi violence and intolerance of dissent deepened, open church-based resistance to the German state was becoming impossible – at least, that is, unless one was willing to go directly to the concentration camp.

**Second Escape and Return to Resistance (Summer 1939–April 1943)**

On the eve of Nazi Germany's invasion of Poland, which started World War II, Bonhoeffer escaped Germany a second time. He was again invited to New York, with the prospect of pastoring, teaching, and/or doing refugee work. For most, it would have been a dream come true. Those seeking escape from Germany in the frantic days of summer 1939 numbered in the millions.

But he had hardly arrived before he knew it had been a mistake to leave his homeland. There had been very, very good reasons to leave Germany and go to America. War was inevitable. Bonhoeffer knew he could not serve in Hitler's army, but that his refusal would not only get him imprisoned or shot but would damage the reputation of his beloved Confessing Church. The latter was his gravest concern. Indeed, returning to Germany was an almost certain path to death. But Bonhoeffer went back anyway. He knew that home was where he belonged, come what may. Of all the decisions Bonhoeffer ever made, I personally find this one – to return to Germany in July 1939 – the most remarkable of all.

*Fifth inflection point*: Bonhoeffer did not always know the right thing to do. On at least two occasions, this one most famously, he used his extraordinary connections to flee Germany. The first escape was to London in October 1933; the second was to New York in June 1939. His desire to escape helps humanise him, for who among us can wonder why escape looked appealing? But the fact that in each case he realised that he must return – this again heroises him. If you could leave Nazi Germany in summer 1939, *you did not go back*. He went back.

On 1 September 1939, the war began. It was rally-round-the-flag time. Many who opposed Nazism volunteered anyway to prove their patriotism. Bonhoeffer surprised people when he appeared to do the same, though in a most unusual way. He joined the German military intelligence agency, the Abwehr, where his brother-in-law Hans von Dohnanyi was a top official. The case for Bonhoeffer's appointment to the Abwehr was that his extensive international contacts could be helpful to military intelligence.

But the new post was a cover for conspiracy. Dietrich Bonhoeffer had become a double agent. The Abwehr was a centre of the remaining resistance to Hitler. It included many senior German military officials who had long opposed Hitler, and whose resistance only deepened once the war began and atrocities against civilians immediately took place. The Abwehr contained principled military men who knew a better Germany – and who also knew much of what the Nazi regime planned, as well as the evils it was already doing.

This remarkable assignment was only possible because of Bonhoeffer's family connections, in this case to Dohnanyi. At first, he appears to have had little to do and was able to continue to quietly support illegal Confessing Church pastors and also to work on my favourite of his books, his extensive but unfinished *Ethics*.[13] Eventually Bonhoeffer was dispatched several times, to Norway, Sweden, and Switzerland, as a double agent under Abwehr cover. His primary clandestine work was to liaise with Western representatives and to communicate to them the names and intentions of the conspirators who planned to bring Hitler down, by assassination if necessary. His job was to convince the Allies that principled, high-level resistance to Hitler remained significant and to help prepare the way for recognition of a post-Hitler government.

*Sixth inflection point*: Bonhoeffer returned to Germany to join a high-level anti-Nazi conspiracy within the military. Christian ministers just don't do things like this. There is a clergy sphere and a government elite sphere, and they rarely meet – at least, not like this. But Bonhoeffer, as we noted earlier, was born into the kind of family that lived and moved in elite governmental circles. His decision to become a theologian/pastor was the outlier move in that family. So, in joining the conspiracy Bonhoeffer stepped out of the theologian sphere and back into the government elite sphere, his family's native environment; of course, this particular government service role was to become part of an anti-Nazi government elite trying to resist Hitler. This is quite remarkable. But it helps to remember that as a man of draft age Bonhoeffer eventually would have had to serve somewhere in the military or die for refusing. He indeed served – as he and his friends believed true patriotism required.

### Imprisonment and Execution (April 1943–April 1945)

On 5 April 1943, Bonhoeffer was arrested, along with several other members of the conspiracy. He never saw freedom again. He faced harsh interrogations, possibly including torture. By all accounts, despite tremendous stresses and fears, Bonhoeffer behaved with dignity and courage throughout his two years in prison. Other prisoners later recalled him as a source of hope and strength.

We know of Bonhoeffer's time in prison mostly from his letters. Some of these letters are pedestrian but others are extraordinary at both interpersonal and theological levels. Many are to his very young fiancée Maria, to whom he had become engaged in January, just months before his arrest. The great majority he wrote to his best friend Eberhard Bethge, who had married Bonhoeffer's niece Renate Schleicher.

Bethge later compiled some of these prison missives into a book, *Letters and Papers from Prison*.[14] It is clear from the letters that Bonhoeffer's thought was moving in more radical directions during his prison days. In my view, the prison

[13] Dietrich Bonhoeffer, *Ethics* (Dietrich Bonhoeffer Works, Volume 6: Minneapolis: Fortress, 2005).

[14] Dietrich Bonhoeffer, *Letters and Papers from Prison* (Dietrich Bonhoeffer Works, Volume 8: Minneapolis: Fortress, 2010).

writings reflect disillusionment with traditional theology, religion, and the mainstream German Church. God had not intervened to stop radical human evil. The Church had failed to stand up consistently for Jesus or for Nazism's victims. Bonhoeffer suggested the need for a new worldliness focused on responsible action on behalf of other people here and now. He hypothesised that we were entering a world "come of age," one "without the working hypothesis called 'God.'" Such an age would require a "religionless Christianity."

*Seventh inflection point*: The Bonhoeffer who wrote *Ethics* (1940–March 1943) was trying to reconstruct a Christian ethics grounded in Scripture and tradition but having the hard lessons of the Nazi era. The prison Bonhoeffer strikes me as reflecting deep disillusionment with a generally worthless church as well as the consequences of prison life, with death on the horizon.

On 20 July 1944, the conspiracy came close to assassinating Hitler, but failed. Hitler's vengeance was fierce, and Bonhoeffer seems to have sensed that the failed assassination sealed his fate. The war dragged on, with Germany's defeat increasingly assured. Bonhoeffer was moved from prison to prison and eventually his letters stopped. As the Allies continued to advance in the spring of 1945, Hitler ordered the deaths of the conspirators.

On 9 April 1945, Bonhoeffer and six other resisters were hanged at Floossenbürg concentration camp. Hitler committed suicide in his Berlin bunker just three weeks later. Bonhoeffer's family only found out about his death on a BBC radio broadcast that summer.

## Conclusion

My teacher Glen Stassen continually returned to Dietrich Bonhoeffer as a source of inspiration and insight over the entire course of his career. I have found myself doing the same thing over the decades, and my mind and heart turn to him again as I write during the coronavirus lockdown of spring 2020.

Perhaps what the appeal of Bonhoeffer comes down to is the combination of his mastery of the Christian intellectual tradition, his vibrant, disciplined personal faith, and his willingness to do the right thing in national public life even at the ultimate cost. Bonhoeffer inspires me as a scholar to never stop learning. He inspires me as a Christian to never stop growing. And he inspires me as a scholar-Christian-citizen to never stop engaging American public life on behalf of what is right and just.

This coronavirus pandemic is going to leave behind a changed nation and world. Those who survive will have so very much to do. Even as I write – on 23 March 2020 – I am attempting to bring to bear the best resources of the Christian intellectual tradition, the deepest wellsprings of my faith, and the most faithful expression of Christian witness in relation to public policy. And long after this immediate crisis is over, that is the work that all serious Christian scholars, especially ethicists, will continue to do. Murray Dempster has been and will continue to be one of them.

## Discussion Questions

1. What particular dynamics in German culture does Gushee identify as setting the stage for Bonhoeffer developing a moral witness?
2. Gushee's second inflection point is set in Harlem, New York, where, following the thought of Reggie Williams, Gushee states that Bonhoeffer developed the notion of Jesus as suffering, liberating, and "black." How did such a perspective of Jesus change Bonhoeffer's view of a moral witness? How might such a view influence our concept of a moral witness?
3. Which of the inflection points identified by Gushee do you see as the most significant to Bonhoeffer's developing ethic?
4. Gushee states that culture has been changed as it has responded to the coronavirus. What specific ways do you see culture having been changed and how does Bonhoeffer's witness speak to those changes? What other elements within contemporary culture could be positively engaged through the moral witness of Bonhoeffer?

## Bibliography

Bonhoeffer, Dietrich. "The Church and the Jewish Question." In *A Testament to Freedom: The Essential Writings of Dietrich Bonhoeffer*. Eds Geffrey B. Kelly and F. Burton Nelson. New York: HarperCollins, 1990.

Bonhoeffer, Dietrich. *Act and Being*. Dietrich Bonhoeffer Works, Volume 2. Minneapolis: Fortress, 1996.

Bonhoeffer, Dietrich. *Life Together*. Dietrich Bonhoeffer Works, Volume 5. Minneapolis: Fortress, 1996.

Bonhoeffer, Dietrich. *Discipleship*. Dietrich Bonhoeffer Works, Volume 4. Minneapolis: Fortress, 2003.

Bonhoeffer, Dietrich. *Ethics*. Dietrich Bonhoeffer Works, Volume 6. Minneapolis: Fortress, 2005.

Bonhoeffer, Dietrich. *Sanctorum Communion: A Theological Study of the Sociology of the Church*. Dietrich Bonhoeffer Works, Volume 1. Minneapolis: Fortress, 2009.

Bonhoeffer, Dietrich. *Letters and Papers from Prison*. Dietrich Bonhoeffer Works, Volume 8. Minneapolis: Fortress, 2010.

Gushee, David P. and Colin Holtz. *Moral Leadership for a Divided Age: Fourteen People Who Dared to Change Our World*. Grand Rapids, MI: Brazos Press, 2018.

Hitler, Adolf. *Mein Kampf*. Trans. Ralph Manheim. Boston: Houghton Mifflin, 1943.

Luther, Martin. "On the Jews and Their Lies, 1543." Luther's Works, Volume 47.. Philadelphia: Fortress, 1971, 121–306.

Reuther, Rosemary Radford. *Faith and Fratricide*. Boston: Seabury Press, 1974.

Schlingensiepen, Ferdinand. *Dietrich Bonhoeffer 1906–1945: Martyr, Thinker, Man of Resistance*. London: T&T Clark, 2010.

Williams, Reggie L. *Bonhoeffer's Black Jesus: Harlem Renaissance Theology and an Ethic of Resistance*. Waco, TX: Baylor University Press, 2014.

# Chapter 9

# Desire Redirected: Hermeneutical Shifts Regarding War and Peacemaking

Kenneth J. Archer

> Our citizenship is not here, but in heaven. Phil. 3:10 … Indeed we love our country, and hope for peace and prosperity but to level guns and mow down our enemies like grass and hasten their souls to hell is not the spirit of our Master … We are not cowards but we want to follow the example of and teaching of our Lord.
>
> A.J. Tomlinson, "The Awful War Seems Near"[1]

> The Christian's true citizenship is in heaven … Patriotism is unfortunately allowed to run wild in so many believers … We fear that a perverted patriotism is far more deeply rooted in most of our hearts than becometh citizens of the heavenly kingdom of our Lord Jesus Christ; and if we are not careful it can make us very traitors to the true body of Christ.
>
> Donald Gee, "War, the Bible, and the Christian" [Part 2][2]

**Abstract**

Pentecostals in the United States over time shifted from an officially pacifist community, practising nonviolence, to one that officially recognised actions of warfare as consistent with Pentecostal life. Early Pentecostals stated that their commitment to nonviolent pacifism was plainly taught in Scripture and that such action valued human life. This shift away from official commitments to pacifism included a hermeneutical paradigm shift. Various reasons have been identified by historians for the shift in practice by Pentecostals. These reasons are outlined, though they are not the focus of the essay. Rather, the essay presents suggestions for the re-engagement of hermeneutical practices that value the recovery and advancement of nonviolent peacemaking within Pentecostal practices. Among these are revisiting and reviving the concept of Jesus as Prince of Peace, visiting anew admonitions of Scripture, articulating an eschatological orientation toward peacemaking, and reviving the Pentecostal testimony or story of peacemaking that confirms the eschatological community of the saints.

---

[1] Michael G. Long, *Christian Peace and Nonviolence: A Documentary History* (Maryknoll, New York: Orbis Books, 2011), 145, citing A.J. Tomlinson, "The Awful War Seems Near," *Church of God Evangel* (31 March 1917), 1.

[2] Donald Gee, "War, the Bible, and the Christian" [Part 2], *The Pentecostal Evangel* (15 November 1930), 2–3, in Brian K. Pipkin and Jay Beaman (eds), *Early Pentecostals on Nonviolence and Social Justice: A Reader* (Eugene, OR: Pickwick, 2016), 139–40.

## Hermeneutical Shifts Regarding War and Peacemaking

Generally, but not unanimously, the early Pentecostals, especially the leaders, were committed to a consistent application of nonviolence when it came to human life. Many affirmed that "taking human life was prohibited" by God and thus immoral.[3] This theological understanding, they said, was *plainly taught* in Scripture.[4] In North America, most of the new forming Pentecostal denominations declared themselves to be a pacifistic church.[5] "Even though the Pentecostal movement was not a monolithic group of individual pacifists," writes Pentecostal social ethicist Murray Dempster, "at the official level the Pentecostal church was a pacifist church."[6]

About three weeks after the United States entered World War I, the General Presbytery of the newly organised Assemblies of God (1914) sent a letter to President Wilson requesting that their ministers be eligible to claim conscientious objector status.[7] Along with the cover letter was the A.G. resolution which stated:

> While recognizing Human Government as of Divine ordination and affirming our unswerving loyalty to the Government of the United States, nevertheless we are constrained to define our position with reference to the taking of human life.

---

[3] "General Council of the Assemblies of God," in Michael G. Long (ed.) *Christian Peace and Nonviolence: A Documented History* (Maryknoll, NY: Orbis Books, 2011), 143. An important work that had influenced early leaders of Pentecostalism was Arthur Sidney Booth-Clibborn, *Blood Against Blood* (3rd edition, New York: Charles C. Cook, 1914).

[4] For one example, see the AG resolution below, note 8.

[5] See the seminal piece by Jay Beaman, *Pentecostal Pacifism: The Origin, Development, and Rejection of Pacific Belief among Pentecostals* (Hillsboro, Kansas: Center for Mennonite Brethren Studies, 1989). For a convenient collection of essays by early Pentecostal leaders addressing nonviolence, see Pipkin and Beaman (eds), *Early Pentecostals on Nonviolence and Social Justice: A Reader* (Eugene, Oregon: Wipf and Stock, 2016). For a sustained analysis of the Assemblies of God see Paul Alexander, *Peace to War: Shifting Allegiances in the Assemblies of God* (Telford, Pennsylvania: Cascadia Publishing House and Scottdale, Pennsylvania: Herald Press, 2009). See also, Charles H. Mason, "The Kaiser in the Light of the Scriptures," in Mary Mason (recomp.) and James Courts (ed.), *The History and Life Work of Elder C.H. Mason, Chief Apostle, and His Co-Laborers*, (Memphis: Church of God in Christ, 1987).

[6] Murray W. Dempster, "Pacifism in Pentecostalism: The Case of the Assemblies of God," in Jeffrey Gros and John D. Rempel (eds), *The Fragmentation of the Church and Its Unity in Peacemaking* (Grand Rapids, MI and Cambridge, UK: Eerdmans, 2001), 140. For a brief introduction to pacifism as it relates to Pentecostalism, see D.J. Wilson, "Pacifism," in Stanley M. Burgess (ed.), *The New International Dictionary of Pentecostal and Charismatic Movements* (Grand Rapids, Michigan: Zondervan, 2002), 953–55.

[7] The Assemblies of God was organised in Hot Springs, Arkansas, in 1914 as a fellowship of ministers. "Combined Minutes of the General Council of the Assemblies of God, 1914–1917" (St Louis, Missouri: Gospel Publishing House, n.d.), 1–5, https://ag.org/About/About-the-AG/History, accessed 6 January 2023.

WHEREAS, in the Constitutional Resolution adopted at the Hot Springs General Council, April 1–10, 1914, we plainly declared the Holy Scriptures to be the all-sufficient rule of faith and practice, and

WHEREAS the Scriptures deal plainly with the obligations and relations of humanity, setting forth principles of "Peace on earth and good will toward men" (Luke 2:14); and

WHEREAS we as followers of the Lord Jesus Christ, the Prince of Peace, believe in the implicit obedience to the Divine commands and precepts which instruct us to "Follow peace with all men," (Heb. 12:14); "Thou shalt not kill," (Exod. 20:12); "Resist not evil," (Matt. 5:29); "Love your enemies," (Matt 5:44); etc., and

WHEREAS those and other Scriptures have always been accepted and interpreted by our churches as prohibiting Christians from shedding blood or taking human life;

THEREFORE we, as a body of Christians, while purposing to fulfill all the obligations of loyal citizenship, are nevertheless constrained to declare we cannot conscientiously participate in war and armed resistance which involves the actual destruction of human life since it is contrary to our view of the clear teachings of the inspired word of God, which is the sole basis of our faith.

April 28th, 1917.[8]

Prior to, during, and after WW1, the majority of Pentecostal leaders' stance on violence and killing was clear. They practised nonviolence, a kind of active pacifism, because they saw it plainly taught in Scripture, and they valued human life.[9] They believed the taking of human life and the activity of war itself were immoral for several reasons, not the least being its impact upon global evangelism.[10] They encouraged members if drafted to appeal and declare themselves as conscientious objectors.

Pentecostals desired to be faithful followers of Jesus. Nonviolence was a central understanding of following Jesus as a way of life. "It was grounded in the Bible, in the teachings of Jesus and the apostles, the teaching and example of the early church" and relationally grew out of the greatest commandment to love God and others, including your enemies (Matt. 22:37-40).[11] Early Pentecostal pacifists would have agreed with a pithy and provocative contemporary Brethren

---

[8] Cited in Dempster, "Pacifism in Pentecostalism," 137–38.

[9] For a helpful discussion on the word *pacifism* as it relates to early Pentecostalism, see Alexander, *Peace to War*, 31–33. See also Pipkin and Beaman (eds), *Early Pentecostals on Nonviolence and Social Justice*, xvii.

[10] Murray W. Dempster, "'Crossing Borders': Arguments Used by Early American Pentecostals in Support of the Global Character of Pacifism," *EPTA Bulletin: The Journal of the European Pentecostal Theological Association* 10:2 (1991), 63–80. See also Zachary M. Tackett, "Early Pentecostalism in Black and White: American Pentecostals Engaging Peace During World War I" (presentation, 40th Annual Meeting for the Society of Pentecostal Studies, Memphis, TN, 10–12 March 2011), and his "As Citizens of Heaven: Peace, War, and Patriotism Among Pentecostals in the United States during the First World War," in Gordon L. Heath (ed.), *American Churches and the First World War* (Eugene, OR: Pickwick, 2016), 71–86.

[11] Pipkin and Beaman, *Early Pentecostals on Nonviolence and Social Justice* (2016), xvi.

bumper sticker which reads, "When Jesus said, 'Love your enemies,' I think he probably meant don't kill them."[12] In today's language they were truly "pro-life" from womb to tomb.[13]

Even though today most Pentecostals in the USA are committed to pro-birth, they are no longer committed to nonviolence as the way of the Christian life. They simply reject pacifism of any kind, and now more than ever are avid defenders of the "right to bear arms." It is not uncommon to find safety courses advertising concealed weapon permit training at their church conferences, and weaponised security service as a ministry of a local church.[14]

Clearly, classical Pentecostal denominations in the USA are no longer officially committed to pacifism. Most classical Pentecostal denominations, like the Assemblies of God (A.G.) and the Church of God (CG), Cleveland, Tennessee, changed their official pacifistic statements more than fifty years ago.[15] In 1967 the AG adopted a revised statement on members' response to military service:

---

[12] Lauren Seganos, "On the Bumper Sticker: 'When Jesus Said "Love Your Enemies," I Think He Probably Meant Don't Kill Them,'" State of Formation, 13 March 2014, https://stateofformation.org/2014/03/on-the-bumper-sticker-when-jesus-said-love-your-enemies-i-think-he-probably-meant-dont-kill-them/ (accessed 18 Jul2 2022).

[13] In the USA, Pentecostals are generally pro-birth in working to overturn Roe vs Wade more so then pro-life. Today, the majority would reject national health care, affirm the practice of capital punishment, and "would not" discourage members from enlisting in military service but instead encourage it as a patriotic responsibility. Military chaplaincy is enthusiastically supported for it is understood as a ministry of the church to military personnel and their families as both a means of evangelism and moral spiritual support. For an example of a fully pro-life perspective, see Ronald J. Sider, *Completely Pro-life: Building a Consistent Stance on Abortion, the Family, Nuclear Weapons, the Poor* (Eugene, OR: Wipf and Stock, 2010).

[14] "DeSantis Signs Bill Allowing Concealed Carry at Churches that Share Land with Schools," NWF Daily News (30 June 2021), https://www.nwfdailynews.com/story/news/local/2021/06/30/desantis-signs-florida-bill-allowing-concealed-carry-in-churches-share-land-with-schools/7813477002/ (accessed 18 Jul2 2022); Jacob Paulsen, "Should I Conceal Carry in Church?" ConcealedCarry (28 April 2021), https://www.concealedcarry.com/law/concealed-carry-in-churches/ (accessed 18 Jul2 2022). From the AG see, "Concealed Carry and Church Safety," AGFinancial, accessed 11 February 2022, https://www.agfinancial.org/resources/article/concealed-carry-church-safety; an Ordained Bishop in the Church of God, Cleveland, Tennessee, specialises in security ministry that includes use of weapons; see Dwayne Harris, "How to Operate an Armed Church Security Team," Full Armor: Church Safety Solutions, accessed 11 February 2022, https://www.fullarmorchurch.com/operating-armed-church-security-team/. Of course, these church-sanctioned ministries do offer other important nonviolent security measures, yet the consistent agreement is that deadly force is the best way to bring down an active shooter; thus, if it is legal to do so, then you should have armed security in the church services.

[15] See Murray W. Dempster, "Reassessing the Moral Rhetoric of Early American Pentecostal Pacifism," *Crux* 25:1 (March 1990), 23–36. For the AG's move from pacifism to pro-military, see Alexander, *Peace to War.* In the list of teachings in the Church of God, Cleveland, Tennessee, up through the 39th General Assembly (1944),

> As a movement we affirm our loyalty to the government of the United States in war and peace.
>
> We shall continue to insist, as we have historically, on the right of each member to choose for himself whether to declare his position as a combatant, or a noncombatant, or a conscientious objector.[16]

In less than fifty years most Pentecostal denominations reworded their official positions on pacifism. In doing so they dropped the early argument for a nonviolent, pacifistic way of life, which was originally grounded in their covenantal relationship with God through Christ. Scripture was understood to teach such a way of life *clearly* and *plainly*. Of special emphasis was the teachings and nonviolent lifestyle of Jesus. Now they affirm the individual's right to choose based solely upon his/her personal conscience. It is now acceptable and encouraged to *voluntarily* join the military and serve in *combatant* roles, create weaponised security ministries for local churches and carry concealed weapons.[17] Often the clergy are leading the way in weaponising the laity with deadly force.[18]

The denominations within early Pentecostalism did *re-affirm* that members whose choice is to be conscientious objectors can remain in good standing in the *church*. That is, one could be a noncombatant conscientious objector, or a pacifist committed to nonviolence, and remain an honourable member of the community. Assuming a conscientious objector would not voluntarily join the military but, if drafted, a person could appeal to serve in noncombat roles or governmental-approved alternative service.[19] However, I concur with the insightful and mournful statement made back in 1980 by Murray Dempster. In his editorial for

---

teaching 29 declares that the CG is "against members going to war in combative service." The Scriptures used to support their teaching were Romans 12:19, Matthew 5:38-48, and Matthew 18:10, 11. In 1945 at the 40th Assembly, teaching 29 was "struck out" and replaced with, "The Church of God believes that nations can and should settle their differences without going to war; however, in the event of war, if a member engages in combatant service, it will not affect his status with the Church. In case a member is called into service who has a conscientious objection to combatant service, the Church will support him in his constitutional rights." Interesting that individual consciousness provides the moral rationale for such a decision, with constitutional rights being the political reason for the church supporting the person. Scripture is not referenced.

[16] Cited in Murray W. Dempster, "Peacetime Draft Registration," in *AGORA: A Magazine of Pentecostal Opinion* 3:4 (Spring 1980), 8–9.

[17] One could take the threats of the community seriously, and have security, a form of nonviolent resistance to evil doers, without guns.

[18] Ken Pegano, the pastor of New Bethel [AG] Church, Louisville, Kentucky, sponsored a celebration of the Second Amendment during Sunday worship in 2009, "Pastor Asks Members to Bring Guns to Church: A Kentucky Pastor is Inviting His Flock to Bring Guns to Church to Celebrate the Fourth of July and the Second Amendment," NBC News, 4 June 2009, https://www.nbcnews.com/id/wbna31111096.

[19] See Zachary Michael Tackett, "Brothers in Non-Combatant Service: Civilian Public Service and Pentecostals During World War Two" (presentation, 48th Annual Meeting for the Society of Pentecostal Studies, Washington, DC, 28 February–2 March 2019), for some early examples.

*Agora*, he wrote, "The poverty of explicit biblical thinking in this rationale is an utter embarrassment to people who give first priority in a 'Statement of Faith' to affirming the authority of Scripture."[20] Basically the AG original resolution with Scripture references supporting the value of human life and thus practising nonviolence was simply removed. For example, the AG resolution adopted in 1967 replacing the former of 1917 lacked scriptural references.[21] The new resolution begins the same as the former, affirming their loyalty to the U.S. government in peace but now, unlike the former, adds "in war."[22] The point is that Scripture might have been used to support the new position, but was not, nor was there any explanation as to why the original was being abandoned for a pro-military and pro-war statement (or at least affirming that their members would support the war efforts of the USA) which now includes combative military service, meaning the killing of human lives. The irony here is clear. The new resolution was antithetical to the very rationale for the original resolution. They originally argued that "we cannot conscientiously participate in *war and armed resistance* which involves the actual destruction of human life, since this is contrary to our view of the clear teachings of the inspired Word of God, which is the sole basis of our faith."[23]

A hermeneutical paradigm shift took place in less than fifty years among these early Pentecostal denominations. World War I was the immediate impetus for the formulation of official statements encouraging a nonviolent stance on the

---

[20] Dempster, "Peacetime Draft Registration," 9.

[21] See footnote 16, above. The CG did the same thing.

[22] See the "Minutes Revised Constitution and Bylaws the Thirty-Second General Council, Long Beach, California, August 24–29, 1967" (Springfield, MO: General Council of the Assemblies of God, 1967), 35. The full resolution reads as follows:
WHEREAS the ideal world condition is that of peace, we as Christian citizens should use our influence in promoting peaceful solutions to world problems; and,
WHEREAS we live in a world in which there may arise international emergencies which will lead our nation to resort to armed conflict in defense of its ideals, freedom, and national existence; and
WHEREAS, our first loyalty is to God, we recognize nevertheless that human government is ordained of God, and that these are obligations of citizenship which are binding upon us as Christians; and
WHEREAS, we acknowledge the principle of individual freedom of conscience as it relates to military service; therefore be it
RESOLVED, That article XXII of the General Council Bylaws be deleted and replaced with the following article:
Article XXII Military Service
As a movement we affirm our loyalty to the government of the United States in war or peace. We shall continue to insist, as we have historically, on the right of each member to choose for himself whether to declare his position as a combatant, noncombatant, or a conscientious objector.

[23] "Resolution Concerning the Attitude of the General Council of the Assemblies of God Toward Any Military Service which Involves the Actual Participation in the Destruction of Human Life," in "Combined Minutes of the General Council of the Assemblies of God in the United States of America, Canada, and Foreign Lands 1914–1917," (St Louis, Missouri: Gospel Publishing House, n.d.), 11, digital copy available through Flower Pentecostal Heritage Center, https://ifphc.org.

taking of human life through war and armed resistance. These early Pentecostals were shaped theologically by their holiness backgrounds, and their desire to restore early or so-called Spirit-empowered New Testament Christianity.[24] In doing so they were citizens of heaven which meant they were also loyal to their earthly government's laws as long as those governmental laws and practices did not conflict with the clear teaching of Scripture. In the words of William Seymour, the famous Azusa Street pastor, Christians like others "must 'submit themselves to governors' (1 Pet. 2:14) … so far as they shall not interfere with, or contravene, the claims of divine law … remembering that God's claims are supreme.'"[25]

However, the US government's emphasis on nationalistic conformity during and following the wars helped accelerate change in attitudes about patriotism and to the official policy on pacifism. During the presidency of Woodrow Wilson, Congress passed two laws to help with the war effort: the Espionage Act of 1917 and the Sedition Act of 1918 which "criminalized any 'disloyal, profane, scurrilous, or abusive language' about the US government or military, or any speech intended to 'incite insubordination, disloyalty, mutiny, or refusal of duty.'" [26] The continuous pressure placed upon leaders, including threats and actual imprisonment, meant that they took extra caution in how the wars were discussed in their publications and pulpits.[27] In the end, many classical denominations more forthrightly adopted rationalistic arguments which "enshrined 'the principle of individual freedom of conscience as it relates to military service.'"[28] The sad irony was that on the one hand early nonviolent peace theology that forbade the taking of human life did not have time to further develop and was then officially aborted altogether. On the other hand, it was not replaced with serious reflection upon character formation of individuals enlisting, nor upon the theological practice of just war theory. Members were simply left to decide on whether it was morally acceptable to take another person's life based upon their personal preference and understanding of Scripture on the subject matter. The only good news was that the AG and CG did not completely deny to their membership the option to be committed to nonviolence when it comes to human life, an option few today in these denominations are encouraged to consider.

The hermeneutical paradigm shift was a consequence of various factors fuelled by active legal pressure placed upon them by the U.S. government. These

---

[24] See Kenneth J. Archer, "Pentecostal Theology as Story: Participating in God's Mission," in Wolfgang Vondey (ed.), *The Routledge Handbook of Pentecostal Theology* (London and New York: Routledge, 2020), 40–50.

[25] Pipkin and Beaman, *Early Pentecostals on Nonviolence and Social Justice,* 27.

[26] Dave Roos, "The Sedition and Espionage Acts were Designed to Quash Dissent During WWI," History, accessed 2 May 2022, https://www.history.com/news/sedition-espionage-acts-woodrow-wilson-wwi.

[27] See Alexander, *Peace to War,* 132–38, 331; also Pipkin and Beaman, *Early Pentecostals on Non-Violence*, xv-xvii.

[28] Dempster, "Pacifism in Pentecostalism," 138; see Roger Robbins, "A Chronology of Peace: Attitudes Toward War and Peace in the Assemblies of God: 1914–1918," *Pneuma: The Journal of the Society of Pentecostal Studies* 6:1 (Spring 1984), 24.

factors coalesce into a significant modification of an early Pentecostal narrative of identity. The loss of certain early convictions about Jesus as the nonviolent Prince of Peace and commitment to nonviolence as a way of life were seen by some as both healthy and necessary modifications, for it led to an endorsed active political engagement. This became even more so with the rise of the religious right and its close cooperative relationship with the Republican party.[29] I, like others, believe it was much more harmful to Pentecostal theological identity and practice, for it skewed the early history of the Pentecostal tradition along with their more holistic social ministries concerns.[30] This is a history that most likely would have been lost without the active recalling by academic Pentecostal historians, theologians, ethicists, and educators, through their academic publications, preaching, and teaching. Murray Dempster is just one such important person. It is not an overstatement to say that most Pentecostals today have no idea that their Pentecostal denomination was once committed to pacifism as articulated by their arguments against the taking of human life and opposition to war.

The demise of and occasional outspoken disdain for early Pentecostals' commitment to pacifism in the USA have been the subject of some recent significant analysis.[31] Reasons offered for the demise are often based upon sociological, cultural, economic, historical, political, and theological perspectives. The following arguments have been put forth to explain the hermeneutical paradigm shift.

- An argument that early Pentecostals' accommodation into the evangelical religious middle class and mainstream culture transformed their perspective.[32]
- An argument that two pragmatic impulses resided in early Pentecostalism, one being a qualified pacifism, and the other being indifference which is not to be confused with the development of just war theory.[33]

---

[29] See Randall Balmer, *The Making of Evangelicalism: From Revivalism to Politics and Beyond* (Waco, Texas: Baylor University Press, 2010); and Kevin M. Kruse, *One Nation Under God: How Corporate America Invented Christian America* (New York, NY: Basic Books, 2015).

[30] For my attempt to offer a corrective see Kenneth J. Archer and Andrew S. Hamilton, "Anabaptism-Pietism and Pentecostalism: Scandalous Partners in Protest," *Scottish Journal of Theology* 63:2 (2010), 185–202; Kenneth J. Archer and Andrew S. Hamilton, "Scandalous Partners in Protest: A Continuing Dialogue," in Paul Nathan Alexander (ed.), *Pentecostals and Nonviolence: Reclaiming a Heritage* (Eugene, OR; Pickwick, 2012), 308–20; and "Liberating Hermeneutics: Toward a Holistic Pentecostal Mission of Peace and Justice," co-authored with Richard E. Waldrop, *Journal of the European Pentecostal Theological Association* 31:1 (2011), 65–80.

[31] The first sustained study was Jay Beaman, *Pentecostal Pacifism: The Origin, Development, and Rejection of Pacific Belief among Pentecostals* (Hillsboro, Kansas: Center for Mennonite Studies, 1989). For a more recent and comprehensive analysis which focuses exclusively upon the AG, see Paul Alexander, *Peace to War.*

[32] Jay Beaman, *Pentecostal Pacifism.*

[33] Grant Wacker, *Heaven Below: Early Pentecostals and American Culture* (Cambridge, Massachusetts and London, England: Harvard University Press, 2001), see especially chapter 14, "War."

- Somewhat consistent with the first, yet from a more robust social-theological-ethical analysis is the argument that, although most of the leadership objected to war, the absolute pacifistic leaders were in the minority and in a short period of time their influence waned.[34]
- An important argument put forth is that as Pentecostals became more influenced by dispensational premillennialism and American exceptionalism their pacifism became more passive in practice. Some still discouraged Christians from participating in war or killing if conscripted while a significant portion of denominational leadership was affirming the necessity of Christian responsibility to support positively and patriotically the USA in the war effort.[35]
- Somewhat supporting the previous perspective is the insightful argument that the American progressive era's influence on the shaping of Pentecostals' perspectives on war and patriotism led to conflicting models of understanding.[36]

I believe all these arguments have merit, and many overlap and reinforce one another, especially the first and last two. The various explanatory reasons for the demise of pacifism among Pentecostals speak to the contextualised complexity of the issues; however, it does not negate, nor should it minimise, the fact that "the literature of early Pentecostals indicates that they were generally, but not universally, pacifists"[37] who grounded their view on the *plain meaning of Scripture*. Also, the reorientation of desire towards justifiable use of violence seems to take place in such a way as to suggest that their primary lens through which Scripture was interpreted shifted. The early Pentecostals' commitment to Jesus as central, his teachings as taking precedent, and the gospel as prominent, no longer was the theological hermeneutical key through which the church should read the rest of the Bible. Furthermore, the socio-political context created by the passing of the Espionage and Seditious Acts facilitated the further departure from nonviolence through coercive efforts by the USA government. The government targeted key outspoken leaders and put pressure on the denominational leadership to be cautious as to what they might publish concerning the war effort. The early denominational leaders, such as those in the AG, would clearly and loudly affirm their loyalty to the USA even as some affirmed more quietly the objection to the use of lethal violence.

Disdain for early Pentecostal pacifism is still heard today. Sometimes early Pentecostal pacifism is referred to as an example of Pentecostals' lack of involvement in public policy and politics. For example, the popular magazine called *Charisma* ran an essay by John Stemberger, who makes such a claim.[38]

---

[34] Murray Dempster affirms much of Beaman's arguments yet augments them in important ways. See Dempster's "Pacifism in Pentecostalism."

[35] Wilson, "Pacifism," 953–55.

[36] Tackett, "As Citizens of Heaven."

[37] Wilson, "Pacifism," 953.

[38] John Stemberger, "The Rising Tide of Influence: How Pentecostalism is Changing the Dynamics of American Politics," *Charisma Magazine* (1 November 2011), 1–5, http://www.charismamag.com/index.php/features/32030-the-rising-tide-of-influence (accessed 18 July 2022).

Stemberger, in his essay titled "The Rising Tide of Influence: How Pentecostalism is Gradually Changing the Dynamics of American Politics," writes, "Historically Pentecostals have been pietists and not reformers, meaning they've traditionally remained unengaged in matters of public policy and politics. With a focus on robust worship, church life and spiritual gifts, they've held a natural disposition against engaging in 'the things of the world' such as politics." To some degree I would agree with him. It is the next sentence which is used to support his statement that I find problematic. Stemberger continues, "This was evident during World War I when most Pentecostals were pacifists." Here, pacifism is used as a negative example that contributed to Pentecostals' lack of engagement with USA politics. The unstated implication is that pacifism is not a favourable option for Pentecostals, for it encourages one to withdraw from national politics. The following sentence further illustrates his point. "In the mid-1950's [sic] for example, Pentecostal leaders had little to say about the pressing issue of the day – nuclear disarmament – yet many preached 'boldly' on the importance of not playing sports on the Lord's day."[39] As I said, I agree that for the most part Euro-white Pentecostals in the USA did not take official stands on public policy, such as nuclear disarmament in the 1950s nor the civil rights movement in the 1960s.[40] However, one could argue that it was a result of the loss of an *active form* of pacifism which contributed to USA Pentecostal leadership's silence on the issues of nuclear disarmament.

The early Pentecostal literature demonstrates that they were struggling with being faithful followers of Jesus and patriotic citizens. A few leaders were, however, presenting powerful prophetic critiques upon the First and even Second World War. Early Pentecostal pacifistic clergy and laity could not stem the growing tide of patriotism gone to seed. The fruit is Nationalism and Exceptionalism, and this in turn becomes a reciprocating means to fully identify with an evangelicalised Republican party and the religious right.[41]

Stemberger's essay shows that white USA Pentecostals have become full-fledged missionaries to Retake the Country for God and to stand shoulder to shoulder with the religious right and the Republican Party, something that he celebrates and encourages.[42] In fairness, his essay does lift up a few "minority" Pentecostals who are active in politics that cross party lines.

I think historians, theologians, and ethicists have shown that the early pacifistic literature written by Pentecostals had a more prophetic eschatological

---

[39] Stemberger, "The Rising Tide of Influence," 1.

[40] There was one very important noticeable exception, and that was the Pentecostal leader Donald Gee, UK citizen, and continuous objector to war. He did address the importance of nuclear disarmament.

[41] Charismatics and Pentecostals vocally supported the Presidency of Donald Trump. See John Fea, *Believe Me: The Evangelical Road to Donald Trump* (Grand Rapids, MI: Eerdmans, 2018).

[42] Stemberger writes, "Across the board, Pentecostals tend to be politically conservative, especially on moral and social issues. As a result, they predominately identify with and register as republicans – with the primary exception to this being black Pentecostals … among the Church of God in Christ (COGIC), for example, most are registered Democrats." Stemberger, "The Rising Tide of Influence," 2.

critique of nationalism, unchecked capitalism, concern for social issues, and more serious reflection upon Scripture than many realise. At least early pacifism was consistent with the Pentecostal Full Gospel and the importance for evangelism.[43] Yet now, and especially in the predominately white Pentecostal denominations, Pentecostalism has moved to being generally but not universally patriotic supporters of active military service and political advocates of the middle-class evangelical religious right.[44] The abandonment of the "Prince of Peace" and being soldiers for the cross was replaced by being Christian soldiers for God's justifiable country and cause. Without the prophetic outcries and pacifistic voices, white Pentecostalism followed other evangelical traditions in embracing a qualified kind of American civil religion.[45] What should have happened is that a more robust critique of the political parties, including the Republicans, should have been offered to the Pentecostal communities. The Pentecostal traditions should engage in more critical assessment of the ongoing and growing subtle narrative of Manifest Destiny, systemic racism, and unquenchable thirst for guns as the means for a safer America. Ironically the early Pentecostals' passion for the Reign of God was harnessed into an unflinching passion for American civil religion.

Story plays a significant role in understanding identity and practice of communities. The controlling convictions of a community might be identified through its central narrative convictions. For Pentecostals, the assessment of these storied convictions and practices is primarily through the means of Scripture and experience.[46] Testimonies are the means through which the experienced beliefs are shared with others. Also, the relationship of the community with Christ would always want to ground all normative beliefs and practices in Scripture. The Pentecostal communities can reassess, dismiss, and/or modify the core convictions and practices. This is clearly demonstrable in the case of those denominations that had officially affirmed that they were a pacifistic church and then later would significantly modify it. Without a consistent formative narrative of nonviolent peacemaking, the community forgets how to negotiate what it means to be a Pentecostal community whose citizenship is in heaven yet lived out on earth for the sake of the nations. The lack of such a narrative has led to the wholesale embrace of the "individual right"

---

[43] The Full Gospel is the testimonial confessions that Jesus is the Saviour, Sanctifier, Healer, Spirit Baptiser and King coming soon. Variations of this theme can still be heard in most Pentecostal churches. See Kenneth J. Archer, "Full Gospel," in Adam Stewart (ed.), *Handbook of Pentecostal Christianity* (DeKalb, Illinois: Northern University Press, 2012), 89–91.

[44] A few Pentecostal scholars have worked on developing a Pentecostal Just War Theory that attempts to remain faithful to early Pentecostalism while holding to early twenty-first-century concerns. For an example, see Michael Beals, "Toward a Pentecostal Contribution to the Just War Tradition," in Paul Alexander (ed.), *Pentecostals and Nonviolence: Reclaiming a Heritage* (Eugene, Oregon: Pickwick, 2012), 229–49.

[45] See Kenneth D. Ward and Allison Calhoun-Brown, *Religion and Politics in the United States* (6th ed., Lanham, Maryland and Plymouth, United Kingdom: Rowman and Littlefield Publishers, 2011), chapter 3, "One Nation Under God: A Civil Religion."

[46] See Archer, "Pentecostal Theology as Story," 40–50.

to defend oneself to the point of killing, and that all US involvement in wars has been justifiable. This is simply a given for many Pentecostal folks today.

The good news is that there is a growing awareness among younger Pentecostals of the early position of classical Pentecostalism on pacifism. Along with this comes the discovery of testimonies of Pentecostals who were conscientious objectors to war and some serving courageously in noncombative roles. Hence nonviolent peacemaking is not a cowardly flight from moral responsibility to protect others,[47] nor a withdraw from the world, but instead a courageous means of being willing to engage nonviolently with evil practices both on personal and systemic levels. One is willing to die resisting evil doers but not kill for one's earthly country or family. This is an active engagement with systemic evils in society, not a passive withdrawal from it.

The early Pentecostal testimonies were always grounded in Scripture and in particular the Gospels. As a result of being Spirit-empowered followers of Jesus, they felt that it was necessary for them to practise nonviolent resistance when it came to military service.[48] Along with the historic reality, the influential testimonies and growing number of influential academic Pentecostals and Charismatics embracing various forms of nonviolent peacemaking,[49] there seems to be a real stirring of the Spirit of Life to rediscover and rekindle a passion for God's kingdom through active participation in nonviolent peacemaking rooted in the teaching and ministry of Jesus.[50] The Pentecostal and Charismatic peacemakers are retrieving and seriously revisioning early Christian, Anabaptist and Pentecostal practices of peacemaking.[51] Biblical Pentecostal-Charismatic

[47] Contra Eric Patterson argued that C.S. Lewis "succinctly refuted pacificism as irresponsible." The charge that pacifism is irresponsible is one step from declaring pacifism as immoral. Patterson's quote of C.S. Lewis addresses a withdrawal passivity. Patterson does not even recognize various kinds of pacifism, simply assuming that pacifism is withdrawal and retreat from evil altogether. See Patterson, "Moral Clarity in a Time of Terror," *Providence: A Journal of Christianity and American Foreign Policy* 2 (Winter 2016), 5–7.

[48] They really did not like the word pacifist. Alexander, *Peace to War*, 334.

[49] See Martin William Mittelstadt and Brian K. Pipkin (eds), *Mennocostals: Pentecostal and Mennonite Stories of Convergence* (Pentecostals, Peacemaking, and Social Justice Series, Book 12: Eugene OR: Pickwick, 2020); and Martin William Mittelstadt and Geoffery William Sutton (eds), *Forgiveness, Reconciliation, and Restoration: Multidisciplinary Studies from a Pentecostal Perspective* (Pentecostals, Peacemaking, and Social Justice Series, Book 3: Eugene, OR: Pickwick, 2010).

[50] For work being done in South Africa by Pentecostals, see Marius Nel, *Pacifism and Pentecostals in South Africa: A New Hermeneutic for Nonviolence* (London and New York: Routledge, 2018). Also, certain significant voices in North American evangelicalism have helped Pentecostals as well. For one example see the collection of essays edited by Bruce Ellis Benson and Peter Goodwin Heltzel in *Evangelicals and Empire: Christian Alternatives to the Political Status Quo* (Grand Rapids, MI: Brazos Press, 2008).

[51] For an important examination of the early church, see Alan Kreider, *The Patient Ferment of the Early Church: The Improbable Rise of Christianity in the Roman Empire* (Baker Academic, 2016).

models for nonviolent engagement for peacemaking are emerging.[52] Such a narrative with sustaining practices will help stem the growing tide of nationalism and encourage a robust holistic mission of the Full Gospel.[53] With the globalisation of Pentecostalism, such a narrative reasserting that Jesus is the Prince of Peace is crucial for Pentecostal identity as a contrast society who lives and ministers in the world but is not of the world. If, or hopefully when, Pentecostal denominational magazines once again start running serious essays affirming biblical models of peacemaking, along with testimonies of heroic contentious objectors, and the need for spiritual discernment in matters of national wartime, we will be witnessing another major hermeneutical paradigm shift – for the better.

In the following I will offer some suggestions that may help with the ongoing work in nonviolent peacemaking. These suggestions are an attempt at retrieving early Pentecostals' passion for the Kingdom of God where Jesus serves as the Prince of Peace and King. Retrieval alone is not enough; constructive practitioners and theologians will need to revision, recontextualise, and represent the perspectives in fresh ways that speak to particular issues.

First and foremost, Pentecostals should retrieve the centrality of Jesus Christ as Prince of Peace. Such a perspective will help them further appreciate the importance of a full gospel ministry, one that also addresses social ills of society in active resistance through nonviolent ways.[54] Early Pentecostals interpreted Scripture, both the Old and New Testament, in a Jesus-centric manner.[55] Such readings affirmed nonviolence as the Christian way of life. Hence the Pentecostal peacemaking is a Spirit-empowered and Jesus-shaped cruciform way of life.[56]

The remaining are not placed in a hierarchical order, but instead should be understood more as multiple concerns. When brought together they form a gestalt of sorts – a clear, cohesive, and coherent narrative theology. Pentecostals should return to Pentecost and retrieve a pneumatological grounding for their theological development of peacemaking. Surely the Lord and Giver of Life is essential to such a task and should be the source of such an empowered way of life.

---

[52] Along with this has been a positive movement to re-examine "just war theory" and move to a more serious critique of the use of violence. Often "Just Peacemaking" is found to be better studied by those engaging in Peace Studies. See Glen H. Stassen, *Just Peacemaking: Transformative Initiatives for Justice and Peace* (Louisville, KY: Westminster John Knox Press, 1992); and Glen H. Stassen (ed.), *Just Peacemaking: The New Paradigm for the Ethics of Peace and War* (Cleveland, OH: Pilgrim Press, 2008).

[53] See the Pentecostals, Peacemaking, and Social Justice Series edited by Paul Alexander and Jay Beaman for further helpful resources.

[54] See Dario Lopez Rodriguez, *The Liberating Mission of Jesus: The Message of the Gospel of Luke* (trans. Stefanie E. Israel and Richard E. Waldrop; Eugene, Oregon: Pickwick, 2012).

[55] See Chris E.W. Green, *Sanctifying Interpretation: Vocation, Holiness, and Scripture* (Cleveland, TN: CPT Press, 2015), 116–18.

[56] See Michael J. Gorman, *Reading Paul* (Eugene, Oregon: Cascade Books 2008), chapter 1.

Pentecostals should return to Scripture and retrieve from it the importance of being a pilgrim people. This in turn would help reshape their desire away from a patriotic at best and nationalistic at worst love for country.[57] Hopefully a responsible citizenry will always affirm their place is first and foremost the kingdom that is yet to be consummated, while also being morally responsible nonviolent citizens of a state working positively for social justice and peace. Hence glossolalia will serve as the language of the kingdom, a language that deconstructs all human intelligible languages as it reorients the passion of God's people through a shared and common heavenly language.[58]

In turn this should lead naturally to an eschatological orientation. Pentecostals are people of the Way (Acts 9:2) who long for the return of Jesus, yet such longing generates great hope in God. An inaugurated eschatological vision strengthens their baptismal vow and encourages a concern for caring for all God's creation. As an eschatological missionary people, Pentecostals should retrieve the early Christian understanding of being a counter-cultural and charismatic community. Such an ecclesiastical understanding would encourage a more robust understanding of the importance of a flourishing community that ministers out of abundance and not scarcity.

Finally, Pentecostals should retrieve and revise their basic story, one that affirms that they are people of the "Latter Rain" (Acts 2) in continuity with the saints gathered in the upper room, and the Christians faithful throughout the centuries.[59] If such efforts can cause a reorientation of desire, then Pentecostal pacifists would publicly proclaim their allegiance to Jesus Christ as the cruciform way of life through nonviolently and actively resisting evil systems, and persons.

Such a nonviolent way of life does not dismiss personal, and/or corporate sin, nor the importance of Jesus as our substitutionary atonement. Yet it does take seriously the *Christus Victor*, and his community as the body of Christ, the bride of Christ, and the temple of the Holy Spirit. This community (Christ's community) is the "one nation under God" that is found in and among all the earthly nations (1 Pet. 2:9; Eph. 2:11-22). A nation of sojourners who are longing for the permanence of the land that is promised them when Jesus Christ returns (glorified earth and heaven united).

## Discussion Questions

1. What actions within the US government and within Pentecostalism does Archer identify as contributing to Pentecostals' hermeneutical shift regarding nonviolence?
2. Archer identifies but does not expound upon several theories presented by historians for a theological shift within American Pentecostalism. If you

---

[57] See James K.A. Smith, *Desiring the Kingdom: Worship, Worldview, and Cultural Formation* (Grand Rapids, MI: Baker Academic, 2009).

[58] I am indebted to Daniela C. Augustine for this significant insight. See her *Pentecost, Hospitality, and Transfiguration: Toward a Spirit-inspired Vision of Social Transformation* (Cleveland, TN: CPT Press, 2012).

[59] See Archer, "Pentecostal Theology as Story."

were to give further attention to one or more of these theories, which one(s) would you like to consider further?

3. Archer asks the reader to consider whether "the reorientation of desire towards justifiable use of violence" has not shifted Pentecostal hermeneutics. Thereafter Archer presents several suggestions for advancing nonviolent peacemaking. Which of these suggestions do you see as most compelling?

## Bibliography

Alexander, Paul. *Peace to War: Shifting Allegiances in the Assemblies of God.* Telford, Pennsylvania: Cascadia Publishing House and Scottdale, Pennsylvania: Herald Press, 2009.

Archer, Kenneth J. "Pentecostal Theology as Story: Participating in God's Mission." In *The Routledge Handbook of Pentecostal Theology*. Ed. Wolfgang Vondey. London and New York: Routledge, 2020, 40–50.

Archer, Kenneth J. and Andrew S. Hamilton. "Anabaptism-Pietism and Pentecostalism: Scandalous Partners in Protest." *Scottish Journal of Theology* 63:2 (2010), 185–202.

Archer, Kenneth J. and Andrew S. Hamilton. "Scandalous Partners in Protest: A Continuing Dialogue." In *Pentecostals and Nonviolence: Reclaiming a Heritage*. Ed. Paul Nathan Alexander. Eugene, OR; Pickwick, 2012, 320–32.

Archer, Kenneth J. and Richard E. Waldrop. "Liberating Hermeneutics: Toward a Holistic Pentecostal Mission of Peace and Justice." *Journal of the European Pentecostal Theological Association* 31:1 (2011), 65–80.

Augustine, Daniela C. *Pentecost, Hospitality, and Transfiguration: Toward a Spirit-Inspired Vision of Social Transformation.* Cleveland, TN: CPT Press, 2012.

Balmer, Randall. *The Making of Evangelicalism: From Revivalism to Politics and Beyond.* Waco, TX: Baylor University Press, 2010.

Beals, Michael. "Toward a Pentecostal Contribution to the Just War Tradition." In *Pentecostals and Nonviolence: Reclaiming a Heritage*. Ed. Paul Alexander. Eugene, OR: Pickwick, 2012, 229–49.

Beaman, Jay. *Pentecostal Pacifism: The Origin, Development, and Rejection of Pacific Belief among Pentecostals*. Hillsboro, KS: Center for Mennonite Brethren Studies, 1989.

Benson, Bruce Ellis and Peter Goodwin Heltzel, Eds. *Evangelicals and Empire: Christian Alternatives to the Political Status Quo*. Grand Rapids, MI: Brazos Press, 2008.

Booth-Clibborn, Arthur Sidney. *Blood Against Blood.* 3rd ed. New York: Charles C. Cook, 1914.

"Combined Minutes of the General Council of the Assemblies of God, 1914–1917." St Louis, Missouri: Gospel Publishing House, n.d.

"Concealed Carry and Church Safety." AGFinancial. Accessed 20 June 2022. https://www.agfinancial.org/resources/article/concealed-carry-church-safety.

Dempster, Murray W. "Peacetime Draft Registration." *Agora: A Magazine of Pentecostal Opinion* 3:4 (Spring 1980), 8–9.

Dempster, Murray W. "Reassessing the Moral Rhetoric of Early American Pentecostal Pacifism." *Crux* 25:1 (March 1990), 23–36.

Dempster, Murray W. "'Crossing Borders:' Arguments Used by Early American Pentecostals in Support of Global Character of Pacifism." *EPTA Bulletin: The Journal of the European Pentecostal Theological Association* 10:2 (1991), 63–80.

Dempster, Murray W. "Pacifism in Pentecostalism: The Case of the Assemblies of God." In *The Fragmentation of the Church and Its Unity in Peacemaking*. Eds Jeffrey Gros and John D. Rempel. Grand Rapids, MI and Cambridge, UK: Eerdmans, 2001, 137–65.

Fea, John. *Believe Me: The Evangelical Road to Donald Trump*. Grand Rapids, MI: Eerdmans, 2018.

"General Council of the Assemblies of God." In *Christian Peace and Nonviolence: A Documented History*. Ed. Michael G. Long. Maryknoll, NY: Orbis Books, 2011, 143.

Gorman, Michael J. *Reading Paul*. Eugene, OR: Cascade Books, 2008.

Green, Chris E.W. *Sanctifying Interpretation: Vocation, Holiness, and Scripture*. Cleveland, TN: CPT Press, 2015.

Harris, Dwayne. "How to Operate an Armed Church Security Team." Full Armor: Church Safety Solutions. Accessed 11 February 2022. https://www.fullarmorchurch.com/operating-armed-church-security-team/.

Kreider, Alan. *The Patient Ferment of the Early Church: The Improbable Rise of Christianity in the Roman Empire*. Grand Rapids, MI: Baker Academic, 2016.

Kruse, Kevin M. *One Nation Under God: How Corporate America Invented Christian America*. New York, NY: Basic Books, 2015.

Long, Michael G. *Christian Peace and Nonviolence: A Documentary History*. Maryknoll, New York: Orbis Books, 2011.

Mason, Charles H. "The Kaiser in the Light of the Scriptures." In *The History and Life Work of Elder C.H. Mason, Chief Apostle, and His Co-Laborers*. Recomp. Mary Mason and ed. James Courts. Memphis, TN: Church of God in Christ, 1987.

"Minutes Revised Constitution and Bylaws the Thirty-second General Council, Long Beach, California, August 24–29, 1967." Springfield, MO: General Council of the Assemblies of God, 1967.

Mittelstadt, Martin William and Brian K. Pipkin, eds. *Mennocostals: Pentecostal and Mennonite Stories of Convergence*. In Pentecostals, Peacemaking, and Social Justice Series, Book 12. Eugene, OR: Pickwick, 2020.

Mittelstadt, Martin William and Geoffry William Sutton, eds. *Forgiveness, Reconciliation, and Restoration: Multidisciplinary Studies from a Pentecostal Perspective*. In Pentecostals, Peacemaking, and Social Justice Series, Book 3. Eugene, OR: Pickwick, 2010.

Nel, Marius. *Pacifism and Pentecostals in South Africa: A New Hermeneutic for Nonviolence*. London and New York: Routledge, 2018.

"Pastor Asks Members to Bring Guns to Church: A Kentucky Pastor is Inviting His Flock to Bring Guns to Church to Celebrate the Fourth of July and the Second Amendment." NBC News. 4 June 2009. https://www.nbcnews.com/id/wbna31111096 (accessed 18 July 2022).

Patterson, Contra Eric. "Moral Clarity in a Time of Terror." *Providence: A Journal of Christianity and American Foreign Policy* 2 (Winter 2016), 5–7.

Paulsen, Jacob. "Should I Conceal Carry in Church?" ConcealedCarry (28 April 2021) https://www.concealedcarry.com/law/concealed-carry-in-churches/ (accessed 18 July 2022).

Pipkin, Brian K. and Jay Beaman, eds. *Early Pentecostals on Nonviolence and Social Justice: A Reader*. Eugene, OR: Pickwick, 2016.

"Resolution Concerning the Attitude of the General Council of the Assemblies of God toward any Military Service which Involves the Actual Participation in the Destruction of Human Life." In "Combined Minutes of the General Council of the Assemblies of God in the United States of America, Canada, and Foreign Lands 1914–1917," 11. Accessed 20 November 2020. Digital copy available through Flower Pentecostal Heritage Center, https://ifphc.org.

Robbins, Roger. "A Chronology of Peace: Attitudes Toward War and Peace in the Assemblies of God: 1914–1918." *Pneuma: The Journal of the Society of Pentecostal Studies* 6:1 (Spring 1984), 3–26.

Rodriguez, Dario Lopez. *The Liberating Mission of Jesus: The Message of the Gospel of Luke*. Trans. Stefanie E. Israel and Richard E. Waldrop. Eugene, OR: Pickwick, 2012.

Roos, Dave. "The Sedition and Espionage Acts Were Designed to Quash Dissent During WWI." *History* 21 September 2020. Accessed 2 May 2022. https://www.history.com/news/sedition-espionage-acts-woodrow-wilson-wwi.

Seganos, Lauren. "On the Bumper Sticker: 'When Jesus said, "Love your enemies," I think he probably meant don't kill them.'" *State of Formation* (13 March 2014). https://stateofformation.org/2014/03/on-the-bumper-sticker-when-jesus-said-love-your-enemies-i-think-he-probably-meant-dont-kill-them/ (accessed 18 July 2022).

Sider, Ronald J. *Completely Prolife: Building a Consistent Stance on Abortion, the Family, Nuclear Weapons, the Poor*. Eugene, OR: Wipf and Stock, 2010.

Smith, James K.A. *Desiring the Kingdom: Worship, Worldview, and Cultural Formation*. Grand Rapids, MI: Baker Academic, 2009.

Stassen, Glen H. *Just Peacemaking: Transformative Initiatives for Justice and Peace*. Louisville, KY: Westminster John Knox Press, 1992.

Stassen, Glen H., ed. *Just Peacemaking: The New Paradigm for the Ethics of Peace and War*. Cleveland, OH: Pilgrim Press, 2008.

Stemberger, John. "The Rising Tide of Influence: How Pentecostalism is Changing the Dynamics of American Politics." *Charisma Magazine* (1 November 2011), 1–5, http://www.charismamag.com/index.php/features/32030-the-rising-tide-of-influence (accessed 18 July 2022).

Tackett, Zachary Michael. "Early Pentecostalism in Black and White: American Pentecostals Engaging Peace during World War I." Paper presented at the 40th Annual Meeting of the Society of Pentecostal Studies, Memphis, TN, 10–12 March 2011.

Tackett, Zachary Michael. "As Citizens of Heaven: Peace, War, and Patriotism Among Pentecostals in the United States during the First World War." In *American Churches and the First World War*. Ed. Gordon L. Heath. Eugene, OR: Pickwick, 2016, 71–86.

Tackett, Zachary Michael. "Brothers in Non-Combatant Service: Civilian Public Service and Pentecostals during World War Two." Paper presented at the 48th Annual Meeting of the Society of Pentecostal Studies, Washington, DC, 28 February–2 March 2019.

Wacker, Grant. *Heaven Below: Early Pentecostals and American Culture*. Cambridge, MA and London, England: Harvard University Press, 2001.

Ward, Kenneth D. and Allison Calhoun-Brown, *Religion and Politics in the United States*. 6th ed. Lanham, MD and Plymouth, United Kingdom: Rowman and Littlefield Publishers, 2011.

Wilson, D.J. "Pacifism." In *The New International Dictionary of Pentecostal Charismatic Movements*. Ed. Stanley M. Burgess. Grand Rapids, MI: Zondervan, 2002, 953–55.

# Chapter 10

# Toward Individual Conscience: The Assemblies of God and World War II

Zachary Michael Tackett

**Abstract**

The Assemblies of God in the United States during World War I identified as a peace church. Pentecostals stated in their official statements that the Spirit through the biblical witness calls the church to sustaining human life, that the intentional taking of human life, including in times of war, is not consistent with the gospel. Thus, the Presbytery of the AG asserted to the federal government that their members should be recognised as conscientious objectors (COs). Such objection, however, included the possibility of serving as a noncombatant. The Presbytery of the AG also noted that some if not many members may choose to serve as combatants; the AG would be supportive of their decision. During the years after WWI and prior to the Second World War, the church maintained her commitment to pacifism. As late as 1940, the Superintendent of the AG publicly identified the denomination as pacifist. Yet, when the war began, many in the AG chose to serve as combatants. Further, the AG in their publications shifted from prioritising pacifism toward emphasising support of her members that were serving as combatants. The present essay argues that this change was the result of a shift from emphasising the actions based upon the beliefs of a community of faith to prioritising actions that emerge from individual conscience. Pentecostals who had been encouraged as a community of faith to serve as conscientious objectors to war during the First World War, in the Second were encouraged to embrace a personal conscience. As a result, the church would shift from a community ethic to an individual ethic as the primary determinative factor regarding participation in war as a conscientious objector, noncombatant, or combatant.

## Introduction

The Assemblies of God (A.G.) of the United States in 1967 made a change in their polity regarding participation in armed conflict, articulating "the right of each member to choose for himself whether to declare his position as a combatant, a noncombatant, or a conscientious objector."[1] From 1917 until 1967 the AG identified as a pacifist community. The position of the church from 1917

[1] General Council of the Assemblies of God, "Minutes (August 24–29, 1967)," 35, Flower Pentecostal Heritage Center, www.ifphc.org.

forward was that the taking of human life was not appropriate. The Pentecostal community was committed to peacekeeping. Thus, the church encouraged conscripted members to serve as noncombatants or conscientious objectors. The denomination also recognised that some of her members would choose to serve in combatant roles; their decisions would be honoured by the Pentecostal community. The church in 1967 officially shifted from a community that prioritised pacifism, including noncombatant service, to prioritising an individual's choice based upon individual conscience regarding participation in armed conflict.[2] While the resolution accurately noted that the choice of members had always been recognised and honoured, the implication that the AG had always been a church that prioritised individual conscience was an overstatement. The AG since 1917 had advocated for pacifism, either through conscientious objection to war or though noncombatant service. The AG at that time and after also indicated that they would support their members who would choose combatant service. Yet, the priority from early on, as identified by the Presbytery's letter of 1917 to the federal government, lay in challenging war through pacifism.

The AG commitment to pacifism reached back to the first years of the Assemblies of God as a denomination. The denomination was formed in 1914. As the United States in 1917 began conscription for World War I, the Executive Committee identified the AG as a peace church. The Secretary of the AG forwarded a notice of the church's pacifist commitment to the federal government, that constituents who would declare as conscientious objectors to participation in armed conflict would receive church support.[3] The denomination as well as most American Pentecostal communities challenged the war in Europe as detrimental to society. Pentecostals identified the taking of human life as antithetical to their gospel mission.

As the Second World War raged in Europe during the late 1930s, the issue of armed or combatant service was renewed. The General Superintendent of the AG, E.S. Williams, in the summer of 1940, published an address to the AG constituency. Therein he reiterated that the AG was a peace church. The federal government reinstituted conscription shortly thereafter, in September of 1940. Williams may have been anticipating this renewal of conscription. Williams pointed to *The Pacifist Handbook* of 1939 and to the US Census figures of 1936. These documents identified the Assemblies of God as the third-largest peace church in the United States, alongside communities such as Brethren, Mennonites, Quakers, and Churches of Christ.[4]

The leadership and constituency of American Pentecostals, including those in the AG, began changing immediately before World War II. Pearl Harbor played

---

[2] "Minutes," 35.

[3] "The Pentecostal Movement and the Conscription Law," *The Weekly Evangel* (4 August 1917), 6, Flower Pentecostal Heritage Center, www.ifphc.org.

[4] E.S. Williams, "The Conscientious Objector," *The Pentecostal Evangel* (15 June 1940), 4, Flower Pentecostal Heritage Center, www.ifphc.org. Williams referenced, but did not source, the 1936 census and *The Pacifist Handbook: Questions and Answers Concerning the Pacifist in Wartime, Prepared as a Basis for Study and Discussion* (Fellowship of Reconciliation, 1939).

a significant role in a shift in priorities. The Second World War in the early 1940s was followed by an extended Cold War. This concluded hot conflicts in Korea during the early 1950s and in Vietnam during the 1960s and early 1970s. At the nadir of the Cold War, during the fray of the Vietnam War, the AG changed its polity to meet what had become the dominant practice of her constituents. The AG shifted from a community in WWI whose leadership prioritised conscientious objection, to a church whose polity in the late 1960s came to prioritise individual conscience. Significant to that shift were the events of Pearl Harbor and the United States entering World War II. The AG's response to the dynamics of the Cold War continued that shift.

## Establishing Assemblies of God Polity

The United States in 1940 resumed conscription, anticipating the United States' direct participation in the growing conflicts in Europe and the Pacific. Stanley Frodsham as editor of the *Pentecostal Evangel*, the official oracle of the AG, spoke to AG constituents, particularly those who may be facing the draft, regarding AG polity. The article does not have a byline, so it may have been written by another at the *Evangel*. Yet, Frodsham certainly approved its publication. Significantly, Frodsham had been the secretary of the AG in 1917 when the policy of prioritising noncombatant service and conscientious objection was adopted. He had penned the letter to the federal government in 1917 wherein the AG officially declared itself to the government as a peace church. Frodsham made clear in this writing twenty-three years later, in 1940, that the commitment to pacifism made in 1917 remained the standard within AG polity. Because of the universal feeling in the ranks of the AG that military service is incompatible with the gospel of Jesus Christ, Frodsham affirmed, and that a Christian cannot fully follow the teachings of his Lord and Master if he engages in armed conflict, the General Presbytery of the Assemblies of God drew up a statement in the year 1917. This pacifist statement, Frodsham emphasised, has never been rescinded.[5]

The article continues by emphasising that a person contending for conscientious objector status should not simply identify himself as a member of a peace church, the AG, but should embrace and declare a personal objection to war. These are the two historic requirements for responding to conscription by claiming conscientious objection to war. Yet, the article's emphasis upon a person holding a personal objection to war, in addition to the church's objection to war, reflects a reality that, while the official position of the church was that of a peace church, the AG constituency was not universally committed to pacifism. The emphasis of the article on persons identifying their personal objection to war also recognises that a shift toward individual conscience was developing within Pentecostal practice.

The AG and other Pentecostal communities after World War I, between the conflicts of the First and Second World Wars, did not struggle with the

[5] "The New Conscription Law," *The Pentecostal Evangel* (12 October 1940), 13, Flower Pentecostal Heritage Center, www.ifphc.org.

theological implications of participation in war. The church debated issues such as the personhood of Jesus, the nature of the Trinity, the relationship of speaking in tongues to Spirit baptism, and the nature of sin to the process of redemption (soteriology and sanctification). Yet, the issue of participation in war received little attention in theological discussions. The AG had written a statement against participation in war in 1917 but had not followed this by developing a theology regarding participation in war.

The adoption of the 1917 statement on pacifism had served as an emergency measure, though it was not identified as such. The statement was approved by the Executive Committee rather than the General Council; that is, the measure was passed by the executive leadership but was not addressed by the General Council in session: a meeting and vote of all ordained clergy and church delegates. The Executive Committee represents the leadership of the denomination; they are subject to the General Council. In 1917 there would not have been time for the General Council in session to take up the issue of participation in war prior to the government's implementation of a draft. Thus, the Executive Committee drafted a statement on pacifism and presented it to the federal government so that members of the AG could claim conscientious objection. The action of the Presbytery served as established policy until 1967. The issue was not taken up again, this time by the General Council, until that year.

The adopted 1967 bylaw prioritised an individual's conscience regarding participation in armed conflict. Further, the 1967 statement declared that this was the historic position of the AG.[6] Associate Professor of Social Ethics Murray Dempster of the AG's Southern California College, now Vanguard University, objected in a 1980 editorial. The shift, he contended, was not consistent with precedent, as the 1967 statement asserted, but instead abandoned the Pentecostal heritage of pacifism. Moreover, the 1967 statement shifted the reasoning for participation in armed conflict. "Apparently, the Pentecostal believer's conscience on war," lamented Dempster, "no longer needed to be formed specifically by biblical teaching but was now to be informed by knowledge of certain political, theological and ethical propositions."[7] Dempster's lament highlights that the shift that began during World War II had been solidified during the Vietnam War era.

## As a Peace Church

The United States on 6 April 1917, declared war on Germany, wherewith the US officially entered the Great War. Six weeks later the United States passed a conscription law, which included a clause for limited conscientious objection. Conscription, stated the law, could not constrain a person for service who was "a member of any well-recognised religious sect or organisation ... whose existing creed or principles forbid its members to participate in war in any form

---

[6] Minutes, 35.

[7] Murray W. Dempster, "Peacetime Draft Registration and Pentecostal Moral Conscience," *Agora* 3:4 (1980), 3.

and whose religious convictions are against war or participation therein."[8] Thus, the federal regulation on conscientious objection during WWI had a two-fold requirement. First, conscripts claiming exemption needed to show a personal conviction against participation in armed conflict. Second, conscientious objectors were required to demonstrate membership of a church or organisation that engaged a historic commitment to pacifism. Pentecostals objected to war but, as they were new communities, they had little historic precedent. Thus, demonstrating that the church as a community objected to participation in armed conflict might be difficult for Pentecostals to verify. Pentecostalism, however, was a child of holiness-evangelicalism that had a longstanding tradition of advocating for the marginalised and often challenged the appropriateness of war. Further, some within Pentecostalism had roots in pacifist Quaker communities. The AG resolution of 1917 was intended to demonstrate Pentecostals' historic commitment to pacifism.

*The Pentecostal Evangel* (PE) published the resolution and the letter that was sent to the federal government. The church intended to fulfil the "obligations of loyal citizenship." At the same time the AG objected to members being required to participate "in war and armed resistance which involves the actual destruction of human life."[9] The writer of the article, possibly the secretary of the AG, Stanley Frodsham, explained this action to the AG constituency. "From the very beginning," stated Frodsham, "the [Pentecostal] movement has been characterized by Quaker principles."[10] Moreover, the pacifist commitment of the AG was part of Pentecostals' global expression of pacifism. Among global Pentecostals who advocated pacifism, he stated, were German, British, and Canadian Pentecostals.[11] This perspective was consistent with the declared positions of most Pentecostal denominations in the United States. For example, the Church of God in Christ asserted, "We believe the shedding of human blood or taking of human life to be contrary to the teaching of our Lord and Saviour, and as a body, we are averse to war in all its various forms."[12]

Notwithstanding Frodsham's implications of univocal objection to participation in war, not all Pentecostals were committed to pacifism, with some and perhaps many in the United States and globally choosing to participate in armed conflict. To this point, Murray Dempster has challenged the validity of identifying a universal commitment to pacifism during WWI. Dempster even

---

[8] Section 4 of Conscription Act, 18 May 1917, cited by Jeffrey Kovac, *Refusing War, Affirming Peace: A History of Civilian Public Service at Cascade Locks* (Corvallis, OR: Oregon State University Press, 2009), 23.

[9] "The Pentecostal Movement and the Conscription Law," *The Weekly Evangel* (4 August 1917): 6, Flower Pentecostal Heritage Center, www.ifphc.org.

[10] "The Pentecostal Movement and the Conscription Law," 6.

[11] "The Pentecostal Movement and the Conscription Law," 6.

[12] In "Rev. Charles Harris Mason" [sic], held by Special Collections, University of Memphis Libraries, Tolbert-COGIC collection, box 9. See also, Theodore Kornweibel, Jr, "Race and Conscientious Objection in World War I: The Story of the Church of God in Christ," in Theron F. Schlabach and Richard T. Hughes (eds), *Proclaim Peace: Christian Pacifism from Unexpected Quarters* (Urbana and Chicago: University of Illinois Press, 1997), 62.

questions whether pacifism was the majority position within the constituency of the AG. That is, while church leadership identified the Assemblies of God as a peace church, the majority of the membership may not have been pacifists.[13]

### Between the Wars

The AG in their magazines during the armistice between WWI and WWII published a few articles related to participation in war. These articles prioritised conscientious objection. *The Pentecostal Evangel* (*PE*), representing the AG, and *The Latter Rain Evangel* (*LRE*), a publication of one of the AG's most prominent churches, Stone Church in Chicago, published a handful of articles on this subject. Commonly these were short news or informational pieces. One such article made brief references to practices in the early church, to the early church theologian Tertullian, and to Friends co-founder George Fox as opposing taking up the sword.[14] Another brief article contended that conscientious objection provides an embodied critique to society.[15]

Some articles engaged testimonies of conscientious objectors. The most comprehensive story is that of Robert McClay, whom *The PE* in 1932 featured on the cover. Having been conscripted during WWI, McClay reported to duty with the intention of declaring for noncombatant service. "I felt that a Christian could not possibly take human life, but that perhaps I could work as a stretcher bearer or in hospital work."[16] The article continued by detailing McClay's life in a military camp. The title of the article – "Standing True to Scriptural Principles" – evoked the thought that conscientious objection is built upon standards developed within Scripture. Eventually, recalls McClay, "I was handed my papers of discharge on the ground that I was mentally unfit. So seven months from the time God promised to deliver me, He made good His promise."[17]

The *LRE* published a sermon by Donald Gee, a British Pentecostal known for his pacifist commitments. Gee recounted, "I suffered for being a conscientious objector. I envied my brethren in prison. I never went along the street but what I was scoffed at." Most people, he stated, did not speak to him favourably about his objection to war. A few, however, appreciated his embodied critique. "[T]here was a little group of Christians down there who took us to their hearts when everybody reviled us," related Gee. "They took us into their homes and loved us when others scorned. You love friends who are friends in days like

[13] Murray W. Dempster, "Pacifism in Pentecostalism: The Case of the Assemblies of God," in Theron F. Schlabach and Richard T. Hughes (eds), *Proclaim Peace: Christian Pacifism in Unexpected Quarters* (Urbana: University of Chicago Press, 1997), 33.
[14] "War and Christianity," *The Pentecostal Evangel* (23 September 1939), 10, Flower Pentecostal Heritage Center, www.ifphc.org.
[15] "Conscientious Objectors," *The Latter Rain Evangel* (October 1933), 13, Flower Pentecostal Heritage Center, www.ifphc.org.
[16] Robert McClay, "Standing True to Scriptural Principles," *The Pentecostal Evangel* (6 February 1932), 8, Flower Pentecostal Heritage Center, www.ifphc.org.
[17] McClay, "Standing True to Scriptural Principles," 9.

that."[18] Gee had introduced this story by stating, "I have joy, even though carrying my cross, because of the joy that awaits me at the end of the journey – the joy of victory and fellowship with Christ."[19]

A third published story tells of a conscript from World War I who "registered as a conscientious objector, offering himself for hospital work or any kind of non-combative service."[20] In contrast to Gee and McClay, the soldier was not approved for noncombative status; instead, he was required to serve in the infantry. In that role, he chose not to discharge his weapon. "He had carried ammunition and had been faithful in his duties but had never fired a shot."[21] Significant to each of these identified stories that were published in *The PE* and *The LRE* during the armistice era, pacifism was highlighted as a Christian value for the Pentecostal community and correspondingly was underscored as an embodied critique to society.

## World War II

Pearl Harbor awakened the United States, thrusting the US Congress toward declaring war in the Pacific and in Europe. Pearl Harbor also served to push some clergy and constituents in the AG toward reconsidering their commitments to pacifism. In that not all Pentecostals had roots in the historic peace churches and in that the AG during the armistice years had some but not extensive engagement in developing their theological commitments to pacifism, many quickly shifted toward accepting the appropriateness of combatant service. Many Pentecostals identified the actions of the Japanese Navy at Pearl Harbor in December of 1941 as justifying taking up arms as a means of national self-defence. Opined General Secretary J. Roswell Flower in the spring of 1942, "[T]he traditional position of the Assemblies of God on war and armed conflict has received serious reconsideration by a number of our members. If there be any excuse for a Christian going to war, that excuse has been furnished by the present situation, so some have reasoned."[22]

At least three actions taken by the AG during WWII may be identified as demonstrating the changing attitudes toward the war. First, changing perspectives on conscientious objection to war and changing views regarding noncombatant service may be demonstrated in changing actions regarding official and financial support of conscientious objection. Second, the AG began thinking of warfare differently. Some described war primarily as a spiritual encounter with evil. From this perspective, armed conflict becomes an extended action of a larger spiritual battle. Third, the AG extended direct support to

---

[18] Donald Gee, "The Fruit of the Spirit is – Joy," *The Latter Rain Evangel* (March 1932), 10, Flower Pentecostal Heritage Center, www.ifphc.org.

[19] Gee, "The Fruit of the Spirit," 10.

[20] "Never Fired a Shot," *The Latter Rain Evangel* (August 1935), 22, Flower Pentecostal Heritage Center, www.ifphc.org.

[21] "Never Fired a Shot," 22.

[22] Flower to Fellow-Minister[s], Assemblies of God Ministers' Letter, 16 March 1942, Flower Pentecostal Heritage Center, www.ifphc.org.

combatant soldiers and sailors in a variety of ways. These three concepts are addressed in the following pages.

### *The General Secretary of the AG, the Conscientious Objector, and Alternative Service*

J. Roswell Flower, as general secretary of the AG, in his quarterly minsters' letter that encouraged the church to support the young men of the AG who were embodying a critique to war via conscientious objection, was sent to all AG clergy. Flower used these letters and articles he wrote for *The Pentecostal Evangel* to address various concerns of conscientious objectors and concerns of sailors and soldiers serving in combatant and noncombatant roles. In the spring 1942 ministers' letter, a few months after the United States entered the Second World War, Flower identified the need to support conscientious objectors to the war. "Numerous letters have been received [in the General Secretary's office] from pastors, and many of our Christian young men as well, in which expressions are found indicating difficulties encountered by them to reconcile their calling as servants of Christ with the militaristic spirit that is necessary to fight and win at war."[23] Here Flower advocated for those conscripts who had chosen conscientious objection. Others had chosen noncombatant status. But most AG conscripts, Flower noted, had chosen to answer conscription by accepting combatant roles. Flower explained,

> Quite a large number of our young men have appealed for and obtained classification as noncombatants … Not more than twenty of our young men have taken the extreme conscientious objector view so far …
>
> By far the larger number of the young men who are members of the Assemblies of God have permitted themselves to be inducted, waiving all claims for exemption on the grounds of conscience. Many of these have weighed carefully their conscientious scruples against war with the right of the government to exercise authority over them, and have gained consent of conscience to yield themselves unreservedly to their government for armed conflict. Others have not been able to do this, but the decision has been left with the individual in every case.[24]

The dilemma faced by the Pentecostal conscript, contended Flower, was whether or not the potential personal actions of a soldier or sailor in taking human life would conflict with his Christian faith. "He has been taught to believe that as a follower of Christ he is commissioned to save lives and not to destroy them. It is therefore with abhorrence [that] he contemplates the prospect of being required to deprive men of life in armed conflict."[25] Flower juxtaposed the responsibilities of the state over against the responsibilities of the individual person. Many conscripts from the AG were now approaching war through lenses that saw war as the responsibility of the state. They "have reached the conclusion

---

[23] Flower to Fellow-Minister[s], 16 March 1942.

[24] J. Roswell Flower, "The Plight of the Christian in the Present World War," *The Pentecostal Evangel* (12 June 1943), 6, Flower Pentecostal Heritage Center, www.ifphc.org.

[25] Flower, "The Plight of the Christian in the Present World War," 6.

that upon induction into the armed forces personal responsibility ceases."[26] Here Flower invoked the notion that fighting evil in war extended beyond human actions. Those who have chosen to serve as combatants and have weighed the issues, reasoned Flower, "believe that the present war is a conflict between Christ and paganism, that we are not merely fighting against flesh and blood but against principalities and powers, against the rulers of the darkness of this world, against wicked spirits incarnate."[27] Moreover, serving in the military might provide positive dynamics regarding evangelism. Once in military service, reasoned Flower, many of these men "have found many opportunities to witness for the Lord … Some stories of remarkable conversions are coming out of the training camps."[28] Flower as secretary of the AG in his ministerial letters and in his articles in *The PE* was attempting to navigate the waters of AG polity that rejected war and advocated for the conscientious objector but at the same time clearly identified his Pentecostal community as supporting the United States as patriots and valued the service of those members who would choose to serve as combatants.

Early in the war, Flower as a spokesperson for the denominational leadership advocated for the AG clergy and constituency to support an alternative to combatant and noncombatant military service that had become available shortly prior to the United States entering World War II. The peace churches, including the Assemblies of God, prior to the war had petitioned the federal government to recognise and value service to the United States that did not require participation in war, an action that had not been available during the Great War. The government approved such a plan, authorising Civilian Public Service (CPS) camps. COs could actively support the United States via firefighting, building parks, and providing humanitarian service in local communities. The camps were not supported by tax-payer dollars but by the conscientious objectors themselves and through private contributions, primarily through the peace churches. One Pentecostal CO explained why he chose CPS service over noncombatant service:

> I can understand why you would take the stand that you have [that of advocating noncombatant service over absolute pacifism]. As for myself, I cannot take part in non-combatant service and do as I feel the Lord would have a child of God to do. One in non-combatant service would not be taking a life directly, but I feel they would be indirectly. I love the stars and stripes[,] but I would rather serve our country by building up our land than to engage in any phase of military service.[29]

Flower implored the AG to help fund camps, noting that their fellow Pentecostals were faithful workers in the camps. "In most instances, [these men] were taken from home and placed in the camps and forgotten … [They are] [m]isunderstood by their friends, often by members of their own families, and by their churches of which they are members."[30] Moreover, in contrast to those

---

[26] Flower, "The Plight of the Christian in the Present World War," 6.
[27] Flower, "The Plight of the Christian in the Present World War," 6–7.
[28] Flower, "The Plight of the Christian in the Present World War," 6–7.
[29] Unidentified CO, in Flower to Fellow-Minister[s], 16 March 1942.
[30] J. Roswell Flower, "The Plight of the Conscientious Objector in the Present World Conflict," *The Pentecostal Evangel* (3 July 1943), 2.

serving in the Army and Navy, these civilian service workers were conscripted but had not been compensated financially. They were working for the betterment of the nation at war but unlike conscripts in the military were not being compensated for their service. "Soldiers are cared for by the US Government and are paid wages ..." In contrast, the civil service workers in camps "must labor in forestation and other public projects without pay. In addition, [the worker] is charged for board and room at the rate of thirty dollars per month."[31] Upon this argument, Flower challenged the constituents of the AG to stand with the peace churches in financially supporting the CPS camps. "The question we are now facing is whether we ought to throw the full responsibility for the support of these men who claim membership in the Assemblies of God upon the three historic peace churches, or to share with them the burden of caring for these men who have been assigned to them by the draft boards."[32] "We believe we owe it to all of these boys to stand back of them in every way possible."[33] Flower in 1942 identified about twelve AG sons who were serving in camps.[34] In 1943, he identified about twenty AG men in the camps.[35] Pentecostals from communities other than the AG also served in the camps.

Limited financial contributions came from AG churches, falling well short of the final support needed for AG COs in the camps. Roswell Flower, as secretary of the Assemblies of God, encouraged the AG constituency to support COs as an expression of their Pentecostal faith and in support of patriotic commitments. Such support recognised the church's advocacy of peace and at the same time supported the societal needs of the United States during war. While the argument was consistent with AG polity, the argument gathered little traction in the churches.

### *Warfare in the Heavenlies*

"[T]he conflict raging in Europe, Asia, and Africa," is predicated by, is the result of, evil, spiritual forces, contended an unnamed writer for *The Pentecostal Evangel*. Written during the summer of 1941, prior to Pearl Harbor, the writer approached the war in a manner that might be viewed as a popularisation of Plato's ideal. The physical warfare between nations reflected a greater spiritual warfare within the heavenlies. "The saints are equipped with heavenly armor, and armed with heavenly weapons to fight spiritual wickedness in the heavenly places."[36] Weapons of warfare do not have value in this war in the heavenlies. "Do not use carnal weapons for spiritual warfare. They are worse than useless."[37] The prayers of the Pentecostal faithful become spiritual weapons to engage and defeat evil, so that the weapons of physical warfare will be defeated. "Let us pray for our rulers, that they may be fortified of God against these hosts of evil spirits

---

31 Flower, "The Plight of the Conscientious Objector in the Present World Conflict," 2.
32 Flower, "The Plight of the Conscientious Objector in the Present World Conflict," 2.
33 Flower to Fellow-Minister[s], 16 March 1942.
34 Flower to Fellow-Minister[s], 16 June 1942.
35 Flower, "The Plight of the Christian in the Present World War," 6.
36 "Universal Warfare," *The Pentecostal Evangel* (19 April 1941), 4, Flower Pentecostal Heritage Center, www.ifphc.org.
37 "Universal Warfare," 4.

that purpose the destruction of millions."[38] Limited mention in this spiritual analysis was made of the war on the ground, air, and sea. The writer implied that the present physical activity of waging war is be influenced by spiritual forces through prayer. The writer made no mention of the Pentecostal community's responsibility regarding physical warfare. Correspondingly, the writer did not address conscription, the taking up of arms by the conscript, nor taking pacifist actions.

A little over a year and a half later, after the US was fully engaged in a global war, William I. Evans addressed Assemblies of God's Central Bible Institute (CBI), providing a similar message. "The issues of warfare are decided in the spiritual realm where spiritual forces are locked in combat," asserted Evans.[39] "How little the world realises the presence of mighty supernatural forces controlling and directing the human forces that appear to be determining the issues of the present war."[40] Evans continued by invoking the words of the Apostle Paul that we do not wrestle with flesh and blood, but "against wicked spirits in heavenly places." Evans surmised, "Spiritual forces are engaged in [the present] combat [in Europe, North Africa, and the Pacific]."[41]

Evans, however, did not limit his discussion to the heavenlies, going beyond the implications of the intersection of spiritual and physical warfare. He spoke of soldiers on the ground, destruction on earth, and an overarching, superintending heavenly battle. The earthly results of the spiritual war in the heavenlies were gruesome.

> Our soldier boys go in their bravery and their devotion to God and country, willing to lay down their lives physically to win battles on the field where the fighting is against flesh and blood. Hosts of men are slain. Flesh and blood goes [sic] down in gory streams. Whole villages and towns are depopulated. Men, women and children are slaughtered by the thousands. But the issues of the battles are not decided on earth's fields. The issues of warfare are decided in the spiritual realm where spiritual forces are locked in combat.[42]

Evans called upon the ministerial students at CBI to participate in the war through the spiritual warfare of prayer. "[O]ur place in this warfare is in the heavenly realms where spiritual forces are battling, and our responsibility is to find our place under the leadership of the Holy Ghost in this conflict."[43] Within this context of addressing prospective AG clergy, Evans addressed conscientious objection for clergy but failed to address the availability to laity who had been conscripted to identify as conscientious objectors. Stated Evans, "It is a wonderful thing that the Government of the USA makes provision in this world war that young men who are devoting themselves to the Christian ministry have practically permanent deferment from physical military service."[44] Evans failed

---

[38] "Universal Warfare," 4.

[39] W.I. Evans, "How the Issues of War Will Be Settled," *The Pentecostal Evangel* (2 January 1943), 2, Flower Pentecostal Heritage Center, www.ifphc.org.

[40] Evans, "How the Issues of War Will Be Settled," 2.

[41] Evans, "How the Issues of War Will Be Settled," 2.

[42] Evans, "How the Issues of War Will Be Settled," 2.

[43] Evans, "How the Issues of War Will Be Settled," 2.

[44] Evans, "How the Issues of War Will Be Settled," 2.

to note, however, that AG polity recognised all members of the AG who were subject to conscription as eligible for conscientious objector status – clergy and laity alike.

Darbian dispensationalist undercurrents can be seen in some of the writings that addressed warfare in the heavenlies. One of the more obvious expressions of those dispensationalist undercurrents may be found in an article written by J. Narver Gortner titled, "Why Does Not God Intervene and Stop This War?" Using language adopted from dispensationalism, Gortner identified the current era as a "dispensation of grace" in which the present war was being used by God to chastise the nations. In a reference to the ancient northern kingdom of Israel, but also implying the present nations at war, Gortner warned, "Every nation that has fallen[,] has fallen as a result of sin. War is divine judgment … The eyes of God are upon the nations today. He is working all things after the counsel of His own will."[45] Gortner concluded with a prophetic statement reflective of the prophetic charges that had populated Pentecostals' critique of the First World War. "It is time for the nations to repent … America should repent, should turn from every evil way, and should seek the face of God."[46]

### *In Support of the Troops*

The general secretary of the AG, Roswell Flower, oversaw a variety of projects that were designed to provide encouragement and care for sailors and soldiers. Such was the case of the December 1942 letter, encouraging clergy to make it easy for soldiers to find AG churches. With the goal of providing support to AG members in the military, the AG took a variety of actions in support of the troops. This included establishing a servicemen's department, encouraging qualified persons to become chaplains in the Army, creating a newsletter for soldiers named *Reveille*, and the publishing of articles about military service in *The PE*.[47] Among the simplest items were identified ways that clergy could extend support to the troops by welcoming them into their churches.

> Soldiers complain that when they try to find Assemblies of God [churches] in the communities near which they are stationed, they have the utmost difficulty … Assemblies of God boys who are away from home yearn for fellowship, sympathy and understanding. Let us do all in our power to encourage them.[48]

"The Servicemen's Department … has been a beehive of activity for months … The tabulation of names and addresses of Servicemen who are members of the Assemblies of God or else connected with families who are members, has now passed the 20,000 mark."[49] The Servicemen's Department of the AG was

---

[45] J. Narver Gortner, "Why Does Not God Intervene and Stop This War?" *The Pentecostal Evangel* (6 February 1943), 6, Flower Pentecostal Heritage Center, www.ifphc.org.

[46] Gortner, "Why Does Not God Intervene and Stop This War?" 6.

[47] For example, "Helping the Service Men," *The Pentecostal Evangel* (21 February 1942), 1, 6, Flower Pentecostal Heritage Center, www.ifphc.org.

[48] Flower to Fellow-Minister[s], Assemblies of God Ministers' Letter, 16 December 1942, appendix, Flower Pentecostal Heritage Center, www.ifphc.org.

[49] Flower to Fellow-Minister[s], Assemblies of God Ministers' Letter, 17 June 1944, Flower Pentecostal Heritage Center, www.ifphc.org.

established following the General Council that met in the summer of 1943. Explained Flower, "The work of spreading the Gospel among the servicemen became too great to be carried as a side-line of the Home Missions Department."[50]

One of the activities of the Servicemen's Department was the distribution of *Reveille*, an occasional periodical that included stories of interest to soldiers and airmen, sailors, and Marines. "Over 4,000,000 copies of Reveille have been printed and distributed ... Over six hundred chaplains of all denominations ... have asked for and distributed huge bundles of Reveille."[51] *Reveille* published stories of soldiers and sailors and incorporated cartoon illustrations in the tradition of Sad Sack[52] or the Korean War favourite Beatle Bailey.[53] The writers of *Reveille* stated its purpose: "This paper has been named *Reveille* because we desire to awaken your interest in those truths which for ages have been the bulwark of the soul."[54]

A second significant action taken by the AG was the encouragement of chaplains in the Army. The Secretary in 1944 reported to the clergy that the AG had been allotted thirty slots for military chaplains, but initially these slots were not able to be filled, primarily because of the limited number of AG ministers who met the educational requirements. Pentecostals had a tradition of schooling pastors in Bible colleges or through mentoring. Military chaplaincy required seminary studies. The secretary lamented that the chaplaincy positions allotted to Pentecostals were no longer available because the Army had filled those positions with chaplains from other denominations.[55]

Perhaps the most significant positive visualisation of the chaplaincy came at the 1943 General Council in session wherein Army chaplain First Lieutenant Clarence P. Smales was a featured speaker. His address was published on the cover of *The PE*.[56] Highlighting the work of Chaplain Smales signalled to the denomination that it was appropriate to lend spiritual support to AG members who were serving in the military and to extend evangelism to all soldiers. Significant to the initial and continuing understanding of the AG regarding conscientious objection, chaplains then and now serve as noncombatants. Their

---

[50] Flower to Fellow-Minister[s], Assemblies of God Ministers' Letter, 24 January 1944, Flower Pentecostal Heritage Center, www.ifphc.org.

[51] Flower to Fellow-Minister[s], 24 January 1944; see also, "Announcing: A Reveille Servicemen's Department," *The Pentecostal Evangel* (29 January 1944), 5, Flower Pentecostal Heritage Center, www.ifphc.org.

[52] Sad Sack was a misfit soldier created by George Baker, published by Harvey Comics in *Yank, the Army Weekly.* Sad Sack Net: The Official Site, accessed 20 February 2018, http://sadsack.org/OriginalComicStrip.htm.

[53] Mort Walker created Beetle Bailey during the Korean War era as a private who outwitted his superiors, published by King Features Syndicate, Comics Kingdom, accessed 20 February 2018, http://comicskingdom.com/beetle-bailey-1.

[54] *Reveille*, Service Bulletin no. 2, p. 1, with full issue republished in *The Pentecostal Evangel* (21 February 1942), 7–10, Flower Pentecostal Heritage Center, www.ifphc.org.

[55] Flower to Fellow-Minister[s], Assemblies of God Ministers' Letter, 24 January 1944, Flower Pentecostal Heritage Center, www.ifphc.org.

[56] C.P. Smales, "Marks of a Good Soldier," *The Pentecostal Evangel* (25 September 1943), 1, Flower Pentecostal Heritage Center, www.ifphc.org.

role, therefore, would have been consistent with the presbyters' call from WWI in which AG members were to serve the US without doing harm to others, without taking the life of another.[57]

## Toward Individual Conscience

The Second World War served as a watershed for a shift in AG practices regarding conscientious objection. It laid the groundwork for a change in policy that would take place two decades later, in the 1960s. The shift in perspective during WWII was predicated upon moving from prioritising the conscience of the community that had been framed by gospel and by the mission and teachings of Jesus, to prioritising the conscience of the individual that is framed by one's own conviction.

As a community during WWI, the AG identified itself as a church that acted upon a historic commitment to pacifism, what Stanley Frodsham identified as having Quaker principles. The foundation of this commitment was the nature of gospel, that armed conflict was inconsistent with the teachings of Jesus. Alongside this commitment to pacifism, the AG declared that they would serve as loyal citizens. Advocacy of patriotism tended to be read by Pentecostals as meaning that COs were willing to serve as noncombatants instead of as absolute pacifists.

Pacifism was retained as AG polity during WWII, but the reading of the pacifist commitment of the AG began to be reinterpreted. Pearl Harbor changed things. Stated General Secretary Roswell Flower, "[T]he traditional position of the Assemblies of God on war and armed conflict has received serious reconsideration." To reiterate, three basic actions were taken during WWII that reflect the changing interpretation of the AG pacifist commitment. First was the attempt to garner support for CPS camps. While some money was raised, the money received was well shy of the expenses of AG men who served the US as civilian conscripts in CPS camps. A common response from the AG clergy was that the men should not serve as absolute COs, but should serve as noncombatants. Second, some writers provided a theological argument that the real battles were fought in heaven, a heavenly war with evil. War was to be waged with evil through prayer. This action of shifting the focus of war to a heavenly battle served to minimise the concern for the atrocities of earthly, physical battle. The third action taken by the AG was to actively support soldiers, airmen, sailors, and Marines through such ventures as the Servicemen's Department, *Reveille*, ministers serving as chaplains, and the publication of articles in *The PE* that kept combatant and noncombatant soldiers and sailors in the thoughts of the readers.

The AG during WWII continued, as they had since World War I, to advocate for the right of their members to identify as conscientious objectors to war. But

[57] The writers of *The Pacifist Handbook* were uncomfortable with identifying chaplains as pacifist. "The chaplain wears the uniform of the army, accepts army pay, is ranked as an officer, and is completely under the authority of the government … It is therefore very difficult to see how a pacifist could become a chaplain" (p.31).

conscripts often were cautioned that they should make sure that they were true conscientious objectors. The AG as a community was beginning to state in subtle and vocalised ways that choosing to serve as a combatant, noncombatant, or pacifist civilian worker was a personal decision based upon individual conscience. Further, the scale was beginning to tip toward prioritising the Christian who would serve honourably and faithfully through military service, including serving in roles of armed, combatant service.

## Discussion Questions

1. What is a primary distinction identified by Tackett between the way the AG leadership approached conscientious objection in the First World War compared how they addressed conscientious objection in the Second World War?
2. What event or events does Tackett identify as having the most influence in Pentecostals' change of approach to pacifism?
3. If you could ask a question to a person who served in one of the Civilian Public Service camps, what would you ask him?
4. How might the Assemblies of God and other Christian communities better develop theologies and practices of peacemaking that honour their past thought and practices, and that address concerns regarding present and future wars?

## Bibliography

### *Primary Sources*

"Announcing: A Reveille Servicemen's Department." *The Pentecostal Evangel* (January 29, 1944): 5. Flower Pentecostal Heritage Center, www.ifphc.org.

Baker, George. *Yank, the Army Weekly.* Harvey Comics. This is digitally republished at *Sad Sack Net: The Official Site*. Accessed February 20, 2018. http://sadsack.org/OriginalComicStrip.htm.

"Conscientious Objectors." *The Latter Rain Evangel* (October 1933): 13. Flower Pentecostal Heritage Center, www.ifphc.org.

Evans, W. I. "How the Issues of War Will Be Settled." *The Pentecostal Evangel* (January 2, 1943): 2-3. Flower Pentecostal Heritage Center, www.ifphc.org.

Flower to Fellow-Minister[s]. Assemblies of God Ministers' Letter. March 16, 1942. Flower Pentecostal Heritage Center, www.ifphc.org.

Flower to Fellow-Minister[s]. Assemblies of God Ministers' Letter. June 16, 1942. Flower Pentecostal Heritage Center, www.ifphc.org.

Flower to Fellow-Minister[s]. Assemblies of God Ministers' Letter. September 21, 1942, appendix. Flower Pentecostal Heritage Center, www.ifphc.org.

Flower to Fellow-Minister[s]. Assemblies of God Ministers' Letter. December 16, 1942, appendix. Flower Pentecostal Heritage Center, www.ifphc.org.

Flower to Fellow-Minister[s]. Assemblies of God Ministers' Letter. January 24, 1944. Flower Pentecostal Heritage Center, www.ifphc.org.

Flower to Fellow-Minister[s]. Assemblies of God Ministers' Letter. June 17, 1944. Flower Pentecostal Heritage Center, www.ifphc.org.

Flower to Fellow-Minister[s]. Assemblies of God Ministers' Letter. March 23, 1945, appendix. Flower Pentecostal Heritage Center, www.ifphc.org.

Flower, J. Roswell. "Concerning the Conscientious Objector." *The Pentecostal Evangel* (March 4, 1944): 7. Flower Pentecostal Heritage Center, www.ifphc.org.

Flower, J. Roswell. "The Plight of the Christian in the Present World War." *The Pentecostal Evangel* (June 12, 1943): 6. Flower Pentecostal Heritage Center, www.ifphc.org.

Flower, J. Roswell. "The Plight of the Conscientious Objector in the Present World Conflict." *The Pentecostal Evangel* (July 3, 1943): 2. Flower Pentecostal Heritage Center, www.ifphc.org.

Gee, Donald. "The Fruit of the Spirit is—Joy," *The Latter Rain Evangel* (March 1932): 10. Flower Pentecostal Heritage Center, www.ifphc.org.

Gortner, J. Narver. "Why Does Not God Intervene and Stop This War?" *The Pentecostal Evangel* (February 6, 1943): 6. Flower Pentecostal Heritage Center, www.ifphc.org.

"Helping the Service Men." *The Pentecostal Evangel* (February 21, 1942): 1, 6. Flower Pentecostal Heritage Center, www.ifphc.org.

McClay, Robert. "Standing True to Scriptural Principles." *The Pentecostal Evangel* (February 6, 1932): 8. Flower Pentecostal Heritage Center, www.ifphc.org.

*Minutes*, General Council of the Assemblies of God (August 24-29, 1967). Flower Pentecostal Heritage Center, www.ifphc.org.

"Never Fired a Shot." *The Latter Rain Evangel* (August 1935): 22. Flower Pentecostal Heritage Center, www.ifphc.org.

Rev. Charles Harris[son] Mason." Held by Special Collections, University of Memphis [TN] Libraries, Tolbert-COGIC collection, box 9.

*Reveille*, Service Bulletin no. 2. In *The Pentecostal Evangel* (February 21, 1942): 7-10. Flower Pentecostal Heritage Center, www.ifphc.org.

Smales, C. P. "Marks of a Good Soldier." *The Pentecostal Evangel* (September 25, 1943): 1. Flower Pentecostal Heritage Center, www.ifphc.org.

"The New Conscription Law." *The Pentecostal Evangel* (October 12,1940): 13. Flower Pentecostal Heritage Center, www.ifphc.org.

*The Pacifist Handbook: Questions and Answers Concerning the Pacifist in Wartime, Prepared as a Basis for Study and Discussion* (Fellowship of Reconciliation, 1939).

"The Pentecostal Movement and the Conscription Law." *The Weekly Evangel* (August 4, 1917): 6. Flower Pentecostal Heritage Center, www.ifphc.org.

"Universal Warfare." *The Pentecostal Evangel* (April 19, 1941): 4. Flower Pentecostal Heritage Center, www.ifphc.org.

"War and Christianity." *The Pentecostal Evangel* (September 23, 1939): 10. Flower Pentecostal Heritage Center, www.ifphc.org.

Williams, E. S. "The Conscientious Objector." *The Pentecostal Evangel* (June 15, 1940): 4. Flower Pentecostal Heritage Center, www.ifphc.org.

### *Secondary Sources*

Dempster, Murray W. "Pacifism in Pentecostalism: The Case of the Assemblies of God." In *Proclaim Peace: Christian Pacifism in Unexpected Quarters*, edited by Theron F. Schlabach and Richard T. Hughes, 31-57. Urbana: University of Chicago Press, 1997.

Dempster, Murray W. "Peacetime Draft Registration and Pentecostal Moral Conscience." *Agora* 3, no. 4 (1980): 2-3.

Frazer, Heather T. and John O'Sullivan. *"We Have Just Begun to Not Fight: An Oral History of Conscientious Objectors in Civilian Public Service during World War II"* (New York: Twayne Publishers, 1996).

Kornweibel, Theodore, Jr. "Race and Conscientious Objection in World War I: The Story of the Church of God in Christ" In *Proclaim Peace: Christian Pacifism from Unexpected Quarters*, ed. Theron F. Schlabach and Richard T. Hughes, 58-81. Urbana and Chicago: University of Illinois Press, 1997.

Kovac, Jeffrey. *Refusing War, Affirming Peace: A History of Civilian Public Service at Cascade Locks.* Corvallis, OR: Oregon State University Press, 2009.

Walker, Mort. *Comics Kingdom.* King Features Syndicate. Accessed February 20, 2018. http://comicskingdom.com/beetle-bailey-1.

# Chapter 11

# A Pentecostal/Charismatic Response to the "Red Scare" as Portrayed in *The Voice of Healing*

Lisa Millen

**Abstract**

*The Voice of Healing* (*T.V.H.*) (1948–1966), primarily edited by Gordon Lindsay, was a herald for the American Pentecostal Healing Movement. It chronicled the ministries of Oral Roberts, Jack Coe, A.A. Allen, William Branham, T.L. Osborn, Raymond T. Richey, W.V. Grant, and others. For the editors of *T.V.H.*, communism posed a political threat to the United States and a spiritual threat to Christianity. The editors of *T.V.H.*, basing their observation on their reading of biblical prophecy and engaging a Pentecostalised dispensationalist rubric, desired to warn their readers of this two-fold threat. This essay, engaging articles in *T.V.H.* from 1948 to 1960 and a few pamphlets prominently advertised in *T.V.H.*, considers how the healing revivalists, as portrayed in *T.V.H.*, and the *T.V.H.* itself called the nation to defeating communism.

## Introduction

In the fall of 1953 Robert Faussett snapped a few photographs of the latest shipment for his Pennsylvania company's records. Faussett and his coworkers noticed a strange circular apparition in the sky. Although it hovered in the air for an unusual length of time, the men gave it little thought, but when the prints were developed Faussett found something unexpected in the photograph. Not only was the apparition present, but its symbol was unmistakable. A large hammer and sickle, the symbol of communism, was clearly visible. Gordon Lindsay, editor of *The Voice of Healing* periodical, included the photo in the November 1953 issue of the magazine. The headline read: "Signs in the Heavens." The story reminded readers that Luke had warned at the end of time "fearful sights and great signs" would be visible in the heavens. It was no coincidence the sign depicted in the article was the symbol of Communist Russia.[1]

For the editors of *The Voice of Healing* (*T.V.H.)* communism posed, not only a political threat, but a spiritual one as well. The editors of *T.V.H.* did not think Americans rightly understood the diabolic nature of communism, but the editors did. Thanks to their grasp of biblical prophecy, they also understood communism's plans for the world, as well as God's plans for communism,

[1] Gordon Lindsay, "Signs in the Heavens," *TVH* (November 1953), 18.

including its ultimate defeat, aided, in part, by the healing revivals. I will first address *TVH*'s use of biblical prophecy to explain the nature of communism, its plans for the world, and God's plans for communism. Next, I will examine the way in which *TVH* understood the role of the healing revivals in defeating communism. Finally, I will draw conclusions based on my research. Research for this article comes from *TVH*, 1948 to 1960, as well as a few pamphlets prominently advertised in *TVH*.

## The Nature of Communism

Gordon Lindsay thought Americans were naïve regarding the sinister nature of communism. *TVH* wanted readers to understand the truth. Communism was clearly anti-God and anti-Christ.[2] Lindsay identified Russia as the "Beast Power" of Revelation 13 and Daniel 9. By 1949 humanity was just beginning to experience the "sinister character" of this satanic Beast Power, which could understand "dark sentences" and "wear out the saints."[3] Dr George Dewey, a columnist for *TVH*, explained that the driving force behind communism was not born in the mind of Karl Marx but in the heart of hell.[4] Communism had been "spawned in a hatred of all that is good and holy,"[5] and these "followers of the Son of Perdition" received their inspiration from hell.[6] In his monthly column *Prophecy Marches On!* Howard Rusthoi told readers that Russian billboards showed people eating the flesh of Jesus and drinking his blood. Communists burned effigies of Jesus and worshipped statues of Judas Iscariot.[7] Russia, "ever drunk with satanized intrigue," was the devil's henchman, and communism was his bosom friend.[8] If *TVH* readers thought communism was not a threat, such ideas were staunchly crushed. Lindsay wrote, "If the world knew what was in the minds of the men in the Kremlin, they might well turn sick with horror at the diabolical schemes being hatched in the minds of men who prefer to be devils rather than human beings."[9] *TVH* understood what its readers did not.

## Communism's Plan to Overtake the World

One way of helping *TVH* readers to fully appreciate communism's evil nature was to explain the communists' diabolical plans to control the world. Dominion of the earth was the Russian leaders' "one absorbing aim" and they would use any means necessary to achieve it, even if it meant joining with Adolf Hitler,

---

[2] Gordon Lindsay, "The Rise of the Red Terror," *TVH* (October 1948), 14.
[3] "The Month in Prophecy …" *TVH* (April 1949), 13.
[4] George Blomgren Dewey, "Russia's Plans for 1952," *TVH* (May 1952), 19.
[5] Gordon Lindsay, "In the Last Two Years," *TVH* (February 1952), 20.
[6] Dewey, "Russia's Plans," 15.
[7] Howard Rusthoi, "Prophecy Marches On!" *TVH* (February 1954), 22.
[8] B. Lauster, "Tent Filled with 22,000 People, Scene of Great Hicks Campaign in Germany," *TVH* (December 1957), 14 and Gordon Lindsay, "The Orange Tide of the Red Dragon," *TVH* (January 1951), 14.
[9] "Russia has the Atomic Bomb," *TVH* (November 1949), 15.

whom *TVH* suggested might possibly still be alive. The communists have never deviated from their goal but were driven by the power of demons to achieve it.[10] Just as the early church had a missionary vision, so the communists had a vision, to spread their gospel throughout the world.[11]

In May of 1952, George Dewey detailed Russia's plans for the year, which included taking over the world.[12] The Chinese had already fallen to communism in February 1949 when the communists overthrew the Chinese general Chiang Kai-shek, which Lindsay blamed on the Americans, and now the world had to fear the "orange tide," as well as the "red tide." China was now a mixture of communists and those "degenerate bandit hordes of the yellow race," who, unfortunately, had never been reached with the gospel.[13] However, China's fall to communism fulfilled prophecy because, according to Revelation 16, it "made way for the kings of the East" to participate in the final battle.[14]

*TVH* laid out what they believed to be Russia's plans for Israel, Iran, and Germany. Rusthoi often wrote about Russia's plans to invade Israel and provided evidence, such as when he pointed out an eclipse that occurred around 1952, the shadow of which moved from Palestine to Russia and showed the exact path of Russia's imminent invasion of Israel.[15] Likewise, Lindsay connected Russia with both "Gog" and "Rosh," mentioned in Ezekiel 38 and 39, and explained how Russia would invade Israel. He unpacked the hidden meaning of a Russian stamp from 1930, in which Russia inadvertently announced her plans for an Israeli invasion.[16] *TVH* commented on developments in Iran as well, since Russia would have to move through Iran to invade Israel. For those interested in finding out more about the relationship between Russia and Iran, *TVH* offered a free copy of Rusthoi's "detailed, secret report" of events taking place throughout the Middle East.[17] When Stalin announced in June 1952 that it was time to unify Germany and thus bring all of the country under communist control, Rusthoi considered its prophetic significance. Citing Daniel, Revelation, and Ezekiel, he demonstrated how, before the Antichrist appeared, Russia would dominate all of Germany to the Rhine River, the ancient boundary of the Roman Empire.[18] Prophecy showed that Germany (Gomer) would be on the side of the communists in the battle of Armageddon.[19] These are just a few examples of *TVH*'s dozens of attempts to unpack Russia's plans in light of biblical prophecy.

---

[10] "The Mystery of Hitler's Disappearance," *TVH* (May 1949), 12.

[11] Velmer Gardner, "When God Fights Russia," *TVH* (March 1954), 4.

[12] Dewey, "Russia's Plans," 9. Dewey's source for this material was an information service in
London which had five Russian spies in top governmental positions in Russia.

[13] Lindsay, "The Orange Tide," 15. Note Lindsay's derogatory language.

[14] Howard Rusthoi, "Prophecy Marches On!" *TVH* (July 1954), 18.

[15] Gordon Lindsay, "The Mysterious Darkening of the Sun and Moon," *TVH* (March 1952), 16.

[16] Gordon Lindsay, "Is it Peace or is it War?" *TVH* (July 1953), 27. There are many more examples in *TVH* of prophecy regarding Russia and Israel.

[17] Howard Rusthoi, "Prophecy Marches On!" *TVH* (July 1953), 29.

[18] Howard Rusthoi, "Prophecy Marches On!" *TVH* (June 1952), 22.

[19] Howard Rusthoi, "Prophecy Marches On!" *TVH* (July 1954), 18.

*TVH* wanted readers to know that communism had plans for America as well. George Dewey warned that, by the end of 1952, America would have given up her way of life.[20] Evangelist Velmer Gardner told readers communists were already in here. "Yes, friends, Russia is on the march to control our land. They would like to influence our schools and churches, and get into the hearts of the youth of our land with their Satanic doctrine." As an example, Gardner wrote that communists were infiltrating the labour unions, in order to destroy the nation from within. One communist who held an important union position was witnessed shaking his fist at the American flag and shouting, "I hate it" and "the constitution of the United States be damned!" Not all union leaders were communist, Gardner acknowledged, but one could not be too careful.[21] Communists were at work in America and *TVH* readers needed to be aware.

Lindsay insisted that America was already at war, and this war would invariably lead to Armageddon. In fact, Lindsay's prophecy charts showed that World War II had never actually ended but would escalate into World War III.[22] Any suggestion that Russia wanted peace rather than war was not to be believed. "Serious Bible scholars" knew it was a false peace. Only those unversed in biblical prophecy could ever hope for a peaceful resolution to the world situation.[23] Rusthoi agreed that Russian talks of peace were not trustworthy; Russia was secretly preparing for war. The uncertainty and anxiety the Russian "peace" offensive caused could be explained by properly deciphering biblical prophecy that said in the last days there will be "distress of nations with perplexity. Luke 21:25."[24] Lindsay concluded in 1953 that Western leaders were finally beginning to understand what *TVH* already knew; communism does not really want peace. If they had only studied their Bibles, Western leaders could have avoided making tragic political mistakes.[25]

## God's Plan for Communism

Lindsay reminded his readers that, "God rules and overrules. He sits on his throne controlling the destinies of the nations."[26] Likewise, Rusthoi wrote that the entire world is subject to the "incomprehensible and inscrutable" will of God.[27] However, while Lindsay believed God's will was incomprehensible, he

---

[20] Dewey, "Russia's Plans," 9.

[21] Gardner, "When God Fights Russia," 4.

[22] Lindsay, "The US in Prophecy," 2.

[23] Lindsay, "The Year 1952 in Prophecy," 14.

[24] Howard Rusthoi, "Prophecy Marches On!" *TVH* (June 1953), 29.

[25] Lindsay, "Is it Peace or is it War?" 26. Lindsay continued to be suspicious of any talk of peace. When in 1959 Khrushchev proposed a plan to disarm the world within four years, Lindsay believed Russia could not be trusted. While the rest of the world was disarming, Khrushchev would be secretly building up Russian arms. Besides, Lindsay warned, the four years of Khrushchev's plan were suspiciously close to the three and a half years of tribulation mention in Daniel 9:27. Gordon Lindsay, "The Prophetic Significance of the Khrushchev Visit," *TVH* (November 1959), 5.

[26] "The Rise of the Red Terror," 16.

[27] Howard Rusthoi, "Prophecy Marches On!" (July 1953), 29.

also believed he understood God's plan better than most Christians, particularly in regard to divine timing. Lindsay saw prophetic events arranged around sets of 666 days. They included the beginning of World War I, the attack on Pearl Harbor and the North Atlantic pact, and Eisenhower's election, significant because he would be instrumental in America's relationship with the communists.[28] The number 1290 was also significant as it was the number of desolation in Daniel 2:11.[29] Likewise, the number seven held significance because it was the number of perfection. Seven years equalled 2,520 days, so Lindsay created a chart that demonstrated how important events occurred at that increment. At the time of his writing, the next set of 2,520 days would culminate in November 1948. Something prophetically noteworthy was bound to happen.[30] These facts, Lindsay concluded, proved that world events happen by divine design as well as in relation to each other.[31]

Lindsay was confident he understood how that divine timetable worked. When Truman announced in October 1949 that Russia possessed an atomic bomb, Lindsay reminded his readers that *TVH* had already predicted Russia had the atomic bomb several months earlier based on a careful study of the divine time measures. The divine timetable showed a climax would occur within a matter of months and would involve atomic destruction. The United States government was not as dependable as the divine timetable because it failed to consider the amount of aid Russia received from German scientists, as well as the mass infiltration of Russian spies into American government. Most importantly, it failed to take into account biblical prophecy.[32]

Not only did Lindsay understand divine timing, he also recognised divine motive. According to *TVH*, Russia was to be God's reckoning rod for a wayward America. *TVH* posited that in many ways America was a favoured nation because of her Christian foundation, a reoccurring theme. Although Russia controlled 53% of the world's population, while only 7% lived in America, America had 93% of all schools, industries, and churches because she was a product of the gospel of Christ.[33] America also had the secrets of atomic power. However, in a prophecy republished from the *Texas Herald*, Jesus asked the question, "Do you think that you are favored people that cannot fall?" America certainly would fall, Jesus answered, if she was not obedient.[34]

In 1948, *TVH* printed a prophecy that foretold the coming of World War III and that it would take place on American soil. E.B. Echols told America, "You

---

[28] Lindsay, "The World in Prophecy," *TVH* (August 1948), 12.

[29] Exactly 1290 days after the Russians entered World War I, they turned their backs on the allies and prepared the way for the Communist Revolution. Gordon Lindsay, "Do World Events Happen by Chance or Are They Timed?" *TVH* (Aug. 1950), 14.

[30] Gordon Lindsay, "November 1948 in Prophecy," *TVH* (November 1948), 15.

[31] Lindsay, "The Year 1952 in Prophecy!" 15.

[32] Lindsay, "This Month in Prophecy," *TVH* (November 1949), 14. Atomic destruction was inevitable. Lindsay equated the atomic bomb, often referred to as the "a-bomb" with "abomination of desolation" of Daniel 9:27. It might just be coincidence that they sound alike, but the evidence seemed to point to this.

[33] Dewey, "Russia's Plans," 8.

[34] "A Prophecy Given in the Spirit to America," *TVH* (September 1954), 8.

must soon drink your cup of judgment: for your gross iniquities and sins are ripe for judgment and punishment."[35] Another prophecy stated that, although God had made Americans victorious in battle, they had forgotten their promises made during the war. Therefore, America would face judgement for her sins of immorality, materialism, and collaborating with the enemy.[36] In 1950, *TVH* printed a vision George Washington had received at Valley Forge concerning the coming destruction of America. In it an angel sprinkled ocean water over Europe, Asia, and Africa. As black clouds arose over them, they become one great land mass from which a "DARK RED LIGHT" shown (*TVH* emphasis). *TVH* identified the light as Communist Russia. Hordes of soldiers moved with the cloud, over the ocean to encase America. Washington could hear the sounds of battle as American cities were destroyed.[37] Later, *TVH* printed Conrad G. Feige's vision of the atomic destruction of America for her sin of materialism. After referencing Washington's vision, Feige recounted seeing explosions of Russian bombs over the Pacific Northwest. Then the Russians re-enacted Pearl Harbor at San Francisco.[38] Regular readers of *TVH* could be assured that Armageddon was coming, it would happen on American soil, and it would be well deserved.

God's plan was clearly laid out in prophecy, and one was negligent not to read and understand the signs. His "sane and coherent" plan would be fulfilled in the present generation. The struggle between heaven and hell was reaching its climax, but the victor had already been declared when God had "pledged to destroy the destroyers," and communism would be defeated.[39] It was clear to *TVH* that God hated communism as much as communists hated God. When Christ returned to the earth, Velmer Gardner reported, it would be to defeat Russia. He wrote,

> … The Lion of the Tribe of Judah will come back to fight Russia's Bear. The Communists will begin to scream with horror, as fire and brimstone falls from Heaven upon them. They will then kneel in the dirt at His feet and cry for the rocks and mountains to fall upon them to shield them from his face.[40]

Several prophecies foretold of a divine defeat of communism and noted a distinctly American victory. In Washington's vision, as America was being destroyed, the angel blew his trumpet, and a great light penetrated the dark cloud of communism. The word UNION was emblazoned over the angel's head, and he carried the American flag and a sword. The angel and "legions of bright spirits" aided America in her fight. The cloud rolled back, the invaders retreated, and the angel told the American people, "While the stars remain that the heavens send down dew upon the earth so shall the republic last." The angel admonished

---

[35] E.B. Echols, "Approximate Horrors of Next World War," *TVH* (June 1949), 14.
[36] Lindsay, "The US in Prophecy," 3.
[37] "The Famous Vision of George Washington," *TVH* (May 1950), 14. The vision is a fictional story published in 1861 by Charles Wesley Alexander.
[38] Conrad G. Feige, "Vision of Atomic Destruction in America," *TVH* (April 1955), 6, 19. America retaliated, and Feige concluded the resulting destruction was a fulfilment of Isaiah 24:19, 20
[39] Charles O. Benham, "World War III in Prophecy," *TVH* (October 1950), 5.
[40] Gardner, "When God Fights Russia," 5.

Washington to "let every child of the Republic learn to live for his God, his land and union."[41]

Dr Charles Benham encouraged his readers that this was a wonderful time for Christians. "The stern reality of Red Communism's attacks upon Christian civilization means that our living Christ and the adversary are now coming to grips. It is the most exciting drama of the ages."[42] It would all be over soon. Russia would be defeated and the righteous protected. Only the Christian could look forward to the days ahead, knowing with certainty that "not a hair of his head will perish."[43] Gardner summed up his thoughts on the world situation by saying, "O what a day of triumph this is going to be for the children of God, but what a day of horror for those who have rejected him ... What crowd are you going to be in on that day?" Gardner asked his readers.[44]

## Role of the Healing Revivals

The rise of communism was also a call for Christians everywhere to spring into action. The people of the world faced two great challenges: communism was on the advance, and Christ's return was imminent. The challenges were interconnected because at any moment communism might overrun a nation, thus limiting the opportunity that the gospel might be heard. Nations must be reached before they succumbed to the communist threat. When Cuba faced the threat of communism, Lindsay wrote that the "one best hope" to keep it from advancing was a healing revival.[45] Bob Finley, who had visited Korea before the war, reported that a great healing revival had occurred. He concluded that the revival had kept South Korea from turning to communism. The communists might have decided it would be nearly impossible to communise Christians, he suggested.[46] Likewise, F. Burke declared that only a mighty revival could combat the flames of Communism.[47]

Evangelising the world had to occur before the atomic destruction the final battle against communism would bring.[48] Lindsay questioned, "We are in a race against time, which will happen first – the coming of unrestricted atomic war

---

41 "The Famous Vision of George Washington," *TVH* (May 1950), 15.

42 Charles O. Benham, "God Answers the Present World Crisis with Miracles of Healing," *TVH*
(April 1949), 4.

43 "The Month in Prophecy," *TVH* (March 1949), 13.

44 Gardner, "When God Fights Russia," 5.

45 Gordon Lindsay, "The 1960s – What May God's People Expect in the Coming Decade?" *TVH* (February 1960), 4.

46 Bob Finley, "What Happened in Korea," *TVH* (Oct. 1950), 5.

47 F. Burke, "Shall Communism Overrun the 'Dark Continent'?" *TVH* (February 1953), 19.

48 Although no one knew when this would occur, the year 1953–54 was put forth as a year of significance and promoted as the "zero" hour. Although Christ did not return in that year, Lindsay still considered the year significant in moving the world toward Armageddon, in which Communists would fight against God. Gordon Lindsay, "The Amazing Year of 1953–54." *TVH* (January 1954), 26–28.

which might depopulate the earth, or a revival which will evangelize the billion souls who have never heard the gospel?"[49] Likewise, A.A. Allen urged his readers, "If we would spare ourselves the agonies of an atomic war, we MUST enter into the plan of God to reach the entire world with the gospel."[50] As far as *TVH* was concerned, the healing revivals were God's plan.

Lindsay told readers that, in the face of advancing communism, the greatest service they could offer their nation and their fellow citizens was to repent and turn to God.[51] They should do it quickly, Jaggers added, because the rumblings of the foundations of civilisation could already be heard, and the "dark waters of judgment long impounded against a crumbling dam lap impatiently, waiting for the moment when they shall break their barriers."[52] Healing revivals were the most promising sign that national repentance might take place in America. The president would never be able to protect America, but individual citizens could through repentance.[53] A few lackadaisical prayers would not suffice, nor would a National Day of Prayer. Anguished cries and "deep searching repentance" were necessary, and the main venue for such activity was the healing revivals.[54]

The distinguishing characteristic of the healing revivals was the restoration of the charismatic.[55] Only supernatural intervention could make a difference in the crisis the world faced; therefore, all Christians needed to cooperate with God's chosen means for revival. This would be the last great move of the Spirit before the final conflict. The church needed immediately to accept these 'supernatural aspects of worship," Lindsay warned.[56] Charles Benham wrote, "Miracles flood the scene in these revivals promoted by God's faith-heroes, because He wants to give the world a demonstration of the final exhibition of Satanic fury meeting head-on with Holy Spirit power."[57] The *TVH* evangelists were leading the way in world evangelism. They hoped to reach a thousand million souls, and a presentation of the supernatural was a very effective means of communication.[58]

Unique to this revival was the Pentecostal message of Spirit baptism. In a letter to *TVH* readers, evangelist O.L. Jaggers urged that the only thing that would save the nation from chaos and atomic war was the Pentecostal message and the spiritual awakening it brings. Healings only came about through the Holy Spirit, which Jaggers specifically tied to Holy Spirit baptism. Jaggers requested support for a radio broadcast so he could share the Pentecostal message globally.[59] Saving the world required repentance, water baptism, and Holy Spirit

---

[49] Gordon Lindsay, "The Prophetic Significance of the Meeting of the Big Four," *TVH* (August 1955), 17.

[50] A.A. Allen, "Allen Revival Hour: 140 Million Spanish Speaking People Must Be Won!" *TVH* (January 1955), 22.

[51] Lindsay, "The Orange Tide," 15.

[52] O.L. Jaggers, "Dear Voice of Healing Readers," *TVH* (April–May 1951), 5.

[53] Lindsay, "The Coming Election," 21.

[54] Lindsay, "The Orange Tide," 15.

[55] Lindsay, "The Orange Tide," 15.

[56] Lindsay, "The Orange Tide," 15.

[57] Benham, "God Answers the Present World Crisis with Miracles of Healing," 4.

[58] Lindsay, "The Prophetic Significance of the Meeting of the Big Four," 17.

[59] O.L. Jaggers, "Dear Voice of Healing Readers," 5.

baptism according to B.E. Echols. The Holy Spirit was the saving, delivering, sanctifying, and keeping power of God. Only those who were filled and gifted by the Holy Spirit would be able to stand in the gap between an angry God and a guilty world.[60] George Dewey concluded that in order to maintain American democracy two things would need to happen before 1952 ended. First, a strong European defence system must be built to protect the continent from communism. Second, America must experience an "old-fashioned, Holy Ghost conscience-plowing revival." To fail on either of these accounts would cause America to succumb to communism.[61]

In light of the world situation, it was difficult to tell how long the revivals would last, and Lindsay suggested that their time might be coming to a close. Therefore, it was important to make good use of whatever time remained.[62] Lindsay admonished those who supported the revival to separate themselves from those who denied it. Readers needed to both pray for the revivals and support them financially.[63]

## Conclusions

It is not my intent to excuse any of the evils perpetrated by the communists or any military during these years. Nor is it my intent to invalidate the suffering of any involved. Neither do I dismiss the miracles that occurred during the revivals, nor do I discount the overwhelming multitude of personal testimonies of healing presented in *TVH*. However, I would like to draw two conclusions based on my research.

First, the editors of *TVH* were responsible for the spread of misleading, untrue, and conspiratorial information. Whether through articles Lindsay or Rusthoi had written, or through the reprinting of other works, much misinformation was spread throughout the Christian world.[64] Through Lindsay's numerical cycles, the suggestion that Hitler might still be alive, the reprint of Washington's vision, and the suggestion that 1953–54 was the "zero" hour, readers were fed a steady stream of unfounded ideas presented as truth. Although Lindsay often stated that *TVH* did not want to be divisive or dogmatic on prophetic issues, he still offered far-reaching suggestions. *TVH* also presented itself as being privy to inside information or knowledge that was not accessible to its readers. The writers suggested they possessed a special understanding of the mind of communist leaders and of God's plans. Lindsay regularly sent an unspoken message to readers that *TVH* knew more than the experts in the field. Now the readers had that information as well.

What made these prophetic pronouncements appear credible to *TVH* readers? One possible cause may have its roots in the theology of faith healing. Those

---

60 Echols, "Approximate Horrors of the Next World War," 15.

61 Dewey, "Russia's Plans," 19.

62 Lindsay, "Has the Hour of Judgment Come?" 3.

63 Lindsay, "The US in Prophecy," 13.

64 In one meeting alone, 1,500 copies of *TVH* were distributed. Rev. G. Greatorex, "Evangelists John and Olive M. Kellner Minister to the Needs of the People in Kitchener, Ontario," *TVH* (January 1955), 12.

who came for healing were continually encouraged to disregard their symptoms. Rather they were to have faith that they were healed. For one example among many in *TVH*, in an article, "Faith Ignores the Symptoms," readers were warned not to look for symptoms after they had prayed for healing. He told the story of a man who had been healed of a hernia that continued to swell. The swelling never went away, according to the author, because the man continued to wear a truss, thus proving he expected the hernia to return. Looking and preparing for signs of returning symptoms is a sure way to cause them to return. Faith requires one to ignore what one sees. "If you look to see IF you are healed, you may easily find that you are not." Do not look to see if symptoms have returned, readers were admonished. Rather, "ignore symptoms and rejoice in faith."[65]

The second source of credibility for these writers was the spiritual authority surrounding them. The periodical overflowed with reports of the supernatural. Prophetic articles were placed alongside page after page of healing testimonials, many attributed to various evangelists. Many evangelists reported receiving their gift of healing following visions of Christ or through the visitation of an angel. Although Lindsay himself was not an evangelist per se, as editor of *TVH*, he was tightly associated with the evangelists and often participated in their meetings. The prophetic and the miraculous were so tightly woven together, that to challenge one implied challenging the other. If the Holy Spirit was working in one area, he must be working in the other, and no Pentecostal wants to quench or blaspheme the Spirit. Additionally, healing and prophecy are often seen as two sides to the same gift of the Holy Spirit. Both are functions of "the Word of the Lord." Therefore, it did not seem usual for a person who functioned as a healer to also function as a prophet.

My second conclusion is that through *TVH* salvation was expanded from freedom from sin and sickness to include freedom from a political ideology. The revivals not only freed people from sin but also freed and protected them the threat of communism by encouraging repentance and sowing the gospel of Christ. Additionally, Christians were instrumental, indeed necessary, in bringing about that freedom. Yet, it was only certain Christians who could help accomplish this goal; those who were Spirit-filled, more specifically, those connected with the healing revivals. Several more conclusions could be drawn, but there is insufficient space to address them.

For the editors of *TVH*, the world of the 1940s and 50s was divided into two distinct realms, democracy in the West and communism in the East, representing spiritual polar opposites and forever irreconcilable. *TVH* occasionally addressed the prophetic significance of communism throughout the 1960s. There was ongoing concern that Communist China might have an atomic bomb or that Cuba might pose a communist threat to America. Yet, these topics became sidelights rather than cover stories. Overall, the communist threat seemed to disappear from

---

[65] Rev. Horton, "Faith Ignores Symptoms," *TVH* (November 1952), 16, on to 18. There are many more examples of this idea scattered throughout *TVH*. For example, in a reprint of Andrew Murray's sermon on divine healing, Murray reminds his listeners that, even if the symptoms get worse, don't pay any attention to them, because they were on a path to healing. "Andrew Murray's Message of Divine Healing," *TVH* (September 1949), 12.

*TVH* in the 1960s. Entire issues never even broached the subject. However, the diabolical nature of communism continued to signal danger in the minds of those involved in *TVH.*

## Discussion Questions

1. Identify two or three ways that the editors of *TVH* built upon the concerns of Americans; concerns that extended beyond the churches, translating those concerns into prophetic statements? How did the editors use these concerns to develop the perception of credibility?
2. What actions did the editors take to shift divine healing from beyond physical healing and healing of community to develop political ideologies?
3. How did the editors shift the concerns to evangelism and care for others, such as for Chinese and Russians, to visualising those not allied with the United States as pawns of evil?
4. What are ways that the contemporary church addresses the relationship of spiritual and political dynamics in light of current geopolitical interests?

## Bibliography

"A Prophecy Given in the Spirit to America." *TVH* (September 1954), 8.

Allen, A.A. "Allen Revival Hour: 140 Million Spanish Speaking People Must Be Won!" *TVH* (January 1955), 21–22.

Benham, C.O. "God Answers the Present World Crisis with Miracles of Healing." *TVH* (April 1949), 4.

Benham, Charles O. "WWIII in Prophecy: Our Book of the Month." *TVH* (October 1950), 4–5.

Burke, F. "Shall Communism Overrun the 'Dark Continent'?" *TVH* (February 1953), 18–20.

Dewey, George Blomgren. "Russia's Plans for 1952." *TVH* (May 1952), 8–9, 19.

Echols, Elder B.E. "Approximate Horrors of Next World War." *TVH* (June 1949), 14–15.

"Events to Come in Russia and Israel." *TVH* (January 1957), 9.

"The Famous Vision of George Washington." *TVH* (May 1950), 14–15.

Feige, Conrad G. "Vision of Atomic Destruction in America." *TVH* (April 1955), 6, 19.

Finley, Bob. "What Happened in Korea Just Before War Broke Out?" *TVH* (October 1950), 5.

Gardner, Velmer. "When God Fights Russia." *TVH* (March 1954), 4–5.

Horton, Reverend. "Faith Ignores Symptoms." *TVH* (November 1952), 16, 18.

Jaggers, O.L. "Dear Voice of Healing Readers." *TVH* (April–May 1951), 5.

Lauster, B. "Tent Filled with 22,000 People, Scene of Great Hicks Campaign in Germany" *TVH* (December 1957), 14.

"Letters to the Editor." *TVH* (September 1951), 16.

Lindsay, Gordon. "November 1948 in Prophecy." *TVH* (November 1948), 14–16.

Lindsay, Gordon. "Editorial … The Year 1949." *TVH* (January 1949), 7.
Lindsay, Gordon. "Do World Events Happen by Chance or Are They Timed?" *TVH* (August 1950), 14–15.
Lindsay, Gordon. "The March of Prophecy as Fulfilled in the Year 1949." *TVH* (February 1950), 14–15.
Lindsay, Gordon. "Has the Hour of World Judgment Come?" *TVH* (September 1950), 2–4.
Lindsay, Gordon. "The Orange Tide of the Red Dragon." *TVH* (January 1951), 14–15.
Lindsay, Gordon. "The US in Prophecy." *TVH* (March 1951), 2–3,13.
Lindsay, Gordon. "The Mysterious Darkening of the Sun and Moon." *TVH* (March 1952), 16–17.
Lindsay, Gordon. "The Coming Election and Prophecy." *TVH* (June 1952), 20–21.
Lindsay, Gordon. "The Year 1952 in Prophecy!" *TVH* (February 1953), 14–15, 22.
Lindsay, Gordon. "The Year 1953–54 in Prophecy!" *TVH* (March 1953), 18–19, 21.
Lindsay, Gordon. "Is it Peace or is it War?" *TVH* (July 1953), 26–27.
Lindsay, Gordon. "Signs of the Ending of the Age." *TVH* (December 1953), 19–21.
Lindsay, Gordon. "The Amazing Year of 1953–54." *TVH* (January 1954), 26–28.
Lindsay, Gordon. "The Prophetic Significance of the Meeting of the Big Four." *TVH* (August 1955), 4, 17.
Lindsay, Gordon. "The March of Prophecy in the Year 1955." *TVH* (March 1956), 5–6, 22.
Lindsay, Gordon. "The Prophetic Significance of the Krushchev Visit." *TVH* (November 1959), 4–5.
Lindsay, Gordon. "The 1960s – What May God's People Expect in the Coming Decade?" *TVH* (February 1960), 4–5, 9, 11.
Lowenberg, P.E. "I Saw Hiroshima." *TVH* (August 1951), 18–19.
"The Month in Prophecy …" *TVH* (April1949), 13.
"The Month in Prophecy …" *TVH* (March 1949), 13.
"This Month in Prophecy …" *TVH* (November 1949), 14–15.
"The Mystery of Hitler's Disappearance." *TVH* (May 1949), 12–13.
"The Rise of the Red Terror." *TVH* (October 1948), 14, 16.
Rusthoi, Howard. "Prophecy Marches On!" *TVH* (June 1952), 22.
Rusthoi, Howard. "Prophecy Marches On!" *TVH* (June 1953), 29.
Rusthoi, Howard. "Prophecy Marches On!" *TVH* (July 1953), 29.
Rusthoi, Howard. "Prophecy Marches On!" *TVH* (February 1954), 22.
Rusthoi, Howard. "Prophecy Marches On!" *TVH* (July 1954) 18.
Rusthoi, Howard. "Prophecy Marches On!" *TVH* (Oct. 1954), 17.

# Chapter 12

# Why Should Pentecostals Engage in Social Ethics? Ecumenical Considerations

Jean-Daniel Plüss

**Abstract**

Compassion ministries, as expressions of social ethics, were at the heart of early Pentecostals. Social ethics worked alongside spiritual practices as integral expressions of Pentecostal faith. This dual dynamic waned during the mid-century but was revived in the latter part of the twentieth century as Pentecostals began interacting with historic churches that emphasised social ethics. Pentecostal ethicists and missionaries called the Pentecostal church to her roots in valuing social ethics alongside spiritual practices. Social ethics was renewed as a spiritual practice. Today Pentecostals are engaging in political debate, prophetically calling for justice and peace, challenging economic exploitation, uplifting marginalised peoples, and caring for creation. Pentecostals are challenged to work with other Christians and all people for the good of humanity and as an expression of God's love for humanity and creation.

## A Turning Point on My Faith Journey

It was in early 1996 when I was invited by Murray W. Dempster, Byron D. Klaus and Douglas Petersen to present a paper at a conference on the globalisation of Pentecostalism in San José, Costa Rica. I came as a West European intellectual, steeped in phenomenology, addressing issues of Pentecostals facing secularisation and musing about globalising trends. I was all for evangelism, but I had no deep convictions about the nature of mission, except that seeking to contact those yet unreached with the gospel was a good thing to do. Similarly, my ethical considerations were mostly focused on the individual, "the human person adequately considered."[1] This all would be challenged when Murray Dempster and his friends invited us to visit the Latin America ChildCare school in Linda Vista, in those days a settlement of the poor southeast of the capital of San José. There I saw what it meant to give hope to children by providing them with one warm meal a day, clothing, education, and spiritual nourishment. On the following Sunday I attended a small Pentecostal congregation where I noticed a girl of about thirteen years of age, dressed in provocative garments. What was she doing in church? Apparently, she found shelter and solace for a

[1] The focus on the human person adequately considered was introduced by Prof. Louis Jennsen of the Catholic University of Leuven, where I did my post-graduate studies.

few hours before she had to return home and most probably return to forced prostitution. It was on that visit that I realised that the gospel had to be incarnate, and that mission was not only to preach but to engage practically for the good of the people.

In the same year my regular engagement in ecumenical conversations with mainline churches began. I was challenged by representatives of non-Pentecostal churches who argued that my kind of church seemed to do little in terms of social engagement and opposition to injustice and violence. This in turn led me to a deeper study of the roots of Pentecostalism as well as current expressions of Pentecostal ministries in the world, especially in the Global South. The argument that I would like to present in this paper is on the necessity of including socio-ethical engagement in ecumenical relations. It is important to share one's faith in Christ, to appreciate each other's traditions and to share spiritual gifts with one another,[2] but if Christians want to be credible witnesses of their faith in the twenty-first century, it is of paramount importance that besides proclaiming the gospel they would seek ways for common action in the name of Christ, the Servant of God.

## Social Ethics: Pentecostal Beginnings

Any student of Pentecostalism will sooner or later realise that already early leaders of the movement were aware of the social implications of their spirituality. This would, for instance, be William J. Seymour and his vision of unity for all of God's children regardless of ethnic background, class, gender, or church affiliation, who clearly included an ethical dimension in his preaching.[3] Frank Bartleman, an early witness of the Azusa Street revival and prolific writer, "spoke publicly on a wide range of social, economic, political and ecclesial issues … Bartleman literally inundated the Pentecostal press with his strident assessments … [H]e [did] critique Federal spending programs, question whether the U.S. had a free press, harangue artificial market supports, plea for food give-away programs, and rebuke certain economic and militaristic practices in his day."[4]

Similarly, the socio-ethical dimension is clearly visible as the Pentecostal movement began on the European continent. Thomas Ball Barratt, an English-born Norwegian Methodist pastor, who shared his experience of being baptised in the Holy Spirit in his church in Kristiania/Oslo on the second day of Christmas in 1906 was a social worker at heart. Lewi Pethrus, who was the first Pentecostal

---

[2] The sharing of spiritual gifts is an important aspect in what is called receptive ecumenism, as we will see further down.

[3] See for instance Dale T. Irvin, "Drawing All Together in One Bond of Love: The Ecumenical Vision of William J. Seymour and the Azusa Street Revival," *Journal of Pentecostal Theology* 3:6 (April 1995), 25–53; and Cecil M. Robeck Jr, "William J. Seymour and the 'Bible Evidence,'" in Gary B. McGee (ed.), *Initial Evidence: Historical and Biblical Perspectives on the Pentecostal Doctrine on Spirit Baptism* (Peabody, MA: Hendrickson,1991), 81.

[4] Cecil M. Robeck Jr, "Pentecostals and Social Ethics," *Pneuma* 9:3 (Fall 1987), 105–106.

leader in Sweden, became nationally known for starting a ministry for the poor in his church. Later he initiated a newspaper, a radio station, a school, and a political party.[5]

One could present countless examples of how early Pentecostal missionaries engaged in social activity. Their ethical engagement was congruous with their experience of being baptised in the Holy Spirit, which is the Spirit of Jesus Christ incarnate. Preaching the good news naturally included praying for the sick. One example would be the compassion ministries of Lillian Trasher who founded the first orphanage in Egypt and became known as the "Nile Mother." Later she also helped to set up a home for widows and a place for the blind. Interesting for our ecumenical reflection is that her work, although basically funded by the Assemblies of God, became a cause that merited the support of Presbyterian churches and other Christian, humanitarian, and government organisations.[6] Today, the Episcopal Church remembers her example of Christian social engagement in its calendar of saints on 19 December each year.[7]

## Social Ethics: An Ecumenical Necessity

In order to argue my point, it will be necessary to give a short introduction to the ecumenical vision and its developments. What we will see is that there has been a shift from ecumenical positions to ecumenical relations, and that is where social engagement comes in.

The ecumenical movement, as it developed in the twentieth century, focused primarily on finding, wherever possible, agreement in doctrine and ecclesial cooperation. An example of this process has been the formation of United or Uniting Churches, where different church traditions like Reformed, Methodist, Presbyterian and other bodies found a way of being church together.[8] Another example of classical ecumenism has been the publication of common documents like the *Joint Declaration on the Doctrine of Justification* between the Lutheran World Federation and the Pontifical Council for the Promotion of Christian

---

[5] Joel Halldorf, "Lewi Pethrus and the Creation of a Christian Counterculture," *Pneuma* 32:3 (2010), 354–68. David Bundy, "Social Ethics in the Church of the Poor: The Cases of T.B. Barratt and Lewi Pethrus" (paper presented at the 10th conference of the European Pentecostal Charismatic Research Association in Leuven, Belgium), accessed 26 November 2019, www.ipcrach.2001-leueven.html.

[6] For instance, for information on the Lillian Trasher Orphanage as well as a listing of contributing partners, "Lillian Trasher Orphanage," Hands along the Nile Development Services, https://www.handsalongthenile.org/causes/lillian-trasher-orphanage-assiut/; and "Contributing Partners," Hands along the Nile Development Services, accessed 26 November 2019, https://www.handsalongthenile.org/about/contributing-partners/.

[7] "December 19: Lillian Trasher, Missionary in Egypt, 1961," *Standing Committee on Liturgy and Music of the Episcopal Church* (19 December 2010), https://standingcommissiononliturgyandmusic.org/2010/12/19/december-19-lillian-trasher-missionary-in-egypt-1961/.

[8] Examples are the Churches of North and South India or the Uniting Church in Australia.

Unity or the Faith and Order Document on *Baptism, Eucharist and Ministry* by the World Council of Churches.[9]

Pentecostals have, since the early 1970s, engaged in bilateral dialogues aimed at finding greater understanding between different church traditions. A good number of documents have been published since; especially those generated by the Roman Catholic–Pentecostal dialogue have received attention.[10] The first common document of the Reformed–Pentecostal dialogue illustrates the method and style of the classical ecumenical documents. The first round of this dialogue took place from 1996 to 2000. The ensuing document was entitled *Word and Spirit, Church and World: The Final Report of the International Dialogue Between Representatives of the World Alliance of Reformed Churches and Some Classical Pentecostal Churches and Leaders 1996–2000*.[11] This title illustrates the tensions that were felt at the time. What is of the essence, the Spirit or the Word? Where is the focus of attention, the church or the world? Although the two teams professed much in common, statements like "Reformed Christians affirm …" and "Pentecostals focus more on …" pointed to various differences in conviction and emphasis. To name differences is, in and of itself, not wrong, but one is left with the impression that this document was basically an overview of the state of affairs. This was an ecumenical statement on positions. We can put the issue at stake differently. One could ask, where does the "ecumenical" rubber hit the road? Would it be on variant understandings about baptism and the precise notion of God's grace or the nature of the church?

There are, however, a few paragraphs that point in another direction. Under the titles "Service to the Word" and "Spirit, Kingdom, World," we read:

> 75. The grace of the Holy Spirit, given to us by Jesus Christ through the proclamation of the reign of God, prompts us to serve and participate in the mission of God in the world. This mission includes both proclamation and social engagement, which cannot be separated. Mission is concerned with the righteousness of our horizontal relationship with our neighbors and nature, as well as the vertical relationship with God.
>
> 76. We recognize that the understanding of mission varies with the social location of the given situation. The Holy Spirit empowers and leads us to work for the structural transformation of society as well as the individual transformation of ourselves without committing the church to a specific political ideology …

---

[9] The Joint Declaration on the Doctrine of Justification was originally signed in 1999. This document has in the meantime been received by the World Methodist Council (2006), the Anglican Consultative Council (2016), and the World Communion of Reformed Churches (2017). The Faith and Order paper no. 111 on Baptism, Eucharist and Ministry is considered to be a major ecumenical achievement. To my knowledge there is no aspect of this document that has resulted due to Pentecostal influence.

[10] See for instance, *The Holy See*, accessed 26 November 2019, Dialogue Documents (christianunity.va) accessed 13 January 2023.

[11] The text of this report and various responses, both Reformed and Pentecostal, can be found in, "Word and Spirit, Church and World: The Final Report of the International Dialogue Between Representatives of the World Alliance of Reformed Churches and Some Classical Pentecostal Churches and Leaders 1996–2000," *Pneuma* 23:1 (Spring 2001), 9–43.

> 94. Pentecostals differ on how they view the role of the Holy Spirit in sustaining, reforming, or transforming human society. Some Pentecostals interpret reality dualistically … Others identify the role of the Spirit as one who invites Christians to engage in the reforming and transforming of society.[12]

At the time Reformed members of the dialogue were pushing for the inclusion of social engagement as part of the proclamation of the reign of God whereas some Pentecostals felt that, although socio-ethical responsibility was certainly part of Christian discipleship, the emphasis on the transformation of human society was shifting the focus away from proclaiming the gospel for the salvation and reconciliation with God. The word "social gospel" still conjured uncomfortable notions of liberal Christianity (whatever that meant). About twenty years have passed since that document was crafted and I believe that many more Pentecostals see a necessity of including ethical, social, and ecological concerns in the conversations on what the proclamation of the gospel is all about. That not because of any theological watering down of the salvific essence of the faith, but rather because Pentecostals and other Christians can agree that the Kingdom of God is to be lived as far as possible here on earth and not only to be expected in a life to come. Issues of peace and justice matter if our faith is to be expressed in credible ways.

I see three reasons why Pentecostals are now engaging more clearly in social justice issues. First, there is a fuller appreciation of how God's reign is described and fought for in both the Old and New Testament. Second, Pentecostals in the Global South are facing more issues of injustice, violence, and destruction than their sisters and brothers in the North. It matters to them personally. And third, the secularisation of many traditionally Christian nations in the North forces active believers to answer fundamental issues of humanity if they want to be credible witnesses of Jesus in the public square, rather than withdrawing into a self-centred community with a more or less closed system of belief. Let us look at these three points more closely.

Murray Dempster wrote an important article in 1986 with regard to a new appreciation of the Scriptures in matters of social justice.[13] He argued that the Old Testament advocates five basic theocentric features of social ethics and that these build the principal foundation for the life of the people of Israel.[14] Dempster then goes on, with the help of Roger Stronstad's *The Charismatic Theology of St Luke*,[15] to say that this Jewish heritage was lived out in the public ministry of Jesus (Luke 4:16-21) and was commissioned on Pentecost by the power of the Holy Spirit to the new church. Dempster then concludes by saying that the

---

[12] "Word and Spirit, Church and World: The Final Report," *Pneuma*, 23:1 (Spring 2001), 31, 36.

[13] Murray W. Dempster, "Pentecostal Social Concern and the Biblical Mandate of Social Justice," *Pneuma* 9:2 (Fall 1987), 129–153.

[14] These are: the fact that humans are created in the image of God, that Israel is a covenant people, that there was a prophetic tradition of social criticism, and that the religious books suggested Jubilee teachings.

[15] Roger Stronstad, *The Charismatic Theology of St Luke* (Peabody, MA: Hendrickson, 1984).

experience of Spirit baptism holds therefore a great promise for the church's mission and ministry.[16]

The second reason why Pentecostals are now engaging more in social justice issues is based on the fact that matters of sexual abuse, domestic violence, corruption, supporting people at the margins, etcetera are more immediate concerns in the Global South than in the relatively affluent countries of the North. David and Beth Grant, for instance, created some twenty years ago *Project Rescue* in India to give hope to a "young generation ensnared by drugs, gangs, and prostitution."[17] Another example is the *Shalom Project* championed by Janice and Rick Waldrop. They work in Latin America with educational institutions in order to promote social transformation through advocacy, awareness-raising and peaceful direct action.[18] The Waldrops have also been involved in helping refugees. The reason these two examples are mentioned is that such projects are of general interest and are ecumenically relevant. Especially, once a project reaches a certain size, it would be a luxury to try to manage such involvement for the common good by one church alone, particularly as common proclamation and action are a more powerful witness of the churches to their faith in Christ.

A third reason why Pentecostals engage more in socio-ethical activities is the fact that many countries in the North experience a secularisation at the expense of past common values that were basically expressions of Christian convictions. Secular humanism is an attractive alternative in these post-Christian societies. Individualism exacerbates the divide. Why be a Christian if humanist personal values are making people just as happy? Furthermore, why listen to Christian voices if they are apparently hopelessly divided among themselves? In my opinion, the only option for Christians is to proclaim their faith in Christ together and to demonstrate it by common actions of compassion and justice relevant to the society they live in. To give a recent example, new ways towards the common good were explored by different churches in Zurich and other cities in Switzerland. Under the name "Love in Action" people from Catholic, Reformed, Evangelical, and Pentecostal churches decided to be visible in their city by engaging in a number of activities that benefitted others without considering any "return on investment," i.e. ecclesial benefit.[19]

In all of this, however, Pentecostals will ask about the spiritual dimension of such activities. They would agree that the time of separating evangelism and social concern as an either/or issue has passed. They would to a large extent embrace a both/and approach. Nevertheless, they would raise the legitimate

---

[16] Dempster, "Pentecostal Social Concern," 149.

[17] David and Beth Grant, for instance, created some twenty years ago Project Rescue in India to be on a mission to "rescue and restore victims of sexual exploitation through the love and power of God." Project Rescue, accessed 28 November 2019, https://www.projectrescue.com/our-story.

[18] The Shalom Project, accessed 28 November 2019, https://theshalomprojectinternational.org/mission-and-vision/.

[19] The programme of "Love in Action" is created by the grass roots and facilitated by the churches. See Love in Action, accessed 29 November 2019, https://loveinaction.today/.

concern that engagement for education, healthcare, justice and peace, or ecology can easily be detached from values that are more important to them; namely, the call to be reconciled to God. It is precisely at this juncture that the social engagement of Pentecostals is of ecumenical significance. Let me therefore turn your attention to present examples where Pentecostals who are involved in ecumenical activities face interesting challenges with regard to evangelism and social concern.

## Examples of Ecumenical Relevance

The following examples will show that interaction between different churches with regard to socio-ethical involvement can not only lead to a stronger witness; it may also bring about synergies previously not envisaged.

### *Healing in Madagascar*

The official international dialogue between the Lutheran World Federation and classical Pentecostals began in 2016 under the motto of Luke 4:18-19,

> The Spirit of the Lord is upon me, because he has anointed me to bring good news to the poor. He has sent me to proclaim release to the captives and recovery of sight to the blind, to let the oppressed go free, to proclaim the year of the Lord's favor.

The idea was that the two teams would explain to each other their sense of calling and mission. The group began to speak about their sense of identity (he has sent me to proclaim). In 2017 the focus was on proclamation (he has anointed me to bring the good news). In 2018 the dialogue met in Chile to gain an appreciation of how the two church traditions engage with the poor (to bring the good news to the poor). And in 2019 they met in Madagascar to learn more about healing and deliverance (to proclaim release to the captives and recovery of sight to the blind, to let the oppressed go free).

The reason for meeting in Madagascar was that the Malagasy Lutheran Church has been part of a lasting revival which emphasises evangelism, prayer for healing, casting out of demons and prophetic ministry. This movement is called Fifohazana, which simply means revival. It began in 1894, where a retrograde indigenous Lutheran evangelist was miraculously healed of a severe illness. Dada Rainisoalambo had been trained by Norwegian Lutherans. He was a gifted communicator. But he lapsed back to his indigenous religion and made his living as a traditional medicine man. When he got very ill, the story goes, he had a vision of Christ and remembered what he had been taught. He prayed to Jesus that his leprosy might be healed. The next morning, after having been restored, Rainisoalambo began to proclaim the gospel again and a revival began soon after.

There are several reasons why this Fifohazana movement is noteworthy. First, it had from the very beginning a strong indigenous expression.[20] Second, it has

[20] The shepherds of this movement (charismatically gifted lay men and women who minister as evangelists and counsellors) wear long white robes to this day as an expression of humility and Malagasy identity, cf. Cynthia Holder Rich, *The Fifohazana:*

had an influence across the different churches in Madagascar. Today, about 75% of the Malagasy Lutheran Church count themselves as being part of this revival movement. It has also influenced the union of Reformed churches known as Church of Jesus Christ in Madagascar. The Catholic Church and the Anglican Communion do also have relations with this revival. In other words, because of its strong Malagasy identity this movement was able to be intentionally ecumenical long before the ecumenical movement developed there in the second half of the twentiethcentury. Third, the past four leaders of the Fifohazana were two men and two women. It is an egalitarian movement. Like in early Pentecostalism, if the Holy Spirit calls someone to be a prophet or apostle, the gender is secondary to the vocation and the confirmation of that person's ministry by the fruit that becomes evident. Fourth, although Rainisoalambo preached repentance to Christ, prayed for healing, and delivered people from occult oppression, he valued at the same time hygiene, orderliness, economic sharing, and service to the poor and sick. When the Lutheran–Pentecostal dialogue group visited one of the Fifohazana stations, they participated in a worship service that included preaching, prayers for healing, and the casting out of demons. In the same compound there were teaching facilities and a medical station for people suffering from mental illness. This combination of a spiritual and a practical approach, emphasising divine healing and receiving professional medical help, is an integrative and viable approach that has convinced many.[21] A good number of Pentecostals still separate the spiritual and secular approaches. But I believe that social ethicists promoted by people like Murray Dempster, Byron Klaus, Douglas Petersen, Rick Waldrop, and others have contributed to a more holistic understanding of service to one's neighbour. The charismatic and social ministry of the Fifohazana movement is an example that resonates well with Pentecostals.

The 2019 ecumenical encounter between Pentecostals and the Malagasy Lutheran Church has resulted in another discovery. The Lutherans consider the Fifohazana movement as part of their identity. So far, they have had little contact with classical Pentecostals even though there are so many similarities in spiritual praxis. The reason may lie in a cautious position towards missionaries from former colonial powers. Nevertheless, the president of the Malagasy Lutheran Church, Rev. Dr David Rakotonirina, Rev. Dr Joseph Randrianasolo, professor at the Lutheran Graduate School of Theology in Fianarantsoa, Madagascar, and Rev. Dr Noel Rabemanantsoa, who attended the dialogue talks, were unanimous in their opinion that conversations with Pentecostals should be pursued. On the Pentecostal side it became clear that a bit of history re-writing was necessary. In

*Madagascar's Indigenous Christian Movement* (Amherst, NY, Cambria Press, 2008), 20.

[21] The Fifohazana leader Ms Nenilava had a conversation with the King of Norway in 1973 remarking, "I preach the gospel, I attend to the mentally insane, I educate young delinquents, I raise infants and take care of the old" (Je prêche l'évangile, soigne les aliénés mentaux, éduque les jeunes délinquants, élève les nourrissons et les vieillards). Quoted by Sébastien Fath, "Nenilava, Prophétesse de la Délivrance," *Regards Protestants* (15 July 2018), https://regardsprotestants.com/francophonie/nenilava-prophetesse-de-la-delivrance/ (accessed 1 December 2019).

the 15 November 1930 issue of *The Pentecostal Evangel*, an article with the title "How Pentecost Came to Madagascar"[22] told the story of a woman evangelist by the name of Ravelonjanahary. She began her evangelistic ministry in 1910 that was accompanied by many miraculous events. That in fact was the second leader of the Fifohazana revival that began as mentioned in 1894. What we have here is yet another Pentecostal-like revival preceding the Pentecostal events of Topeka, Kansas, in 1900, and the Azusa Street revival in Los Angeles that began in 1906.[23]

### *Empowerment in Cambodia*

After the civil war had ravaged Cambodia (1968–1975), the country was rife with domestic and community violence. Human trafficking, slavery, and abuse have been affecting women and children especially. Pierre Tami, who had been sent by the Swiss Pentecostal Mission, realised that the young women in the brothels of Phnom Penh did not want to go back home because usually the situation was worse for them there. Believing in a God of compassion, as illustrated by the story of Hagar, the Egyptian domestic worker that was sent away by Abraham, he realised that more needed to be done than preaching the gospel in order to give these people a chance to find healing, be restored, and regain human dignity. He set up rescue shelters and was able to find plots of land where the unwed mothers could live with their children and work the land to

---

[22] "How Pentecost Came to Madagascar," *Pentecostal Evangel* (15 November 1930), 1. Here the story is told of woman called Ravelo (her full name was Ravelonjanahary) who began a ministry of evangelism, healing, and exorcism after she personally was raised from the dead, and the healing ministry of a man called Rajaofera who became a well-known preacher in the 1930s. The sisters Watkins (?) who reported these events simply shared how Pentecost came to Madagascar. The background story, however, is that Rajaofera was groomed by the Norwegian Missionary society and that he had a strong impact on the Protestant churches of that country. Flower, Pentecostal Heritage Center, https://ifphc.wordpress.com/2019/11/15/pentecost-came-to-madagascar-in-1910-in-a-revival-of-signs-and-wonders/?fbclid=IwAR2YeY_nCBntL2Yc-r2RYqegALPCI-XJ0jpq01Oc-AlQeSiJ3W75YfF2pZk (accessed 28 November 2019). The *Pentecostal Evangel* carries an article entitled "Rajaofera, the Miracle Worker of Madagascar," wherein J.H. Egeberg tells the story somewhat differently and with more detail; namely that Ms Ravelonjanahary lay dying and miraculously learned to read the Bible. And that Rajaofera was the son of a native Lutheran pastor and had a great influence on the people trained at the Lutheran Mission College. J.H. Egeber, "Rajaofera, the Miracle Worker of Madagascar," *Pentecostal Evangel* (7 December 1940), 8. Flower Pentecostal Heritage Center, https://archives.ifphc.org/pdf/PentecostalEvangel/1940-1949/1940/1940_12_07.pdf#Page8 (accessed 28 November 2019). The affinity between Pentecostal spirituality and the Fifohazana movement seems to continue. In 1954, the Swiss Pentecostal magazine *Die Verheissung des Vaters* (The Promise of the Father) reported of an Indigenous woman called Nenilava who ministered powerfully with the gifts of the Holy Spirit. Nenilava is the name of the third leader of that Malagasy revival! "Zwei Bemerkenswerte Flugzeug-Geschichten," *Die Verheissung des Vaters* 4 (1954), 8.

[23] Other examples being the nineteenth-century folk revivals in Scandinavia, Pandita Ramabai's Mukti Mission in India in 1905, the Hebden Mission in Toronto 1906–1910, and the indigenous Pentecostal revival among the Methodists in Chile in 1909.

produce more than they needed for subsistence. He set up schools, and later care programmes and training centres so that the children would be able to have a realistic chance in life. Today Hagar International is a humanitarian work that is active in Cambodia, Afghanistan, Vietnam, and other countries.[24] It is supported by governments, international agencies like the United Nations, the World Bank, and the World Economic Forum, and is funded by various religious organisations.

Pierre Tami also began a project that is called Shift360.[25] He realised that, in order to help people in the long run, a paradigm shift is necessary that needs to take place in society by working towards a common good through job creation and skills empowerment to improve the livelihood and dignity of vulnerable people in the Greater Mekong Subregion. Job creation in the tourism sector, for instance, by the establishment of the Academy of Culinary Arts Cambodia is an initiative that empowers young people to get stable employment. In the past the Swiss Pentecostal Mission[26] sent out missionaries that in one way or another were involved in church planting. With Pierre Tami the missions board went another way. Their contribution is simply that they provide for his basic salary with no strings attached. They are convinced that Tami's projects in Asia are one way of working towards the Kingdom of God being manifest in this world. They are focusing on the flourishing of human lives, of people that have been created in the image of God. In fact, the work we have described here goes beyond a Christian socio-ethical engagement with an ecumenical relevance; it is promoting the common good and involves all people of good will. It is therefore also of interreligious significance.

## Conclusion

We have seen that compassion was already at the heart of early Pentecostals. Although there was a strong emphasis on preaching the gospel so that "souls could be saved," it was not their only motivation because they cared and believed in a merciful God. By running orphanages, by nursing the ill, providing for education etc. there was usually an emphasis on the person, but not exclusively so. It was also a declaration of hope against evil structures in society. When Pentecostals began to pay attention to socio-ethical issues the focus was widened to address systemic evil. Today we find Pentecostals publicly engaging in political debate, prophetically calling for justice and peace, challenging economic exploitation, taking the side of marginalised people, and urging for action with regard to creation care. More than ever before, Pentecostals are challenged to work together with other Christians and all people of good will to

[24] "Hagar: The Whole Journey," Hagar International, accessed 2 December 2019, https://hagarinternational.org/.

[25] "Who We Are," Shift360, accessed 2 December 2019, https://shift360.ch/about-shift360/.

[26] Now also known as the Pentecostal Assemblies of Switzerland. For more about the work of Pierre and Simonetta Tami, see Schweizerische Pfinstmission, www.pfingstmission.ch/was-wir-tun/ (click on "Greater Mekong Subregion"), accessed 13 January 2023.

address such issues. If they do not, then they would be living under the illusion that they can handle the challenges of life on their own. As people who believe in the work of the Holy Spirit, they would commit the error of believing that God is only at work in their circles. And finally, and perhaps most profoundly, they will not be credible witnesses of Christ who called the church to unity so that the world may believe.

## Discussion Questions

1. Identify three or four specific expressions of social engagement as identified by Plüss within early Pentecostalism. How was compassion and social uplift congruous with Pentecostal faith as it was identified and practised within early Pentecostalism?
2. Plüss contends for three reasons that Pentecostals are now engaging more clearly in social justice issues. Explain one or more of those reasons.
3. Name two or three specific expressions of ecumenical dialogue that were significant to Pentecostals embracing social ethics anew.
4. Which of the examples of social uplift provided in the latter half of Plüss's essay do you find most compelling?

## Bibliography

Bradelma, "December 19: Lillian Trasher, Missionary in Egypt, 1961." Standing Committee on Liturgy and Music of the Episcopal Church. 19 December 2010. https://standingcommissiononliturgyandmusic.org/2010/12/19/december-19-lillian-trasher-missionary-in-egypt-1961/ (accessed 28 November 2019).

Bundy, David. "Social Ethics in the Church of the Poor: The Cases of T.B. Barratt and Lewi Pethrus." In *Journal of the European Pentecostal Theological Association* 22:1 (2002), 30–44. https://www.tandfonline.com/doi/abs/10.1179/jep.2002.22.1.003; Paper presented at the 10th conference of the European Pentecostal Charismatic Research Association, Leuven, Belgium, 17–21 July 2001. http://www.epcra.ch/2001-leuven (accessed 13 Jan 2023). https://www.handsalongthenile.org/about/contributing-partners/.

Dempster, Murray W. "Pentecostal Social Concern and the Biblical Mandate of Social Justice." *Pneuma* 9:2 (Fall 1987), 129–53.

Egeber, J.H. "Rajaofera, the Miracle Worker of Madagascar." *The Pentecostal Evangel* (7 December 1940), 8. Flower Pentecostal Heritage Center, https://archives.ifphc.org/pdf/PentecostalEvangel/1940-1949/1940/1940_12_07.pdf#Page8 (accessed 28 November 2019).

Fath, Sébastien. "Nenilava, Prophétesse de la Délivrance." *Regards Protestants* (15 July 2018). https://regardsprotestants.com/francophonie/nenilava-prophetesse-de-la-delivrance/ (accessed 1 December 2019).

Hagar International. "Hagar: The Whole Journey." Accessed 2 December 2019. https://hagarinternational.org/

Halldorf, Joel. "Lewi Pethrus and the Creation of a Christian Counterculture," *Pneuma* 32:3 (2010), 354–68.

Hands Along the Nile Development Services. "Contributing Partners." https://www.handsalongthenile.org/about/contributing-partners/ (accessed 26 November 2019).

Hands Along the Nile Development Services. "Lillian Trasher Orphanage." Accessed 26 November 2019. https://www.handsalongthenile.org/causes/lillian-trasher-orphanage-assiut/.

The Holy See. Accessed 26 November 2019. Dialogue Documents christianunity.va (accessed 13 January 2023).

Rodgers, Darrin J. "How Pentecost Came to Madagascar." *The Pentecostal Evangel* (15 November 1930), 1. Flower Pentecostal Heritage Center, https://ifphc.wordpress.com/2019/11/15/pentecost-came-to-madagascar-in-1910-in-a-revival-of-signs-and-wonders/?fbclid=IwAR2YeY_nCBntL2Yc-r2RYqegALPCI-XJ0jpq01Oc-AlQeSiJ3W75YfF2pZk (accessed 28 November 2019).

Irvin, Dale T. "'Drawing all Together in One Bond of Love': The Ecumenical Vision of William J. Seymour and the Azusa Street Revival." *Journal of Pentecostal Theology* 3:6 (April 1995), 25–53.

Love in Action. Accessed 29 November 2019. https://loveinaction.today/.

Project Rescue. https://projectrescue.com/our-work (accessed 28 November 2019).

Rich, Cynthia Holder. *The Fifohazana: Madagascar's Indigenous Christian Movement*. Amherst, NY: Cambria Press, 2008.

Robeck, Cecil M. Jr. "Pentecostals and Social Ethics." *Pneuma* 9:3 (Fall 1987), 105–106.

Robeck, Cecil M. Jr. "William J. Seymour and the 'Bible Evidence.'" In *Initial Evidence: Historical and Biblical Perspectives on the Pentecostal Doctrine on Spirit Baptism*. Ed. Gary B. McGee. Peabody, MA: Hendrickson,1991, 72–95.

Schweizerische Pfinstmission. www.pfingstmission.ch/was-wir-tun/ (accessed 2 December 2019).

"Spirit, Church and World: The Final Report of the International Dialogue between Representatives of the World Alliance of Reformed Churches and Some Classical Pentecostal Churches and Leaders 1996–2000." *Pneuma* 23:1 (Spring 2001), 9–43.

Shalom Project. Accessed 28 November 2019. https://theshalomprojectinternational.org/mission-and-vision/.

Shift360. "Who We Are." Accessed 2 December 2019. https://shift360.ch/about-shift360/.

Stronstad, Roger. *The Charismatic Theology of St Luke*. Peabody, MA: Hendrickson, 1984.

Von Wirken des Geistes Gottes in aller Welt," *Die Verheissung des Vaters*, 4 (1954): 6. Report taken from *Pentecost* 27 (1954), edited by Donald Gee.

# Chapter 13

# Manifest Lament: Pentecostals, Lukan Hospitality, and Indigenous Decolonisation

Martin W. Mittelstadt


## Abstract

The multidisciplinary writings of Elaine Enns and Ched Myers interrogate Canadian colonisation of Indigenised communities. In this essay Mittelstadt draws heavily on Enns' assessment of Mennonite settlement and then reflects on Pentecostal participation and responsibility. This examination of Pentecostal praxis includes a postcolonial reading of Lukan hospitality. The result is a call for Pentecostals to enlarge their vision of healing toward Indigenous neighbours.


## Introduction

2020 was a year like no other. Since my move to the United States in 2000, I have long pontificated against the mythic "American Dream." I teach relentlessly the need for Pentecostals to address consumerism, colonialism, nationalism, militarism, and racism. To do so, I often hook my students through interrogation of Canada, a nation more complex than its international perception as a rich mosaic of hospitality. In 2020, the COVID-19 pandemic slowed everyone. The murder of George Floyd, the 2020 election, and the 6 January 2021 insurrection launched a new season for reflection and research. I began serious study of critical race theory to better understand my Canadian story. In my quest to further understand the tension between racism and being racialised, I turned specifically to the plight of the Indigenous. I stumbled on what would become a life-changing read by Mennonite scholar Elaine Enns and her husband Ched Myers. Amid a voracious spring and summer of reading on Indigenous life in Canada, the horrific news of unmarked grave sites at residential schools went national and international.[1] I knew it was time to write my reflections, and the invitation to participate in this *festschrift* in honour of fellow Canadian Murray Dempster provides a perfect moment. I first encountered Murray through his articles on social justice and Pentecostalism. We met at the Society for Pentecostal Studies, where he became a hero and a mentor from afar.

---

[1] The first of many recent revelations came out of Kamloops, BC, and broke in late May (see Courtney Dickson and Bridgette Watson, "Remains of 215 Children Found Buried at Former BC Residential School, First Nation Says," CBC News (27 May 2021), https://www.cbc.ca/news/canada/british-columbia/tk-eml%C3%BAps-te-secw%C3%A9pemc-215-children-former-kamloops-indian-residential-school-1.6043778 (accessed 22 July 2021).

In this essay, I revisit my Canadian Pentecostal story with my attention fixed solely on my Indigenous neighbours. First, I centre my new discoveries upon the multidisciplinary work of Enns and Myers. In their *Healing Haunted Histories*, Enns locates her family (hi)story within the larger narrative of Mennonite migration and settlement in Canada on land made available through displacement of Indigenous peoples. Myers, an American New Testament scholar, interrogates European migration to North America with a postcolonial reading of Luke 9:1-6 and 10:1-12.[2] Together, their stories inspire another turn in my journey as a Lukan scholar in the Mennocostal tradition.[3] Ahead of my re-entry into Canadian and Pentecostal history, I draw heavily on various Mennonite attempts to revisit their efforts to address complicity. Upon doing so, I turn in the second half of this essay to tentative possibilities for further Pentecostal reflection and action. I must state up front that this is by no means a finished project, but an unfolding life story. Since I cannot make this journey alone, I invite my fellow Pentecostals to walk with me.[4]

## Living Haunted Lives: Concerning Peace, Dust, Decolonisation, and Hospitality

Elaine Enns rehearses a common Mennonite story. Her grandparents on both sides fled Ukraine to "settle" on the Canadian prairies. With their perspective of God's guidance and provision, the Mennonites "purchased" land made "available" by the Canadian government. However, as these Mennonites celebrated their rescue from Eastern Europe, they seemed oblivious to or unconcerned over the violent displacement of Indigenous peoples ahead of their arrival. Enns laments the untold impact of Mennonite (and other European) settlers. Successful settlement, better stated as colonisation, entailed a manifold assault on Indigenous peoples. After the rapid and mass slaughter of the bison starved Indigenous people off their lands, Mennonites and others were recruited to domesticate the prairies through an unrelenting push for a new agrarian economy. The Canadian government forced displaced Indigenous peoples onto reservations and targeted their children for aggressive assimilation through residential schools. Enns captures what ought to be the Mennonite tension. On one hand, the Mennonite story is one of persistent trauma, the saga of ongoing

[2] Elaine Enns and Ched Myers, *Healing Haunted Histories: A Settler Discipleship of Decolonization* (Eugene, OR: Cascade Books, 2021).

[3] See my "Spirit and Peace in Luke-Acts: Possibilities for Pentecostal/Anabaptist Dialogue," *Didaskalia* 20 (Fall 2009), 17–41; "My Life as a Mennocostal," in Paul Alexander (ed.), *Pentecostals and Nonviolence: Reclaiming a Heritage* (Eugene: Wipf & Stock, 2012), 316–334; "Reading Luke-Acts in the Mennocostal Tradition: Pentecostals, Mennonites, and Prophethood," in Martin Mittelstadt and Brian Pipkin (eds), *Our Lives as Mennocostals* (Eugene, OR.: Pickwick, 2019), 14–28.

[4] Throughout this chapter, I refer to "Pentecostal" through the lens of my Anglo-Canadian spiritualities and settler discipleship; I am well aware of the multiethnic and diverse expressions of Pentecostalism in Canada, not least among First Nations. I employ the term "Indigenous" to identify the diverse expressions of "First Nations," those who lived in the Americas ahead of European advancement.

migration because of religious persecution. On the other hand, these same Mennonites settled "next door" to their Indigenous neighbours too often with little communication and with unawareness of the damage they had caused.

Enns uses her story to implore Mennonites (and other settler communities) to rethink "settler discipleship" by way of three extended storylines. First, *landlines* must describe more than the geographic migration from lands left behind to arrival on a new homeland. Landlines must include the complicated motives for migration, such as voluntary or forced, individual or communal, and during peace or war. Such stories must also address similar questions concerning the fate of peoples on the land where the migrants have settled. Second, *bloodlines* cannot refer only to biological ancestry, but a more convoluted narrative. Bloodlines encompass not simply family trees, but the problematic trauma fuelled by the respective departure and resettlement of Mennonites and Indigenous communities. Bloodlines must consider immediate and extended racial, ethnic, gender, and political backstories. Mennonite migration from the "old country" must be read not only through privilege, but as trauma, and the fresh start for Mennonites must take into account the traumatic impact dealt upon Indigenous communities. Finally, *songlines*, not least for Christians, must recount stories of accommodation and resistance that tell of celebration, recovery, rescue, and healing. In haunting fashion, Enns interrogates Mennonites who settle only for testimonies of their rescue. Instead, she calls her fellow Mennonites to listen to the plight of their Indigenous neighbours who, though "migrating" only miles from their previous homeland, share similar songlines of persistent suffering.

In a lengthy theological excursus, Myers weaves Mennonite arrival to Canada alongside centuries of Christian mission to Indigenous people. In the (in)famous words of Desmond Tutu: "When the Missionaries arrived, we natives had the land, and they had the Bible. They taught us how to pray with our eyes closed. When we opened them, they had the land, and we had the Bible."[5] These words launch Myers' postcolonial reading of Luke 9 and 10. Myers imagines a very different witness if Christians had followed Jesus' commission to announce, "peace to this house!" (Luke 10:5). Instead, Christians too often fused the cross and the sword, conversion and conquest, evangelisation and subjugation, and displacement with settlement. To the detriment of Indigenous peoples, European missionaries bought into the "Doctrine of Discovery," the idea that the lands encountered by explorers were uninhabited and simply "there for the taking."[6] The Lukan Jesus indicates that, where missionaries are welcomed, they are to remain as guests until they "leave from that place" (Luke 9:4). According to Myers, if not welcomed, missionaries "don't move around looking for a better

---

[5] Enns and Myers, *Healing Haunted Histories*, 132.

[6] See Mitzi Smith's "Resisting the Great Co-mission," a chilling poem and commentary on the collusion of the gospel and empire, in Steve Heinrichs (ed.), *Unsettling the Word: Biblical Experiments in Decolonization* (Winnipeg, MB: CommonWord, 2018), 184–90; Mark Charles and Soong-Chan Rah, *Unsettling Truths: The Ongoing, Dehumanizing Legacy of the Doctrine of Discovery* (Downers Grove, IL: Intervarsity Press, 2019); and George E. Tinker, *Missionary Conquest: The Gospel and Native American Cultural Genocide* (Minneapolis: Augsburg, 1993).

deal, [they] don't demand special treatment," but "shake the dust off" their feet (Luke 10:11).[7]

Indigenous communities were naturally hospitable; they generally accepted strangers as part of their interconnectedness with all of creation.[8] However, the arrival of Europeans did not result in acceptance of guests, but settlers bent on conquest. Myers turns again to Jesus, who sends his disciples not as self-sufficient travellers, but as vulnerable visitors dependent on their hosts. Though Jesus does not address the prospect of permanency, Myers suggests that the Christian missionary must advance on the terms of the host community, so that the gospel might indigenise. Malaysian American Pentecostal Amos Yong states further that "the roles of guests and hosts are fluid, continuously reversable."[9] Honourable hosts must provide for the needs of their guests and avoid insulting and failing to protect them. Similarly, guests must not usurp the role of host, refuse what is offered, or request more than what is offered. Given the Indigenous understanding of land not in terms of ownership, but as a resource to be used for "all your relations," Myers can only imagine contemporary Christianity if Christians had practised guest-initiated approaches instead of Manifest Destiny.

Enns and Myers locate Mennonite migration with settler discipleship. Mennonites migrate not as guests, but as "settlers." Though they do not come via the sword, they are no less beneficiaries of violent displacement. Mennonite sociologist Leo Driedger agrees: "[Mennonites] settle in large concentrations on the Canadian prairies only because the Canadian government had cleared away the Indians and Métis in the West."[10] To his chagrin, Mennonite invaders were generally not only unaware of their participation in the displacement of earlier residents, but they "looked upon their indigenous neighbors with disrespect and condescension."[11] Such displacement based upon colonial conquest raises serious ethical problems. How does a minority community committed to love of their neighbours participate in the invasion of another minority and destroy their predecessors' way of life? How does Mennonite cooperation with governments to secure land compromise their belief in separation of church and state? How do nonresistant Mennonite minorities benefit from lands and protection obtained by government through violent advancement without compromising one of their elementary principles? Finally, Eileen Klassen Hamm brings these questions into the present: "What is a peace church on the prairie to do with such knowledge? How might we share such a burden as we journey forward?"[12]

---

[7] Enns and Myers, *Healing Haunted Histories*, 132.

[8] Jeanine Leblanc Lowe, "Indigenous Hospitality: Gaining Wisdom and Learning Practices from Cultures That Welcome," *NAIITS* 7 (2009), 48.

[9] Amos Yong, *Hospitality & The Other: Pentecost, Christian Practices, and the Neighbor* (Maryknoll, NY: Orbis Books, 2008), 124.

[10] Leo Driedger, "Native Rebellion and Mennonite Invasion: An Examination of Two Canadian River Valleys," *Mennonite Quarterly Review* 46:3 (July 1972), 290.

[11] Driedger, "Native Rebellion," 299.

[12] Eileen Klassen Hamm, "Truthtelling and Reconciliation on the Prairies," *Vision* 14:2 (2013), 50.

## "Unsettling" Reflections of a Canadian Pentecostal

In the second half of this essay, I turn from Mennonite storylines to my fellow Pentecostals. Since Pentecostals are a people driven by mission, they unsurprisingly moved quickly to convert their Indigenous neighbours. In 1907, Winnipeg's earliest Pentecostal congregation embarked upon outreach to Indigenous communities. By the 1970s, the Pentecostal Assemblies of Canada (PAOC) peaked at 130 Indigenous congregations and currently sits at roughly 80. Aaron Mix Ross suggests that "the story of Pentecostalism among Indigenous people belongs to Indigenous people more than it belongs to Euro-Canadian missionaries. And, in fact, it is a thoroughly indigenous movement."[13] I must admit my apprehension with such uncritical praise.

If Pentecostals are to address their settler discipleship, we must first revisit our Canadian history. The Canadian story I received as a child and young adult cannot remain the meta-narrative. It is time to re-engage our historic national and religious storylines. Adam Barker exposes the Canadian settler narrative:

> The essence of internal colonization ... is not the appropriation of labour (as in slavery), for this has been peripheral, of depopulation (genocide), for indigenous populations have increased threefold in this century, or even the appropriation of self-government (usurpation), for at different times indigenous peoples have been permitted to govern themselves within the colonial systems (as in the early treaty system and perhaps again today).[14]

Instead, the underlying storyline describes the Indigenous as archaic, without history, and with limited capacity to progress, and reveals the desire for assimilation that at its root sought their disappearance.[15]

A path forward requires more than biblical and theological education. I offer the following recommended readings outside of my discipline. Beyond the life-changing work by Enns and Myers, I suggest two multidisciplinary introductions on the politics of racism. Richard Delgado's *Critical Race Theory* and Nathan Cartagena's four-part podcast *What is Critical Race Theory* provide solid introductions from two perspectives, one secular and the other Christian.[16] They

---

[13] Aaron Mix Ross, "The PAOC and Indigenous Peoples," in David Wells (ed.), *Picture This! Reflecting on 100 Years of the PAOC* (Mississauga: PAOC, 2018), 126. I admit that Ross has recently completed a dissertation about to be published. I was not able secure a copy from him. See further Clinton Westman, "Pentecostalism and Indigenous Culture in Northern North America," *Anthropologica* 55:1 (2013), 141–56.

[14] Adam Barker states further: "By not attempting the physical or political extermination of Indigenous peoples but instead forcing them into the role of the 'aboriginal,' colonization achieves the end goal of establishing a stable social order based on a stratification analogous to that presented in George Orwell's *Animal Farm*: all are equal, but some are more equal than others" ("The Contemporary Reality of Canadian Imperialism: Settler Colonialism and the Hybrid Colonial State," *American Indian Quarterly* 33:3 (2009), 336).

[15] Brian Gobbett, "Mission Christianity in Canada and the 'Problem' of Indigenous Christianity," *Direction* 43:2 (2014), 170.

[16] Richard Delgado, *Critical Race Theory: An Introduction* (2nd ed., New York: New York University Press, 2016); for Nathan Cartagena's podcast follow the links at, "Critical Race Theory with Nathan Cartagena, Pt 1: What IS it, Actually?" Gravity

deliver definitions, historical context, and the multidisciplinary web necessary to position authentic Christian witness in an ever-political world.

Second, I suggest revisiting Canadian history. I read Donald Wright's *Canada: A Very Short Introduction* and Olive Patricia Dickason and William Newbigging's *Indigenous Peoples Within Canada*.[17] Wright produces a wide-ranging postcolonial history that addresses the plight of the marginalised. Dickason and Newbigging centre specifically on Indigenous life ahead of and in the path of settler advancement. I also completed a thirteen-week course titled "Indigenous Canada" hosted by Tracy Bear, assistant professor at the University of Alberta.[18] Bear pulls together Indigenous educators, storytellers, and artists to produce a beautiful, yet saddening storyline. In the spirit of story, akin to Pentecostal (counter) testimony, I recommend Thomas King's *The Truth About Stories*. In this publication of his 2003 Massey Lectures, he untangles a native narrative from a disconcerting Anglo-Canadian construction of Indigenous life. He gives a chilling rehearsal of terms meant to popularise the North American picture of an "Indian." For a "vision" of Indigenous life, I commend the films by acclaimed Canadian director Alanis Obomsawin. Many of her more than fifty films are public domain with the National Film Board of Canada. Her films, whether several minutes long or full-length documentaries, focus on community life, the land, culture, politics, spirituality, and so much more. Finally, I suggest Michelle Good's award-winning novel. In her *Five Little Lambs*, she envisions the experiences of five survivors from a residential school in British Columbia. Published in 2020, the book addresses not only their lives in residential schools, but their tumultuous re-entry into society. Given the recent (inter)national headlines concerning residential school travesties, I cannot imagine a more appropriate time for Pentecostal congregations to become more knowledgeable of Indigenous Canadian storylines. The cumulative effect of my re-education has produced sadness, tears, and anger that I can only describe as "groans too deep for words" (Rom. 8:26). Though I remain unsure of my future action, I require further and deeper personal transformation. Lament is "less about managing a crisis than descending into the depths of that crisis; less about damage control, than facing, admitting, and even embracing the damage and devastation that confronts us."[19] The recent discovery of unmarked graves reveals that the pain, loss, and impact upon our Indigenous neighbours remain raw and deep. In

---

Leadership, 11 May 2021, https://gravityleadership.com/podcast/critical-race-theory-what-in-the-world-is-it-anyway-w-nathan-cartagena/ (accessed 20 June 2021).

[17] Donald Wright, *Canada* (Oxford, UK: Oxford University Press, 2020); Olive Patricia Dickason and William Newbigging, *Indigenous Peoples Within Canada* (4th ed., Oxford, UK: Oxford University Press, 2019). For my American friends, I suggest Roxanne Dunbar-Ortiz, *Indigenous Peoples' History of the United States* (Boston, MA: Beacon Press, 2016).

[18] For further information, see Paul L. Gareau, "Indigenous Canada," University of Alberta, accessed 23 June 2021, https://www.coursera.org/learn/indigenous-canada.

[19] Chanelle Robinson, "'Papa Don't Preach': Imagining a Theology of Apology in Canada," *Toronto Journal of Theology* 35:1 (2019), 11.

witnessing their grief, "Our hearts should be broken wide open to make room for transformation."[20]

In that vein, my lament turned swiftly to ongoing repentance. On the one hand, I drew heavily from responses I have already learned from afar, namely, my personal recollection of confessing communities in Germany, South Africa, and Rwanda. Canada's recent Truth and Reconciliation Commission also proved timely. We have much to learn from common stories of exploitation, oppression, and violence. If we call our churches to repent, we must first learn the plight of our Indigenous neighbours. When we call our churches to repent, we must not only re-examine our larger national storylines, but our regional and local settler storylines.[21]

The call to repentance among (Canadian) Pentecostals will not come without difficulty. Indeed, my conversations with fellow Pentecostals elicit common responses: "We [my generation] weren't the colonists! We did better than our predecessors! Pentecostals didn't lead residential schools!" I have learned from my Mennonite friends that these answers are too simple and dismissive. Instead, I am compelled to ask with them, "What might a church open to decolonisation look like?" I resonate with Michael Wilkinson and Linda Ambrose:

> The PAOC continued to employ colonial patterns and critical attitudes toward Indigenous Pentecostal leaders while ignoring the realities of the trauma of residential schools and the racism that many experienced … [Along the way] PAOC leaders worked to establish and maintain their own organizational culture and … failed to recognize and respect Indigenous cultures and ways.[22]

Pentecostals must no longer deny our complicity in Canada's prolonged colonial history. Like Mennonites, we must revisit our early commitment to peace and own up to a mythic storyline of Canadians as benevolent peacemakers. "For too long, Canadian settlers like to remember that while the United States conducted 'Indian wars,' Canada enjoyed a more benign settlement process made possible by treaty negotiations with Indigenous groups."[23] Sadly, the Canadian "war" persists as a perpetual history of broken treaties.

---

[20] Hamm, "Truthtelling", 49. Length restrictions do not allow further commentary on the growing debate over the Sixties Scoop, namely, the aggressive fostering and adoption movement. Children born to Indigenous parents, many of whom were survivors of residential schools, were "scooped" into Euro-Canadian families. Young Indigenous mothers and fathers wounded by their past lose their children not to residential schools, but another form of assimilation.

[21] Matt Jones (in Paulette Regan's *Unsettling the Settler Within: Indian Residential Schools, Truth Telling, and Reconciliation in Canada* (Vancouver, BC: UBC Press, 2011)) suggests the following guidelines for public and ecclesial repentance and apology; 1) records officially in writing; 2) names the wrongs in question; 3) accepts responsibility; 4) states regret; 5) promises non-repetition; 6) does not demand forgiveness; 7) is not hypocritical or arbitrary; and; 8) undertakes – through measures of publicity, ceremony, and concrete reparation – both to engage morally those in whose name the apology is made and to assure the wronged group that the apology is sincere (180).

[22] Michael Wilkinson and Linda M. Ambrose, *After the Revival: Pentecostalism and the Making of a Canadian Church* (Montreal: McGill University Press, 2021), 146.

[23] Hamm, "Truthtelling," 50.

To be sure, there are no uncomplicated solutions. I am drawn to the words of Pentecostal scholar Adam Stewart: "The idea that there exists some measurable quantity or even quality of apologies, commemorations, healing, education, or money that might somehow represent the end of reconciliation between Settlers and Indigenous people is not a Christian idea." Instead, Pentecostals must remain open to "the operation of God's grace in our lives and in the world" and commit to reconciliation as "a continuous work of dynamic trans-immanent cooperation" with the Holy Spirit.[24] Nimi Wariboko's caution that "the destination may move before the journey is completed" calls for more than the squaring of accounts; it calls for a lifelong path of discipleship.[25]

As part of this journey, Pentecostals must own their employment of settler discipleship. In the context of Jesus' commissioning in Luke 9, we came not as guests, but claimed the role of healers and exorcists. Sadly, we failed to recognise God's activity ahead of us, and we embarked upon immediate healing and deliverance of a people we scarcely understood. Native American Pentecostal Angela Tarango offers harsh criticism: "Many Pentecostals … view the power that Native peoples assign to the land on which they live on as suspect, dark, or even demonic."[26] Settler disciples fail to recognise that "[t]he land's power isn't some actual power that is unknown, magical, spooky, and therefore to be feared; its power lies in the way it holds the memory and therefore the culture of the people."[27] Even as we attack Indigenous spiritualities, cultures, and customs and instinctively label them demonic, perhaps we are the ones in need of an exorcism. As settled Pentecostals perhaps we need healing from our imperialist mindset, from thinking we know what is best for others. Do we require deliverance from the racism that lives and breathes in the institutions and activities of our everyday lives? Why do we get defensive when Indigenous peoples speak up for themselves and question the inequalities they face in housing, employment, education, healthcare, safe water, and access to their lands? I declare my need for healing from denial that colonialism has shaped my family, my church, my workplace, and my community. We should be honest about how we have benefitted from the Canadian colonial enterprise.[28]

Pentecostals need healing and courage to reimagine mutual relationships with Indigenous neighbours.[29] Perhaps Pentecostal and Indigenous spiritualities share

---

[24] Adam Stewart, "The Unfinished Work of Reconciliation: The Truth and Reconciliation Commission of Canada, Neoliberal Liability Amelioration," *NAIITS* 16 (2018), 117. See the open-ended Mennonite response: "Statement of Anabaptist Church Leaders: Truth and Reconciliation Commission Hearings," Edmonton, Alberta, March 2014, *Direction* 43:2 (2014), 243–45.

[25] Nimi Wariboko, *The Pentecostal Principle* (Grand Rapids, MI: Eerdmans, 2011), 97.

[26] Angela Tarango, "The Land is Always Stalking Us," *Pneuma* 36:3 (2014), 403.

[27] Tarango, "The Land," 404.

[28] For a helpful collection of essays, see Nestor Medina, Alison Hari-Singh, and HyeRan Kim-Cragg (eds), *Reading In-Between: How Minoritized Cultural Communities Interpret the Bible in Canada* (Eugene: Pickwick, 2019). For an introduction to Indigenous worldviews and theologies, see Clara Sue Kidwell, Homer Noley, and George E. Tinker, *A Native American Theology* (Maryknoll, NY: Orbis Books, 2001).

[29] Hamm, "Truthtelling," 52.

underexamined affinities. According to Tarango, "[Pentecostalism] offers a message of power, through the Holy Spirit, that is appealing to converts, Native and non-Native." Though she affirms that Pentecostal growth among "Native tribes both in North and South America has been rapid and profound," she also interrogates Pentecostals for their pride and their denial of participation in the initial conquest and colonisation of the Americas. Pentecostals "continue to propagate ideas regarding racial inferiority, which is inevitably tangled up in beliefs of spiritual inferiority and an inability to understand the land as a place of power and memory that transcends Christian conversion."[30] Like Enns and her Mennonite ancestors, Pentecostals may not be directly responsible for the displacement of their Indigenous neighbours, but we must not "settle" for the conversion of individuals alone. We must imagine a holistic soteriology that recognises, supports, and acts on behalf of our Indigenous neighbours. Pentecostals must work alongside Indigenous peoples in their resistance to the "homogenizing moral colonization of empire" and their quest for "differential relationships to land."[31]

I suggest with Ray Aldred that only upon re-education will it be possible for "mission organizations [to] start changing their understanding of missions to First Nations from something done to or for First Nations to something done in partnership with them."[32] Ojibwa activist Wab Kinew concurs: "The truth about reconciliation is this: It is not a second chance at assimilation. It should not be a kinder, gentler evangelism, free from the horrors of the residential school era. Rather, true reconciliation is a second chance at building a mutually respectful relationship."[33] In the spirit of the Lukan Jesus, a Pentecostal reading of Luke 9 and 10 requires as much or more attention to guests and hosts than to healers and exorcists. Beyond our insatiable pursuit of conversions, we must reverse our settler strategies and engage in hospitable and mutually constructive theological exchange. This involves embracing the call of a prophetic movement: "To participate in strategies that would ensure that Indigenous populations have access to community-based programmes focused on recovering language, identity, spirituality, and land."[34] A quick and episodic response will not work: there are no short cuts!

---

[30] Tarango, "The Land," 399. She challenges Pentecostal misunderstanding and abuse of the indigenous church principles penned by Assemblies of God missiologist Melvin Hodges (first published in 1953 and republished as *The Indigenous Church* (Springfield: Gospel Publishing House, 2012)): "The land each tribe lives on defines their particular traditional beliefs as well as their rituals, lifeways, customs, and memory. Until Pentecostals understand the full meaning of the land in Native American terms, they will never be able to understand fully the complexity of Native culture, and they will not be able fully to enact the indigenous principle." (400–401).

[31] Barker, "Canadian Imperialism," 336.

[32] Ray Aldred, "Missions to Native People: Moving from Charity to Justice," *Direction* 43:2 (2014), 199.

[33] Cited by Kerry Baisley, "Residential Schools and the Reports of Unmarked Graves," *Diocese of New Westminster Newsletter,* 18 July 2021, https://www.vancouver.anglican.ca/blog/residential-schools-and-the-reports-of-unmarked-graves (accessed 22 July 2021).

[34] Robinson, "Don't Preach," 22.

Even as I write, I have committed to a one-year seminar hosted by Steven Heinrichs, director of Indigenous–Settler Relations, for the Mennonite Church of Canada. He and Esther Epp-Tiessen recently published *Be It Resolved*, a 500-page documentary history of more than ninety documents from 1966 to 2020 that detail Anabaptist commitments to Indigenous justice and decolonisation.[35] The "Be It Resolved" conference will encourage personal and congregational reflection and attention toward the specific actions addressed to religious bodies in the Calls to Action in the Truth and Reconciliation Commission of Canada (#48–49, 59–60).[36] As I embark on this journey, I am already imagining a similar Pentecostal compilation, a documentary history of PAOC interactions by way of newsletters, *The (Pentecostal) Testimony*, as well as General and District Conference decisions and minutes. I am convinced that the revelation of an unsettling history will produce collective Pentecostal lament, repentance, and decolonising strategies.

I am further inspired by the recent addition of "P293 Indigenous Ministry" as a required course for several ministerial training programmes at Horizon College in Saskatoon, Saskatchewan. The course is taught by James Thunder, adjunct professor and founder of Reconciliation Thunder, a non-profit that uses social media to teach and implement the results of Canada's Truth and Reconciliation Commission. The "Course Description" and "Relationship to Horizon's Mission" from his April 2021 syllabus demonstrate similarities to the Mennonite reflections above:

> Course Description: This course prepares students for success in ministry with Indigenous Peoples by contrasting recent and historical failed mission attempts with efforts that produced positive outcomes. Students examine various Indigenous ways of contextualizing the core tenets of Christian faith as well as the history leading up to the Truth and Reconciliation Commission's calls to action. Students also explore ways to act on these calls within the context of ministry.
>
> Relationship to Horizon's Mission: The college's mission is: Advancing God's Kingdom by Preparing Competent Christian Leaders for Spirit-Empowered Life and Ministry. Competent leaders are those who constantly strive to learn more about Indigenous Peoples and who understand that advancing God's kingdom does not mean advancing a moral foundation for western imperialism but rather advancing the progressive voices of justice, healing, hope, and radical change that come through sharing the love of Jesus. Informed, Spirit-empowered ministry is best done in partnership with Indigenous leaders and should take into consideration their current political, social, and economic situations and support Indigenous Peoples where possible.

I am encouraged that such a course may have helped to avoid two of my own unsettling stories. In the mid-1990s, I was a pastor in southern Manitoba. While immersed in ministry and dissertation research, I received my first invitation to

---

[35] For information and further resources, see Steve Heinrichs and Esther Epp-Tiessen (eds), "Be it Resolved Challenge," Mennonite Church Canada, accessed 23 June 2022, https://www.mennonitechurch.ca/event/11787-2021-06-01-be-it-resolved-challenge.

[36] Access "Truth and Reconciliation Commission of Canada: Calls to Action" at https://ehprnh2mwo3.exactdn.com/wp-content/uploads/2021/01/Calls_to_Action_English2.pdf (accessed 11 August 2021).

teach an adjunct course on "The Gospels" at Central Pentecostal College (now Horizon College) in Saskatoon, Saskatchewan. I taught at the short-lived Native Bible College, an extension of the main campus. I received no training in First Nations' worldviews, history, and spiritualities or their relationship to the PAOC, and in fairness, it never dawned on me that I needed such an orientation.[37] I would be a scholar of the Gospels! I had been well-schooled in historical-critical methodologies. Though I had recently embraced narrative criticism, I could not have imagined the rise of reader-response theories and the future impact of decolonising theologies. Though I cannot redo the past, I would jump at an opportunity to use my ongoing re-education to re-teach and learn alongside those same Indigenous Pentecostal students.[38] During this same season I led two "short-term missions" trips to Oxford House, a fly in Cree reservation 570 miles north of Winnipeg. My students and I led one-week vacation Bible school programmes. To this day, the experience ranks among the most cross-cultural experiences of my life. Like the story above, I was ill-prepared and, in hindsight, presumptuous to bring the "gospel" to these neighbours.

In the spirit of Luke 9 and 10, I can only wonder how different my first teaching experience and northern Manitoba adventures would have turned out if I had been a guest under Jimmy Thunder's instruction. In the spirit of Enns and Myers, I implore my fellow Pentecostals to address our haunted histories and pursue prophetic storylines built on the discipleship of decolonisation.

## Discussion Questions

1. In the section, "Living Haunted Lives," Mittelstadt draws on Elaine Enns to address three concerns regarding colonialism and Christian discipleship. Which of these concerns piques your interest? Reflect upon positive and negative interactions between European-Canadians and Indigenous peoples. Consider Christian participation in this process.
2. In the section, "Living Haunted Lives," hospitality plays a major role, particularly through Mittelstadt's engagement of the thought of Ched

[37] Follow Reconciliation Thunder on Facebook, https://www.facebook.com/ReconciliationThunder/, or the website, Reconciliation Thunder: Leaders Helping Leaders Promote Reconciliation, https://reconciliationthunder.org/?fbclid=IwAR2USh-MN4rvBH16KC-tSvqR0WLL3qunZkaHD-OtlqLBo2DsKlfc18sBH4Q (accessed 23 June 2021). See James Thunder's Spring 2021 syllabus for Indigenous Ministry (P293) at https://www.horizon.edu/wp-content/uploads/2021/04/SYLLABUS-P293-Indigenous-Ministry-Summer-2021-Thunder.pdf (accessed 23 June 2021).

[38] See Ekaputra Tupamahu's "The Stubborn Invisibility of Whiteness in Biblical Scholarship," Political Theology Network, 12 November 2020, https://politicaltheology.com/the-stubborn-invisibility-of-whiteness-in-biblical-scholarship/ (accessed 22 June 2021). Tupamahu captures the Euro-American obsession with the Synoptic Problem: "The longer I study it, the more I realize that this is an exclusively white 'problem.' The Synoptic Problem is a retrojection of whiteness into biblical texts." According to Tupamahu, the Synoptic Problem makes copyright and "ownership" of the text the primary concern of the Gospels. Such a reading "gives many white men … a headache but produces little or no concern to our Indigenous readers."

Myers. Reimagine how a Lukan hospitality might encourage European-Canadians to fresh engagement with Indigenous peoples.

3. In the final paragraph Mittelstadt calls upon Pentecostals to reimagine their story as a backdrop for action. Considering his call to action, how might Pentecostals in the present context engage Lukan hospitality as a prophetic statement for present interactions with Indigenous peoples?

## Bibliography

Aldred, Ray. "Missions to Native People: Moving from Charity to Justice." *Direction* 43:2 (2014), 192–201.

Baisley, Kerry. "Residential Schools and the Reports of Unmarked Graves." *Diocese of New Westminster Newsletter* (18 July 2021). https://www.vancouver.anglican.ca/blog/residential-schools-and-the-reports-of-unmarked-graves (accessed 22 July2021).

Barker, Adam. "The Contemporary Reality of Canadian Imperialism: Settler Colonialism and the Hybrid Colonial State." *American Indian Quarterly* 33:3 (2009), 325–51.

Cartagena, Nathan. "Critical Race Theory with Nathan Cartagena, Pt 1: What IS it, Actually?" *Gravity Leadership* (11 May 2021). https://gravityleadership.com/podcast/critical-race-theory-what-in-the-world-is-it-anyway-w-nathan-cartagena/ (accessed 20 June 2021).

Charles, Mark and Soong-Chan Rah. *Unsettling Truths: The Ongoing, Dehumanizing Legacy of the Doctrine of Discovery*. Downers Grove, IL: Intervarsity Press, 2019.

Delgado, Richard. *Critical Race Theory: An Introduction*. 2nd ed. New York: New York University Press, 2016.

Dickason, Olive Patricia and William Newbigging. *Indigenous Peoples Within Canada*. 4th ed. Oxford, UK: Oxford University Press, 2019.

Dickson, Courtney and Bridgette Watson. "Remains of 215 children Found Buried at Former BC Residential School, First Nation Says." *CBC News* (27 May 2021). https://www.cbc.ca/news/canada/british-columbia/tk-eml%C3%BAps-te-secw%C3%A9pemc-215-children-former-kamloops-indian-residential-school-1.6043778 (accessed 22 July 2021)

Driedger, Leo. "Native Rebellion and Mennonite Invasion: An Examination of Two Canadian River Valleys." *Mennonite Quarterly Review* 46:3 (July 1972), 290–300.

Dunbar-Ortiz, Roxanne. *Indigenous Peoples' History of the United States*. Boston, MA: Beacon Press, 2016.

Enns, Elaine and Ched Myers. *Healing Haunted Histories: A Settler Discipleship of Decolonization*. Eugene: Cascade Books, 2021.

Facebook. "Reconciliation Thunder." https://www.facebook.com/ReconciliationThunder/ (accessed 11 August 2021).

Gareau, Paul L. "Indigenous Canada." University of Alberta. https://www.coursera.org/learn/indigenous-canada (accessed 23 June 2021).

Gobbett, Brian. "Mission Christianity in Canada and the 'Problem' of Indigenous Christianity." *Direction* 43:2 (2014), 166–79.

Hamm, Eileen Klassen. "Truthtelling and Reconciliation on the Prairies." *Vision* 14: 2 (2013), 47–53.

Kidwell, Clara Sue, Homer Noley, and George E. Tinker. *A Native American Theology*. Maryknoll, NY: Orbis Books, 2001.

Lowe, Jeanine Leblanc. "Indigenous Hospitality: Gaining Wisdom and Learning Practices from Cultures That Welcome." *NAIITS* 7 (2009), 47–59.

Medina, Nestor, Alison Hari-Singh, and HyeRan Kim-Cragg, Eds. *Reading In-Between: How Minoritized Cultural Communities Interpret the Bible in Canada*. Eugene: Pickwick, 2019.

Mennonite Church Canada. "Be it Resolved Challenge" Edited by Heinrichs, Steve and Esther Epp-Tiessen. . Accessed 23 June 2022. https://www.mennonitechurch.ca/event/11787-2021-06-01-be-it-resolved-challenge.

Mittelstadt, Martin W. "Spirit and Peace in Luke-Acts: Possibilities for Pentecostal/Anabaptist Dialogue." *Didaskalia* 20 (Fall 2009), 17–41.

Mittelstadt, Martin W. "My Life as a Mennocostal." In *Pentecostals and Nonviolence: Reclaiming a Heritage*. Ed. Paul Alexander, 316–34. Eugene, OR: Wipf & Stock, 2012.

Mittelstadt, Martin. "Reading Luke-Acts in the Mennocostal Tradition: Pentecostals, Mennonites, and Prophethood." In *Our Lives as Mennocostals*. Eds Martin Mittelstadt and Brian Pipkin. Eugene, OR.: Pickwick, 2019, 14–28.

Reconciliation Thunder: Leaders Helping Leaders Promote Reconciliation. Accessed 23 June 2022. https://reconciliationthunder.org/?fbclid=IwAR2USh-MN4rvBH16KC-tSvqR0WLL3qunZkaHD-OtlqLBo2DsKlfc18sBH4Q.

Regan, Paulette. *Unsettling the Settler Within: Indian Residential Schools, Truth Telling, and Reconciliation in Canada*. Vancouver, BC: UBC Press, 2011.

Robinson, Chanelle. "'Papa Don't Preach': Imagining a Theology of Apology in Canada." *Toronto Journal of Theology* 35:1 (2019), 9–24.

Ross, Aaron Mix. "The PAOC and Indigenous Peoples." In *Picture This! Reflecting on 100 Years of the PAOC*. Ed. David Wells. Mississauga: PAOC, 2018, 124–139.

Smith, Mitzi. "Resisting the Great Co-mission." In *Unsettling the Word: Biblical Experiments in Decolonization*. Ed. Steve Heinrichs. Winnipeg, MB: CommonWord, 2018, 184–190.

"Statement of Anabaptist Church Leaders: Truth and Reconciliation Commission Hearings." *Direction* 43:2 (2014), 243–45.

Stewart, Adam. "The Unfinished Work of Reconciliation: The Truth and Reconciliation

Commission of Canada, Neoliberal Liability Amelioration." *NAIITS* 16 (2018), 105–19.

Tarango, Angela. "The Land is Always Stalking Us." *Pneuma* 36:3 (2014), 397–406.

Thunder, James. "P293 Indigenous Ministry" syllabus (Spring 2021). Horizon College and Syllabus. https://www.horizon.edu/wp-content/uploads/2021/04/SYLLABUS-P293-Indigenous-Ministry-Summer-2021-Thunder.pdf (accessed 23 June 2021).

Tinker, George E. *Missionary Conquest: The Gospel and Native American Cultural Genocide*. Minneapolis: Augsburg, 1993.

Truth and Reconciliation Commission of Canada. "Calls to Action." Winnipeg, MB: Truth and Reconciliation Commission of Canada, 2015. Accessed 23 June 2022. https://ehprnh2mwo3.exactdn.com/wp-content/uploads/2021/01/Calls_to_Action_English2.pdf.

Tupamahu, Ekaputra. "The Stubborn Invisibility of Whiteness in Biblical Scholarship." *Political Theology Network* (12 November 2020). https://politicaltheology.com/the-stubborn-invisibility-of-whiteness-in-biblical-scholarship/ (accessed 22 June 2021).

Wariboko, Nimi. *The Pentecostal Principle*. Grand Rapids, MI: Eerdmans, 2011.

Westman, Clinton. "Pentecostalism and Indigenous Culture in Northern North America." *Anthropologica* 55:1 (2013), 141–56.

Wilkinson, Michael and Linda M. Ambrose, *After the Revival: Pentecostalism and the Making of a Canadian Church*. Montreal: McGill University Press, 2021.

Wright, Donald. *Canada*. Oxford, UK: Oxford University Press, 2020.

Yong, Amos. *Hospitality & The Other: Pentecost, Christian Practices, and the Neighbor*. Maryknoll, NY: Orbis Books, 2008.

# Chapter 14

## The Value of the Human Soul: Radicalising Adolf von Harnack's Social Gospel

Frank D. Macchia

### Abstract

Harnack's social gospel focuses on the infinite value of the soul in God and the communion of saints built around it. The church is the fellowship or "brotherhood" bound together by the eternal life of their souls in God. In this way, the church embodies the eternal gospel. Building upon the notion of the work of God through Jesus and now the work of God via the Spirit, Harnack's analysis of the church as fellowship is evaluated. The church embodies the kingdom message of Jesus in voice and practice. The essay values Harnack's understanding of the church as a socially-just fellowship; yet we are to be concerned with Harnack's contention that the church should seek limited help from the gospel in its social witness. The churches confront institutional racism, sexism, and economic injustice as an implication of their gospel in its social witness. This mission is a significant component of Jesus setting at liberty those who are oppressed. The essay continues by outlining the understanding of the church as Harnack's strength regarding the social nature of the gospel. Yet, Harnack's approach to corporate evil as limited and in need of a more radical application of the historical-critical method. We must ask, in light of Harnack's analysis of the church, what it means that the church is a social community that addresses a social gospel.

### Reflection on Murray Dempster

I offer this study of Adolf von Harnack's social gospel in deep appreciation for the life and scholarship of Murray Dempster. He has been a professor, a mentor, and a friend to me ever since I first met him as my professor at Vanguard University back in the fall of 1973. His impact on my life has been significant, more so than he will ever know. I am sure that he has influenced countless students in much the same way and that his scholarly work will continue to impact the church and the academy for years to come.

## Introduction

When most people think of the social gospel, they think of Walter Rauschenbusch.[1] Less known is the fact that at the turn of the twentieth century the leading historian of dogma and icon of liberal theology, Adolf von Harnack (1851–1930), had a social gospel as well. Harnack was a pivotal figure in this tradition in the late years of the nineteenth and early years of the twentieth centuries; its heyday existing prior to the advent of the world wars. He was one of Karl Barth's most cherished professors and the one to whom Barth turned most directly against when writing his Romans commentary.[2]

Harnack was born in the Baltic German town of Dorpat where his father taught homiletics and historical theology. His father had strong pietist leanings that his son never adopted. Later, his father opposed him for doubting the deity and pre-existence of Christ. Undaunted by his father's criticism, Harnack applied himself to his scholarship with passion, talent, and rigour. He became enormously prolific. Besides countless articles and professional papers, his multi-volume *History of Dogma* established him as a towering figure in historical scholarship. His works on Marcion and Gnosticism were groundbreaking at the time they appeared, and his classic *What is Christianity?* went through fifteen editions between 1901 and 1950. He was also a leading public figure. In 1903 he became president of the Evangelical Social Congress. In 1906 he was granted the directorship of the Royal Library, and in 1911 he was elected to the presidency of the Emperor's Royal Academy of Sciences.[3]

His version of the social gospel took on a unique blend of conservative Lutheranism and an advocacy of justice for the poor, a blend that gave him a broad-based appeal. Interestingly, Harnack advocated ideas that if applied more deeply would have led to a more "radical" social gospel, but that didn't happen and was unlikely to have happened given his times and personal biography. By "radical" I mean an approach to the social gospel that digs more deeply into the roots of the issues one discusses, thereby avoiding superficial solutions that mask or evade the causes of suffering. Yet, pressing an author of the stature and influence of a Harnack toward a more radical version of himself makes for an interesting academic exercise. I will examine Harnack's social gospel with the goal of pushing his thoughts in a more radical direction but still in ways true to their basic impetus.

---

[1] E.g. Walter Rauschenbusch, *A Theology for the Social Gospel* (New York: Macmillan Company, 1917); Rauschenbusch, *Christianity and the Social Crisis* (New York: Macmillan Company, 1920).

[2] Karl Barth notes that Harnack's anthropocentrism, though imbalanced, contained an element of truth that Barth had not adequately addressed in the years surrounding the writing of his Romans commentary. Barth even wrote, "I should indeed have been somewhat embarrassed if one had invited me to speak on the humanity of God – say, in the year 1920, the year in which I stood up in this hall against my great teacher, Adolf von Harnack." Karl Barth, "The Humanity of God," in *The Humanity of God* (Richmond, VA: John Knox Press, 1960), 38.

[3] W.C.H. Fend, "Church Historians of the Early Twentieth Century: Adolf von Harnack (1851–1930)," *The Journal of Ecclesiastical History*, 52:1 (January 2001), 83–84.

## Historical Criticism

A social gospel depended in Harnack's day (and beyond) on historical criticism. Historical criticism assumed that the church and its message are historically conditioned and, therefore relative, subject to critical analysis and change in the light of new social challenges. A social gospel will thus ally itself with historical criticism in resistance to the notion that any theological formulation is absolute and invulnerable to critical analysis as to its social or cultural conditioning and function. Historical criticism will do the same for social systems and institutions and the cultural ideologies that they preserve. The Bible is not invulnerable to its reach, and neither is the church as an institution. As Dorothee Soelle notes, the German historical-critical method of which Harnack was a part was not only used to historically situate and critically analyse ancient texts but to submit our theological and institutional appropriation of them to critical analysis as well.[4] Harnack stands out in the early twentieth century as the most able and passionate defender of the use of historical criticism in theology as an academic discipline. His voluminous *History of Dogma* is a monumental effort toward this end.[5] He summarised the results of his critical analysis of the history of Christian thought compellingly in his classic, *What is Christianity?*, a book described by Karl Barth as the climax of liberal theology in the nineteenth century.[6] In it Harnack defends theology as a critical discipline, the goal of which is to rediscover the original faith beneath the outmoded crustations of historic doctrines. This faith may then be recast in more socially relevant formulations.

Harnack starts his classic *What is Christianity?* by defending the role of historical criticism in the task of a socially relevant theology. He notes that seminary theology cannot fail to be self-critical; it cannot be given over to Christian apologetics that defends dogmatic formulations at the cost of recognising their relative and limited nature, "or else historical research will be brought into complete discredit."[7] Prior to the widespread influence of historicisation which impacted other areas of study besides theology, German Lutheran faculties of theology offered courses in church history for largely apologetic purposes or to grant students the support and conceptual tools necessary for identifying heretical movements and critiquing them effectively. But all of that changed with the entry of theology into university settings. Historicisation legitimated that entry.[8]

But the relativising of historical traditions in the search for a socially relevant theology does not leave theology with nothing enduring with which to work. The thought was that there is an essential kernel beneath the temporal husks that requires discovery using critical tools. It is then this kernel that requires recasting

---

[4] Dorothee Soelle, *Political Theology* (Philadelphia: Fortress, 1974), 11–18.

[5] Adolf von Harnack, *History of Dogma*, 7 vols (reprinted as 4) (Mineola, NY: Dover Pub, 1961).

[6] Harnack, *What is Christianity?* (New York: Harper & Row Torchbook, 1957); Karl Barth, "Evangelical Theology in the Nineteenth Century," in *The Humanity of God*, 14.

[7] Harnack, *What is Christianity?* 7, italics original.

[8] Johannes Zachhuber, *Theology as Science in Nineteenth-Century Germany: From F.C. Baur to Ernst Troeltsch* (Oxford: Oxford University Press, 2013), 1–4.

in fresh husks. In the German liberal tradition, this kernel was typically found in the soul's immediate relation to the divine, what Friedrich Schleiermacher called "absolute dependence" on the Infinite, an "immediate consciousness of the Deity as He is found in ourselves and in the world."[9] As we will explain below, Harnack will focus on the soul's immediate relation to the divine as well, except he will draw out its social implications. For Harnack the soul is dignified with infinite worth and is placed by Jesus within a "brotherhood" that influences culture by exemplifying a new understanding of human community. Of relevance at this juncture is the fact that Harnack argued that if theology is ahistorical, then it will confuse time-bound formulations with the eternal life of the soul in God to which they seek to bear witness, potentially eclipsing "eternal life in the midst of time."[10] The changing cultural situations caused people to look at past temporal formulations as outmoded and conclude that the church has nothing socially relevant today to offer. The church too can lack awareness of the cultural and social relevance of its gospel. They can neglect to see that the eternal life of the soul in time is still in *time*, having "fellowship" with (or involvement in) the intellectual life of the mind and the social and economic life of humanity.[11]

The phrase "in fellowship with" distinguishes the life of the soul from temporal contexts and challenges but also views these as the realm in which the soul is affected and must respond. This soul reveals its significance as an enduring reality in changing times that binds us all as one despite our varying stations in life. When it comes to the gospel of the human soul promoted by Jesus, Harnack writes: "I am convinced, rather, that at bottom we have to do here with something that is common to us all, and which in the course of history has struggled up out of torpor and discord into unity and light."[12] References to the soul correspond with the deepest yearnings of all of humanity and are the only hope for human unity. Thus, it becomes urgent to rethink it time and again in the context of the most relevant expressions of human culture. Yet, it must be recontextualised to live anew (be rekindled afresh) in a way that is relevant to human life as it is concretely lived. The gospel for Harnack "is not a question of a 'doctrine' being handed down by uniform repetition or arbitrarily distorted; it is the question of a *life*, again and again kindled afresh, and now burning with a flame of its own."[13]

## Harnack's Gospel of the Valued Soul

As noted above, Harnack argues that the gospel promoted by Jesus points essentially to the loving fatherhood of God and the "brotherhood" or fellowship of humanity ennobled by having a soul that exists in relation to this God – "God

---

[9] Friedrich Schleiermacher, *On Religion: Speeches to its Cultured Despisers* (trans. John Oman; New York: Frederick Ungar Publishers, 1965), 82.

[10] Harnack, *What is Christianity?* 8.

[11] Harnack, *What is Christianity?* 9.

[12] Harnack, *What is Christianity?* 9.

[13] Harnack, *What is Christianity?* 11.

as the Father and the human soul so ennobled that it can and does unite with him."[14] Jesus not only uniquely stressed God as Father, he is also the first to have brought the value of the human soul to light, a truth that can no longer be denied.[15] Jesus' message of the kingdom of God refers to the powerful presence of God in the human heart, which "is nothing but the treasure which the soul possesses in the eternal and merciful God."[16] For Harnack, the enduring core truth of Christianity is the value and dignity of human beings. This insight is the core of his social gospel.

The gospel of Jesus that is rediscovered by historical criticism and rekindled afresh within a new context was alive most clearly in the life of Jesus. Christ comes to be defined by this life of the soul dignified by its relation to God; he embodied it. "He lived in religion, and it was breath to him in the fear of God; his whole life, all his thoughts and feelings, were absorbed in the relation to God."[17] From the vantage point of this all-consuming relationship to God, Jesus grasps the core truth of Christianity; in fact, of human history, which has its "end," *telos*, or fulfilment in this all-encompassing relationship of Jesus to his Father. For Harnack, the history of Christian doctrine has unfortunately served to eclipse this living core. "It is only the religion which has been built up into an intellectual system that does not make this emphasizing of the end all-important; without such emphasis no actual religion is conceivable, whether it springs up anew like a sudden flame or glows in the soul like a secret fire."[18] Harnack points to Christ as a place in history where the God–soul relation to which a social theology points was clearly and adequately manifested in time. Harnack was confident that historical investigation can be used to uncover and analyse Christ's life and teaching and then use them as the standard against which to critically judge all future witnesses to this life in the church.

For Harnack, as for the liberal tradition in general, it is the impact of the life of Jesus that explains Jesus' enduring role for our socially relevant theology. Atonement and resurrection play no necessary role in this theology. One would think that the incarnation of the Word of the Father in human flesh might have played a role in this intimate relation of the soul to God for Harnack. But such a confession also falls to the knife of historical criticism. In fact, he arrives at the astounding conclusion from his historical investigation that the "Gospel as Jesus proclaimed it, has to do with the Father only and not with the Son."[19] Jesus perfectly lived this gospel and became its chief criterion for the churches, but he is not necessary to its content. Indeed, for Harnack, the Son is meant to be nothing more than a transparent witness to this gospel; he means to churches only the path to the knowledge of it.[20] Christ bears witness to and teaches this gospel. But this gospel is not about him. The Son is not the subject of this gospel: "He desired no other belief in his person and no other attachment to it than is

[14] Harnack, *What is Christianity?* 63.
[15] Harnack, *What is Christianity?* 67–68.
[16] Harnack, *What is Christianity?* 77.
[17] Harnack, *What is Christianity?* 34–35.
[18] Harnack, *What is Christianity?* 42.
[19] Harnack, *What is Christianity?* 144.
[20] Harnack, *What is Christianity?* 128.

contained in the keeping of his commandments."[21] In my view, Harnack implies that the social gospel is lived primarily within a fellowship that follows the teachings and life example of Jesus, though it could feasibly continue on by focusing on more relevant examples.

## The Barrier of Dogma

As noted above, securing the ecclesial and, by implication, social relevance of Jesus' gospel requires removing the person of Jesus as necessary to the fellowship of human souls. Historic dogma stands in the way of Christ's instrumental and nonessential role as witness to this social gospel. More importantly, an institutionalised church that secures its power through dogma stands in the way. So, the removal of church dogma allows us to discover Jesus anew outside the church's misuse of him. However, eliminating Jesus as necessary to the new community and its social gospel had devastating consequences. Harnack draws a straight line from Jesus' elevation of the human soul in his life example to its ecclesial realisation without interruption. The influence of Christ moves effortlessly through the time between Jesus and the founding of his church without any need for atonement or resurrection. There are no barriers to overcome, no gulf of sin and death to traverse. Christ's human life witness is adequate to carry the power of "redemption" within itself and to deliver it directly to the church. The dedicated soul of a chiefly religious person carries this redemption. Harnack's social gospel ends up based on the triumph of religion and the fellowship of the church is a powerful example of its outcome. Though Harnack may use terms like "redemption" and "regeneration" he had largely gutted these terms of their biblical meanings. They now mean an awakening within the church of the need to follow Jesus' life example.

Harnack does grant the historical Jesus an important role to play in mediating the knowledge of the valued soul to the church. Harnack even believes that Jesus had "messianic consciousness" since his baptism. He had unique knowledge of God the Father and defined his life's mission as sharing such knowledge with humanity.[22] When Harnack encounters the verse in John's Gospel which says that the Father loved the Son before the foundation of the world (17:24), he emphatically responded, "Here all research must stop."[23]

Historical-critical research in Harnack's hands is more than willing to stop those who view John 17:24 within a Trinitarian framework! As for the atonement, Harnack notes that Jesus' death remains "efficacious" for all time. But he quickly adds that this efficaciousness is no different from the influence that Jesus exercised in impacting people throughout his life. Harnack strongly rejects any idea that Jesus' gospel of the "fatherhood" of God and the "brotherhood" of humanity ennobled by God changed in any way due to his death and resurrection.[24] He says almost nothing about what death and

---

[21] Harnack, *What is Christianity?* 125.
[22] Harnack, *What is Christianity?* 131–40.
[23] Harnack, *What is Christianity?* 129.
[24] Harnack, *What is Christianity?* 143, 145.

resurrection might then mean for Jesus outside of his mission to exemplify and proclaim God's valuation of the human soul. He maintains that the view of his death as an expiatory sacrifice was part of an outmoded religious culture and is best translated into a symbol of Jesus' sacrificial love for humanity.[25] We should not be surprised then that Harnack doubts that the resurrection of Jesus had historically occurred. Harnack interprets the idea of Jesus' resurrection as transcending death. As such it is a mere symbol of the transcendent value of the soul in God.[26] Everything boils down to the value of the soul. Jesus' permanent relevance is not to be located in his death or alleged resurrection, but rather in him being the "personal realization" and "strength" of the gospel of the soul's value throughout time.[27] In playing this limited role, Christ for Harnack "has as yet yielded his place to no man."[28] But what is to stop this from one day occurring? Harnack doesn't say.

For Harnack, the historical path to Christological and Trinitarian dogma was a tragic detour from Jesus' simple gospel of the soul's value. The development of Christological and Trinitarian dogma was the result of the Hellenisation of the gospel, and not a natural devolvement of the historical Jesus' core understanding of the gospel. Harnack holds that this was largely due to Paul's influence. The infant church began to fall under the alien influence of Greek thinking, shifting the gospel from the ennobled soul to Christ as Redeemer. Christ Jesus became the central content of the gospel itself rather than merely its chief witness. This wayward Christocentricity allegedly began when Paul reduced the whole of the gospel to the events of Christ's atoning death and resurrection, thus turning the attention of Christian proclamation to the person of Jesus rather than to the truth about God's valuation of the human soul as modelled by Jesus. Eventually, Christ was turned into a doctrine or a "speculative idea," rather than the example of the new life of the soul, but not right away.[29] Fortunately, Paul's Christological emphasis was mainly ethical and not theoretical, making the chief outgrowth of his gospel a life patterned after Christ. But among others taken with Greek metaphysics, Paul's gospel quickly morphed into a doctrine that Christ was a divine being entering into the world to save humanity. This Hellenisation of the gospel gave rise to debates about Jesus' divine and human "natures," transforming the gospel into a speculative doctrine about Christ and removing its concrete relevance to human life.[30]

Harnack argued that, during the early centuries of Christianity beyond the New Testament era, a "fatal connection" was forged between the Greek desire for immortal life and the Christian message. The message became that Christ was a divine "Logos" made flesh so that all flesh could become immortal in him. Christ's witness to a simple gospel that promotes love for God and neighbour is completely lost in this development according to Harnack. It is replaced by a

[25] Harnack, *What is Christianity?* 157–58.
[26] Harnack, *What is Christianity?* 161–62.
[27] Harnack, *What is Christianity?* 145.
[28] Harnack, *What is Christianity?* 130.
[29] Harnack, *What is Christianity?* 153–54.
[30] Harnack, *What is Christianity?* 184–85.

mythological Christ who has been deified so as to deify others.[31] The eternal life in time was replaced by an eternal life beyond time. The value of the soul was replaced by the value of an exalted being. The value of a soul in life was replaced by the value of dogma. Harnack's evaluation of this dogmatic trend was harsh. He stated, "it is a perverse proceeding to make Christology the fundamental substance of the Gospel."[32]

I am amazed that Harnack, who was a Lutheran theologian, could write such a thing given how Christocentric Luther was. But Harnack views himself as more of a historian and theologian of culture than a confessional theologian. The critical application of historical science will save the day for Harnack and Christianity by bringing Christian theology back to Jesus and to the core truths of his gospel. The goal of historical science is to aid theology in rediscovering the original gospel of Jesus beneath the distortions of it that exist in both Scripture and the dogmatic heritage of the church. This gospel offers the church the core truth by which it is to live. Jesus' simple message is: God's Fatherhood and the soul's infinite value. Harnack's Lutheran colours only shine through in his conviction that the gospel is materially the critical principle of the biblical canon and dogma. This material principle keeps historical criticism true to the gospel. It is the kernel beneath the changing husk.

## Harnack's Social Gospel

We need to expand our study to look at some of the specifics of Harnack's social gospel beyond its core in the infinite value of the human soul. In his *Essays on the Social Gospel*, Harnack starts by noting that the core of the gospel has essentially to do with the soul and is thus primarily about repentance, new life, and life eternal rather than social improvement.[33] The eternal soul precedes earthly relevance in Harnack's gospel. The church awakened to its infinite value in God is the direct and primary consequence of the gospel. This insight results in raising people beyond the earthly conflicts of success and distress. There is to be a "holy indifference" to earthly affairs because of the conviction that we possess life eternal in our souls. Yet there is also wedded to this principle of material indifference an enduring and this-worldly love of one's neighbours. The latter became the rule of character for all those devoted to the religion established by Jesus Christ.

Early Christianity formed an early "brotherhood" around this principle of material indifference and love for one's neighbour by bearing witness to it among all with whom they had contact. Holy indifference was not to be directed to people, for the gospel nowhere teaches that our relationship to our neighbours should be characterised by indifference. And neither is the spiritual to be completely divorced from material life in how we show love. The gospel "draws no fine distinction between body and soul" in the church's act of showing love and mercy towards those in need. Jesus said to his followers that they give him

[31] Harnack, *What is Christianity?* 236.

[32] Harnack, *What is Christianity?* 184.

[33] Harnack, *Essays on the Social Gospel* (New York: G.P. Putnam's Sons, 1907), 9.

drink when giving it to others and claimed that his gospel would result in the liberation of the poor. Indeed, "in the simplest and most emphatic terms possible, Christians are urged to help the needy and the miserable with all the strength of love."[34] Holy indifference in the end is limited to "what the individual soul should feel towards the world with all its weal and woe."[35] Christianity seemed to offer the world a unique social gospel, "scorn earthly want and misery, and earthly prosperity alike, and yet relieve distress of every kind."[36]

This dialectic of worldly indifference and a passion to help those who require it means that the church does not seek to enter the conflicts of worldly politics. The Bible offers no specific programme or set of laws for the common welfare or for the economic system that a society should adopt.[37] Selling all that one has to give to the poor, not building treasures on earth, or following Jesus rather than settling the affairs of one's inheritance describe holy indifference to wealth but did not grant us an economic system. Jesus' harsh statements about wealth are due to the fact that in his ancient setting capital was almost always hoarded in a useless way as a dead thing. Harnack points out that, at the turn of the twentieth century, capital is a great economic force in the world. How the New Testament specifically guides us in this new context is not clear for Harnack. He believes that capitalism and the insights of both Christianity and the Enlightenment into human freedom and dignity have inspired much greater freedom in the world. Yet he knows that suffering is still great among many. The only theological guidance he offers is this: "You are accountable to God for all the gifts you have received, and so for your possessions also; you are bound to use them in the service of your neighbor."[38] And "where he clearly perceives that any economic condition has become a source of distress to his neighbor, he is bound to seek for a remedy, for he is a disciple of the Saviour."[39] He is not against challenging institutions out of love for the oppressed, but does not believe that the gospel of Jesus offers us any direct guidance. Harnack is especially against the attempt to justify social revolution in Christ's name.

Harnack turns to the early church for further guidance. He highlights three methods of pursuing a social gospel that may be helpful in the modern era. The first is appealing to the Christian conscience "in such a way as to awaken strong, regenerate, self-sacrificing personalities." This method is basic, for the kingdom of God "must be built upon the foundation, not of institutions, but of individuals in whom God dwells and who are glad to live for their fellow men."[40]

The second is to build congregations of believers into communities "full of active charity and bound by brotherly love; for without such a love all effort is sporadic."[41] In other words, Christian love must be "institutionalised" in the

---

[34] Harnack, *What is Christianity?* 12.
[35] Harnack, *What is Christianity?* 11.
[36] Harnack, *What is Christianity?* 12.
[37] Harnack, *What is Christianity?* 13.
[38] Harnack, *What is Christianity?* 14.
[39] Harnack, *What is Christianity?* 15.
[40] Harnack, *What is Christianity?* 16.
[41] Harnack, *What is Christianity?* 16.

fellowship of the church so as to allow the church to be a united, organised, and enduring witness to Christian charity in the world of misery and destitution.

The third has to do with the "arrangement of the world" and its "ordinances." When it comes to this third level, the church's response to corporate evil, Harnack reveals a degree of ambivalence. He notes that the early church sought to exert its influence "against so much of the existing order of things as was in fact disorder and sin."[42] They appealed to rulers to intervene so as to avoid abuses of power and unjust treatment of the poor. But, Harnack adds, "as far as I can see, the limit of their interference was clearly defined: It did not occur to them to propose economic improvements or to attack fixed institutions such as slavery."[43]

Early Christianity did not justify slavery, nor should it have done so according to Harnack, because of the demands of charity and respect for the value of the soul. But the early church shows us that the church is not to be a revolutionary force in the world of corporate evil. It is rather to prepare the minds and wills of people to respond to corporate roots of suffering and consequent revolutions in a way that maximises charity and justice for all from within social systems in which we find ourselves. Corporate evil will endure no matter what we do, so our efforts should be focused on helping souls endure and flourish in the midst of this evil world, adjusting well to social changes and circumstances.

The major enemy that requires overcoming is the power of evil within the soul, causing the church to concentrate there and to view its social function (beyond charity and fellowship) as reactive spiritually to social changes: "A religion which aims at saving the soul and transforming the inner man, and which regards a change in outward circumstances as but a small matter in comparison with the power of evil, can only follow in the wake of earthly changes and exercise an after-influence."[44] Therefore the soul is to be indifferent to the material world but loving to those who suffer.

Harnack is aware of how his teaching concerning worldly indifference and charity in the midst of abuses of power can be misused to support human misery. He warns that churches are not to submit to a conservatism that makes them indifferent to the plight of their neighbours due to the shortcomings of an economic system, "lest they should become in a bad sense conservative and indolent, and should hide this indolence under cover of very lofty conceptions of their creed." In other words, in the face of misery do not point the poor only to the "lofty creed" of life eternal in order to justify the status quo. He continues, "Instead of helping their poor brother, they preach to him that 'pious indifference' with which individuals should regard their own earthly fortunes."[45] So, in the midst of a misuse of power do not just point those who suffer to the need for "pious indifference." Be indifferent to your own possessions and help them! The church should not be surprised at behaving hypocritically if it remains vulnerable to getting caught up in the conflict between quietism and its counter-

---

[42] Harnack, *What is Christianity?* 17.
[43] Harnack, *What is Christianity?* 17.
[44] Harnack, *What is Christianity?* 19.
[45] Harnack, *What is Christianity?* 19.

response of radicalism. Only an unfailing witness of deep concern and charity can spare the church from succumbing to these extremes.[46]

In *What is Christianity?*, Harnack also tries to navigate his way between radicalism and quietism. Against radicalism, he notes that the eternal value of the individual soul is indeed the basis of the social gospel. The gospel was for Jesus "profoundly socialistic as it was individualistic because it establishes the infinite and independent value of every human soul."[47] Religion is thus the soul, and morality is its body.[48] Jesus taught love not only for God but also for our neighbours, which necessitates caring for them in their misery.[49] This individual ethic finds embodiment in the community of faith. Jesus' gospel "aims at founding a community among men as wide as human life itself and as deep as human need."[50] But one cannot draw this church into the world of politics without tragic consequences. This message cannot be overtaken by the struggle between competing political voices. The gospel wishes to establish a "socialism" based on "consciousness of spiritual unity" rather than social unity won by the settling of "conflicting interests" in the social or political sphere.[51] Neither is the church to support revolution. Though Jesus proclaimed "solidarity and brotherliness, in favor of the poor," he was no social revolutionary.[52] The gospel has implications for politics but cannot be reduced to a political ideology. We should fight for equal rights for the poor in the world, "but do not let us expect the Gospel to afford us any direct help."[53] The gospel gives rise to a spiritual "brotherhood," and this inspires bold measures in the direction of charity and equal regard for all people.

In Lutheran fashion, Harnack separates the realms of God and Caesar, "two powers as separate and divorced from each other … two quite different provinces." In this separation, the soul belongs to God alone and is judged as valued by God in a way that secular powers cannot succeed in denying.[54] In the midst of denials of human dignity, the poor can be assured that God will bring justice at the end of time. Meanwhile, they are not to aggressively assert their rights in this world but rather to show love to their enemies.[55] The life of the church, however, is different. The church is to establish a community where justice is indeed achieved, though not by law or force but by love and persuasion.[56] "The Gospel makes its appeal to the inner man, whether he is well or wounded."[57] The focus on the infinite value of the soul in God gives rise to

[46] Harnack, *What is Christianity?* 19.
[47] Harnack, *What is Christianity?* 99–100.
[48] Harnack, *What is Christianity?* 73.
[49] Harnack, *What is Christianity?* 99.
[50] Harnack, *What is Christianity?* 100.
[51] Harnack, *What is Christianity?* 100.
[52] Harnack, *What is Christianity?* 101–102.
[53] Harnack, *What is Christianity?* 116.
[54] Harnack, *What is Christianity?* 105.
[55] Harnack, *What is Christianity?* 110.
[56] Harnack, *What is Christianity?* 112.
[57] Harnack, *What is Christianity?* 115.

the idea that our holy indifference to the trials and social and political conflicts of life is to be wedded to a passionate effort to help the poor and the oppressed.

## Summary and Response

By way of summary, Harnack's social gospel focuses on the infinite value of the soul in God and the communion of saints built around it. He depends on historical criticism to eliminate or reinterpret any biblical or dogmatic traditions that could end up eclipsing this simple gospel or the call to live in it. This includes the deity of Christ, the atonement, the resurrection, and any belief that makes the dogma of Christ's person the object of attention. Christ only points beyond himself. He is not necessary to the social gospel he founded, though he is its chief witness. Following Jesus and his command to love our neighbour by granting them infinite value is the totality of this social gospel.

Harnack uses this trimmed-down gospel to account for the rise of the church. In trimming down the gospel in this way, historical criticism implicitly calls into question the church as an institution-based entity that uses elaborate dogma and rituals as the gateway to admission. The church is rather to be the fellowship or "brotherhood" bound together by the eternal life of their souls in God. In this way, the church may be said to embody the eternal spirit of its gospel. Since all of humanity is bound together by their souls in God, the church is to extend its social gospel outwardly into the world, caring for the downtrodden and inviting them to come together with others in a life fashioned after the example of Jesus. Faith in God means nothing else than regard for the infinite value of others. There is no other creed for the faith than this for Harnack.

But extending this social gospel into the world does not mean reducing the gospel to a social or political ideology; neither does it mean turning the church into a revolutionary force. The gospel will indirectly guide Christian involvement for justice in the world but not directly. This protects the gospel from being exploited by social forces and conflicts. The church is protected from this exploitation by securing its identity and enduring relevance in its gospel of eternal life, the infinite value of the soul in God, and a fellowship that transcends social differences. The church is to be "holy indifferent" to the positive or negative effects of social and material life. Yet, the church is not to be indifferent to the suffering of others. They are to do what they can to help them materially and to aid in their own discovery of their infinite worth before God. Love requires nothing less.

My response is this: the gospel is indeed "social." Though the term "social gospel" is understandably no longer current, I will not spend time discussing the pros and cons of that fact. I will focus rather on the substance of Harnack's arguments. It must be admitted that he is provocative at points. In fact, he is sometimes problematic precisely where he is provocative. The value of the human soul can indeed be *a* focal point of a social gospel and I would not oppose the assumption that the soul takes precedence over all other dimensions of human life. In fact, social injustice and oppression cut deeply because they attack one right down at the very depths of one's soul, which is why the oppressed must dig deep to find strength precisely at the core of their being. There is no question that social oppression is penetratingly dehumanising. Thus, Harnack's repeated assertion that every soul is equally valued by God and that the oppressed must realise their connection with God down in the depths of their being is a truth of which many among the oppressed have testified. The life of the soul is indeed of highest worth. Humankind shall not live by bread alone! In fact, to attempt to live by bread alone is a living death. In gaining freedom, the oppressed cannot simply be content with attaining a bigger piece of the material pie. The highest value is one's spiritual life. And this is true. Harnack's remarks here, for all of their shortcomings, still speak to me.

Furthermore, Harnack, the great critic of Gnosticism, repeats time and again that the life of the soul, though distinct from the body, is not separable from it. He also notes time and again that we are historically conditioned and must be understood as such. But has he understood these truths deeply enough? Has he applied them radically enough? After all, the "body" is not abstract and generalised but specific and diverse. Yet Harnack, the great historian, still speaks in the abstract of "souls" or "bodies," not realising that there are no such abstractions. There are soulish bodies and embodied souls whose very existence in the world is mediated by the realities of race, sex, and class (among other things). Pentecost means that this diverse embodiment of living souls is affirmed by God as integral to the unity of the church, for unity does not eclipse diversity (Acts 2:17-18). Whenever diversity is eclipsed, one has assimilation to the dominant culture rather than attained a just unity. The argument for a purely "spiritual" unity of eternal souls serves the interests of the socially privileged. The many tongues of Pentecost are thus implicitly subversive. This diversity is not dissolved by the Spirit (Acts 2:4); all tongues share equally in the Christian witness, and they remain significant before God's throne (Rev. 7:9). A historical criticism that does not just condition but *really situates* people historically would involve this insight. Historical situatedness regards a church that ignores such issues to be supportive of an oppressive ideology. Harnack the great historical critic wasn't critical enough. He needed to push his critical method deeper and then turn it upon himself.

Moreover, I agree that "holy indifference" to both prosperity and need is a noble goal, so long as it is not taken to mean that we are indifferent to human suffering. In all fairness to Harnack, he attempted to distance his doctrine of holy indifference from this abuse. And his concern was biblical. Paul sought after holy indifference and achieved it (Phil. 4:12-13). But one is never to speak lightly about such matters, especially from a position of privilege. It is much easier to be "indifferent" to both prosperity and need from a historical situation of privilege than from a situation of oppression. Again, historical situatedness contextualises our theological speech and this contextualisation needs to be taken into consideration when we speak. Holy indifference pursued by an apostle who gave up everything to serve the advancement of the gospel in the world, and suffered both unjustly and greatly in doing so, takes on a different meaning when it is promoted by someone living in the lap of luxury. For someone from a situation of luxury to advise those who suffer injustice to be indifferent to the source of their misery has a very different ring to it, even if one is careful to qualify it, as Harnack did, by urging the comfortable to concentrate on being indifferent to their wealth by sharing it. Is it not naïve to assume that the privileged would follow his advice to the point of being existentially challenged as deeply as those who seek indifference to material need? Again, had Harnack thought deeply enough about the historical situatedness of theology?

As for the church, I like the way Harnack attempts to ecclesially mediate his social gospel. The church is to embody the kingdom message of Jesus before the world, embody it as a just fellowship that loves its neighbours. Harnack does not skip over the mediation of the church so as to draw a straight line from Jesus to the secular relevance of his gospel. Within such a secular gospel that bypasses the needed mediation of the church, the church is called to serve the kingdom of God in the world at the cost of its role as the necessary and chief sign of its arrival. This sign involves the church's kerygmatic, sacramental, charismatic, diakonic, and missional functions, which are anchored in redemption and renewal through Christ and the gift of the Spirit. These functions are not to be demythologised and translated into a secular idiom in a way that reduces the church to a social agency. Such a social gospel would be reductionistic. There is truth to Harnack's warning not to simply identify the gospel with a political ideology or party, nor with any particular social system or economic plan.

But to say that the church's involvement in social issues receives no direct help from the gospel goes too far. We dare not use Luther's two-kingdoms doctrine to grant the gospel direct relevance only to the life of the soul or the fellowship of the church.[58] Since evil is embodied in social systems, the gospel must be allowed to speak a word of both judgement and hope to those who benefit or suffer from them. The gospel speaks above all else to the life of the soul, but not exclusively. If the churches do not confront socialised institutional racism, sexism, and economic injustice with the direct help of their gospel, then their gospel will not have an adequate witness to the kingdom of God in the world. Jesus did indeed come to set at liberty those who are oppressed in every sense of that word (Luke 4:18). The gospel will have profound implications for social, political, cultural, and economic matters. Such implications will be debated in the churches, to be sure. If following the gospel given for the liberation of the oppressed, such debates would give preference to the voices of the oppressed. In intrachurch debates, such matters are too important to grant preference to the judgements of those who have every reason to leave the status quo in full force and, worse, to affirm it. Again, situating the church historically would have exposed such a matter and subordinated it to critical analysis. I don't find a clear grasp of these matters in Harnack. Again, the historical critic isn't critical enough.

Harnack is weak on the church's social witness in relation to corporate evil. He argues that we are not to be indifferent to those who suffer, but aren't we guilty of such indifference if we neglect to attack the roots of their suffering in systemic evil? Merely appealing to rulers or suggesting cosmetic changes to institutions are not enough. Harnack's social gospel is mainly a survivalist gospel. The gospel of Jesus and the fellowship of the saints is for Harnack our

[58] This doctrine viewed the church and the world as separate and parallel kingdoms of God, the former governed by grace and forgiveness and the latter by law and retribution.

haven in a heartless world. His social gospel is geared mainly to helping folks withstand the lure of prosperity and survive the misery of social oppression. The church is the social infirmary for sin-sick souls. Holy indifference towards the negative effects of prosperity and poverty and care for the suffering are for Harnack the means by which people can be protected from the world. His social gospel is effective only as a band-aid for the body and kool-aid to the soul but not as a source of change for the disadvantaged. Though Jesus cannot be reduced to the role of a social revolutionary, his gospel was nevertheless revolutionary in its impact. The crucifixion and resurrection of Jesus relativised the ruling power of sin and its threat of death and placed God's judgement upon them. Sin and death are not just embodied in personal lives but also even more powerfully in social systems and institutions. An interpersonal love ethic is not able to adequately resist sin on this level, proclaim God's judgement upon it, or apply pressure for change. Redemption as it exists in the kingdom of God promises hope not only for the eschatological bliss of the soul but also for just communion within a new world, a heavenly city that embodies the righteousness of the kingdom and fulfils the fellowship of the church. The church seeks to be a sign of this kingdom and to work for analogies of it in the world, all the while looking forward in hope to the day of its full realisation in the new creation.

Lastly, what about how the world is "situated" in the biblical narrative? God in Harnack's version of the social gospel plays the part of a distant actor who does not do much other than guarantee the infinite value of the human soul. Christ does not do much other than bear witness to it. The Spirit inspires the soul or fellowship but is otherwise hidden in Harnack's gospel narrative as well. Harnack's theology is anthropocentric. He has thereby removed from the church the most profound theological resources imaginable for promoting its social gospel.

The church is indeed situated in history, but it is even more profoundly and determinatively situated in the biblical narrative. What Karl Barth described as the "strange new world within the Bible" is a narrative that focuses above all else on the God who turns with grace to humanity in the incarnation, life, death, and resurrection of Christ and in his pouring out of the Spirit upon all flesh. Christ and not the human soul is thus the central point of this narrative, the one who carries redemption to its fulfilment. The social gospel is due to the triumph of Christ and his Spirit; it is not the triumph of religion or the value of the soul. Switching the centre of the gospel to its lesser theme (the value of the soul) as the superior focus bankrupts one's social gospel theologically.

Harnack is correct that Jesus evokes discipleship as a way of life. A mere confession or dogmatic formulation alone is not faith by a long shot. And there is something to say about the way in which the history of dogma was in danger of abstracting the gospel from the life of faith and worship in which it originally lived, moved, and had its being. Yet, discipleship without the dogmatic truths preoccupied above all else with the work of the Triune God in the world lacks theological depth, guidance, and eschatological reach.

How could God's love for humanity have triumphed without the Father sending the Son into flesh by way of the Spirit in the Virgin's womb so as to redeem and renew all flesh? The mere fact that all souls exist in immediate relation to God does not come close to probing the depth and victory of love revealed in the incarnation. And what about the cross? That the eternal Son of the Father went to the cross under the leading of the Spirit and bound himself to humanity at the point of their greatest need, their captivity to darkness, despair, and death. The cross does not just exemplify love, it makes it possible as a present and eschatological victory in a world under captivity to sin and death. Redemption is not secured merely in discovering the eternal value of the human soul! Basing redemption in the immortal soul is a Hellenised gospel if I ever saw one! The chief critic of the Hellenisation of the gospel ends up being the chief Helleniser! Moreover, historically situating the cross brings to the fore an unjust murder, what James Cone rightly called a "lynching."[59]

The oppressed are made to look to the cross as a source of hope and are made to repent of their resignation in the face of evil and the lure of taking the role of the oppressor if given the chance. But it also brings to the fore the sin of the oppressor and calls their self-justifying abuse of power into account, offering hope for them as well. As Miroslav Volf has noted, the cross is the point of reconciliation between both, a break in the cycle of violence, offering redemption for oppressor and oppressed, even the elements of both in all of us.[60] The resurrection fulfils the victory of the cross and creates the possibility of a just community in Christ and in the Spirit (Rom. 4:25; 1 Tim. 3:15). The cross and the resurrection make us worthy of the Spirit (Gal. 3:14), releasing and enabling the many tongues in their glorification of God and in their work together through many diverse gifts to bear witness to the new humanity in Christ. Viewing the cross and the resurrection as unnecessary shifts the power of mediation from God to the strength and endurance of the human soul.

For all of his shortcomings, Harnack used his scholarly gifts with tireless passion to support a social gospel that made an important impact throughout his realm of influence, which was wide. I read him with appreciation as well as criticism. In the end, I found myself wondering what is it that situates us historically. What does it mean to call our gospel "social?" I know that Harnack thought long and hard on such questions. The fruit of his labour, though having shortcomings, also had points worth considering with utmost seriousness by the churches today. If only Harnack had followed the path of his inquiry to more radical conclusions! The historical critic needed to become more critical in his historical analysis and the Lutheran more Lutheran in his Christology! In saying this, I do not merely stand over him pronouncing judgement. I stand next to him in appreciation, being receptive to judgement as well.

## Discussion Questions

1. What problems did Harnack identify in the way history had been written concerning its relationship to apologetics and the relativising of historical

---

[59] James Cone, *The Cross and the Lynching Tree* (Maryknoll, NY: Orbis Books, 2011).

[60] Miroslav Volf, *Exclusion and Embrace: A Theological Exploration of Identity, Otherness, and Reconciliation* (Nashville: Abingdon Press, 1996).

analysis? Is his concern applicable to contemporary writings of history? Explain.
2. Explain the path taken by Harnack to navigate between radicalism and quietism.
3. How does Harnack engage the infinite value of the soul in God and the communion of saints to develop a social gospel?
4. Macchia concludes by stating that he appreciates Harnack while also holding judgement with regard to the social implications of gospel. How might we best engage what Macchia identifies as the points of appreciation for the development of a gospel that addresses cultural concerns within contemporary society?

## Bibliography

Barth, Karl. *The Humanity of God.* Richmond, VA: John Knox Press, 1960.
Cone, James. *The Cross and the Lynching Tree*. Maryknoll, NY: Orbis Books, 2011.
Fend, W.C.H. "Church Historians of the Early Twentieth Century: Adolf von Harnack (1851–1930)." *The Journal of Ecclesiastical History* 52:1 (January 2001), 83–102.
Harnack, Adolf von. *Essays on the Social Gospel.* New York: G.P. Putnam's Sons, 1907.
Harnack, Adolf von. *What is Christianity?* New York: Harper & Row Torchbook, 1957.
Harnack, Adolf von. *History of Dogma*, 7 vols (reprinted as 4). Mineola, NY: Dover, 1961.
Rauschenbusch, Walter. *A Theology for the Social Gospel.* New York: Macmillan Company, 1917.
Rauschenbusch, Walter. *Christianity and the Social Crisis*. New York: Macmillan Company, 1920.
Schleiermacher, Friedrich. *On Religion: Speeches to its Cultured Despisers.* Translated John Oman. New York: Frederick Ungar Publishers, 1965.
Soelle, Dorothee. *Political Theology*. Philadelphia: Fortress, 1974.
Volf, Miroslav. *Exclusion and Embrace: A Theological Exploration of Identity, Otherness, and Reconciliation.* Nashville: Abingdon Press, 1996.
Zachhuber, Johannes. *Theology as Science in Nineteenth-Century Germany: From F.C. Baur to Ernst Troeltsch.* Oxford: Oxford University Press, 2013.

# Chapter 15

# CARE (Christian Action Research and Education) as a Model for Social Action

William K. Kay

**Abstract**

Christian Action Research and Education (CARE) found initiating impulse in Britain during the early twentieth century as a Pentecostal community committed to missionary action. The community began taking actions of social concern in the post-war years of the mid-century with particular attention initially given to assisted-living homes. The community increasingly committed itself to actions of social justice but saw itself philosophically distinct from the organisations that identified as culturally or philosophically liberal. The late twentieth century saw CARE developing as a social justice agency that was distinctly Pentecostal in practices and in the theology that drove those practices.

**Reflection on Murray Dempster**

My memories of Murray Dempster are fragmentary. I believe we met in 1986 when I first visited the USA and gave a talk to the faculty of Southern California College, Los Angeles, California (now Vanguard University). The Society for Pentecostal Studies (SPS) provided other opportunities for discussion but the longest and most significant conversation we had was after Murray left Vanguard and we dissected the state of Pentecostal higher education together. I had bought, read, and enjoyed *The Globalization of Pentecostalism: A Religion Made to Travel* in the 1999 Regnum edition and marginalia in the copy in my bookcase shows that I read it with some care. So, thank you, Murray, for enriching my life and helping me to understand more of the global phenomenon that is the Pentecostal movement.

**Prelude**

The Pentecostal movement in Britain began in the first part of the twentieth century. Elim was founded in 1915 and Assemblies of God (AG) in 1924. Both these classical groups, as well as the Apostolic Church in Wales, were involved in mission and church planting in their own ways. Elim grew through the centralised crusading and healing ministry of George Jeffreys (1889–1962), while Assemblies of God was more localised. Both groups operated an annual conference for ministerial discussion and decision-making. There was little emphasis on social action. Jeffreys believed revival was the cure of all social ills and national problems. Assemblies of God, differentiating itself from liberal denominations, had an abhorrence of the "social gospel," which it considered to be a watered-down version of the real evangelical thing.

In the post-war period from about 1960 onwards, responding to the vision of individual pastors rather than to conference decisions, the AG did take social action. Two assisted living homes were founded as well as a Pentecostal Child Care Association (c. 1960 and 1977). In the same way, Elim in its preaching and teaching had always supported a lifestyle that excluded participation in sport, the reading of novels, dancing, attendance at the cinema or theatre, and other similar activities. These were not specifically expressions of social concern, but they showed an awareness of wider society and its preoccupations and distractions. And, especially during the 1930s when war was brewing in Europe, they kept abreast of British politics in their denominational magazine and prayed for the nation. Even so, Pentecostalism as a whole never felt impelled to debate or preach a theology of social action or political engagement, though in this respect it was no different from other sections of evangelicalism.

The end of the war marked the start of a new historical phase. There was a birth-rate boom for a few years after 1945 and the generation born post-war did not complete any national service (i.e. compulsory military training). Further, they were not required to take part in war as their fathers and grandfathers had been required to do. The post-1945 generation lived through the grey and conformist 1950s, years of post-war reconstruction. As the 1960s dawned, instead of going abroad to fight, they found themselves in an era of full employment and lifted up in a wave of cultural renewal expressed, among many other things, by drug-fuelled new music. In 1966 they were at last entitled to vote and they voted in a young Labour government zealous for social change.

The late 1950s and the 1960s saw a series of liberalising legal revolutions. In 1959 Penguin Books won a court case entitling it to print an unexpurgated version of D.H. Lawrence's *Lady Chatterley's Lover*, a book containing detailed descriptions of sexual intercourse. In 1961 the contraceptive pill became available on the National Health Service. In 1965 capital punishment was abolished and in 1967, despite intense opposition, abortion was permitted, also on the National Health Service. In the same year the Lord Chamberlain's powers of censorship of theatre were ended and homosexuality was decriminalised between consenting males over the age of 21. In 1969 the Divorce Reform Act altered conditions for the dissolution of marriage: a no-fault divorce could now occur by consent after only two years. A "new morality" came into vogue though, as its critics pointed out, "the new morality is only the old immorality." Sexual norms rapidly shifted, encouraged, so it seemed, by pornographic enactments in literature or on the stage and screen; and, when marriages struggled, it became easier to end them rather than to persevere. In 1969, the voting age in Britain was lowered to 18, a signal that youth and not age was in the ascendant.

Broadcasting had become increasingly important as a result of the sale of affordable televisions. The BBC, the biggest and most trusted broadcaster in the country, began to popularise satire in the 1960s.[1] Programmes which essentially mocked the previous generation were given airtime and the young, and others, enjoyed poking fun at the buttoned-up members of the ruling classes. In 1963 the heroism of wartime officers and soldiers was made a matter of pathos and ridicule[2] and one commentator thought the Labour Party only came to power in 1964 courtesy of the BBC.[3]

The person appointed Home Secretary was Roy Jenkins (1920–2003), a clever Welshman who, in a 1959 book setting out a case for Labour, persuasively argued for social change across a wide spectrum: prison, capital punishment, homosexuality, theatrical performances, marriage, the licensing of alcohol, divorce – all the topics eventually changed by the spate of legislation in the 1960s.[4] Jenkins also wanted to support the arts with public money and believed "the permissive society was the civilised society." It has been said that when people lose religion, they turn to art for meaning and this appears to be the position with Jenkins. When he joined the cabinet and became Home Secretary he initiated or stood behind the social legislation of the 1960s without necessarily making this a matter of government policy. He supported many "private members' bills" which allowed individual backbench Members of Parliament (MPs) to initiate legislation. Normally private members' bills fail to become law but Jenkins by supporting them made sure that many of them did.[5] This became a mechanism and driver of the moral revolution of 1960s: many people who equated legality with morality accepted that once a particular behaviour was permitted by law it must also be moral.

The arguments in Parliament, when they occurred, almost always avoided high principles. Essentially they were utilitarian: freedom was not an absolute value but only desirable for the good consequences it can bring; abortion was necessary to protect the life of the mother and to prevent the trade of the backstreet abortionist;[6] it was assumed that the ready availability of contraception would reduce the need for abortion; it was argued (unconvincingly) that easier divorce stabilised marriage instead of undermining

---

[1] Independent television, funded by advertising, only started in 1955. The BBC remained the major player in broadcasting, especially as it ran a national radio network alongside its TV output.

[2] *Oh! What a Lovely War* was a stage show in 1963 and was filmed in 1969.

[3] Mary Whitehouse, *Most Dangerous Woman?* (Tring: Lion, 1982), 62. The remark is Brian Walden's.

[4] Roy Jenkins, *The Labour Case* (Harmondsworth: Penguin, 1959), see chapter 9.

[5] Roy Jenkins, *A Life at the Centre* (London: Macmillan, 1991), 196, found time to speak in favour of David Steele's abortion bill on a free vote.

[6] Dominic Sandbrook, *White Heat: A History of Britain in the Swinging Sixties* (London, Little, Brown, 2006), 658, reckons there were 100,000 backstreet abortions a year in the previous decades though he provides no explanation of how this number was calculated, a point that needs to be made because it does not come from any set of official statistics. According to an archive of historical statistics, "Historical Abortion Statistics, United Kingdom," compiled by William Robert Johnston, http://www.johnstonsarchive.net/policy/abortion/ab-unitedkingdom.html (accessed 10 January 2023), 53,643 *legal* abortions took place in 1969, which makes it difficult to believe 100,000 *illegal* abortions took place three years previously.

it; that a rise in sexually transmitted diseases was not especially linked to permissiveness; capital punishment was an ineffective deterrent, and so on.[7] Parliament resisted moral or theological arguments and was much more interested in arguments about money – how much an abortion service would cost or what would be the financial consequences to the nation of divorce.

## Christian Responses

For many years Christians had thought about the relationship between Christianity, culture, and politics. During the 1939–45 war violent pagan European dictatorships attacked democracies that could loosely be said to be Christian or, at the very least, endorsed religious rights and freedoms which, in and of themselves, enabled the churches to make a legitimate contribution to national life. Religious freedom in the UK was manifested in the diversity of religious groups enjoying the protection of law and, during wartime, in the recognition that Christian pacifism was a valid vocation. Pacifists were not imprisoned nor discriminated against.[8]

During the dark early days of the war the Archbishop of Canterbury, William Temple, published a well-regarded and widely read paperback, *Christianity and Social Order* (1942). In it he deduced social and economic policy from broad Christian values and principles. From Christian sympathy for those who suffer he deduced policies that addressed bad housing, malnutrition, and unemployment. From a consideration of eschatology, he deduced the social order is "our school master to bring us to Christ;"[9] it should be planned with human destiny in mind. From Christian ethics he deduced that there must be a respect for all of humanity and this entails a respect for human freedom. From a consideration of the nature of human beings as made in the image of God and yet sinful he deduced, "the art of government in fact is the art of so ordering life that self-interest prompts what justice demands."[10] Indeed, while political systems veer between excessive individualism and enforced collectivism, only Christianity provides a basis for a community that also cherishes the flourishing of the individual.

Other Christian writers in the decades that followed drew attention to damaging cultural trends. C.S. Lewis in a series of brilliant publications exposed the shallowness and hard-heartedness of fashionable anti-Christian worldviews. His famous *Screwtape Letters* uncovered the dangers of inverting morality; his defence of miracles in a Newtonian universe reconciled divine freedom with mechanistic models of causation; and his critique of vivisection and humanistic

---

[7] Christie Davies, *Permissive Britain: Social Change in the Sixties and Seventies* (London, Pitman, 1975), e.g. 27, 55.

[8] There were 59,000 conscientious objectors in the UK in World War II, almost four times as many as in World War I. Andrew Billen, "World on Fire," *The Times* (20 September 2019), https://www.thetimes.co.uk/article/world-on-fire-the-new-second-world-war-tv-drama-that-doesnt-take-sides-fhwqfbssr (accessed 10 January 2023).

[9] William Temple, *Christianity and Social Order* (Harmondsworth: Penguin, 1942), 43.

[10] Temple, *Christianity and Social Order*, 42.

theories of punishment all made cogent philosophical and far-reaching points.[11] More direct and probably equally influential at the time was Francis Schaeffer, who provided generalised analyses of Western culture that demonstrated how worldviews had radically shifted in the period since the Reformation.[12] Among other things he drew attention to the torrent of abortions resulting from the 1973 Roe v. Wade case in the United States and he warned that, if abortion was normalised, all kinds of other pernicious consequences would follow including pressure for euthanasia or assisted dying. He saw (prophetically) how a doctrine of rights that placed some rights above others was bound to lead to the devaluation of those rights that were effectively superseded and, in this way, to result in a kind of moral tyranny perpetrated in the name of liberalism.[13]

### *Mary Whitehouse*

The moral and social transformation of British society in the 1960s was mirrored in television broadcasting. Plays, discussion programmes, films and other shows all began to reflect or promote libertarian values undermining the previous generation. The BBC was funded by a tax (or licence fee) on all viewers with the intention of making it independent of commerce and government. Its very independence, however, dulled its response to democratic sensitivities with the result that, when a liberal elite took control of its board and management, there was little the ordinary listener or viewer could do.

One woman, a schoolteacher who noted the impact of BBC sex-educational programmes on the girls in her school, was shocked and angered by what was happening. Mary Whitehouse (1910–2001) had been a convert to the Moral Re-Armament Movement in the 1930s. She began to write to the BBC and hold public meetings.[14] Her "Clean-up TV" campaign in 1964 gave way to the founding of the National Viewers' and Listener's Association (NVLA) the following year. This was essentially a campaigning organisation dependent upon her own letters to government, the newspapers, and the BBC, but with a vocal membership of around 150,000 people at its height. Although she faced derision and, in some quarters, became a "hate figure" involved in several court cases, her influence was considerable and long-lasting. She drew attention to sexual explicitness and gratuitous violence as well as to blasphemy. She was vituperatively opposed by legal challenges as well as by satirical mockery, but

---

[11] C.S. Lewis, *Miracles* (London, Godfrey Bles, 1942); C.S. Lewis, "The Humanitarian Theory of Punishment," *The Twentieth Century: An Australian Quarterly Review* 3:3 (1949), 5–12.

[12] H.R. Rookmaaker, *Modern Art and the Death of Culture* (Leicester: IVP, 1970), provided a similarly convincing analysis, especially as it was confined to a single discipline.

[13] Francis A. Schaeffer, *How Should We Then Live? The Rise and Decline of Western Thought and Culture* (Old Tappan, NJ: F.H. Revell, 1976).

[14] Mary Warnock, "Mary Whitehouse," in *Oxford Dictionary of National Biography* (Oxford: Oxford University Press, 2022), https://www.oxforddnb.com/view/10.1093/ref:odnb/9780198614128.001.0001/odnb-9780198614128-e-76525 (accessed 10 January 2023).

she gradually found what sort of tactical victories could be achieved in the pursuit of godly causes.

*Nationwide Festival of Light*

While Mary Whitehouse focused her attention on the slide in moral standards in broadcasting, the Nationwide Festival of Light was a wider movement that took its crusading exuberantly out into the streets and squares of public life.[15] It sought to re-assert the Judaeo-Christian framework for public morality and, with Raymond Johnston as its director from 1974 to 1985, the spontaneous campaigning zeal of evangelical Christians was given intellectual muscle by his string of eloquent publications.[16] Johnston argued that the erosion of public morality could only undermine the traditional nuclear family which was itself the essential building block of a healthy society.[17] Abortion and pornography, as well as being intrinsically damaging to human dignity, were driven by covert and manipulative commercial interests.[18] Moreover, because he was concerned with the Judaeo-Christian framework, Johnston and the NFOL were prepared to work with Jewish and Roman Catholic advocates to create a broad coalition. All this became apparent as the coalition was assembled. It contained broadcasters like Malcolm Muggeridge and the high-profile saint, Mother Teresa, as well as intellectuals like Francis Schaeffer and John Stott. Its signature events primarily were public rallies or marches in the centre of London during the 1970s and early 80s. There was also a dramatic series of beacon fires across the land in an echo of warnings that had historically alerted the population to the dangers of foreign invasion; though, in this instance, it was also the fulfilment of a vision received in charismatic prayer.

## The Work of CARE

Institutions perpetuate values. Institutions express values by embodying them and arguing for them in the public forum. Out of the Nationwide Festival of Light in 1983 came the impulse to found CARE (Christian Action Research and Education). Lyndon Bowring, a minister ordained in the Elim Pentecostal Church who had become the Executive Chairman of the Nationwide Festival of Light now became the executive chairman of CARE, and its director was Raymond Johnston. Johnston, however, died suddenly of cancer in 1985 and so

---

[15] John Capon, ... *And There Was Light* (London, Lutterworth Press, 1972).

[16] Andrew Atherstone, "Christian Family, Christian Nation: Raymond Johnston and the Nationwide Festival of Light in Defence of the Family," in John Doran, Charlotte Methuen and Alexandra Walsham (eds), *Religion and the Household* (Martlesham, UK: Boydell Press, 2014).

[17] We appear in 2022 to have reached a point when the majority of British people no longer think that the family is the building block of society: John Bingham, "Marriage No Longer the Foundation of Family Life," *The Telegraph* (10 September 2013), https://www.telegraph.co.uk/news/uknews/10296611/Marriage-no-longer-the-foundation-stone-of-family-life.html (accessed 10 January 2023).

[18] A point made in various places in *Pornography: The Longford Report* (London: Coronet Books, 1972), e.g. 222.

Bowring and close colleague Charlie Colchester took on the directorship. Bowring remained in the role for more than thirty years and became one of the most influential Pentecostals in Britain.

By now the legislative changes of the 1960s were beginning to take effect. Despite the 1967 safeguards – that abortion was only permissible to protect the life and health of the mother on the advice of two medical practitioners – it quite quickly became apparent that requests for abortion were almost always granted.[19] "The total number of annual abortions more than doubled between 1969 and 1971."[20] The soaring figure of 86,565 in 1970 climbed further reaching 139,702 by 1975.

The question was how CARE should react to the deluge of changes now coming through. According to Bowring the legislative enactments of the 1960s had occurred while evangelicals had been "asleep."[21] What was to be done? An address by the evangelical Anglican, John Stott, had put the case to CARE and its supporters that, while social action was not part of the gospel, it was part of the church's mission. So CARE began to encourage Christians to "engage" with the altered cultural landscape, to persuade and advocate reform in the arenas where public opinion was formed and expressed. Campaigns and marches were held, placards were brandished, and rallies convened. We were, said Bowring, "full of truth." As the years went on, however, attitudes altered so that militant Christians recognised the need to be "full of grace *and* truth." The slogan "abortion kills" was replaced by "both lives matter."

In 1987, twenty years after abortion was legalised and permitted on the National Health Service, a rally was held at the Royal Albert Hall.

> We calculated how many abortions had taken place since 1967 and we had permission to drop paper petals from the dome[,] one for every known aborted child. It went on and on and on and we were sobbing our hearts out. People [were] standing with their head and shoulders covered with these petals.

Graham Kendrick's hymn was sung with deep emotion.[22]

> Who can sound the depths of sorrow
> In the Father heart of God
> For the children we've rejected
> For the lives so deeply scarred?
> And each light that we've extinguished
> Has brought darkness to our land
> Upon our nation, upon our nation
> Have mercy, Lord.

---

[19] Abortion following incest or rape could be covered by reference to the pregnant woman's mental health.

[20] "UK Abortion Statistics: Facts and Figures relating to the Frequency of Abortion in Great Britain," Abort73, accessed 21 September 2019, https://abort73.com/abortion_facts/uk_abortion_statistics/.

[21] I interviewed Lyndon Bowring (16 August 2019).

[22] Graham Kendrick, "Who Can Sound the Depths of Sorrow?" (hymn), "Graham Kendrick, Songs That Help the Church to Sing," https://grahamkendrick.co.uk/who-can-sound-the-depths-of-sorrow/, Accessed 13 April 2023.

Public opinion before the 1967 Abortion Act was sensitive to circumstances surrounding the health of a mother or unborn child or of consequences to other children in a family when an abortion was or was not permitted. In 1965 polling showed 66% of adults thought abortion should be legal in some circumstances while 24% thought it should be illegal in all circumstances.[23] Over time public opinion has liberalised and become predominantly "situationalist"; though many people have taken refuge in the "don't know" category and the number of people at the ends of the scale who would "always" or "never" allow abortion is small. One commentator has argued that abortion is a "sad but inevitable fact of modern living" while another (a pro-abortionist) has viewed abortion "a moral wrong but a pragmatic choice."[24] The attitudinal slide towards an acceptance of abortion is statistically correlated with a decline in religious belief in the general population, so that one conclusion might be that only by reviving religious life in Britain will public opinion be changed. But another conclusion might be that the uncommitted "don't knows" are persuadable, with the consequence that continued campaigning on the issue is merited. Bowring put it this way, "although we partly lost on abortion, we are never going to take it lying down. Our aim is to get to the place where abortion is unthinkable."

Despite the strident and absolutist claims of abortionists, there remains a variability of opinion in different parts of the United Kingdom and this variability has been reflected in the divergent legislative provisions made by Irish, Welsh, and Scottish politicians. In Northern Ireland where religious life is most traditional and fervent, the Belfast assembly (Stormont) has restricted abortion to a narrow range of cases and resisted political pressure to conform to the criteria applied elsewhere in the UK. The current efforts of CARE are directed towards protecting Northern Ireland from Westminster politicians, especially those with extreme views about the permissibility of abortion even at a very late point in the pregnancy, much later than is allowed on average in other European countries; but unfortunately, in the turbulence of British politics brought about by Brexit negotiations, it failed. Even so, careful exposition of the current legal position is given by CARE on its website and, in addition to this, summaries of the evidence concerning the "difference between the mental health outcomes of women with unwanted pregnancies who gave birth from those who had abortions." Indeed, "there is no available evidence to suggest that abortion has a therapeutic effect in reducing the mental health risks of unintended pregnancy." Similarly, CARE answers questions about freedom of choice as it affects women with unwanted pregnancies. The debate, in other words, has widened. In its earliest days it focused almost exclusively upon killing unprotected and unborn children and thus included contention about the moment a human life actually begins. Now debate takes note of risks to the mental health of women and other matters over which agreement between contesting parties can more easily be reached.

---

[23] Ben Clements and Clive D. Field, "Abortion and Public Opinion in Great Britain: A Fifty-Year Retrospective," *Journal of Beliefs and Values* 39.4 (2018), 429-44.

[24] Quotations taken from Clements and Field, "Abortion and Public opinion in Great Britain," 429–44.

Over the years following the initial campaigning against legalised abortion, CARE has developed practical help for women faced by unplanned pregnancies. These include simple prayer points, initiatives to create a supportive environment within churches and the founding of a separate pro-life charity that combines advocacy with nationwide practical assistance. All this is alongside support for traditional marriage and informed opposition to pornography, prostitution, and human trafficking – activities often accompanying sexual abuse and therefore traumatic pregnancy.

These widening concerns show CARE is not a single-issue pressure group. It is much more than a campaigning organisation because of its strong connections with churches on one side and, in recent years, with Parliament on the other. Even in the 1980s it brought approximately 300 interdenominational church groups into existence; these met to pray and show appreciation for members of Parliament. The groups would pray for the MP's family or would write to him or her before crucial votes in parliament became due. Prayer was always woven into the CARE'S activities and part of its ethos. Resilience was needed and inspiration was taken from the very long campaign William Wilberforce conducted in the nineteenth century against slavery.[25] Time and again Wilberforce introduced bills to Parliament and time and again he was defeated. He was told repeatedly the economy depended on slavery and the Bible endorsed it until, just as his life ended, abolition was finally secured. The aged John Wesley had written to the young Wilberforce in 1791, "Unless God has raised you up for this very thing, you will be worn out by the opposition of men and devils. But if God be for you, who can be against you?"[26] And one might say the same thing about CARE.

So how does CARE decide which causes to pursue? The answer here is that decisions are taken after several trustees feel a "burden" for a particular issue. So the causes are generated through prayer and spiritual discernment. There is then a feedback loop involving supporters and beneficiaries. This consultative method of operation keeps CARE where it should be as a leader of opinion with a servant heart.

> CARE measures the success of its strategies by setting objectives at the beginning of each year to progress its strategy and by reviewing progress on a regular basis. This is done based on both specific measurable targets and using feedback from supporters and those benefiting from CARE's work.[27]

Contemporary revelations provide an example. Until very recently there were no specific British laws governing human trafficking. As CARE's website points out,

---

[25] There is a fine painting of Wilberforce in one of the meeting rooms of CARE's offices.

[26] Rick Hogaboam, "John Wesley's Final Letter to William Wilberforce, Slavery, and the Sanctity of Life" (12 January 2017), https://medium.com/@rickhogaboam/john-wesleys-final-letter-to-william-wilberforce-slavery-and-the-sanctity-of-life-571538291c16 (accessed 10 January 2023).

[27] Trustees' report for the year ended 31 March 2018, 4.

> an estimated 600,000–800,000 people are trafficked across international borders each year with more trafficked within their own countries. The Government estimates there could be as many as 10,000–13,000 men, women and children in modern day slavery in the UK each year.[28]

The trade is thought to be worth $32 billion a year internationally.[29] There were charities offering help on a piecemeal basis, but no charitable or Christian institution had examined the legal loopholes by which traffickers managed to ply their vile trade. There was no one championing opposition in Parliament; CARE stimulated parliamentary action. A Bill was introduced into the Northern Ireland assembly that ensured a stiff penalty for the traffickers and a period of time for the trafficked person to be rehabilitated – which demonstrates how the beneficiaries of CARE's activism are taken into account. After release from the grip of traffickers, the bewildered and damaged victims need time to come to terms with their predicament in the country where they now live. This whole approach became law and was then picked up in other countries like Canada and India.

Over the years CARE has built up enormous expertise. Even from the 1980s two or three committed lawyers and one legal draughtsman gave their services to Raymond Johnson. This pool of talent has gradually deepened and been complemented by academic and investigative research to calibrate the wording of legal enactments. In the 1980s legislation directed at curbing pornography was successful but, in the last few years, the same explicit images have returned in an online form. As a result, CARE has had to rethink legislative countermeasures. And this it has done as a service to sympathetic parliamentarians. The season of big banner-waving demonstrations is over and the warfare has moved to backrooms. Only recently a bill to legalise euthanasia was quietly introduced with the result that CARE had quickly to mobilise a letter-writing campaign. Had Christians not been awake, the bill might have gained traction. As Bowring pointed out, the generation that legalised abortion is now ironically in danger of being euthanised. Where Christians believe *every* person of whatever age is made in the image of God, the secularist, filled with a hard-line doctrine of evolution, is disposed to accept the dogma of the "survival of the fittest" with all the consequences that might have for the least fit and the weakest.

Unscrupulous financial and criminal organisations use every method they can to make money without regard to human suffering. In fighting these organisations, CARE has to be alert to every new malpractice. It also has to keep pace with technology to build a profile on digital media. For this reason, it is active on Twitter and Instagram while running a Leadership Programme for young interns, some of whom have later gone on to high office.

As an example of the adaptability and freshness of the approach taken by CARE, one only needs to consider the bioethical work now being done. Ethical issues raised by human reproduction include the complexities of surrogate motherhood, gene editing, three-parent children, and artificial insemination by

---

[28] *CARE for What you Believe*, accessed 23 June 2022, https://care.org.uk.
[29] "What do You Care About?" CARE, https://care.org.uk/our-causes/human-exploitation (accessed August 2019).

anonymised donors and the legal rights of their offspring. Bioethics must consider the implications for sex-selection of infants, "designer babies," issues relating to health insurance following DNA testing, and as yet unforeseen questions relating to robotics. These topics and others like them are within the purview of CARE. Nigel de Cameron has written on robotics and explored the implications of artificial intelligence for the job market as well as the questions that arise from "sex robots" and how automation affects the warmth of human interaction and the neural structures and cognitive capacities of children exposed to computer screens from infancy.[30]

Social change is reflected in education. Moral questions arise over what is taught to children in schools about relationships. Young children are now being introduced to sexual concepts that were hardly spoken of in previous generations, and within such teaching are inbuilt moral norms relating to the acceptability of specific behaviours. There is a contradiction – or at the very least a sharp tension – between the values of unrestricted personal liberty on one side and responsibility for mental health on the other, both one's own and that of others. So, while the taking of recreational drugs may provide a temporary high, the long-term consequences upon mental health, including a propensity for psychoticism, are underappreciated.[31] Significant private drug-taking may subsequently require significant public expenditure on psychological support and counselling. Similar principles govern addiction to gambling. Fixed-odds betting terminals allow gamblers to lose large sums of money at one spin. CARE has therefore campaigned to reduce the size of the maximum stake from £100 to £2 to give addicts a chance to exercise self-control – a move that could lead to a re-examination of the scope of personal freedom which, until now, has tended to follow the liberal maxim that everything is allowable so long as it does not harm other people.[32] What is noticeable about CARE's campaign is that it has not attempted to ban betting or outlaw fixed-odds terminals or in other ways limit human freedom. Rather, it has attempted to improve the circumstances in which gambling addicts find themselves. In essence, CARE is prepared to gaze into the future to attempt to head off the worst consequences of current trends.

CARE is also prepared to gaze backwards at the UK tax system and its discrimination against married couples, a matter taken up by Nola Leach, CARE's chief executive, after the tax laws were changed in 2000.[33] Despite political promises that the family would be protected by the tax system, there is little evidence that these promises have been fulfiled. There are even possible

---

[30] Nigel Cameron, *Will Robots Take Your Job? A Plea for Consensus* (London: Polity Press, 2017); Nigel Cameron, "The Robots are Coming," CARE, 2017, https://care.org.uk/news/latest-news/care-hosts-major-robotics-conference (accessed August 2019).

[31] E.g. Rob Poole and Kate Brabbins, "Drug Induced Psychosis," *British Journal of Psychiatry* 168:2 (February 1996), 135–38.

[32] Found in J.S. Mill, *On Liberty* (Indianapolis: Hackett Publishing Company, 1859). See also, "Victory as FOBT Stake is Slashed, CARE (17 May 2018), https://care.org.uk/news/latest-news/victory-fobt-stake-slashed (accessed August 2019).

[33] "Marriage and Family," CARE, 2019, https://care.org.uk/our-causes/marriage-and-family/family-and-tax (accessed August 2019).

penalties for marrying, with the result that couples who expect to raise children are deterred from entering the benefits of the marriage state. The stability of parental homes is unrewarded. "In 2012, for example, a one-earner married couple with two children on an average wage bore a tax burden that was 45% greater than the OECD [Organisation for Economic Cooperation and Development] average."[34] It is extraordinary that the cost, both psychological and financial, of weakening the classic nuclear family is not appreciated by radical political advocates: the impression given is that they would rather advance their agenda, whatever the cost, than protect the vulnerable. This was certainly the case when Catholic adoption agencies were shut down because of their refusal to place children in the same-sex homes.

One of the unusual aspects of CARE's total ministry is its ability to bless the creation of brand-new charities that then come to function independently with their own funding streams, directors, websites, and activities. Care for the Family is now a major charity with training materials, books, seminars, and other face-to-face interactive activities to support many kinds of family structures and configurations.[35] Similarly, CARE's Prayer for Schools, while not a separate charity, is an initiative in partnership with other campaigning agencies like Youth for Christ, the Association of Christian Teachers, Prayer Spaces in Schools, Scripture Union, and Churches Together in England.

## Conclusion

CARE is an unusual charity with multiple campaigns that cohere under a theological vision of the kingdom of God. Although it began in England, it has offshoots in other parts of the United Kingdom as well as in Europe. It is not a selfish charity drawing in money competitively for its own aims. Instead, it has fostered the birth of other charities, recognised local variations in culture and jurisdiction and, putting the family at the heart of its practical vision, has sought to fight all those encroachments, whether by drugs or legislative enactment, that damage the individual and devastate the family. This organic and wide vision is combined with a personal and spiritual touch. Members of the organisation are people of prayer as much as they are professional activists. New outreaches to recruit supporters from a younger generation occur within the context of preaching and worship. Members of staff are prepared to testify as they would in an evangelical or Pentecostal meeting and, despite closeness to parliamentary processes, CARE does not operate like a Washington lobbying agency. It is more ecumenical in its attitude and broader in its scope. It accepts the need to work with Members of Parliament from all political parties with the result that one cannot simply read the British or European political scene across into the North American one. There is, for instance, a tradition of Christian socialism in Britain and in Europe there are Christian Democratic parties (originally associated with the Catholic Church). In this respect CARE's political balance is neutral: what matters is to advance the cause of Christ.

---

[34] "Marriage and Family," CARE.

[35] Care for the Family, accessed 23 June 2022, https://www.careforthefamily.org.uk.

## Discussion Questions

1. Kay notes that prior to the 1960s, Pentecostals in Britain were involved in social and political debate, but not in a traditional sense. In what ways does Kay identify early and mid-century Pentecostals addressing societal concerns?
2. How was moral and social transformation were addressed by Mary Whitehouse? How were her perspectives received by the broader culture? How did her approaches either ally or contrast with the Nationwide Festival of Light?
3. How does Kay identify the approaches that CARE has taken toward engaging the unborn? How have they moved beyond a single-issue approach?

## Bibliography

Atherstone, Andrew. "Christian Family, Christian Nation: Raymond Johnston and the Nationwide Festival of Light in Defence of the Family." In *Religion and the Household*. Eds John Doran, Charlotte Methuen and Alexandra Walsham. Martlesham, UK: Boydell Press, 2014.

Billen, Andrew. "World on Fire." *The Times* (20 September 2019). https://www.thetimes.co.uk/article/world-on-fire-the-new-second-world-war-tv-drama-that-doesnt-take-sides-fhwqfbssr (accessed 10 January 2023).

Bingham, John. "Marriage No Longer the Foundation of Family Life." *The Telegraph* (10 September 2013). https://www.telegraph.co.uk/news/uknews/10296611/Marriage-no-longer-the-foundation-stone-of-family-life.html (accessed August 2019).

Cameron, Nigel. *The Robots are Coming*. London: CARE, 2017. https://care.org.uk/news/latest-news/care-hosts-major-robotics-conference.

Cameron, Nigel. *Will Robots Take Your Job? A Plea for Consensus*. London: Polity Press, 2017.

Capon, John ... *And There Was Light*. London: Lutterworth Press, 1972.

Care for the Family. Accessed 23 June 2022. https://www.careforthefamily.org.uk.

"Care for What you Believe." CARE Accessed 23 June 2022. https://care.org.uk

Clements, Ben, and Clive D. Field. "Abortion and Public Opinion in Great Britain: A Fifty-Year Retrospective." *Journal of Beliefs and Values* 39:4 (2018), 429–44.

Davies, Christie. *Permissive Britain: Social Change in the Sixties and Seventies*. London: Pitman, 1975.

"Historical Abortion Statistics, United Kingdom." Compiled by William Robert Johnston. Accessed 21 September 2019. http://www.johnstonsarchive.net/policy/abortion/ab-unitedkingdom.html.

Hogaboam, Rick. "John Wesley's Final Letter to William Wilberforce, Slavery, and the Sanctity of Life." 13 January 2017. https://medium.com/@rickhogaboam/john-wesleys-final-letter-to-william-wilberforce-slavery-and-the-sanctity-of-life-571538291c16 (accessed 10 January 2023).

Jenkins, Roy. *The Labour Case*. Harmondsworth: Penguin, 1959.

Jenkins, Roy. *A Life at the Centre*. London: Macmillan, 1991.

Lewis, C.S. *Miracles*. London: Geoffrey Bles, 1942.

Lewis, C.S. "The Humanitarian Theory of Punishment." *The Twentieth Century: An Australian Quarterly Review* 3:3. (1949). 5–12.

Mill, J. S. *On Liberty*. Indianapolis: Hackett Publishing Company, 1859.

Poole, Rob and Kate Brabbins. "Drug Induced Psychosis." *British Journal of Psychiatry* 168:2 (1996), 135–38.

*Pornography: The Longford Report* (London: Coronet Books, 1972).

Rookmaaker, H.R. *Modern Art and the Death of Culture*. Leicester: Intervarsity Press, 1970.

Sandbrook, Dominic. *White Heat: A History of Britain in the Swinging Sixties*. London: Little, Brown, 2006.

Schaeffer, Francis A. *How Should We Then Live? The Rise and Decline of Western Thought and Culture*. Old Tappan, NJ: F.H Revell, 1976.

Temple, William. *Christianity and Social Order*. Harmondsworth: Penguin, 1942.

"UK Abortion Statistics: Facts and Figures relating to the Frequency of Abortion in Great Britain." *Abort73,* accessed Sept 21, 2019. https://abort73.com/abortion_facts/uk_abortion_statistics/.

"Victory as FOBT Stake is Slashed." CARE. London. 17 May 2018. https://care.org.uk/news/latest-news/victory-fobt-stake-slashed (accessed August 2019).

Warnock, Mary. "Mary Whitehouse." In *Oxford Dictionary of National Biography* Oxford: Oxford University Press, 2022. https://www.oxforddnb.com/view/10.1093/ref:odnb/9780198614128.001.0001/odnb-9780198614128-e-76525 (accessed 10 January 2023).

"What Do You Care About?" CARE, London. https://care.org.uk/our-causes/human-exploitation (accessed August 2019).

Whitehouse, Mary. *Most Dangerous Woman?* Herts, England: Lion, 1982.

# Chapter 16

# Saints vs Heroes: The Triumph of Spectacle in American Culture and Film

Robby Waddell

**Abstract**

Comparing and contrasting the character formation in a number of films, this essay raises the question whether popular entertainment is shaping its adherents to be heroes or saints. Heroes are defined as characters whose stories support the narrative of redemptive violence while saints offer an alternative way of being in the world. Heroes occupy the centre of the narrative, unlike saints who defer attention to a greater good. Heroes are celebrated for their virtues and triumphs; saints may not be victorious though they are always faithful. Heroes are often warriors; saints typically are martyrs. Saints may be weak while the flaws of heroes are often superficial. American culture continues to idolise heroes. Christianity, on the other hand, calls for its adherents to embody saintliness.

## Introduction

Although I grew up in a traditional Appalachian-Pentecostal home in Virginia, my family did go to the movies, though I knew it was best for me not to discuss these adventures with my grandmother; we didn't want to disappoint her or cause her any anxiety. On a rare occasion we would go to the drive-in, which held its own distinct experience – sitting in the car, listening to the audio coming from a speaker that was hung on the driver's door window, which at the time seemed like space-age technology. I remember seeing *The Love Bug* featuring Herbie, *Coalminer's Daughter* with Loretta Lynn, and *E.T.* at the Skyview Drive-in. Often we saw movies in a cinema at the Bristol Mall, which was an hour drive from home. The whole pilgrimage was exciting: the dark room, the giant screen, the stereo speaker system, the popcorn, which was an occasional treat due to the added cost. I was captivated by the stories, wowed by the special effects, and inspired by the characters. At the time, I would have never articulated it this way, but it was really a religious experience. Joseph Campbell refers to the movie theatre as the modern temple.[1]

Fascinating that today many "contemporary" Christian worship services mimic the characteristics of this secular temple – dark rooms, large screens, state-of-the-art sound systems, light shows, etc. One of the biggest changes since Campbell's assessment nearly three decades ago is the increasing ubiquity of the

[1] Joseph Campbell, *The Power of Myth* (New York, NY: Doubleday, 1988), 21.

screen. Nowadays people are as likely to watch films, view their television shows, or catch their favourite preacher's sermons on their laptops, tablets, or phones, as they are to travel to the temple/cinema. Not unlike other religious experiences, watching movies no longer requires a trip to the holy house of worship but can be experienced wherever Wifi is available. The millennial axiom: home is wherever your Wifi connects automatically.

Netflix and Amazon Prime have changed the way shows are watched. By releasing entire seasons at once, these delivery platforms have created the phenomenon of binge watching, an immersion experience that enables the message of the show to settle deep into the subconscious of its watchers. Furthermore, the production budgets of television shows have ballooned and have been matched with dramatically improved writing. In fact, the small screen is competing with and in many ways excelling past major motion pictures for the most compelling stories and the most devoted fans – cases in point: Breaking Bad, House of Cards, Orange is the New Black, or Game of Thrones.

Whether in film or television, the metanarratives of the most popular storylines are more than mere entertainment; they have the power to shape culture and form the identities of their adherents. In a 2011 census in the United Kingdom, 176,632 people self-identified their faith as "Jedi Knights," making it the seventh most popular faith, though this represented an over 50% decline in Jedi-ism in the ten years since the previous census.[2] According to a study published by the Pew Research Center in 2021, "Self-identified Christians make up 63% of US population in 2021, down from 75% a decade ago."[3] This data supports Charles Taylor's assessment that secularisation is not merely an increase in antireligious sentiment but rather represents shifts and cross-pressures that are forming identities in new ways.

The relationship between Christianity and the entertainment industry, however, need not be framed solely in negative terms. Stories of creation, depravity, redemption, and community fill popular-culture narratives. Sometimes these stories include messianic protagonists who sacrifice themselves in order to rescue their community. In *The Gospel According to Harry Potter*, Connie Neal defines these similarities as "glimmers of the gospel."[4] These glimmers are subtle and rarely intentional. Neal makes a concerted effort to be clear that she doesn't think *Harry Potter* is a Christian allegory or that Harry is

---

[2] Henry Taylor, "'Jedi' Religion Most Popular Alternative Faith," *Telegraph*, 11 December 2012, http://www.telegraph.co.uk/news/religion/9737886/Jedi-religion-most-popular-alternative-faith.html (accessed 18 July 2022). Previously cited in Greg Garrett, *Entertaining Judgment: The Afterlife in Popular Imagination* (Oxford: Oxford University Press, 2015), 16.

[3] Gregory A. Smith, "About Three-in-Ten U.S. Adults Are Now Religiously Unaffiliated," *Pew Research Center*, 14 December 2021, https://www.pewresearch.org/religion/2021/12/14/about-three-in-ten-u-s-adults-are-now-religiously-unaffiliated

[4] Connie Neal, *The Gospel According to Harry Potter: Spirituality in the Stories of the World's Most Famous Seeker* (Louisville, KY: Westminster John Knox Press, 2002), xi. Previously cited in Greg Garrett, *The Gospel According to Hollywood* (Louisville, KY: Westminster John Knox Press, 2007), xiv.

reducible to a Christological trope. It's a worthy story with its own message and deserves to be read (or in the case of the films, watched) on its own terms. Likewise, I would add that when a "secular" story is analysed for these glimmers of the gospel, the key is to appreciate its narrative framework, its nuances, and its subtleties. Not unlike the interpretation of Scripture, the pop-culture story is not reducible to principles, propositions, or prooftexts, which appear in parentheses at the end of denominational statements of doctrine. As Ralph Wood notes about *Lord of the Rings*, its "religious significance … arises out of its plot and characters, its images and tone, its landscape and point of view – not from any heavy-handed moralizing or preachifying."[5]

Most of my work on the relationship of film and theology could be categorised as a search for glimmers of the gospel. I've preached sermons on *The Matrix*, produced a short video on *Forrest Gump*, delivered conference presentations on Aronofsky's *Noah*, published on eco-eschatological visions found in *Elysium* and *Wall-E* and compared those visions to ones found in 1 Enoch and the Book of Revelation.[6] I have also taught a course on theology and film. In the class, we analysed obvious films in which the presence of gospel-like themes lay on the surface such as Ava DuVernay's *Selma*, Robert Duvall's *The Apostle*, Gabriel Axel's *Babette's Feast*, Krzysztof Kieślowski's *Dekalog* and Aronofsky's *Noah*, which Jeff Lamp, senior professor of New Testament at Oral Roberts University, referred to in a social media comment as "the most Christian movie" he had ever seen.

Notwithstanding my appreciation for film as a powerful medium to shape culture and express deep narratives that give human existence meaning, I have maintained a reoccurring concern that has lately been growing in the back of my mind or in the bottom of my heart about the violence present within these stories, especially the violence perpetrated by the protagonists – which is often celebrated and rarely lamented. I think I can trace the most recent iteration of my concern to January 2015. Two films, both of which were based on the lives of actual people, were released that month that would be nominated for the Academy Best Picture Award: *Selma*, which grossed $52 million, and *American Sniper*, which grossed $350 million. *American Sniper* received mixed reviews regarding its treatment of violence along with the toll that violence takes on its participants, both passive and active. While an argument has been made that Clint Eastwood, the director of *American Sniper*, nuances the effects of war, the popularity of the movie was certainly not a result of a collective appreciation for the evils of war but for a collective appreciation for the tragic story of an American military hero, enormously successful at killing, who was himself the victim of the violence that war wreaks in the hearts, minds, and bodies of its

[5] Ralph Wood, *The Gospel According to Tolkien: Visions of the Kingdom in Middle-Earth* (Louisville, KY: Westminster John Knox Press, 2003), xiv. Previously cited in Garrett, *The Gospel According to Hollywood* , xvii–xviii.

[6] Robby Waddell, "A Green Apocalypse: Comparing Secular and Religious Eschatological Visions of Earth," in A.J. Swoboda (ed.), *Blood Cries Out: Pentecostals, Ecology, and the Groans of Creation* (Eugene, OR: Pickwick, 2014), 133–51.

participants.[7] A fellow Iraq War veteran who suffered from PTSD murdered Chris Kyle, the Navy SEAL whose life inspired the movie. *Selma*, on the other hand, is a slice of the story of America's most famous proponent of nonviolence – the Rev. Dr Martin Luther King, Jr. Neither Ava DuVernay, the film's director, nor David Oyelowo, who played King, were nominated for an Academy Award, an oversight which helped to popularise the #OscarSoWhite hashtag.

My point is not to cast judgement on the moviegoers who chose to see *American Sniper* rather than *Selma* but simply to note that the disparity in the popularity and reception of these films awoke in me a dormant awareness that lying deep beneath the metanarratives of our culture is the myth of redemptive violence.[8] Furthermore, this myth resides, to my chagrin, in many of my favourite movies – movies that I have often celebrated as glimmers of the gospel.

Samuel Wells, in his book *Improvisation: The Drama of Christian Ethics*, draws a distinction between heroes and saints.[9] In this essay I use Wells' distinction to reanalyse the storylines and protagonists of a few of my favourite films to see whether those stories reinforce or deconstruct the myth of redemptive violence. Following this analysis, I reflect on the extent to which the myth of redemptive violence and America's penchant for heroes over saints are shaping a culture of spectacle,[10] an illusion that in turn is shaping our Christology and mission.

## Saints v. Heroes

Drawing on the metaphors of drama and improvisation and building on Hans Urs von Balthasar's *Theo-Drama*, Wells makes a compelling argument for the practice of ecclesial ethics or "ethics for the church," which he distinguishes from deontological ethics (dubbed "ethics for anyone") and utilitarian ethics (identified as "ethics for everyone").[11] Locating the theological enterprise in the practices of the church, Wells' project "is only secondarily about a sacred text, sequence of events, or a set of doctrines; it is primarily about the formation, development, and renewal of sacred *people*."[12] By concentrating on the life of the community rather than texts, history, or doctrines, the focus shifts from simply knowing the sacred narratives – a primary goal for narrative criticism and narrative theology – to enacting the sacred story. Scriptures in this matrix are not reducible to scripts that need to be mimicked, but they are essential in the

[7] Robert Emmet Meagher, *Killing from the Inside Out: Moral Injury and Just War* (Eugene, Oregon: Cascade Books, 2014).

[8] Walter Wink, *Naming the Powers: The Language of Power in the New Testament* (Philadelphia, PA: Fortress, 1984).

[9] Samuel Wells, *Improvisation: The Drama of Christian Ethics* (Grand Rapids, MI: Brazos Press, 2004), 42–44.

[10] Chris Hedges, *Empire of Illusion: The End of Literacy and the Triumph of Spectacle* (New York, NY: Nation Books, 2009).

[11] Wells, *Improvisation*, 28. See also Greg Garrett, *Holy Superheroes!*

[12] Wells, *Improvisation*, 37.

formation of people who are being shaped into the image of Christ and thereby being prepared to improvise faithfully in the power of the Spirit.[13]

Focusing on the formation of readers begs an essential question: "What type of person(s) is the ideal goal?" By contrasting Aristotle and Aquinas, Wells highlights a subtle, though important, distinction between heroes and saints. Aristotle, according to Wells, longed for his readers to be virtuous heroes; Aquinas expected his readers to become saints.

Wells identifies five characteristics that distinguish heroes from saints.[14] First, the stories in which the protagonist is a hero differ from the stories told about saints. As the central character, the hero is the primary actor of his or her story without whom the resolution of the conflict in the narrative would be different and certainly far worse. This point exaggerates a major plot hole in the first instalment of the *Indiana Jones* trilogy: *Raiders of the Lost Ark.* If Dr Jones, played by Harrison Ford, is removed from the storyline the outcome changes very little. Although it was Indiana's mission to prevent the Nazis from obtaining the Ark, they acquire it nonetheless. It's only a divine act of judgement that prevents the Nazis from exploiting the power of the Ark. Despite his efforts, Jones' impact on the outcome is practically nonexistent. Contrary to the role of the hero, a saint may function in a secondary capacity in a narrative that is ultimately about God.

Secondly, the story of a hero commemorates the hero's virtues and/or triumphs. The saint by contrast may or may not achieve a great victory, though he or she is always faithful. This difference may help explain Justin Martyr's apologetic struggle to categorise the Gospels as ancient biographies, because the protagonist does not fit the typical mould of a hero; he hadn't accomplished the sort of feats that would normally merit a literary record.

The third difference between a hero and a saint is their iconic depictions. The hero is often a soldier or warrior, whereas the saint is commonly a martyr. Although the tragic hero may die in battle and thus serve as a sacrifice for his or her community, the saint's death is a result of his or her nonviolent stance. Only an act of God can make sense of the martyrdom of the saint. This is perhaps one of the most significant features of the Christian gospels, and it's the one that distinguishes the story of Jesus from the majority of stories in pop culture that contain a messianic character.

Another difference in these types of protagonists is the extent to which they are flawed and how those flaws are handled in the story. Heroes are often flawless or only superficially flawed. Marvel Comics, in my opinion, does a better job than DC Comics in creating superheroes with believable shortcomings, which provide an extra layer of relatability: perhaps this why a great movie has yet to made about Superman. On the one hand, a serious flaw of a hero may put the story's outcome at risk. On the other hand, a saint may experience a

---

[13] Cf. Chris E.W. Green, *Sanctifying Interpretation: Vocation, Holiness, Scripture* (Cleveland, TN: CPT Press, 2015).

[14] The following description of heroes and saints paraphrases Wells, *Improvisation*, 43–44.

deficiency without stressing the narrative. A saint's weaknesses are simply opportunities for growth and/or divine intervention.

Lastly, the hero stands out as a singular exception to the norm. Only by Herculean effort or virtue does a hero merit his or her story to be told. Wells notes that this point is what is most counterintuitive for modern readers.[15] The sense of democratic equality proposes that everyone has the potential to be a hero – to be the centre of his or her own story. Completing normal expectations becomes a heroic achievement. Saints, on the other hand, are always a part of a community. The New Testament uses the designation "saints" over sixty times, and it's always in the plural.

Wells' differentiation between heroes and saints has implications not only for how sacred texts are read and used in Christian communities, but it also has implications for basic Christology. When Jesus is preached, is he depicted primarily as a hero or as a saint? I would suggest that accounts of Jesus that present him as a hero are more Aristotelian than Thomistic – more akin to pop-culture messiahs than the biblical one.

Before moving to an analysis of films, I want to supplement Wells' discussion of heroes and saints with Joseph Campbell's concept of the *classical monomyth* and particular American variation of it, offered by John Shelton Lawrence and Robert Jewett. Campbell defines the monomyth: "A hero ventures forth from the world of common say into a region of supernatural wonder: fabulous forces are there encountered and a decisive victory is won: the hero comes back from the mysterious adventure with the power to bestow boons on his (or her) fellow (person)."[16] Lawrence and Jewett argue that Campbell's classic definition has taken a unique American shape. They define the *American monomyth*: "A community in a harmonious paradise is threatened by evil; normal institutions fail to contend with the threat; a selfless superhero emerges to renounce temptations and carry out the redemptive task; aided by fate, his (or her) decisive victory restores the community to is paradisiacal condition; the superhero then recedes into obscurity."[17]

The distinction between Campbell's definition and the definition by Lawrence and Jewett is important, and may be illustrated, ironically, by an examination of *Star Wars*, a multi-film saga that was intended to be an expression of Campbell's myth. George Lucas, the creator of *Star Wars*, was significantly influenced by Campbell's book *The Hero with a Thousand Faces*.[18] In fact, Lucas' ranch served as a filming location for segments of the television series on Campbell's *The Power of Myth* with Bill Moyers. Lucas sought to incorporate Campbell's archetypes into his mythology, and Campbell approved of the outcome. Lawrence and Jewett, on the other hand, argue that Lucas' storyline has more characteristics of the *American monomyth* than the more virtuous classical monomyth. "Assuming that the classical monomyth has at least some potential

---

[15] Wells, *Improvisation*, 42.

[16] Joseph Campbell, *The Hero with a Thousand Faces* (New York, NY: Meridian, 1956), 30. Previously cited in John Shelton Lawrence and Robert Jewett, *The Myth of the American Superhero* (Grand Rapids, MI: Eerdmans, 2002), 5–6.

[17] Lawrence and Jewett, *The Myth of the American Superhero*, 6.

[18] Lawrence and Jewett, *The Myth of the American Superhero*, 269.

to provide a new set of narratives and icons coherent with democratic faith," Lawrence and Jewett write, "we find ourselves drumming our fingers while Lucasfilm, Ltd., cranks out more films about oppressed royalty, their loyal multicreatural retinue, and their serialized capers in hacking with magic swords or blasting their enemies with torpedoes and laser pistols."[19]

Criticising *Star Wars* is a precarious task. In terms of popularity and cultural influence, it is the sacred cow of modern pop mythology. In fact, my own children chastised me when they learned that I was presenting a critique of the multi-chaptered series. Perhaps the most ardent evangelist for *Star Wars* has been Frank Allnutt, a former publicist for Walt Disney. He summarises his perspective:

> long before the *Star Wars* movies, in a place far, far away, there were *real* Star Wars, a *true* Force, and *real* Jedi. The ancient Star Wars erupted when the evil Fallen Star (Satan) rebelled against the True Force (God) and later waged war against the Son of the True Force, the Bright Morning Star (Jesus Christ) and His faithful followers, who, in my way of thinking, can be seen as true Jedi for Jesus, or *JEsus DIsciples*.[20]

When framed with discussions of heroes, saints, monomyths, and "redemptive" violence, *Star Wars* and other popular blockbusters such as *Lord of the Rings* and *The Matrix*, which are also personal family favourites, are susceptible to critique.

## Heroes and the Myth of Redemptive Violence in Star Wars[21]

Luke Skywalker and Darth Vader/Anakin Skywalker are classical heroes. Luke's narrative arc in the *New Hope* follows Campbell's description of the hero's journey to a tee. The development of Vader/Anakin, however, is more complex and requires multiple episodes to reveal. Nevertheless, as Qui-Gon Jinn predicts in *The Phantom Menace* (Episode 1), Anakin proves to be the chosen one at the end of *Return of the Jedi*, when he brings balance to the Force by destroying the Emperor. In the story, Luke matures by showing resistance to the Dark Side, evidenced by his refusal to kill his father. Though his love and choice of nonviolence is only effective because Vader enacts violence on the Emperor.

The maturity of Luke and redemption of Vader – not to mention the development of Han Solo from a self-centred smuggler to caring friend – exhibit a level of complexity in the narrative. The film, however, deconstructs its own myth with its oversimplification of moral stereotypes and its uncritical use of redemptive violence. Although Yoda, who is the most saintly of characters, advises Luke in his training "that the Jedi knight seeks wisdom and knowledge

[19] Lawrence and Jewett, *The Myth of the American Superhero*, 268.

[20] Frank Allnutt, *The Force of Star Wars* (Grand Rapids, MI: Fleming H. Revell, 1977), 9. Later republished as Allnutt, *Unlocking the Mystery of the Force* (Denver, CO: Allnutt Publishing, 1999). Previously cited in Lawrence and Jewett, *The Myth of the American Superhero*, 280.

[21] Analysis of the *Lord of the Rings* and *The Matrix* will be included in an extended version of this research.

but not violent action," it is violence rather than wisdom and knowledge that "always trumps evil at the most crucial moments."[22] The indiscriminating classification of everything into the categories of good or evil, the Light Side or the Dark Side, enables the characters in the story to justify complete and utter destruction of the other. *The New Hope* concludes with the nuclear destruction of the Death Star, which Luke, the hero, is capable of because he has forsaken technology and relied on the Force. Luke is the supreme warrior from a special class of people – a superior race through whom the Force moves more readily. It doesn't require too much imagination to reflect on European, twentieth-century history and ask which ideological systems advocated for a superior race that could save the world from the evil empire.

The narrative of *Star Wars* promotes essentialist nostalgia with a desire to return to the good ole days of the republic rather than oppressive days of the empire. Luke's simple agrarian farm life and the forest-living Ewoks represent a wholesome ideal contrasted with the ills of urbanisation as in the bar at Mos Eisly or the palace of Jabba the Hutt. The ways of the republic – democratic negotiation and compromise – are apparently impotent. If the peaceful past with its simple virtues is to be regained, then the only viable option that can secure peace and order is a violent total solution.

Campbell and Lucas have exhibited disdain for politics and the democratic process. Campbell believed that the political process was impotent. Lucas commented in an interview with the *New York Times*: "there's probably no better form of government than a good despot."[23] What's needed according to Lucas is an impressive, rich ruler, "not to oppress the masses, but to impress them … so that they feel good rather than disgusted about being ruled."[24] American culture, in my opinion, is increasingly reflecting the extremism that forms the undercurrent of the *Star Wars* universe. This trajectory is being fuelled by a populist xenophobia, which seems to be a reaction spurred partially by nostalgia for a simpler time and partially by anxiety about a future that fears the effects of multiculturalism, globalisation, pluralism, and secularisation. Not unlike the hapless members of the old Republic, the Federation, or the Rebel Alliance, Americans, according to Stanley Hauerwas, "love order, even order that is based on illusion and self-deception. When we say we want peace, we mean we want order."[25] Law-and-order totalitarianism can justify almost any sort and practically any amount of violence – whether in acts of commission (such as war, drone bombings, or mass incarceration) or acts of omission such as denial of resources or geographical exclusion. From an alternative point of view, Thomas Merton asserts, "The Christian can renounce the protection of violence and risk being humble, therefore *vulnerable* … because he (or she) believes that hidden

[22] Lawrence and Jewett, *The Myth of the American Superhero*, 280.
[23] "I'm a Cynic Who Has Hope for the Human Race" (interview with Orville Schell), *New York Times* (21 March 1999), sec. 2, 28.
[24] "I'm a Cynic Who Has Hope for the Human Race," *New York Times*.
[25] Stanley Hauerwas, *The Peaceable Kingdom: A Primer in Christian Ethics* (Notre Dame, IN: University of Notre Dame, 1991), 144. Previously cited in Garrett, *The Gospel According to Hollywood*, 141.

power of the Gospel is demanding to be manifested in and through his (or her) own poor person."[26]

## The Triumph of Spectacle in American Culture and Film

In his provocative book, *Empire of Illusion: The End of Literacy and the Triumph of Spectacle*, Chris Hedges paints a bleak picture of the American culture, and in my opinion, this book should be required reading for all Christian leaders and students in the USA and perhaps Europe as well. In five chapters, Hedges discusses illusions of literacy (in which he critiques the shallowness of celebrity culture), illusions of love (in which he offers an explicit exposé on the pervasiveness of pornographic culture), illusions of wisdom (in which he challenges the academic and intellectual elitism of higher education and its inability to produce virtuous citizens rather than corporate ladder-climbers), illusions of happiness (in which he denounces positive psychology and the entertainment/amusement culture), and illusions of America (in which he laments both the loss of the ideals of a liberal democracy that preferred the common good and the rise of unfettered capitalism that has commodified all aspects of reality).

Hedges utilises the thoughts of a popular pair of futurists – Ray Bradbury and Neil Postman – to illustrate his vision of an empire of illusion, especially the illusion of literacy. In his iconic dystopian novel *Fahrenheit 451* (published in 1953), Bradbury imagined a future in which people would spend large portions of their days watching police apprehend people. As Hedges notes, "Bradley understood" that life, "once it was packaged and filmed, became the most compelling form of entertainment."[27] With the rise and near ubiquity of celebrity culture and reality TV, a moral nihilism coupled with unfettered capitalism has commodified human lives and valued them, not for their intrinsic worth endued by their creator, but for their ability to entertain the culture's unacknowledged voyeurism.[28]

Over three decades ago, Neil Postman asserted that the future was likely to resemble Aldous Huxley's vision in *A Brave New World* more than George Orwell's in *1984*. Postman writes:

> What Orwell feared were those who would ban books. What Huxley feared was that there would be no reason to ban a book, for there would be no one who wanted to read one. Orwell feared those who would deprive us of information. Huxley feared those who would give us so much that we would be reduced to passivity and

---

[26] Thomas Merton, "Blessed are the Meek," *Faith and Violence: Christian Teaching and Practice* (Notre Dame, IN: University of Notre Dame Press, 1968), 24. Previously cited in Garrett, *The Gospel According to Hollywood*, 143. Analysis of films that include more saints than heroes, such as *Harry Potter*, *Shawshank Redemption*, and *Cool Hand Luke* will be included in a separate section at this point in an extended version of this research.

[27] Hedges, *Empire of Illusion*, 29.

[28] Also see Harvey Cox, *The Market God* (Cambridge, MA: Harvard University Press, 2017), which focuses on the apotheosis of the financial market and its deconstructive effects on society. Cox was one of Hedges' professors at Harvard Divinity School.

> egoism. Orwell feared that the truth would be concealed from us. Huxley feared the truth would be drowned in the sea of irrelevance. Orwell feared we could become a captive culture. Huxley feared we would become a trivial culture, preoccupied with some equivalent of the feelies, the orgy porgy, and the centrifugal of bumble-puppy. As Huxley remarked in *Brave New World Revisited*, the civil libertarians and rationalists who are ever on the alert to oppose tyranny "failed to take into account man's almost infinite appetite for distractions." In *1984*, Orwell added, people are controlled by inflicting pain. In *Brave New World*, they are controlled by inflicting pleasure. In short, Orwell feared that what we hate will ruin us. Huxley feared that what we love will ruin us.[29]

Although the visions of Orwell and Huxley differ in the many ways highlighted by Postman, they share the common expectation that the future is more totalitarian than democratic.

While Hedges does not rule out the possibility of a full-blown European-style totalitarianism, he notes that the USA is presently experiencing what the political philosopher Sheldon Wolin calls *inverted totalitarianism*.[30] "Inverted totalitarianism," writes Hedges, "unlike classical totalitarianism, does not revolve around a demagogue or charismatic leader. It finds expression in the anonymity of the corporate state."[31] Consider Citizens United vs Federal Election Commission, a case in the US Supreme Court, which determined that corporations would be allowed to be treated as individuals, and therefore, could flood the political system with excessive cash. This decision is what legalised super PACs (political action committees).

I have already mentioned the distrust for politics and the democratic system shared by Joseph Campbell and George Lucas; however, an analysis of the politics of *Star Wars* reveals it to be far more fascist than what is regularly acknowledged. Despite the anti-empire vocabulary in the film, Lucas admits that he took inspiration for the final scene in *Star Wars: The New Hope* from the Nazi propaganda film *Triumph of the Will*. The anaemic republic is no match for the Dark Side and thus must be rescued by the heroes and their uncritical use of redemptive violence.

While Katniss Everdeen, the protagonist of Suzanne Collins' *Hunger Games* trilogy, is certainly a hero more than she is saint, the narrative arc of the movies serves as cinematic satire of the Empire of Illusion. Collins reported in an interview that she was inspired to write the books, on which the films are based, one night while she was channel surfing between reality TV and a live broadcast of the war in Iraq. Her epic tale portrays a totalitarian state named Panem, which keeps its citizens from its twelve districts under subjection of the Capitol and President Snow through fear and a limited distribution of food. In a storyline that mimics the ancient story of the Minotaur, children are selected at random to

---

[29] Neil Postman, *Amusing Ourselves to Death: Public Discourse in the Age of Show Business* (New York, NY: Penguin Books, 1985), xix–xx. Previously cited in Hedges, *Empire of Illusion*, 39.

[30] Hedges, *Empire of Illusion*, 146. See Sheldon S. Wolin, *Democracy Incorporated: Managed Democracy and the Specter of Inverted Totalitarianism* (Princeton, NJ: Princeton University Press, 2008).

[31] Hedges, *Empire of Illusion*, 146.

represent their home districts in a battle to the death – the winner receiving fame, wealth, glory, and resources for his or her native district. Perhaps I'm sympathetic to Katniss because she represents the poorest and most remote district 12, located in the Appalachian Mountains.

As Greg Garrett notes, Panem, which is Latin for "bread," takes its name from the Roman slogan *panem et circense* (bread and circuses) – the mantra used to describe the gladiatorial games used to entertain/amuse the general population.[32] The resistance in this film is plagued with many of the same ideological shortcomings as the primary antagonists. They take advantage of Katniss, using her popularity as a symbol for violent resistance. Katniss, however, baulks at this attempt. In the final film, when the resistance is about to win the final battle, some of its leaders fantasise about placing the children from the capitol into a new iteration of the hunger games. Although the film is certainly susceptible to a critique of heroic idealisation and use of redemptive violence, its nuanced acknowledgement of the dangers of power make it, nevertheless, a helpful commentary on our culture.

## Concluding Remarks

I suspect that most of my work relating to film analysis will continue to be a positive engagement. However, having raised the question about heroes and saints and the cultures and communities that they help form, I have become increasingly convinced that our culture and moreover our churches are in need for new stories and new myths that seek to develop saints who resist evil with nonviolent means. The church needs to practise a faithful witness by promoting its ideals, engaging the culture, and resisting the temptation to gaze at the spectacle. While Chris Hedges offers blazing critiques of the Christian Right, he recommends an expression of Christianity, even though he does not self-identify as a Christian, exhibited by Bonhoeffer, Dorothy Day, and Martin Luther King, Jr – saints for times such as these.

## Discussion Questions

1. Waddell gives examples of commonalities that the big screen and television have with the practices of the church. What are other examples of commonalities? Explain.
2. Building on Wells' notion of heroes and saints, Waddell states that the church can confuse heroes and saints. What are examples of ways that you have seen the confusion of these concepts either within the church or within society?
3. What are some positive dynamics of weakness that are characteristic of saints in contrast to heroes?
4. How might the church in its worship, its education, and other practices encourage the stories of saints that might speak positively to the present practices of the church?

---

[32] Garrett, *Entertaining Judgment*, 144.

## Bibliography

Allnutt, Frank. *The Force of Star Wars*. Grand Rapids, MI: Fleming H. Revell Co., 1977.

Campbell, Joseph. *The Hero with a Thousand Faces*. New York, NY: Meridian, 1956.

Campbell, Joseph. *The Power of Myth*. New York, NY: Doubleday, 1988.

Cox, Harvey. *The Market God*. Cambridge, MA: Harvard University Press, 2017.

Garrett, Greg. *The Gospel According to Hollywood*. Louisville, KY: Westminster John Knox Press, 2007.

Garrett, Greg. *Entertaining Judgment: The Afterlife in Popular Imagination*. Oxford: Oxford University Press, 2015.

Green, Chris E.W. *Sanctifying Interpretation: Vocation, Holiness, Scripture*. Cleveland, TN: CPT Press, 2015.

Hauerwas, Stanley. *The Peaceable Kingdom: A Primer in Christian Ethics*. Notre Dame, IN: University of Notre Dame, 1991.

Hedges, Chris. *Empire of Illusion: The End of Literacy and the Triumph of Spectacle*. New York, NY: Nation Books, 2009.

"I'm a Cynic Who Has Hope for the Human Race," Interview with Orville Schell. *New York Times* (21 March 1999), sec. 2, 28.

Lawrence, John Shelton and Robert Jewett. *The Myth of the American Superhero*. Grand Rapids, MI: Eerdmans, 2002.

Meagher, Robert Emmet. *Killing from the Inside Out: Moral Injury and Just War*. Eugene, Oregon: Cascade Books, 2014.

Merton, Thomas. *Faith and Violence: Christian Teaching and Christian Practice*. Notre Dame, IN: University of Notre Dame Press, 1968.

Neal, Connie. *The Gospel According to Harry Potter: Spirituality in the Stories of the World's Most Famous Seeker*. Louisville, KY: Westminster John Knox Press, 2002.

Postman, Neil. *Amusing Ourselves to Death: Public Discourse in the Age of Show Business*. New York, NY: Penguin Books, 1985.

Smith, Gregory A. "About Three-in-Ten US Adults Are Now Religiously Unaffiliated." Pew Research Center. 14 December 2021. https://www.pewresearch.org/religion/2021/12/14/about-three-in-ten-u-s-adults-are-now-religiously-unaffiliated (accessed 18 July 2022).

Taylor, Henry. "'Jedi' Religion Most Popular Alternative Faith." *Telegraph*. 11 December 2012. http://www.telegraph.co.uk/news/religion/9737886/Jedi-religion-most-popular-alternative-faith.html (accessed 18 July 2022).

Waddell, Robby. "A Green Apocalypse: Comparing Secular and Religious Eschatological Visions of Earth." In *Blood Cries Out: Pentecostals, Ecology, and the Groans of Creation*. Ed. A.J. Swoboda. Eugene, OR: Pickwick, 2014, 133–151.

Wells, Samuel. *Improvisation: The Drama of Christian Ethics*. Grand Rapids, MI: Brazos Press, 2004.

Wink, Walter. *Naming the Powers: The Language of Power in the New Testament*. Philadelphia, PA: Fortress, 1984.

Wolin, Sheldon S. *Democracy Incorporated: Managed Democracy and the Specter of Inverted Totalitarianism*. Princeton, NJ: Princeton University Press, 2008.

Wood, Ralph. *The Gospel According to Tolkien: Visions of the Kingdom in Middle-Earth*. Louisville, KY: Westminster John Knox Press, 2003.

# Abridged Curriculum Vitae

## Murray W. Dempster

### Educational Background

PhD University of Southern California – Social Ethics
MA University of Southern California – Social Ethics
BA Southern California College (now Vanguard University) – Ministerial Studies

### University Service

2010–2020 Distinguished Professor of Social Ethics, Southeastern University, Lakeland, Florida
2008–2009 – Chancellor, Vanguard University of Southern California, Costa Mesa, California
2000–2008 – President, Vanguard University
1999–2000 – Provost, Vanguard University
1994–1999 – Vice President of Academic Affairs, Southern California College (Vanguard University)
1987–2009 – Professor of Social Ethics, Vanguard University
1980–1987 – Associate Professor of Social Ethics, Southern California College
1978–1980 – Senior Pastor, First Assembly of God, Fullerton California
1971–1978 – Assistant Professor of Religion and Philosophy, Southern California College

### Professional Service

2016 – Lifetime Achievement Award, Society for Pentecostal Studies
2014–2020 – Founder and director, Global Pentecostalism Center, Southeastern University, Lakeland, Florida
1993–2000 – Editor, *Pneuma: The Journal of the Society for Pentecostal Studies*
1991 – President, Society for Pentecostal Studies
1989–1992 – Executive Committee, Society for Pentecostal Studies
1977–1981 – Co-editor, *Agora: A Magazine of Pentecostal Opinion*

### Books

1999 – Co-editor with Byron D. Klaus and Douglas Petersen. *The Globalization of Pentecostalism: A Religion Made to Travel*. Oxford, UK: Regnum, 1999.

1991 – Co-editor with Byron D. Klaus and Douglas Petersen. *Called & Empowered: Global Mission in Pentecostal Perspective*. Peabody, MA: Hendrickson, 1991.

1989 – Co-writer with Augustus Cerillo, Jr. *Salt and Light: Evangelical Political Thought in Modern America*. Grand Rapids, MI: Baker Book House, 1989.

**Partial Listing of Journal Articles and Book Chapters**

2012 – "'Crossing Borders': Arguments Used by Early American Pentecostals in Support of the Global Character of Pacifism." In *Pentecostals and Nonviolence: Reclaiming a Heritage*. Ed. Paul Alexander and Jay Beaman. Eugene, OR: Wipf and Stock Publishers, 2012, 108–129.

2010 – "Eschatology, Spirit Baptism, and Inclusiveness: An Exploration into the Hallmarks of a Pentecostal Social Ethic." In *Perspectives in Pentecostal Eschatologies: World Without End*, Ed. Peter F. Althouse and Robert C. Waddell. Eugene, OR: Pickwick, 2010, 155–188.

2004 – "The Structure of a Christian Ethic Informed by Pentecostal Experience: Soundings in the Moral Significance of Glossolalia." In *The Spirit and Spirituality: Essays in Honor of Russell P. Spittler*. Ed. Wonsuk Ma and Robert P. Menzies. London and New York: T&T Clark, 2004, 108–140.

2001 – "Pacifism in Pentecostalism: The Case of the Assemblies of God." In *Fragmentation of the Church and its Unity in Peacemaking*. Ed. Jeffrey Gros and John D. Rempel. Grand Rapids, MI: Eerdmans, 2001, 137–165; reprint, in *Proclaim Peace: Voices of Christian Pacifism from Unexpected Sources*. Ed. Theron F. Schalabach and Richard T. Hughes. Champaign, IL: University of Illinois Press, 1997, 31–57.

1993 – "Christian Social Concern in Pentecostal Perspective: Reformulating Pentecostal Eschatology." *Journal of Pentecostal Theology* 1:2 (April 1993), 53–66.

1991 – "Evangelism, Social Concern, and the Kingdom of God." In *Called and Empowered: Global Mission in Pentecostal Perspective*. Ed. Murray W. Dempster, Byron D. Klaus and Douglas Petersen. Peabody, MA: Hendrickson, 1991, 22–43.

1987 – "Pentecostal Social Concern and the Biblical Mandate of Social Justice." *Pneuma* 9:2 (Fall 1987), 129–53.

# Contributors

## Editors

**Kenneth J. Archer**, PhD, University of St. Andrews, Scotland, is Professor of Theology and Pentecostal Studies at Southeastern University, Lakeland, Florida. He is Past President of the Society for Pentecostal Studies. Among his publications are *A Pentecostal Hermeneutic: Spirit, Scripture and Community* (CPT Press, 2009), *The Gospel Revisited: Towards a Pentecostal Theology of Worship and Witness* (Pickwick, 2014), and as co-editor *Constructive Pneumatological Hermeneutics in Pentecostal Christianity* (Charis, 2016).

**Zachary Michael Tackett**, PhD, Southern Baptist Theological Seminary, Louisville, Kentucky, is Professor of Historical Theology at Southeastern University, Lakeland, Florida. He is a former Secretary-Treasurer of the Society for Pentecostal Studies. Publications include journal articles addressing Pentecostalism and cultural engagement.

## Contributors

**Chris E.W. Green**, PhD, Bangor University, Wales; DMin, Oral Roberts University, is Professor of Public Theology at Southeastern University, Lakeland, Florida, and Director for St Anthony Institute of Theology, Philosophy, and Liturgics. Among his publications are *All Things Beautiful: An Aesthetic Christology* (Baylor University Press, 2021) and *Sanctifying Interpretation: Vocation, Holiness, and Scripture* (CPT Press, 2nd edition 2020).

**Jacqueline Grey**, PhD, Charles Sturt University, is Dean of Theology and Professor of Biblical Studies at Alphacrusis University College, Sydney, Australia. She is former President of the Society for Pentecostal Studies. Her publications include *Them, Us and Me: How the Old Testament Speaks to People Today*, *Raising Women Leaders* (Wipf & Stock, 2010) and *Three's A Crowd: Pentecostalism, Hermeneutics and the Old Testament* (Pickwick, 2011).

**David P. Gushee**, PhD, Union Theological Seminary, New York, is Distinguished Professor of Christian Ethics at Mercer University, Macon, Georgia. He is Past President of the American Academy of Religion and the Society for Christian Ethics. His writings include *Righteous Gentiles of the Holocaust: Genocide and Moral Obligation* (Paragon House, 2003) and with Glen H. Stassen *Kingdom Ethics: Following Jesus in Contemporary Context* (Eerdmans, 2nd edition 2017).

**William K. Kay**, PhD, University of Reading; PhD University of Nottingham, is Emeritus Professor of Theology at Wrexham Glyndŵr University, Wrexham, Wales, and Fellow of the Institute of Pentecostal Theology and former Senior Lecturer in the Department of Education and Professional Studies at King's

College, London. He is past editor of *The Journal of the European Pentecostal Theological Association.* He is a recipient of the Lifetime Achievement Award by the Society for Pentecostal Studies. His publications include *Pentecostalism: A Very Short Introduction* (Oxford University Press, 2011) and *George Jeffreys: Pentecostal Apostle and Revivalist* (CPT Press, 2017).

**Byron D. Klaus**, DMin, Fuller Theological Seminary, is Vice President of ChildHope (formerly Latin America ChildCare), and the retired President and Professor of Intercultural Studies of the Assemblies of God Theological Seminary, Springfield, Missouri. Among his publications are, co-edited with Murray Dempster and Doug Petersen, *Called and Empowered: Pentecostal Mission in Global Perspective* (Baker Books, 1991) and *The Globalization of Pentecostalism: A Religion Made to Travel* (Regnum, 1999).

**Peter Kuzmic**, DTh, University of Zagreb, Croatia, is Eva B. and Paul E. Toms Distinguished Professor of World Missions and European Studies, Gordon-Conwell Theological Seminary, Hamilton, Massachusetts. He is former editor of *Izvori*, a Christian journal in the Croatian language. His publications include the textbooks *The Gospel of John* and *Biblical Hermeneutics* (Global University, 1997).

**Wonsuk Ma**, PhD, Fuller Theological Seminary, is Dean of the College of Theology and Ministry and Distinguished Professor of Global Theology at Oral Roberts University, Tulsa, Oklahoma. He is the founder of *Asian Journal of Pentecostal Studies* and former director of Regnum Books International. Among his publications are *David Yonggi Cho: A Close Look at His Theology and Ministry* (Asia Pacific Theological Seminary Press, 2016) and *Until the Spirit Comes: The Spirit of God in the Book of Isaiah* (Sheffield Academic Press, 1999).

**Frank D. Macchia**, DTheol, University of Basel, is Professor of Systematic Theology at Vanguard University, Costa Mesa, California. He is past editor of *Pneuma: The Journal of the Society for Pentecostal Studies*. Among his publications are *Jesus the Spirit Baptizer: Christology in Light of Pentecost* (Eerdmans, 2021) and *The Spirit-Baptized Church: A Dogmatic Inquiry* (T&T Clark, 2021).

**Lisa Millen**, PhD, Regent University, Virginia, is Associate Professor of Church History at Assemblies of God Theological Seminary, Springfield, Missouri. Her area of expertise is medieval spirituality, particularly that of the twelfth century. Other research interests include Pentecostal history and its relationship to the medieval mystical tradition.

**Martin Mittelstadt**, PhD, Marquette University, is Professor of New Testament at Evangel University, Springfield, Missouri. He is Past President of the Society for Pentecostal Studies. Publications include *Reading Luke-Acts in the Pentecostal Tradition* (CPT Press, 2011) for which he received the 2011 Book of the Year Award from the Foundation for Pentecostal Scholarship, and *Mennocostals: Pentecostal and Mennonite Stories of Convergence,* co-written with Brian K. Pipkin, (Pickwick Publications, 2020).

**Douglas Petersen**, PhD, Oxford Centre for Mission Studies, is the Margaret S. Smith Professor of World Mission and Intercultural Studies, Director of Theology and Leadership Graduate Studies at Vanguard University, Costa Mesa, California, and the former President of ChildHope (formerly Latin America ChildCare). Among his publications are, co-edited with Murray Dempster and Doug Petersen, *Called and Empowered: Pentecostal Mission in Global Perspective* (Baker Books, 1991) and *The Globalization of Pentecostalism: A Religion Made to Travel* (Regnum, 1999).

**Jean-Daniel Plüss**, PhD, Catholic University of Leuven, is Chair of the European Pentecostal Charismatic Research Association and participates in various international ecumenical dialogues involving Pentecostals. He also presides the Swiss "Fondation du Forum Chrétien Mondial" which supports the activities of the Global Christian Forum. Among his publications is *Therapeutic and Prophetic Narratives in Worship: A Hermeneutic Study of Testimonies and Visions* (Peter Lang, 1988).

**Ron Sider**, PhD, Yale University, is Distinguished Professor of Theology, Holistic Ministry, and Public Policy at Palmer Theological Seminary, St Davids, Pennsylvania, and is the Founder and President Emeritus of Christians for Social Action. Among his publications are *Rich Christians in an Age of Hunger: Moving from Affluence to Generosity* (Thomas Nelson, 2015) and *Just Politics: A Guide for Christian Engagement* (Brazos Press, 2012).

**Robby Waddell,** PhD, University of Sheffield, is Professor of New Testament and Early Christian Literature and Director of the Global Pentecostalism at Southeastern University, Lakeland, Florida. He is past co-editor of *Pneuma: The Journal of the Society for Pentecostal Studies*. Among his publications is *The Spirit of the Book of Revelation* (Deo Publishing, 2006).

**Nimi Wariboko**, PhD, Princeton Theological Seminary, is Walter G. Muelder Professor of Social Ethics at Boston University School of Theology. He is co-editor of *Pneuma: The Journal of the Society for Pentecostal Studies*. His publications include *The Pentecostal Principle: Ethical Methodology in New Spirit* (Eerdmans, 2011) and *Economics in Spirit and Truth: A Moral Philosophy of Finance* (Palgrave Macmillan, 2014).

**Amos Yong**, PhD, Boston University, Dean of the School of Mission and Theology and Professor of Theology and Mission at Fuller Theological Seminary, Pasadena, California. He is a former President of the Society for Pentecostal Studies and former co-editor of *Pneuma: The Journal of the Society for Pentecostal Studies*. His publications include *Renewing the Church by the*

*Spirit: Theological Education after Pentecost* and *Pentecostal Theology and Jonathan Edwards* (T&T Clark, 2020).

# Index


Abortion, 82, 85, 102, 115, 193, 196, 197, 198, 203, 204
Adultery, 77
Armageddon, 137, 138, 140, 141
Assemblies of God, xvii, 64, 72, 76, 100, 102, 104, 105, 113, 114, 115, 117, 118, 119, 122, 123, 124, 125, 126, 127, 128, 129, 130, 131, 132, 133, 149, 167, 191, 220, 222
Azusa Street, 62, 69, 70, 72, 105, 148, 155, 158
Bourgeois Church, 55
Catholic, 64, 65, 66, 68, 69, 73, 88, 94, 147, 150, 152, 154, 196, 202, 223
Charismatic Renewal, 10, 12, 64, 65, 67, 72, 73
Christocentric, 60, 70, 180
Christology, x, 53, 59, 60, 65, 67, 68, 71, 72, 85, 180, 188, 208, 210, 221, 222
Church of God (Cleveland, TN), 99, 100, 102, 108, 114, 121, 133
Civilian Public Service, 103, 116, 121, 125, 131, 133
Code of Hammurabi, 17, 78
Cold War, x, 119
Combatant, 103, 116
Conscientious Objector, 118, 122, 124, 125, 126, 131, 132, 133
Creation, 8, 149, 158, 207, 216
Critical Race Theory, 163, 170
Decolonisation, 159, 160
Discipleship, 83, 94, 98, 160, 170
Divorce, 77, 192
Doctrine of Discovery, 161, 170
Ecclesiology, 28, 34, 53, 56
Ecumenical, 62, 69, 72, 73, 147, 148, 149, 153, 158
Ecumenism, 59, 62, 73, 74
Eschatology, 3, 8, 9, 11, 220
Espionage Act, 105, 115
Evangelicals, 85, 110, 113
Exclusion, 28, 85, 86, 188, 189
Exclusivism, 60
First Nations, 160, 167, 169
Four-Fold Gospel (Five-Fold Gospel, Full Gospel), 5, 12, 60, 109, 111
Germany, 87, 88, 89, 90, 91, 93, 94, 95, 96, 97, 120, 136, 137, 145, 165, 175, 189
Global South, 67, 68, 148, 151, 152
Glossolalia (tongues), xv, xviii, 2, 10, 11, 62, 66, 70, 120, 185, 188, 220
Godhead, 60, 61
Hermeneutic, 65, 73, 110, 114, 221, 223
Historical criticism, 175
Holiness, 32, 33, 60, 61, 73, 111, 114, 209, 216, 221
Homelessness of God, 29
Hospitality, 27, 28, 29, 33, 34, 70, 74, 112, 113, 159, 160, 162, 171, 172
Improvisation, 208, 209, 210, 216
Indigenous persons/communities, x, 161, 162, 163
Just War Theory, 109
Justice, x, 3, 6, 11, 13, 19, 20, 21, 22, 25, 99, 100, 101, 105, 106, 110, 111, 113, 114, 115, 151, 157, 167, 170, 220
*Kristallnacht*, 95
Manifest Destiny, 109, 162
Mennonite, 100, 106, 110, 113, 114, 159, 160, 161, 162, 163, 165, 166, 167, 168, 170, 171, 223
Murder, 77
Narrative, 8, 11
National Socialism, 87
Nazi, 89, 90, 92, 93, 94, 95, 96, 97, 214
Oaths, 77
Oneness Pentecostal, 61, 73
Pacifism, 100, 101, 102, 105, 106, 107, 110, 113, 114, 116, 121, 122, 130, 133, 220
Peace Church, 120
Pearl Harbor, 118, 123, 126, 130, 139, 140

Pentecostal Assemblies of Canada, xvi, 163
Pentecostals, x, xiii, xiv, 1, 2, 5, 7, 8, 11, 13, 35, 43, 55, 57, 60, 61, 62, 63, 64, 66, 67, 68, 69, 70, 71, 72, 74, 99, 100, 101, 102, 103, 105, 106, 107, 108, 109, 110, 111, 112, 113, 114, 115, 116, 117, 118, 121, 123, 125, 128, 129, 130, 131, 147, 148, 150, 151, 152, 153, 154, 156, 157, 158, 159, 160, 163, 165, 166, 167, 169, 170, 171, 197, 203, 207, 216, 220, 223
Pharisees, 31, 77, 78
Pluralism, 65, 72
Poverty, 63, 72
Progressive Pentecostalism, 44, 46
Protestant Reformation, 64
Providence, 110, 115
Redemption, xvii, xix, 187, 188, 213
Revival, 62, 72, 142, 145, 148, 158, 165, 172
Righteousness, 13, 19, 20, 21
Riverside Church (New York City), 40, 46, 47
Russia (USSR), 88, 135, 136, 137, 138, 139, 140, 141, 143, 145
Sabbath, 76, 77
Second Vatican Council, 65
Sedition Act, 105
Social Gospel, 173, 174, 180, 189
Society for Pentecostal Studies, ix, xi, xv, xviii, 1, 63, 72, 159, 191, 219, 221, 222, 223
Stalin, 75, 137
Ten Commandments, 77
*Theotokos*, 65
Toronto Blessing, 65
Totalitarianism, 214, 217
Trinity, 30, 34, 120
Vietnam War, 119, 120
Violence, 75, 79, 86, 105, 211, 213, 216
World War I, 88, 89, 100, 101, 104, 108, 116, 117, 118, 119, 121, 123, 130, 133, 139, 194
World War II, 95, 117, 118, 120, 123, 125, 133, 138, 139, 194